THE
Content-Based Classroom

Perspectives on Integrating Language and Content

Edited by

Marguerite Ann Snow
California State University, Los Angeles

Donna M. Brinton
University of California, Los Angeles

LONGMAN

The Content-Based Classroom

Longman, 10 Bank Street, White Plains, N.Y. 10606

Editorial director: Joanne Dresner
Senior acquisitions editor: Allen Ascher
Senior production editor: Linda Moser
Cover design: Naomi Ganor

Library of Congress Cataloging-in-Publication Data

Snow, Marguerite Ann.
    The content-based classroom : perspectives on integrating language
and content / Marguerite Ann Snow, Donna M. Brinton.
        p.   cm.
    ISBN 0-201-69513-8
    1. English language—Study and teaching—Foreign speakers.
2. Language arts—Correlation with content subjects.
3. Interdisciplinary approach in education.   I. Brinton, Donna
II. Title.
PE1128.A2S595   1997
428'.007—dc21   97-5531
                                                                             CIP

5678910 — MA — 05 04 03

This book is dedicated to the memory of

Grannie Hope
December 22, 1905, to December 24, 1996

Charles L. Honn
May 26, 1918 to February 1, 1997

MAS

Robert Kenneth Brinton
January 1, 1915, to December 9, 1996

DMB

Contents

Focus on Assessment 187

Focus on Research 213

Focus on Alternative Models 274

Introduction

Content-based instruction is a growing enterprise. Since the publication of Bernard Mohan's seminal book *Language and Content* in 1986, interest in integrated language and content programs has increased dramatically. In designing this volume, we have attempted to capture the complexity of issues associated with content-based instruction as an approach and to reflect on its development with a critical eye, yet a constructive tone. Building on previous work in language and content integration, we decided to look forward rather than retell its history. Throughout the volume, however, we include references to earlier work on content-based instruction. We invite readers to explore these efforts as a broader context, both national and international, for the work represented here.

We had several goals in mind as we assembled the various parts of *The Content-Based Classroom*. We sought to solicit a wide range of perspectives on content-based teaching and to showcase work taking place at all educational levels—elementary, secondary, postsecondary, and adult education—both to illustrate the broad base of the approach and to illuminate experiences and challenges pertinent to different instructional settings.

We also decided to use this opportunity to cast the net widely and show the relationship between content-based instruction and other approaches which are currently generating interest in second and foreign language teaching. Accordingly, we asked experts in such areas as whole language and the teaching of culture and literature to discuss the relationship between their work and content-based instruction. We looked to English for Specific Purposes (ESP), Vocational English as a Second Language (VESL), and sheltered English where the connections are more obvious, in an attempt to uncover the similarities and delineate the differences between these approaches and content-based instruction. This type of bridge-building reveals a strong foundation for content-based teaching at all levels of instruction and suggests a rich collection of strategies for improving instruction for second and foreign language students.

There are three main parts to the volume. Part I presents multiple perspectives on content-based instruction, including a focus on theoretical underpinnings; K–12 instruction; postsecondary education; syllabus, materials, and course design; teacher preparation; assessment; research; and alternative models. Part II covers practical issues. Among these are two prominent themes—collaboration between language and content instructors, and issues in content-based program administration. Part III is made up of short chapters which consider the links between content-based instruction and related approaches. We envisioned this section as an exchange, a dialogue with the authors who brought to bear their own perspectives and experiences with different instructional approaches across various levels of instruction. We expect that course instructors and readers will select from among these three parts those chapters that best serve their interests and needs. Our goal was to create as many interesting and relevant options as possible. Each part concludes with Questions for Follow-Up Thought and Application, which provide readers with issues to consider regarding the chapters within that part. The questions require readers to synthesize information from different chapters and, in some cases, reconcile different points of view.

We'd like to think that this volume represents the "state of the art" in content-based instruction at the present time. We believe that the varied ways in which the principles of integrated language and content teaching are being applied at all educational levels is impressive. It is therefore our hope that the readings encourage those presently teaching in content-based settings to join the dialogue and share their experiences at educational conferences and in local and national publications. For those who are new to this instructional approach, we hope this collection will inspire attempts to try content-based teaching. Finally, although we have designed this book with ESL/EFL teachers and prospective teachers in mind, we hope that readers will share relevant articles with their colleagues in the content areas and in the workplace in an attempt to build the bridges which are at the heart of content-based teaching.

We would like to acknowledge Denise Murray and Dorothy Messerschmitt, former editors of *The CATESOL Journal,* who invited us in 1990 to guest edit a special theme issue on content-based instruction. The theme issue, which was published in April 1992, was the original impetus for this book as we used the opportunity to raise key issues in content-based instruction, describe current content-based practices, and suggest directions in which the approach might evolve in the future. The theme issue was well received but limited in its distribution; thus, we seized on the idea to expand the geographical scope of the special issue and further develop the perspectives represented by the original contributors from California. We are very grateful to Joanne Dresner and Allen Ascher of Addison Wesley Longman for supporting this effort and allowing the original volume to blossom into its present form. We also appreciate the keen eyes of Linda Moser and Alice Vigliani, our editors, who kept us on track and on pace, and the hard work of Kathleen McGrath, who helped us with word processing. Our reviewers provided valuable feedback which helped to shape the volume; we are especially grateful to Neil Anderson of Ohio University for his encouragement. Antony Kunnan's thoughtful review of one of the testing chapters and Grace Burkart's timely help with reference information were much appreciated as well. We also thank the many contributors to this volume, all friends and colleagues who share our interest in integrated language and content teaching. Finally, we express our sincerest appreciation to our students in "Teaching English for Academic Purposes" at Cal State LA, who have inspired us with insights and challenged us with questions about content-based instruction.

List of Contributors

Elizabeth Bernhardt, Stanford University

Anthony Bernier, University of California, Irvine

Richard Blakely, Rhode Island School of Design

Donna M. Brinton, University of California, Los Angeles

Cherry Campbell, Monterey Institute of International Studies

Joan G. Carson, Georgia State University

Martha Clark Cummings, Monterey Institute of International Studies

David E. Eskey, University of Southern California

Laureen Fredella, Latin American Association, Atlanta, Georgia

David Freeman, Fresno Pacific College

Yvonne Freeman, Fresno Pacific College

Young Gee, City College of San Francisco

Marge C. Gianelli, Canutillo Independent School District, Canutillo, Texas

Lynn Goldstein, Monterey Institute of International Studies

William Grabe, Northern Arizona University

Rosemary Henze, ARC Associates, Oakland, California

Sharon Hilles, California State Polytechnic University, Pomona

Christine Holten, University of California, Los Angeles

Martha Iancu, George Fox University

Linda Jensen, University of California, Los Angeles

Ann M. Johns, San Diego State University

Lía D. Kamhi-Stein, California State University, Los Angeles

Anne Katz, ARC Associates, Oakland, California

Dorit Kaufman, State University of New York at Stony Brook

Kate Kinsella, San Francisco State University

Dennis Lynch, Michigan Technical University

Tim Murphey, Nanzan University, Nagoya, Japan

Pat Wilcox Peterson, Mankato State University, Mankato, Minnesota

Lyn Margaret Repath-Martos, University of California, Los Angeles

Marisol Rodríguez-Muñoz, Columbus Public Schools, Columbus, Ohio

Nina Glaudini Rosen, Glendale Community College, Glendale, California

Linda Sasser, Alhambra School District, Alhambra, California

Ken Sheppard, Center for Applied Linguistics, Washington, DC

Deborah J. Short, Center for Applied Linguistics, Washington, DC

Marguerite Ann Snow, California State University, Los Angeles

Carole Srole, California State University, Los Angeles

Fredricka L. Stoller, Northern Arizona University

Gloria M. Tang, University of British Columbia

Josephine A. Taylor, Georgia State University

Annela Teemant, The Ohio State University

Jean Turner, Monterey Institute of International Studies

James F. Valentine, Jr., University of California, Los Angeles

Eva Wegrzecka-Kowalewski, Los Angeles Unified School District

Sara Cushing Weigle, University of California, Los Angeles

Kathleen Wong, City College of San Francisco

Jane Zuengler, University of Wisconsin, Madison

part I

Multiple Perspectives on Content-Based Instruction

The multiple perspectives on content-based instruction presented in Part I are framed by research in second language acquisition and educational and cognitive psychology; they are also based on successful second and foreign language programs, including approaches to language across the curriculum. Following a theoretical overview of content-based instruction, the chapters in Part I offer perspectives from the classroom teacher, the materials developer and course designer, and the teacher educator. Other perspectives cover assessment and research in integrated language and content instruction. Finally, alternatives to the most common models of content-based instruction are explored.

FOCUS ON THEORETICAL UNDERPINNINGS

In Chapter 1, "Content-Based Instruction: Research Foundations," William Grabe and Fredricka Stoller review the research support for content-based instruction and provide a comprehensive rationale for this approach to second and foreign language teaching.

FOCUS ON K–12 INSTRUCTION

In Chapter 2, "Integrating Content-ESL: A Report from the Front," Ken Sheppard reports on the scope of integrated language and content instruction in U.S. elementary, middle, and high school classrooms. Looking specifically at sheltered content classes, in Chapter 3, "Sheltered English: Modifying Content Delivery for Second Language Learners," Nina Glaudini Rosen and Linda Sasser describe instructional practices that are used to make subject matter accessible to English language learners. Complementing this chapter are Kate Kinsella's Chapter 4, "Moving from Comprehensible Input to "'Learning to Learn,'" in Content-Based Instruction," which emphasizes the need in such classroom settings for learner strategy instruction; and Gloria Tang's Chapter 5, "Teaching Content Knowledge and ESL in Multicultural Classrooms," which describes the application of Mohan's knowledge framework in a middle school social studies classroom through the use of graphic representations of text structure.

FOCUS ON POSTSECONDARY INSTRUCTION

Fredricka Stoller and William Grabe present a systematic approach for designing content-based courses in Chapter 6, "A Six-T's Approach to Content-Based Instruction"; they illustrate this approach with a theme-based unit in an intensive language program setting. Historians Anthony Bernier (Chapter 7, "The Challenge of Language and History Terminology from the Student Optic") and Carole Srole (Chapter 8, "Pedagogical Responses from Content Faculty: Teaching Content and Language in History") emphasize the linguistic challenges of successfully teaching content (from both the student and instructor's point of view) and offer pedagogical suggestions for better integrating the teaching of language and content. Adding to these reports from ESL settings is Chapter 9 by Tim Murphey ("Content-Based Instruction in an EFL Setting: Issues and Strategies"), which offers a perspective that is unique to the EFL context.

FOCUS ON SYLLABUS, MATERIALS, AND COURSE DESIGN

In Chapter 10, "Syllabus Design in Content-Based Instruction," David Eskey identifies content as the missing dimension in ESL/EFL syllabus design. He highlights content-based instruction as an approach which offers insights into the historic form/function debate. Marge Gianelli (Chapter 11, "Thematic Units: Creating an Environment for Learning") shares her experience in designing thematic units at the elementary school level. In Chapter 12, "Adapting the Adjunct Model: A Case Study," Martha Iancu addresses the need for ongoing assessment and modification of course design when implementing adjunct instruction at the postsecondary level.

FOCUS ON TEACHER PREPARATION

In Chapter 13, "Knowledge, Skills, and Attitudes in Teacher Preparation for Content-Based Instruction," Pat Wilcox Peterson characterizes the competencies that teachers need to successfully integrate language and content. Offering a model of preservice teacher preparation in Chapter 14, "Collaborative Approaches in Preparing Teachers for Content-Based and Language-Enhanced Settings," Dorit Kaufman describes a collaborative training program for TESOL, science, and social studies teacher candidates.

FOCUS ON ASSESSMENT

Jean Turner (Chapter 15, "Creating Content-Based Language Tests: Guidelines for Teachers") discusses key issues in content-based language assessment and offers a procedure that teachers can follow to develop their own content-based tests. Sara Weigle and Linda Jensen (Chapter 16, "Issues in Assessments for Content-Based Instruction") expand on the issues discussed by Turner, arguing that the most important considerations for content-based assessment are authenticity and interaction. They illustrate these considerations through the example of a content-based ESL exam for matriculated university students.

FOCUS ON RESEARCH

Deborah Short (Chapter 17, "Reading and 'Riting and . . . Social Studies: Research on Integrated Language and Content in Secondary Classrooms") draws on research from the observation and analysis of middle school social studies classes to justify the use of specific instructional strategies and the development of materials which integrate language, content, and critical thinking objectives. In Chapter 18, "How Relevant Is Relevance? An Examination of Student Needs, Interests, and Motivation in the Content-Based University Classroom," James Valentine and Lyn Repath-Martos examine the argument that content-based teaching must be relevant to students' needs and interests. They share insights gained from classroom observation, surveys, and student interviews of ESL students enrolled in a university-level ESL content-based class. In Chapter 19, "Enhancing

Student Performance through Discipline-Based Summarization-Strategy Instruction," Lía Kamhi-Stein reports on research into the summarization strategies of language minority students who participated in an innovative adjunct program for high-risk university students. Arguing that much remains to be done to document changes in linguistic development that result from content-based instruction, Jane Zuengler and Donna Brinton (Chapter 20, "Linguistic Form, Pragmatic Function: Relevant Research from Content-Based Instruction") suggest a research agenda that examines the relationship between linguistic form and pragmatic function.

FOCUS ON ALTERNATIVE MODELS

Richard Blakely (Chapter 21, "The English Language Fellows Program: Using Peer Tutors to Integrate Language and Content") and Marguerite Ann Snow (Chapter 22, "Teaching Academic Literacy Skills: Discipline Faculty Take Responsibility") propose two innovative approaches to integrated language and content teaching that incorporate an expanded role for peer tutors and content-area faculty. Both approaches seek to equip individuals who are not traditionally vested with the responsibility for language instruction with strategies for assisting ESL students in the content areas.

chapter **1**

Content-Based Instruction: Research Foundations

William Grabe and Fredricka L. Stoller

Content-based instruction has been used in a variety of language learning contexts for the last twenty-five years, though its popularity and wider applicability have increased dramatically in the past ten years. Early versions of content-based instruction (CBI) were used in English for Specific Purposes (ESP) programs, second language immersion programs for K–12 students, early foreign language magnet classrooms, and a variety of second language (L2) vocational and workplace instructional contexts. More recently, content-based language instruction has extended into other settings; it has become a widespread approach in K–12 classrooms (in both first language (L1) and L2 contexts), in university-level foreign language instruction, in various bilingual education contexts in Europe, and in English for Academic Purposes (EAP) programs. In short, the development of content-based language curricula is gaining prominence in a wide range of contexts. A number of factors account for the rise in popularity of CBI.

In discussion of CBI many authors refer to successful program outcomes as evidence of its benefits. They either describe a program that they assert as successful; or they discuss teacher and student interests, program enrollments, and successful student adjustment to later academic careers as support for CBI. In this chapter, it is our intention to extend the discussion by examining an extensive body of research from a wide range of fields which argues, directly and indirectly, for the benefits of content-based learning. The research which supports CBI spans the range from studies in second language acquisition, to controlled training studies, to various strands of research in educational and cognitive psychology. After reviewing empirical support for CBI from these different domains, we will examine the effectiveness of different types of content-based classrooms and programs. These program outcomes provide another source of support for CBI. We will conclude our discussion with a set of rationales for CBI and its various approaches.

SUPPORT FOR CBI FROM SECOND LANGUAGE ACQUISITION RESEARCH

A major source of support for CBI comes from second language acquisition research, particularly the work of Krashen, Swain, and Cummins. Krashen's (1982, 1985) comprehensible input hypothesis provided an early rationale for the development of CBI in second language contexts. His argument that language is best acquired incidentally through extensive exposure to comprehensible second language input has not only supported the use of CBI but has, in turn, been supported by the successful results of a number of L2 CBI programs. Canadian immersion programs, U.S. bilingual immersion programs, and the University of Ottawa sheltered programs for second and foreign language learners all provide a degree of support for the importance of comprehensible input for L2 development and L2 content learning (Snow, 1993; Wesche, 1993). Students in Canadian immersion programs, for example, when compared with non-immersion students, have demonstrated equivalent subject matter achievement, equivalent L1 language learning, and near-native L2 learning (particularly in comprehension abilities). Even late-immersion programs, with French immersion instruction beginning in the sixth or seventh grades, have led to the same positive results (Wesche, 1993).

Reassessments of Canadian immersion programs, however, have revealed the limitations of instruction which only promotes comprehensible input. Swain (1988, 1993) provides a more balanced account of integrated language and content instruction in the Canadian context when she points out the additional need to emphasize formal language aspects of the content resources used in immersion contexts. Swain (1985, 1988, 1991, 1995a) has argued persuasively that students in French immersion programs in Canada, despite many years of L2 French input, develop only limited L2 proficiency in the areas of speaking and writing, making numerous errors in their productive use of French. These results have led Swain to argue that the Canadian CBI immersion programs are successful in teaching subject matter content and L2 comprehension skills (listening and reading), but are not as successful in teaching speaking and writing. These skills require explicit attention to formal aspects of language output if students are to acquire native-like proficiency (see also Widdowson, 1993).

As a result of the research on Canadian immersion programs, Swain proposed her output hypothesis to address the limitations noted above (Swain, 1985, 1993, 1995b). The output hypothesis argues that student learning depends on explicit attention to productive language skills (i.e., speaking and writing). A more recent extension of the output hypothesis argues for explicit focus on relevant and contextually appropriate language forms to support content-learning activities in the classroom. As a result of these findings, immersion approaches are now giving greater prominence to language learning activities. The combination of focused language instruction and content teaching is a prominent feature of a number of other CBI approaches as well, partly as a result of Canadian immersion evidence and partly as a result of the findings that follow.

Further extensions of the form-content integration for instruction, as distinct from the "form versus content" debate, are discussed by Garrett (1991), Lightbown and Spada (1994), Swain (1995a), and Tarone and Swain (1995). The central argument raised by these researchers is that both form and meaning (content) are important and not readily separable in language learning (see also Halliday, 1993; Wells, 1994). All meaningful language communication typically combines formal accuracy and relevant content within every utterance or written sentence. The two components work together to serve communication needs. In particular, students and teachers need to negotiate language form (as well as content), a concept that is reinforced by recent discussions of sociocultural approaches to second language acquisition, also known as Vygotskian approaches. Such socio-cultural approaches are generally consistent with CBI.

Recently, Lantolf and others (Aljaafreh & Lantolf, 1994; Donato, 1994; Lantolf, 1994; Lantolf & Appel, 1994; Lantolf & Pavlenko, 1995; McCafferty, 1994; Schinke-Llano, 1993) have shown that the Vygotskian-based concepts of (a) negotiation in the Zone of Proximal Development, (b) private speech (internally directed speech as problem-solving and rehearsing strategies), and (c) student appropriation of learning tasks are important notions in L2 learning. They are also notions which are readily applicable to CBI contexts. Students in CBI classes have many opportunities to negotiate the knowledge that they are learning (rather than simply interact or exchange information) and to extend their knowledge at increasing levels of complexity as more content is incorporated into the lessons. Moreover, students in content-based classrooms have many occasions to engage in private speech while learning language, sorting out input and rehearsing as they interact with more knowledgeable individuals (Lantolf & Pavlenko, 1995). Finally, students have many chances to develop ways of learning from teachers and peers, thereby appropriating activities, strategies, and content in ongoing cycles of learning. Research on sociocultural approaches to second language learning provides strong support for CBI when such instruction incorporates Vygotskian notions. Similar support emerges from studies of Vygotskian orientations in L1 literacy learning in elementary-school contexts (Moll, 1990; Newman, Griffin, & Cole, 1989; Rogoff, 1990; Tharp & Gallimore, 1988).

A final theoretical support from second language learning for CBI follows from Cummins's (1984, 1989) notion of Cognitive Academic Language Proficiency (CALP). He argues that many L2 students learn Basic Interpersonal Communication Skills (BICS) within a relatively short period of time (approximately two years in school). However, these language skills are not sufficient for students to succeed in academic learning contexts. Instead, students need to develop Cognitive Academic Language Proficiency if they are to succeed in academic second language learning contexts. The development of CALP in the L2 can take much longer, from five to seven years or more (Collier, 1989; Wong-Fillmore, 1994). Postponing content instruction while students develop more advanced academic language is impractical and ignores students' complex educational needs. Students need to be learning content information *while* they are acquiring CALP. Moreover, such skills, because they are more academically oriented and require more complex language abilities, are best taught within a framework that manipulates more complex and authentic content. In a sense, the language of CALP *is* the language of academic content areas. Thus, the need for more demanding language abilities suggests that a CBI approach would be the most effective way for students to develop CALP.

SUPPORT FOR CBI FROM TRAINING STUDIES

A number of instructional approaches have been shown to be effective in classroom training research and are commonly incorporated into CBI approaches. When these approaches are incorporated, their demonstrated effectiveness provides additional support for CBI. In particular, research on cooperative learning, metacognitive/learning strategy instruction, and extensive reading are supported by impressive results and are readily incorporated within CBI.

Cooperative Learning

Cooperative learning requires that students work together (typically in small groups of four to six) to learn information and carry out a range of tasks. The purpose is to promote peer group support and peer instruction (cf. Vygotskian learning theory). There are a number of approaches to cooperative learning (Fathman & Kessler, 1993; Stahl, 1994), though the approaches developed by Slavin and his colleagues (see Slavin, 1995) have the strongest research documentation, with well over 100 controlled experimental research studies.

Slavin's research, in particular, has demonstrated strong improvements in student learning when students work in groups that have structured objectives, have group goals and rewards, promote individualized accountability, and provide each student in the group with equal opportunities for success. In two versions of his approach to cooperative learning, STAD and CIRC (Student Teams–Achievement Divisions, and Cooperative Integrated Reading and Composition), results of classroom training studies consistently demonstrate significant gains for students in cooperative learning classes across a range of student groups and grade levels. In the case of STAD, this cooperative learning approach has demonstrated significant gains over control groups in language arts, math, reading comprehension, geography, history, and ESL. Cooperative learning leads to greater student cooperation, higher motivation for learning, more positive student attributions for learning success, better attitudes toward school and learning, and greater self-esteem (Slavin, 1995). Cooperative learning is consistent with the goals of CBI and is readily incorporated into CBI (see also Crandall, 1993; Fathman & Kessler, 1993).

Metacognitive/Learning Strategy Instruction

Reading strategy research has demonstrated that strategy learning works best when it is integrated within the regular curriculum as a consistent feature of content and language instruction. Integrating strategy instruction, as discussed here, means more than including lessons that teach important language learning strategies; rather, it refers to teaching curricula in which strategy awareness and development constitute a daily component of *all* learning activities. Recent research on reading strategies has shown that decontextualized strategy instruction seldom transfers to independent learning contexts and typically is not retained over a longer period of time. However, when strategy instruction is seen as part of daily activities in a subject-area or language curriculum through teacher modeling, student awareness, and teacher guidance, the goal shifts from teaching strategies to developing a strategic reader. Such a goal leads to long-term improvements in strategy use and a gradual transfer to independent learning contexts.

The goals of learner strategy training programs are difficult to carry out, as documented by Duffy (1993a, 1993b), Gaskins (1994), Pressley, El-Dinary, Gaskins, Schuder, Bergman, Almasi, and Brown (1992), and Pressley, Almasi, Schuder, Bergman, Hite, El-Dinary, and Brown (1994); but this approach provides the best opportunity for strategy instruction (Brown, Pressley, Van Meter, & Schuder, 1996; Pressley & Woloshyn, 1995). CBI approaches provide one of the few realistic options for promoting the development of strategic learners within a language-learning curriculum. The content component of a content-based classroom provides the extended coherent material into which strategy instruction can be integrated and recycled on a daily basis. Thus, CBI approaches, which promote the importance of strategy learning, provide the curricular resources for development of the strategic language (and content) learner.

Extensive Reading

Research on the advantages of extensive reading shows that reading coherent extended materials leads to improved language abilities and greater content-area learning. In L1 contexts, Stanovich and his colleagues (West, Stanovich, & Mitchell, 1993) have demonstrated that extensive reading (as "exposure to print") improves reading abilities, vocabulary, and general knowledge (see also Anderson, Wilson, & Fielding, 1988; Nell, 1988). In L2 contexts, Elley (1991) has provided strong evidence that students who engage in extensive reading across a range of topics increase their language abilities in reading, writing, vocabulary, speaking, and listening skills; they also develop greater content knowledge and higher motivation (see also Krashen 1989, 1993). Overall, this reading research provides one of the strongest cases of skills transfer and the potential benefits of a CBI curricular approach.

SUPPORT FOR CBI FROM EDUCATIONAL AND COGNITIVE PSYCHOLOGY

Though somewhat further removed from the language learning classroom, research in educational and cognitive psychology offers some of the most persuasive support for CBI. The following five research areas (which may be seen as potentially interacting) represent a range of contributions: cognitive learning theory; depth-of-processing research; discourse comprehension processing research; motivation, attribution, and interest research; and expertise research. An extended discussion would be required to explore these contributions thoroughly; we will only touch on these areas to suggest the types of support each provides for CBI.

Cognitive Learning Theory

The research on learning theory proposed by Anderson (1983, 1990a, 1990b, 1993) provides strong support for the Cognitive Academic Language Learning Approach (CALLA) described by O'Malley and Chamot (1990), and it suggests a reasonable learning theory to explain the effectiveness of CBI more generally (O'Malley, 1990; see also Estes, 1989). Anderson's theory of learning reinforces teaching approaches which combine the development of language knowledge, practice in using language, and strategy training to promote independent learning. In Anderson's ACT* theory, skills (including language skills) and knowledge follow a general sequence of stages of learning from the cognitive stage, to the associative stage, to the autonomous stage. In *the cognitive stage*, students notice and attend to information in working memory; typically they engage in solving basic problems with the language and concepts they are encountering. In *the associative stage*, errors are corrected and connections to related declarative and productive knowledge are strengthened; the knowledge and skills become proceduralized. Finally, in *the autonomous stage*, performance becomes automatic, requiring little attentional effort, and it is well integrated within a strong network that activates additional information through spreading activation. This final stage frees up cognitive resources for the next cycle of problem solving.

Anderson's ACT* theory provides a strong basis for examining complex skill development; as such, it is a reasonable characterization for academic language learning and a strong learning theory for instruction which integrates attention to content and language (Anderson, 1993; Chamot & O'Malley, 1994; O'Malley, 1990). Although ACT* is a learning theory that can be applied to a wide variety of contexts, its capability for describing complex language learning makes it a strong potential foundation for CBI.

Depth-of-Processing Research

Depth-of-processing research argues that the presentation of coherent and meaningful information leads to deeper processing, and that deeper informational processing results in better learning (Anderson, 1990a; Barsalou, 1992; Stillings,

Feinstein, Garfield, Rissland, Rosenbaum, Weisler, & Baker-Ward, 1987). Numerous features of this research can be directly associated with effective CBI.

First, research reported by Anderson (1990a) shows that information which is more elaborated is memorized and recalled better. Research has demonstrated that students' self-generated elaborations (e.g., adding additional phrases to a sentence, continuing a sentence, or forming a "why" question about a sentence) lead to better recall of factual knowledge. Second, when information is closely related to other information in a text, student recall improves (Anderson, 1990a). For this reason, techniques for revealing connections between ideas in texts (e.g., graphic organizers) lead to better informational recall. Similarly, emotional and affective connections increase memory and recall of information. Third, the spaced study of information, rather than a single massive dose, leads to better memory and recall. Spaced study—the recycling of important related information and the efforts made by students to recall and connect prior information—generates multiple access paths in memory and greater connections to other information. The resulting more complex linkages and pathways lead to better learning and recall (Anderson, 1990a).

Overall, these depth-of-processing research findings are consistent with CBI, an approach that, by definition, promotes extended study of coherent content and relevant language learning activities. Thus, depth-of-processing research provides support for the integration of language and content instruction (see also Menke & Pressley, 1994; Pressley et al., 1992; Woloshyn, Pressley, & Schneider, 1992, for elaborated questioning techniques in L1 literacy contexts).

Discourse Comprehension Processing Research

Research on discourse comprehension processes and text coherence has demonstrated that more coherently presented information, in terms of thematically organized material, is easier to remember and leads to improved learning (Singer, 1990). In particular, text information that directly defines and supports the topic of discourse in the text is easier to learn and recall. Moreover, information that has a greater number of connections to related information promotes better learning. The various ways that information is interconnected also help learners use the information in new situations (Spiro, Vispoel, Schmitz, Samarapungavan, & Boerger, 1987). Finally, research on discourse comprehension has demonstrated the importance of verbal and visual representations of information to improve students' memory and recall (Paivio, 1986; Sadoski, Paivio, & Goetz, 1991). This line of comprehension research supports the use of graphic organizers and visual representations of content information for improved learning.

These research results provide strong justification for CBI, because one of its major goals is to give students multiple opportunities to work with coherently developed sets of content resources and to revisit that information from a variety of perspectives, including exposure to visual representations of information (see also Grabe, 1995; Mohan, 1986). Moreover, as information is learned and recall is improved, the coherence and relatedness of this information with other content allow for more complex language learning activities and for the transfer of learning to new situations—both primary goals of CBI.

Motivation, Attribution, and Interest Research

Motivation, positive attributions, and interest are critical factors which support student success with challenging informational activities and which help them learn complex skills—two important goals of CBI. Research has found that motivation and interest arise in part from the recognition that learning is indeed occurring and that the learning of sophisticated and challenging information justifies the effort. Further, considerable research argues that students who are more motivated, who develop an interest in curricular learning goals and activities, and who perceive themselves as successful and capable students learn more and do better in school (Alexander, Kulikowich, & Jetton, 1994; Krapp, Hidi, & Renninger, 1992; Tobias, 1994; Turner, 1993). In addition, students with high interest and motivation make greater elaborations with learning material, make more connections among topical information, and can recall information better (Alexander, Kulikowich, & Jetton, 1994; Krapp, Hidi, & Renninger, 1992). Thus, motivation and interest also provide an explanation for the relationships between better learning and the depth-of-processing and discourse-processing research discussed above.

In similar respects, interest in content information, and the successes students attribute to content learning (based on past experiences), can lead to powerful intrinsic motivation. As noted by Krapp, Hidi, and Renninger (1992), "situational interest, triggered by environmental factors, may evoke or contribute to the development of long-lasting individual interests" (p. 18). Thus, interest in the content of a course may trigger intrinsic motivation and lead to better learning (see also Crookes & Schmidt, 1991; Csikszentmihalyi, 1990; Csikszentmihalyi, Rathunde, & Whalen, 1993; Dweck, 1989; Renninger, Hidi, & Krapp, 1992). One goal of CBI is to generate interest in content information through stimulating material resources and instruction, leading students to develop intrinsic motivation to learn.

One theory of intrinsic motivation which is relevant to CBI is that of "flow," a theory of optimal experience that is well suited to language learning contexts (Csikszentmihalyi, 1990, 1993; Csikszentmihalyi & Csikszentmihalyi, 1988). Flow is the state of optimal experiences (happiness) brought about when personal skills are matched by high challenge, leading to a narrowed focus of attention, a total absorption in the activity, a sense of timelessness, and a temporary lack of awareness of personal problems. Such optimal experiences lead to increased learning. In his synthesis of twenty-five years of research, Csikszentmihalyi (1990) outlines consistent features of flow, features that more typically derive from work or learning environments than from leisure-time activities. Eight such features are noted (p. 49):

1. Tasks must have a reasonable chance of being completed.
2. Concentration on the task must be possible.

3. The task has clear goals.
4. The task provides immediate feedback.
5. Involvement in the task precludes worries and frustration from ordinary life.
6. The person is able to exercise a sense of control over his/her actions.
7. A concern for self disappears.
8. A sense of duration of time is altered.

Two important consequences of flow experiences are an increase in intrinsic motivation and an ability to carry out tasks at higher levels of complexity. Csikszentmihalyi (1990) states:

> Often children—and adults—need external incentives to take the first steps in an activity that requires a difficult restructuring of attention. Most enjoyable activities are not natural; they demand an effort that initially one is reluctant to make. But once the interaction starts to provide feedback to the person's skills, it usually begins to be intrinsically rewarding. (p. 68)

The ability to engage in increasingly more complex tasks successfully augments intrinsic motivation and improves learning capacity. Thus, flow, as a theory of motivation with application to language learning, provides a strong rationale for engaging in CBI; CBI, in turn, provides many opportunities for the development of intrinsic motivation.

Expertise Research

Finally, research on the nature of expertise provides support for CBI approaches. Recently, Bereiter and Scardamalia (1993) outlined a theory of expertise that supports many of the features of effective CBI. They argue that expertise is a process in which a learner reinvests his/her knowledge in a sequence of progressively more complex problem-solving activities and gains from the increasing challenges that result. Expertlike learners look for increasing complexity in the tasks they engage in; in the process, learning itself improves. This problem-solving activity also leads students to develop intrinsic motivation, in part because they recognize their own growing expertise in the given domain or content area, and in part because they experience successes with the increasing challenges. Expertlike learners also devote much of their energy in learning to knowledge-building goals rather than task-accomplishment goals. Good learners want to understand connections between sets of information and are interested in using various strategies for making appropriate connections. In essence, they want to learn how to become good learners. Of course, in the process, they also learn to accomplish tasks, acquire relevant skills, and carry out progressive problem solving.

Bereiter and Scardamalia's discussion of expertise and expertlike learning makes direct connections with Csikszentmihalyi's notion of flow as well as with discourse comprehension research, depth-of-processing research, and Anderson's ACT* theory of learning. A notion that all five lines of argument share in common is the benefit of *complexity* for increased learning and enhanced motivation. Thus, complexity itself becomes a major theme that can optimize learning in the right educational contexts. Each of the five research perspectives described above emphasizes the need for more complex challenges, reinvestment of skills to meet these challenges, and appropriate educational supports to stimulate optimal learning (Bereiter & Scardamalia, 1993; Carter, 1990). The possibilities for building such motivating yet manageable complexities in language learning are most likely to be developed and maintained through the coherent informational resources used in CBI.

Bereiter and Scardamalia also note that the development of complexity in content information and skills acquisition requires an initial foundation of knowledge: a bootstrapping mechanism that will allow students to experience and develop greater intrinsic motivation, more progressive problem solving, and increased learning opportunities. In general, CBI approaches combine coherent and interesting informational resources to create increasing, but manageable, task complexity. Thus, CBI, through the use of a coherent foundation of information, provides the sort of bootstrapping mechanism that the above research perspectives call for.

The various arguments presented here from research in educational and cognitive psychology represent a fairly unusual set of arguments for CBI. The research reported is typically intended to inform learning theories and instructional practices more generally, but the arguments are directly applicable to language learning and, in particular, to academically oriented language learning at almost any grade level. Taken together, these arguments provide some of the strongest rationales for engaging in a CBI approach to language learning.

SUPPORT FROM CBI PROGRAM OUTCOMES

Additional support for CBI follows from the outcomes of actual CBI programs that have demonstrated successes with combined language and content instruction. Although there have been few controlled empirical studies demonstrating the effectiveness of actual CBI programs, the fact that students exit the programs with improved language skills and content-area knowledge attests, at one level, to the success of CBI. Teachers continue to explore ways to combine content and language learning because of their belief in the approach. In this section, we review documentation from five instructional contexts which suggests both the strengths of CBI and its wide range of applications. These five areas include K–12 ESL contexts, K–12 foreign language contexts, postsecondary ESL contexts, postsecondary foreign language contexts, and language across the curriculum contexts.

K–12 ESL Contexts

Numerous discussions of CBI in North American K–12 contexts have appeared in the past ten years. CBI is used in North American elementary school contexts and secondary school contexts with second dialect and ESL students, though the dynamics are quite distinct at the two school levels. In elementary school settings where language and ethnic minority students and/or immigrant ESL students from mixed language backgrounds represent a significant proportion of the enrollment, the emphasis on CBI is particularly strong. This emphasis follows in part from Cummins's observations that CALP takes many years to develop (and students cannot wait five to seven years before beginning content learning) and in part from an instructional philosophy favoring integrated skills and conceptually meaningful instruction. There are, at present, few empirical studies of the benefits of CBI over alternative approaches at elementary school levels (cf. Crandall, 1987), though informal assessment mechanisms indicate increased learning and improved motivation for learning. Practical information on implementing L2 CBI curricula at elementary school levels is discussed in a number of recent volumes, including Chamot and O'Malley (1994), Crandall (1987), Enright and McCloskey (1988), Faltis (1993), and Peregoy and Boyle (1993).

In middle schools and high schools, the somewhat more constrained curricular structure creates more problems for CBI as a general goal. However, CBI instruction has been widely employed in L2 secondary contexts, most commonly through theme-based ESL programs and sheltered instruction. These programs seek to build students' knowledge of academic English in an environment in which students are able to function academically and also learn important grade-appropriate content information (Chamot & O'Malley, 1987, 1994; Johannsen, 1993; Mohan, 1986; Peitzman & Gadda, 1994; Short, 1994; Spanos, 1993; Tang, 1992, see also Chapter 5 in this volume). Mohan (1986) has argued for the importance of such CBI approaches by pointing out that all content learning is language learning, but not all language learning is content learning because language classes often trivialize content learning (see also Halliday, 1993). In general, secondary-level CBI efforts are an attempt to provide *both* relevant language skills and serious, relevant content instruction. The growing number of such theme-based and sheltered curricula at secondary levels provides a reasonable source of evidence in support of CBI.

An additional CBI approach that has been developed involves the use of one school in a district system as an ESL immigrant school. One of the best known examples of this in the United States is Newcomer High School in the San Francisco area (Stack, 1993). Students enroll in Newcomer High for six months to one year and receive intensive ESL instruction combined with bilingual (or sheltered) math and social studies, and another elective course. All these classes count toward high school graduation requirements. Other exemplary programs and curricular efforts are highlighted in the proceedings of a recent U.S. Department of Education OBEMLA (Office of Bilingual Education and Minority Languages Affairs) conference (OBEMLA, 1993) which focused on language minority instruction in middle and high school contexts (see, in particular, Castaneda, 1993; Lucas, 1993; Reyner & Davison, 1993; Spanos, 1993).

K–12 Foreign Language Contexts

Foreign language instruction in other countries (primarily European) has also made successful use of CBI, though there is little empirical data as supporting evidence. Historically, the learning of content through a second language (e.g., Latin) has a long history in Europe (Brinton, Snow, & Wesche, 1989; Krueger & Ryan, 1993a). In the twentieth century, L2 immersion CBI was initiated in the USSR in the 1960s, and Western Europe has consistently promoted advanced second language studies that involve some form of CBI. More recently, the push for European union has entailed foreign language instruction, with CBI components, in the K–12 curriculum in many West European countries. In addition, a number of regions with minority languages have developed bilingual programs that incorporate some form of CBI (Artigal, 1991; Baetens-Beardsmore, 1993, 1994; Byram & Leman, 1989).

In Central Europe, Hungary has recently initiated dual-language secondary schools. Students take one year of intensive language study before enrolling in a number of subject-area courses in their second language over the next four years of secondary schooling (Duff, 1995). Elsewhere, the government of Hong Kong recently endorsed an English immersion program for 30 percent of its students entering secondary school (see Goldstein & Liu, 1994, for a discussion of efforts taken to help students transition from learning content in Chinese to learning content in English). Even in the United States, foreign language CBI in K–12 contexts is regularly practiced. Rhodes (1995) reports that there are 187 total or partial immersion language programs in the United States, and Christian (1995) reports another 182 two-way immersion programs (see also Met, 1993).

Postsecondary ESL Contexts

Research from a number of postsecondary L2 contexts that endorse CBI curricular approaches has indicated improved English language learning, improved student motivation and interest, and successful mastery of content information (Brinton, Snow, & Wesche, 1989; Iancu, Chapter 12 in this volume; Snow, 1991a, 1993; Snow & Brinton, 1988; Stoller & Grabe, Chapter 6 in this volume). Program evaluations show that theme-based courses, sheltered courses, and adjunct courses all represent appropriate approaches for CBI in advanced L2 learning contexts.

English for Specific Purposes (ESP) and advanced disciplinary English for Academic Purposes (EAP) contexts provide additional support for advanced-level CBI programs. ESP curricula, throughout a history that spans more than forty years, have been designed to teach specific content and language skills to students and professional employees ranging from engineering and medical students to lawyers, business executives, airline mechanics, bank tellers, and hotel employees (see Johns, Chapter 31 in this volume). Although there is typically little empirical evidence of program success, because ESP programs seldom evaluate program results through controlled research methods, the available descriptions of various programs indicate that ESP programs achieve their specific purposes on many occasions. Whether such specific accomplishments by students translate into more general second language abilities is a debate that has continued for the past fifteen years (cf. Hutchinson & Waters, 1987; Johns & Dudley-Evans, 1991; Widdowson, 1983). Nevertheless, the relative degree of success enjoyed by ESP programs supports the use of CBI more generally.

In a related line of instructional practices, advanced disciplinary EAP instruction, typically grounded in the content materials of students' academic majors, provides further evidence of the potential benefits of CBI. Swales (1990) has argued that second language instruction which focuses on students' academic disciplines provides the language and content resources for effective advanced EAP instruction. Swales and Feak (1995) have further argued that such an approach introduces students to the specific discourses of their future professions and motivates students to work with authentic, appropriate, and meaningful language resources. They further argue that such advanced content and language instruction is best developed through extensive use of visual and graphic representations, an approach endorsed by a number of CBI advocates (Grabe, 1995; Mohan, 1986; Stoller & Grabe, Chapter 6 in this volume; Tang, 1992, also Chapter 5 in this volume).

Postsecondary Foreign Language Contexts

Over the past ten years, a number of foreign language CBI programs and courses in North American universities have been documented. In the case of the Canadian L2 adjunct courses at the University of Ottawa, there is strong empirical evidence of success (Hauptman, Wesche, & Ready, 1988; Wesche, 1993). In this program, L2 students have performed as well as L1 students on subject matter tests and have developed strong L2 academic language skills, particularly in the areas of reading and listening. In many cases, however, the level of success of the programs is established not through empirical data collection but by student attitudes, increased interest and enrollment, and student job placement.

One of the most successful U.S. programs, judging by student job placement and ongoing student interest in the program, is the combined German and Engineering program at the University of Rhode Island; students earn a double major in German and engineering while spending time as interns in a German-speaking engineering company and following a curriculum of sheltered and theme-based CBI courses (Grandin, 1993; Wesche, 1993). A second successful foreign language CBI program in the United States is Eastern Michigan University's

Language and International Business program (Krueger & Ryan, 1993a; Palmer, 1993). In this program, students major in a modern language (e.g., Spanish, French, German, or Japanese) and take a combination of theme-based and sheltered courses which emphasize business content. The program has been successful in graduating language majors capable of performing successfully in international business fields.

A number of other programs have successfully used a variety of CBI curricular formats. The Monterey Institute of International Studies integrates international policy studies with language education, typically linking content courses taught in various modern languages with adjunct language-support courses in those languages. The U.S. Foreign Service Institute has successfully used theme-based CBI courses in its intensive training programs. The University of Illinois Italian program has used theme-based CBI courses in its second-year curriculum with considerable success, as measured by sustained interest, high enrollment, and student attitudes (Musumeci, 1993). These programs and others point out the potential strengths and benefits of CBI for foreign language instruction in North America (Krueger & Ryan, 1993b; Straight, 1994).

Language Across the Curriculum and Related Approaches

One of the more common sets of arguments in favor of CBI follows from the Language Across the Curriculum (LAC) movement in England in the 1970s. The movement proposed a curricular approach that designated reading and writing as central components of all content-area instruction throughout the school years. This notion has been a source of continuous debate in England, and it has led to a number of related approaches in the United States and Canada: Writing in the Content Areas for secondary grades, Reading in the Content Areas for secondary grades, and Writing Across the Curriculum (WAC) in North American universities. In all four versions of LAC, the goal is to make language/literacy instruction an essential objective in all classes, since all content is learned through language and a focus on language/literacy skills will improve content learning.

In L1 elementary school contexts, many CBI programs are intended primarily to develop literacy skills and help students begin the transition from "learning to read" to "reading to learn." Particularly in whole language classrooms, teachers work to combine language and content instruction. In L1 secondary contexts, efforts to introduce language across the curriculum, reading in the content areas, and writing in the content areas all have met with some resistance because many subject-area teachers want to maintain strong control over their particular courses and subject matter (Office of Bilingual Education and Minority Languages Affairs, 1993; O'Brien, Stewart, & Moje, 1995). Nonetheless, many schools have developed sheltered curricula for students who have difficulties with the mainstream curriculum, and practical suggestions for the implementation of such programs for L2 students are becoming more readily available (Cochran, 1993; Peitzman & Gadda, 1994; Ruddell, 1993).

Despite the relatively long history of these movements and the strong logical appeal of their arguments, there is little evidence to support the assertion that students learn content better when they read and write about it in greater intensity (cf. Ackerman, 1993; Adamson, 1993; Crandall, 1987; O'Brien, Stewart, & Moje, 1995; Tchudi & Huerta, 1983; Vacca & Vacca, 1993). The phrases "writing to learn" and "reading to learn" have yet to be grounded in empirical evidence. Nevertheless, these notions and the four general movements noted above (LAC, WAC, reading in the content areas, writing in the content areas) have been, and remain, very influential in various CBI efforts as well as in L1 and L2 literacy instruction at all levels. The arguments for these approaches are appealing, but the lack of research support for their claims would suggest that other rationales for CBI may be more persuasive.

CONCLUSION

Content-based instruction is a powerful innovation in language teaching across a wide range of instructional contexts. There is strong empirical support for CBI, and the success of many well-documented programs offers additional support for the approach. Moreover, numerous practical features of CBI make it an appealing curricular approach to language instruction. This practical aspect is well argued by Brinton, Snow, and Wesche (1989):

> In a content-based approach, the activities of the language class are specific to the subject matter being taught, and are geared to stimulate students to think and learn through the use of the target language. Such an approach lends itself quite naturally to the integrated teaching of the four traditional language skills. For example, it employs authentic reading materials which require students not only to understand information but to interpret and evaluate it as well. It provides a forum in which students can respond orally to reading and lecture materials. It recognizes that academic writing follows from listening, and reading, and thus requires students to synthesize facts and ideas from multiple sources as preparation for writing. In this approach, students are exposed to study skills and learn a variety of language skills which prepare them for the range of academic tasks they will encounter. (p. 2)

This quotation reflects a consistent set of descriptions by CBI practitioners who have come to appreciate the many ways that CBI offers ideal conditions for language learning when carried out appropriately. These practical considerations, along with the other support covered in this chapter, lead us to suggest seven strong rationales for CBI:

1. In content-based classrooms, students are exposed to a considerable amount of language while learning content. This incidental language should be comprehensible, linked to their immediate prior learning, and relevant to their needs—all important criteria for successful language learning. Such a setting for learning makes second language learning consistent with most other academic learning contexts as well; that is, most classrooms involve the teaching of some type of content information, and, in those classrooms, language learning also occurs—at least incidentally. In content-based classrooms, teachers and students explore interesting content while students are engaged in appropriate language-dependent activities, reflecting the learning that students carry out in other content-area classes. The resultant language learning activities, therefore, are not artificial or meaningless exercises.

2. CBI supports contextualized learning; students are taught useful language that is embedded within relevant discourse contexts rather than as isolated language fragments. In content-based classrooms, students have many opportunities to attend to language, to use language, and to negotiate content through language in natural discourse contexts. Thus, CBI allows for explicit language instruction, integrated with content instruction, in a relevant and purposeful context.

3. Students in CBI classes have increased opportunities to use the content knowledge and expertise that they bring to class. The use of coherently developed content resources allows students to call on their own prior knowledge to learn additional language and content material.

4. CBI itself promises to generate increased motivation among students; in content-based classrooms, students are exposed to complex information and are involved in demanding activities which can lead to intrinsic motivation. Motivation and interest arise partly from the recognition that learning is occurring and that it is worth the effort, and partly from the appropriate matching of increasing student knowledge of a topic with increasing task (or learning) challenges.

5. CBI supports, in a natural way, such learning approaches as cooperative learning, apprenticeship learning, experiential learning, and project-based learning. It also lends itself well to strategy instruction and practice, as theme units naturally require and recycle important strategies across varying content and learning tasks.

6. CBI allows greater flexibility and adaptability to be built into the curriculum and activity sequences. Because additional subtopics and issues can be incorporated into the course, teachers have many opportunities to adjust the class to complement the interests and needs of both teacher and student.

7. CBI lends itself to student-centered classroom activities; in content-based classrooms, students have opportunities to exercise choices and preferences in terms of specific content and learning activities. Because there are many avenues for exploring themes and topics in content-based classes, student involvement in topic and activity selection is increased.

These rationales, when combined with the empirical research findings and the documentation of program successes summarized in this chapter, provide persuasive arguments in favor of content-based instruction across a wide range of L2 instructional contexts. Yet we must acknowledge that these rationales do not automatically operate in all programs which label themselves as content based. A simple label does not necessarily translate into the operationalization of these rationales, nor does it signify a program grounded in the careful structuring of content, language, and strategy instruction/learning. However, programs that do adopt these rationales, as programmatic foundations and in practice, can develop effective content-based curricula and powerful language and content learning classroom environments.

chapter **2**

Integrating Content-ESL: A Report from the Front

Ken Sheppard

Content-language instruction has many definitions, and classroom practices vary as widely as communities, schools, and personnel do. In most schools that have adopted this approach, however, the ideal is for an ESL and content teacher each to take on part of the other's job: The ESL teacher systematically reinforces the students' understanding of content, and the content teacher builds the students' proficiency in English. Thus, the focus is off form much of the time. In the long run, however, students acquire language they need for content classes by revisiting the material covered in content classes with a teacher who is sensitive to the complexities of communicating about content in an unfamiliar language. Theoretically, in this fashion, the students should gradually improve in all curricular areas, as should their test scores and grades.

In 1991, the Office of Bilingual Education and Minority Languages Affairs (OBEMLA) awarded a contract to the Center for Applied Linguistics (CAL) to describe content-ESL programs, pre-K through 12, across the country. The study's explicit goal was to generate "a descriptive analysis of the nature and scope of content-ESL classroom practices." Its larger purpose was to gain a general understanding of content-ESL policies and practices across the country and to consider how these policies and practices might inform the development of a theory of content-language integration. The study was completed in 1994.[1]

---

[1] Copies of the three study volumes are available from the National Clearinghouse for Bilingual Education (NCBE) at 1-800-321-NCBE. See Burkart and Sheppard, 1994; Kauffman et al., 1994; Sheppard, 1994.

SOME DEFINITIONS

Some years ago, the term *content-ESL* was coined to include both halves of the equation—both content-based ESL and linguistically sensitive content instruction, both the ESL teacher and the content teacher. In the CAL study, the approach was broadly defined to capture as much information as possible about these conceptually diverse programs. In short, a program qualified for inclusion if the following criteria applied:

> There are one or more classes in which the integration of ESL and subject matter (content) learning takes place. These classes may merely make content instruction in English more comprehensible, or they may aim at systematic integration. They may be taught by ESL and/or content teachers with or without the use of a student's primary home language. Administratively, they may form part of a larger structure, such as a bilingual or ESL program, or operate autonomously. (Sheppard, 1994, p. 38)

Furthermore, since the school was chosen as the unit of analysis, a program was defined as school-based and schoolwide. Thus, a large school that contained several programs was deemed to have only one; conversely, a program that spilled over five schools was considered to constitute five separate programs.[2] In essence, the view adopted by the study team was that every school is unique and its culture uniquely determines the shape and direction of the instructional programs it houses.

THE PROCESS

Because no previous study of similar scope had ever been undertaken, no database of content-ESL programs existed. One therefore had to be created. This was accomplished by soliciting nominations of content-ESL programs from ESL professionals across the country, combining those nominated programs with Title VII grantees, and purging duplicates. The resulting database contained 2,992 programs.

The study then proceeded across three broad tasks. First, the programs that had been identified were surveyed by mail. Second, a random sample of the programs responding to the first survey was queried more comprehensively about programmatic policies, instructional practices, the teachers, the students, and so on. Finally, site visits to twenty programs were conducted to acquire firsthand knowledge in still more elaborate detail. Altogether, eleven instruments were used for the study. Their use is described in the following sections.

Task One: Defining the Universe

All 2,992 programs that had been nominated or received funding under Title VII were mailed an Identification Questionnaire (IdQ). Its purpose was to identify the ESL programs from that pool that conformed to the study's definition and

---

[2] For this reason, the terms *program* and *school* are used interchangeably in this chapter.

TABLE 2.1   Distribution of ESL students: Total data set

	Percentage of ESL Students	Number of ESL Students
Type of School[a]		
Primary	10	162
Elementary	44	712
Middle	18	292
High	23	370
School Location		
Large cities	26	
Suburbs	18	
Large towns	24	
Small towns	19	
Rural areas	13	
Family Income		
Moderate to high	5[b]	
Moderate	12	
Low to moderate	31	
Low	77	

[a] The remainder (85) were classified as unknown or multiple grade schools.
[b] Percentages in this section sum to more than 100 because many schools reported the presence of students representing more than a single income category.

to obtain basic information that would inform the selection of program to participate in subsequent stages of the study.

The IdQ contained 24 items addressing basic program features, including the program's structure, content foci, size, longevity, and funding source(s), as well as student, teacher, and community characteristics.

In the end, data from 1,621 schools in all parts of the country, at all grade levels, were received, evaluated, and prepared for analysis. Their distribution approximated the distribution of ESL students across the country as reported by various sources,[3] as Table 2.1 reveals.

Task Two: Querying the Universe

A random subset of the programs that had received IdQs received two follow-up questionnaires called the Information Questionnaire for Administrators (InfoQ:A) and the Information Questionnaire for Teachers (InfoQ:T).

---

[3] See, for example, U.S. Department of Education, *The Condition of Bilingual Education in the Nation* (1992).

The InfoQ:A consisted of 24 items addressing such variables as the program's structure, history, staffing, and enrollment. The InfoQ:T requested information about teachers' assignments, experience, instructional practices (i.e., their instructional approaches, preferred classroom activities, routine modifications in language, and use of cues or aids), choice of materials, and qualifications, and about the students' proficiencies in English, educational backgrounds, and the like. The items relevant to instructional practices asked how often teachers engaged in various practices.

In the end, paired InfoQs (one of each type from every program) were available for 468 programs, or 29 percent of the total data set (1,621). The distribution of ESL students by type of school, school size, community location, and family income is summarized in Table 2.2. In addition, 60 percent of the programs reported that over 75 percent of their students were eligible for free or reduced-cost lunches.

TABLE 2.2   Distribution of ESL students: Subset (29%) of total data set

	Percentage of ESL Students	Number of ESL Students
Type of School[a]		
Primary	9	43
Elementary	38	178
Middle	21	97
High	27	126
Community Size		
Large cities	26[b]	
Suburbs	18	
Large towns	24	
Small towns	21	
Rural areas	10	
School Location		
Midwest	19	
Northeast	21	
Northwest	25	
South	27	
Southwest	25	
Family Income		
Moderate to high	6[c]	
Moderate	13	
Low to moderate	32	
Low	78	

[a] The remainder (14) were classified as unknown or multiple grade.
[b] Percentages in this section sum to more than 100 because some programs reported more than one community size.
[c] Percentages in this section sum to more than 100 because some programs reported students representing more than one income category.

Task Three: Visiting the Schools

Twenty sites representing a cross-section of such variables as region of the country, type of school (i.e., grade levels), the students' primary home languages, and community size were selected for study. Data were collected by observation and personal interview during these visits. To conduct them, pairs were formed from the CAL study team.[4]

Team members created the Post-Observation Checklist to guide and record their observations. Items concerned the following: the classroom environment, including the class's content focus, the type of language accommodation in evidence, the media used, and the number of instructors; activities, including group size, tasks students were asked to perform, students' behavior, and the materials used; and instruction, including variables such as teacher behavior, discourse, content, methodology, and learner behavior. Seven interview protocols guided the collection of supporting data for the classroom observations and, ultimately, the preparation of field reports.

A variety of classes representing a range of curricular emphases and grade levels was observed, approximately 125 in all. The teachers of these classes were interviewed before and after each class about their routine practices and the function and sequence of the classes observed.

THE RESULTS[5]

The study's findings are summarized here under six rubrics: students, teachers, programs, instruction, curriculum and materials, and assessment.

Students

Spanish predominated among the students' native languages, with 81 percent of the programs reporting the presence of Spanish-speaking students and 57 percent reporting that over 50 percent of their students had Spanish as a primary home language. However, more than 170 other primary home languages were represented. Thirty-three percent of the teachers who participated in the survey indicated that the majority of their students read and wrote these languages "adequately"; 29 percent reported that their students read and wrote them poorly.

In 79 percent of the programs, there was no English proficiency requirement for participation. Nine percent said the students should know basic English, whereas 4 percent said the students should be "at an intermediate level." As for the students' informal acquisition experiences, most programs reported that their

---

[4] The team included: Grace Burkart, JoAnn (Jodi) Crandall, Dora Johnson, Dotti Kauffman, Joy Kreeft Peyton, Ken Sheppard (project director), and Deborah Short.

[5] Readers are directed to the final report, *Content-ESL across the USA: A Technical Report* (Sheppard, 1994), for definitions of some terms used here and a full discussion of the study's implications and limitations.

students interacted primarily with native English speakers in organized activities (59%) or in conversation with friends and mentors (53%).

Forty percent of the programs indicated that 75 to 100 percent of their students had been schooled continuously in the United States. In 83 percent of the programs reporting, fewer than 20 percent of the students had experienced refugee education; in 79 percent, fewer than 20 percent had experienced migrant education. The students' socioeconomic status was characterized as low income for 77 percent of the programs. Only 5 percent said that their students came primarily from moderate to high income homes.

Teachers

Sixty-three percent of the teacher respondents taught both English and some form of content. This number, in part, may reflect the large number of ESL teachers queried rather than a national trend—that is, because the database was selective and not random, it is not necessarily the case that most content-ESL instructors are ESL rather than content teachers.[6] Of the rest, 12 percent were English teachers who collaborated with colleagues in content instruction, and 3 percent were content teachers who worked with ESL teachers for the same purpose. There were no significant differences between elementary and secondary teachers with respect to these patterns.

The bachelor's degree was the highest level of educational attainment for 43 percent of the teachers, the master's degree for 55 percent. Eighty percent had received specialized training in content-ESL, although nothing can be inferred from these data as to quality and quantity of this training. The median number of years teachers had been in content-ESL was four.

Programs

While 50 percent of the programs had been in operation fewer than five years, 37 percent had operated for more than six years. Sixty-two percent reported that a rapid influx of ESL students into the community had motivated the creation of their content-ESL programs; only 28 percent indicated that the impetus was a legal mandate.

Instruction

The students' native languages were used for instruction in 50 percent of the programs. However, only slightly more than 10 percent devoted more than 50 percent of class time to instruction in those languages. There was more primary

---

[6] It is, however, possible that content-ESL instruction is still largely the province of the ESL teacher, program, or department. After all, at the very least, it is simpler for a teacher accustomed to working with ESL students to integrate language and content instruction than it is for a teacher for whom language instruction is terra incognita.

home language support reported in the elementary schools than in middle or high schools. No information was secured as to the purposes for which primary home language support was provided.[7]

Elementary school teachers were more likely to use innovative classroom activities and take a learner-centered approach than were high school teachers. Similarly, high school students spent more time on academic subjects, such as math and science, that required reading and writing in English than did elementary school students. According to these reports, secondary and elementary teachers also differed in terms of the resources they used in class, whereas they exhibited no differences in terms of their collaborative patterns.

The results reported thus far say nothing about what distinguished both groups from regular ESL or mainstream teachers in classroom practice. Like teachers of language arts generally, the teachers surveyed, for example, favored a language experience approach and eschewed the language lab. They were also more likely to use textbooks than authentic print materials "always," though the use of authentic material was obviously on the rise and occurred "sometimes" or "often" 68 percent of the time. While many (though not a majority) also acknowledged a preference for such instructional practices as inquiry learning and cooperative learning, these approaches were not devised in response to the specific needs of content-ESL students. Thus, there was little evidence in these data of an emergent "content-ESL specific" approach, in the sense of an approach that is created by content-ESL teachers to meet the specific needs of these programs and their students. Rather, the teachers in these classes have adopted practices that are popular across the board. (See also Part III of this volume.)

More specifically, a few approaches commonly associated with language learning per se were examined separately.

Whole language. Eighty-six percent of the respondents to the initial survey said that a whole language approach had been adopted in their programs. On the subsequent survey, the average teacher said that she used whole language activities "often."

Language experience approach (LEA). This approach was reported slightly less often: Respondents said they used it somewhere between "often" and "sometimes."

Cooperative learning. Cooperative learning was favored by 84 percent of the programs surveyed, and it was used somewhere between "often" and "sometimes."

---

[7] The use of two languages in a content-ESL classroom is of course a complex issue. In general, many programs favor a clear division between instruction in the two languages, although there are many communities in the United States where two languages jostle each other constantly, and extensive code-switching is simply an aspect of the way the community communicates. In those cases, the languages coexist as happily inside class as outside (Zentella, 1978). What is generally discouraged in the literature, though common in practice, is the use of consecutive interpretation. Interpretation is difficult under the best of circumstances: It can disrupt the flow of a class if it is not done well and alienate members of the class who do not speak the dominant PHL (primary home language). Unfortunately, these data give no clear impression of the precise patterns of use, though it is clear that use of the students' primary home languages is only one tactic among many that teachers in these programs employ to clarify the material.

Teachers were also asked how often they employed "a variety of student group-ings," and they said they did so "often." Forty-two percent also claimed to use "cooperative assessment."

Task-based language learning. The question was not addressed directly in the surveys because none of the classes investigated had linguistic development as their sole aim. There was evidence, however, that these programs integrated the four skills, stressed communicative activities, and employed a variety of tasks, on the average somewhere between "always" and "often"—so presumably some-thing similar to task-based activities that require students to negotiate meaning was being used.

The natural approach. Teachers said they use this approach "sometimes" or "often," although the wide diversity in these responses suggests that some programs strongly favored the approach and others rarely used it, if ever.

Total physical response (TPR). In response to the question "How often do you use . . . activities requiring little production (e.g., TPR)?" teachers said they "rarely" used them, on the average. Since TPR is primarily associated in practice with students at stages prior to speech emergence, this result is not surprising.

Curriculum and Materials

Two issues relevant to curriculum and materials were widely discussed. Have programs developed their own materials and curricula that incorporate content and language objectives? Do they use technological media such as computer software and video in their classes for ESL students?

Roughly 54 percent of the programs in the study had developed curricula specifically for content-ESL. Of these, 31 percent had content-ESL science curricula, 28 percent math curricula, and 36 percent social studies curricula. Secondary schools were more likely to use outlines, notes, and handouts than were elementary schools, and elementary schools were more likely to use word banks and audiocassettes. While most programs used material from the regular courses in their classes, the majority (90%) also created materials or activities for their students.

The content-ESL programs under study employed a variety of instructional media in their classes. Fifty-three percent of the programs said that they used computer-assisted instruction. As a practical matter, this could be anything from an occasional word-processing activity on the lone computer in the corner to full-fledged computer-assisted classes in mathematics or science in a computer lab. Of those teachers surveyed by means of the information questionnaire, the mean response to the question "How often do you use . . . computer-assisted instruction?" fell between "sometimes" and "rarely," although the high standard deviation (1.16) suggests wide variance. As for other media, both videos or films and audiocassettes fell close to "sometimes" in frequency of use, as did overhead transparencies. On the whole, nontechnological aids scored higher: Realia, for example, were used "frequently," as one might expect in elementary programs.

Assessment

Even though most programs did not require English proficiency for participation, they used a variety of measures to identify and evaluate students upon admission. They also monitored student progress in a lot of different ways, as the study results reveal in considerable detail. Exit procedures also varied widely, as the school visit reports in particular show.

As for course-related assessment, teachers in over 50 percent of the programs reported using (in descending order of frequency) informal questioning, teacher-made paper and pencil tests, student projects, quizzes, journals, compositions, and simulations or oral reports. Administrators in over 50 percent of the programs reported using teacher-made tests and quizzes, grades, standardized language tests, and standardized content tests. Portfolio assessment was universally popular.

FROM PRACTICE TO THEORY

A secondary goal of the study was to assess the extent to which these programs' practices match up with practices recommended in the growing content-ESL literature. The short answer to this question is that many do: The teachers have adopted practices that are consistent with broad trends in instructional practice generally. These practices moved them, in sum, away from discrete-point ideas about language toward an interaction with general meaning, away from commercially published texts toward the use of authentic and program-specific material, away from teacher-centeredness toward the learner-centered environment, away from reductionist notions about the learner toward a holistic definition, away from materially driven activities toward experiential learning, and away from student passivity toward active investment in the learning process. Many programs are in step with such tendencies. However, many others espouse more conventional approaches to learning and the learner, and there are still many programs that have regrouped students without coming to grips with the need for a realignment in programmatic content. Nevertheless, there is evidence that although content-ESL practitioners may not always be at the cutting edge, many provide their students with instruction that is both sensitive to their needs and responsive to progressive shifts in recommended practice.

Content-ESL is a mélange of strategies and methodologies, materials and activities, policies and practices that share a common purpose: the preparation of ESL students for the English medium content classroom through language and content integration. Since it falls between instruction *in* the language and instruction *through* the language, it opens the door to a variety of instructional modalities from a variety of sources, including (to name only a few) language learning strategies devised by ESL educators, cooperative work in small groups, primary home language integration, generic text-driven approaches from the academic classroom, task-oriented activities, criterion-referenced assessment, alternative techniques of assessment, and experiential learning. Therefore, it is best understood as a blend of instructional procedures whose collective virtues are this diversity, a generalized willingness to experiment, and the concomitant absence of a prevailing orthodoxy. Despite its heterogeneity a few patterns are apparent.

The role of the students' native languages. There is a dawning recognition in these programs, if not in many others, that using the students' primary home language for support is valid. Thus, in half the programs reported on here, the home language is used at least some of the time to support instruction in English. In general, however, the students in these programs listen to and speak English better than they read and write their native languages, if their teachers' reported estimates can be credited. Therefore, despite the primary home language's role in these classrooms, these programs appear to have little more effect on the prevailing subtractive tendency (i.e., the tendency of native languages to be overtaken by English within a single generation).

Patterns of prior schooling. In half the programs, 50 percent or more of the students have been educated continuously in the United States, and students who have experienced interrupted schooling are relatively rare. Indeed, well over half the students have received all their educational services in this country. Few of the students enrolled in these classes are likely to feel out of place because of having had no prior experience with the intricacies of U.S. educational institutions. The number of older students who had no previous schooling and were therefore educated continuously in the United States (though not "from the age of 6 or younger"), the database's elementary school bias, and the mismatch between the primary home languages and school language still constitute a problem.

A mix of conventional and innovative material. Authentic print material is used in programs "often" over 40 percent of the time, according to the teachers surveyed, and nearly half the programs have developed "content-ESL specific" curricula. Ninety percent of the teachers said they had created activities or materials for their classes, and they also said that activities were "determined by textbook or textbook series" only some of the time. As school visits revealed, many teachers are developing modules and activities for their students; many of these have yet to be disseminated, however.

On the other hand, 45 percent of the teachers surveyed reported using textbooks on one survey item, whereas on another, 90 percent claimed that they used some form of "published material," including modified texts and workbooks (27%), texts and workbooks designed for content-ESL instruction (32%), basic skills or remedial material (47%), mainstream materials (53%), and ESL books appropriate to the students' proficiency level(s) (62%). On the average, teachers claimed that they used textbooks somewhere between "sometimes" and "frequently." These facts send a mixed message, but it seems clear that published—and presumably commercially published—material still plays a big role in these classes. In other words, the popular assumption that task-oriented approaches such as cooperative or inquiry learning hold sway in content-ESL finds only modest support in these data. Text-dependent exercises and activities—tried and true fill-in-the-blanks, read-aloud activities[8]—still take up a lot of class time. This conclusion was borne out in the classes observed across the country. In other words, even in those programs where teacher creativity and student initiative were actively rewarded, commercial materials and the rote activities that many of them promote were still part of the school's routine.

A preference for alternative assessment. Judging from evidence accumulated during school visits, alternative forms of assessment such as portfolio assessment are growing in use, though notions of what portfolios are and how their contents might be weighted vary widely. On the whole, the use of alternative assessment does not distinguish teachers and administrators in these programs from their colleagues who deal with highly English proficient students. Rather, its endorsement only lends support to the general impression that content-ESL methodology still owes more to creative, across-the-board teaching methodologies than to innovations in second language education.

A tilt toward methodological innovation. The overwhelming majority of the teachers in these programs have received some form of specialized training for content-ESL instruction, and there is some evidence that the teachers in these programs have adopted relatively progressive strategies in their teaching. For example, 27 percent of the variance in instructional approaches was accounted for by a strategy that encompassed cooperative learning, student research projects, and discovery learning. Similarly, over 40 percent claimed that they "often" take a language experience approach, that is, an approach in which students generate their own texts. They also avoid English language exercises such as drills. However, there is little evidence to suggest that in adopting these strategies, content-ESL teachers differ from their more progressive colleagues in non-content-ESL programs or that a content-ESL methodology that differs from other approaches is emergent. Indeed, while they associate themselves with innovative approaches such as cooperative learning and whole language, and do not always identify with more conventional practices, they may not be ahead of the curve in implementing any of these innovations. Large-scale surveys, however, may not be the best way to obtain detailed information on methodological innovations; and short-term school visits also have limitations, not the least of which is their selectivity.

An expanding social role for schools. In addition to course work, schools today provide an array of social services for immigrant students and their families. By offering help with housing, employment, and legal affairs, as well as evening and weekend classes in everything from drug counseling to driving, schools forge strong links with the neighborhood and reinforce family support for education. At schools, it is often the teacher who knows the family best. Many students we interviewed, for example, had developed exceptionally close relationships

---

[8] Teachers said that they "read aloud from the textbook" "often" or "sometimes," but there was a lot of variation in that response set, as reflected in the standard deviation (1.17), suggesting that this practice is by no means universal.

with their teachers, whom they viewed as friends and counselors, and many of the teachers had assumed wider social roles in their neighborhoods than those normally associated with teachers. By contrast, school administrators were often remote authorities who, despite the best intentions, had little direct contact with the students and their families: They knew less about their lives and antecedents than the teachers did.[9]

Success and the need for more research. Most of the teachers surveyed (79%) said that their students in content-ESL classes learned English listening, speaking, reading, and writing faster than their previous students in conventional grammar-based classes had, and nearly all of them (89%) said that the content-ESL students also learned content faster than their previous students had. Needless to say, this measure is a very indirect and somewhat suspect measure of program effectiveness. A more thorough approach would require both within-school and between-school comparisons. Within-school comparisons would be possible if both content-ESL and traditional ESL were available in a single setting and tests were identical or highly correlated. Between-school comparisons would be extremely difficult to carry out unless the students were comparable in terms of key variables such as socioeconomic status and unless the same standardized tests were used at the schools involved at each grade level. In both cases, controlling for pre-existing differences would be difficult, if not impossible. Nonetheless, such a study is much needed; as a first step, a preliminary study should be conducted to determine which indicators of effectiveness would be most discriminating. Many teachers interviewed during the school visits suggested that programs would willingly participate in such a study because program personnel are frequently asked to justify their practices but have little basis for making a principled comparison of treatments.

CONCLUSION

There is some form of content-ESL in roughly 15 percent of the public schools in the United States.[10] For the most part, these programs exist not because they are less expensive than stand-alone ESL classes but, rather, because of the need to increase achievement among a rapidly expanding ESL population. Similar programs can be expected to grow in size and number in the future. Projections are hard to come by, but if the trend evident in the last decade

---

[9] For that reason, the study team decided after field-testing its instruments to bifurcate the InfoQ. Teachers and administrators had different perspectives on the programs, and they knew different things about the students they served.

[10] The CAL study team conducted an independent random survey of schools across the country to estimate the incidence of content-ESL as an approach. Details are available in *Content-ESL across the USA: A Technical Report* (Sheppard, 1994).

continues,[11] children with limited proficiency in English will enter the public schools in larger numbers and stimulate the creation of still more programs. In the meantime, successful programs will continue to improve and expand as networks for the exchange of information about the approach are established and public awareness is increased. Growing concern over the quality of U.S. education, high dropout rates among minority students, and the conse-quent demand for higher performance standards will further spur their growth.

---

[11] The National Center for Education Statistics, in its November 1993 summary, for example, reported that "the number of persons 5 years old and older . . . who were reported to speak a language other than English at home increased by about 40 percent to about 12 percent of the population between 1979 and 1989" (U.S. Department of Education, Office of Educational Research and Improvement, 1993).

chapter 3

Sheltered English: Modifying Content Delivery for Second Language Learners

Nina Glaudini Rosen and Linda Sasser

As teachers, we all experience satisfaction when we find exactly the right strategy for conveying a difficult concept. When students are not able to grasp course concepts and objectives through conventional methods like the lecture, learner-centered teachers seek out and employ alternative methods. Many seasoned teachers of English language learners have learned to modify the delivery of content material to make concepts accessible and comprehensible for their students. The goal is to turn on the light of understanding so that it is reflected in the work of the classroom. The delivery of content information to English language learners in this way is what many practitioners call sheltered English, known now in some regions as Specially Designed Academic Instruction in English.[1]

In sheltered English, content-area teachers use a variety of language teaching strategies to enhance understanding of grade- and age-appropriate subject-area concepts. Such sheltered lessons provide cognitive and linguistic scaffolds for English language learners: Through modeling, demonstration, and interaction with the teacher and their classmates, students use English language skills to demonstrate comprehension of content-area objectives. Typically, sheltered English courses are taught in the areas of social sciences, life and physical sciences, and mathematics in K–12 settings and in business and technology in vocational/technical educational settings. To succeed in matching activities to the linguistic

---

[1] Specially Designed Academic Instruction in English (SDAIE) is a phrase used in California to describe content courses taught to English language learners. For the position paper on SDAIE endorsed by the California Association of Teachers of English to Speakers of Other Languages (CATESOL), visit the CATESOL web site at http://www.crl/com/~malarak/catesol/html/ or contact Pam Butterfield, CATESOL public relations chair, at Palomar College, 114 West Mission Road, San Marcos, CA 92069.

and cognitive levels of students, teachers require both knowledge and understanding. In addition to knowing their students well, practitioners of sheltered instruction need a repertoire of effective second language strategies and a secure understanding of their content areas.

Sheltered instruction is one approach to content-based instruction (CBI) that calls for teachers to reject the "commonsense notion that the content of a language course should be language," and embraces the premise "that people do not learn languages, then use them, but that people learn languages by using them" (see Eskey, Chapter 10 in this volume). Therefore, although a CBI course may be a language course designed to facilitate the acquisition of English, the content of that course could also be the world—that is, the topics, themes, and ideas which fill our universe. Seen in this way, sheltered instruction and content-based ESL are mirror images of each another.

In sheltered English, teachers use highly specific techniques and strategies to develop concepts and themes. English language learners gain knowledge as well as the language which encodes that knowledge. Classroom examples provide a clear understanding of this process.

I felt like an astronaut in a rocket looking at the constellations.

I learned a whole lot about outer space. Mr. Dorff was amazing. It was a very exciting experience.

These students, enrolled in a fourth-grade sheltered science class at Edison Elementary School in Glendale, California, had just spent an entire day and evening at school with Tom Dorff, a local astronomer. Mr. Dorff had shared slides, told stories, and given students and their parents an opportunity to view the night sky through telescopes. The students' enthusiastic reception of this experience is reflected in their comments.

How did these English language learners access the linguistically and cognitively challenging material presented by Mr. Dorff? Prior to his visit, teachers had prepared the students with a variety of hands-on science activities: They made star charts and models, used flashlights to demonstrate a variety of astral phenomena, and measured and drew the sun and planets to scale on their asphalt playground. The students participated in a star scavenger hunt to locate and share information through the use of reference materials. With colored paper, paints, and chalk the students also made artistic stellar representations. When Mr. Dorff arrived, the students brought this background to the new conceptual experience he was about to provide. Through visual aids, Mr. Dorff expanded the students' existing knowledge; in the darkened room, students focused on the slides and viewed visual images as they listened to the astronomer's explanation of the constellations. The darkened room and the dramatic content of the slides worked together to create a supportive classroom environment. In this stimulating context, the children were not focused on learning a second language but rather on understanding the content or message of Mr. Dorff's talk. Yet while the children were engaged in the unit's sheltered activities, many content learning and language acquisition opportunities were presented.

Such integration of content and language objectives is evident in the overview of the astronomy unit presented in Figure 3.1. As the figure illustrates, this unit for fourth-grade students constantly moves between building concepts

FIGURE 3.1 Content and language objectives in a sheltered unit

Activity	Purpose	Language or Content?	Assessment
K-W-L chart*	to assess student knowledge	content	completion of K-W columns
star and planet charts	to build vocabulary	language	observation: use of resources
	to reformulate data	language	
	to locate information on a chart	language	completion of star charts
	to develop reading skills	language	learning log or journal
astral phenomena with flashlights	to introduce concept of reflected lights	content	learning log or journal
sharing circle	to develop vocabulary	language	oral participation
playground model of solar system	to develop a concept of scale	content	accurate measurements
	to use measurements	content	participation completed model
star scavenger hunt	to locate printed information	language	observation
	to share data orally	language	participation
	to present data in written form	language	written report
artistic star representations	to express understanding in a nonprint medium	content	completion of artwork
story telling	to comprehend a story	language	feedback
	to connect prior and new experiences	content	facial expression
slides of constellations	to build knowledge	content	learning log or journal
viewing the night sky	to identify constellations	content	participation; student questions
	to apply concepts learned	content	completion of K-W-L chart
culminating project (e.g., mural, student-made books, student interviews, research project)	to express the scale of the universe	language	student responses to unit

*What I *know,* what I *want* to know, and what I *learned* chart (see Weaver, 1994).

in the content area and providing students with the language needed to manipulate and apply those concepts. With adults who may already possess conceptual understanding of the solar system, the emphasis would be placed more squarely on language development—but since fourth-grade English language learners need opportunities to use the target language to interact with one another as well as to expand their frames of reference, an integrated unit like this moves between the dynamics of language acquisition and content mastery.

As Figure 3.1 makes clear, teacher assessment of students' language and content development is ongoing. Since learners bring different background knowledge and linguistic proficiency to the classroom experience, formal measures would be inappropriate for several reasons. Formal examinations in a true/false, multiple-choice, or short-answer format measure the learner against a limited set of fixed external criteria. The results of such measures tend to tell us more about what students do not know than about the vast and varied knowledge they may have acquired. For English language learners, such tests may be less about content and more about reading, writing, and/or test-taking skills (see Weigle and Jensen, Chapter 16 in this volume). On the other hand, teachers who observe their students engaged in activity-based learning, who respond to their students' logs, who facilitate oral interaction in sharing circles— in short, teachers who are involved in the learning processes along with their students—know very well how much their students know, have learned, and are likely to learn. By allowing students to select final projects, teachers both stretch and support their students—they stretch by encouraging choice, creativity, and responsibility; they support by providing options through which students of varied skill levels can demonstrate success.

The preceding lesson is but one example of how content can be sheltered in a science class. The visiting astronomer not only used visual aids to support learning but also created a context in which his presentation reinforced the content that had been previously taught. In creating both a positive affective climate and a supportive academic context, Mr. Dorff provided an ideal sheltered learning environment which facilitated success for English language learners.

PEDAGOGICAL NEEDS OF SHELTERED ENGLISH TEACHERS

To empower English language learners with academic skills, sheltered teachers need several sorts of pedagogical understandings:

- *They need to know the subject matter they plan to teach.* This permits them to select key concepts out of the many possibilities in the curriculum. For instance, if the concept of cycles is essential to a deep understanding of life sciences, then the teacher may choose to organize the semester or the term around this key concept, bringing in other elements as they relate directly to the cycles.

- *They need to have a repertoire of instructional strategies which will assist in making grade-level content comprehensible and, therefore, accessible.* Such strategies will be appropriate for the students' developing language skills and will employ a conscious use of appropriate visuals, context clues, graphic organizers, and social interaction.

- *They need knowledge of second language learning processes.* This includes knowledge not only of the cultures represented in their classrooms but also of second language development and of how students are assisted in learning. The greater the teachers' familiarity with diverse cultures and language acquisition theory, the more equipped they are to adroitly guide students to academic success.

- *They need to be able to assess the particular cognitive, linguistic, and social strategies students use.* When students add to their stock of strategies, they become more academically versatile and independent. For instance, during a parent conference at a private elementary school, the sheltered teacher met with each child's parents for an hour. During that time the teacher asked numerous questions about the child's interests, trying to pinpoint the child's learning strategies by asking questions such as, "Does your child like to work with her hands?" "Does your child read on her own? For how long at one time?" The teacher gathered background information about each student and used that information to alter not the content but the delivery of that content to reach each child according to individual learning strategies.

Not all teachers may have the luxury of a lengthy parent interview; in addition, some may be overwhelmed by student numbers. With time limits constraining assessment possibilities, teachers can use observation as a tool to determine the answers to questions such as those listed in Figure 3.2. These questions can assist the teacher in discovering students' learning styles. Working with these questions in mind and keeping a watchful eye on students allows for ongoing informal assessments of students.

FIGURE 3.2 Questions for ongoing information assessment of learning strategies

- In a collaborative group, which students take a leadership role? Which students stay back or prefer spectator roles?
- Which students use a dictionary? Conversely, which students never do?
- Which students write exactly as they speak?
- Which students need constant response or feedback from the teacher?
- Which students shine in oral participation? Which students fade away or hide?
- Which students eagerly volunteer for activities?
- What are students' interests? How do they express these interests?

Sheltered teachers can also employ other, more formal strategies to gain knowledge of student learning strategies and enhance the classroom environment. Some teachers distribute a reading/writing inventory during the first day or week of class. If students are asked for data about their home language, country of origin, language use preferences, and reading/writing habits and preferences, a single piece of paper can provide a classroom ethnography that is rich in data. Other teachers accomplish the same goal by setting up partner interviews; when partners introduce one another and talk about reading/writing behaviors, the presentations provide a mosaic of classroom interests, behaviors, and strategies. Students can also participate in a preference survey of class assignments or rank order a list of activities. Data from such instruments can be presented graphically in a chart and used as the focus of a language lesson on comparatives or a journal entry on the topic of the chart's significance.

The zone of overlap between content and language development activities is constantly shifting. Those who labor in this borderland territory may need to become risk-takers, for it is in this risk-taking that a whole realm of possibility is revealed. Sheltered teachers begin to look at their work anew, asking the questions: What do I do? Why does it work/not work? What is needed at this very minute? How are my students' needs informing my teaching? New possibilities present themselves as the teacher sets forth into the unknown, armed with a firm knowledge of subject matter, a repertoire of sheltered techniques, and a sense of adventure.

In looking at K–12 students being served today, we see a diverse array of young people arriving in our North American classrooms—all needing to learn English, academic skills, and the culture of their adopted nation. Although not every teacher is an ESL or sheltered teacher, the ever-increasing numbers of language minority students in content classrooms force the realization that the teacher's pedagogical understanding of second language processes can serve these students well. School programs can use this understanding of processes and strategies to successfully bridge the gap between language and content instruction.

EXEMPLARY PROGRAMS

In Southern California, the Glendale Unified School District has designed a sheltered program to meet the needs of English language learners in social studies and science. Initially funded by a Title VII grant from the U.S. Department of Education, the Academic Excellence Program provides support to students through a combination of materials and instructional strategies. The program emphasizes the use of visuals and "hands-on" activities. Built into the integrated curriculum are strategies to encourage interaction such as cooperative learning (Johnson, Johnson, Holubec, & Roy, 1984; Kessler, 1992), reciprocal teaching (Palinscar & Brown, 1986), and student pairing (Kagan, 1986; 1988). The program also publishes the *SEA* (Sheltered English Approach) *News* in which teachers share specific activities they have successfully implemented.

Other Glendale programs have adopted similar methods for improving teaching strategies and helping English language learners succeed in the content areas. Denise Evans, who works in the Emergency Immigrant Education Assistance Program (a federally funded program), teaches her English language learners history and science. Speaking slowly and articulately, she explains that the idea of popping corn was discovered by Native Americans and has her students duplicate the ancient procedure. After the students have completed the process and are contentedly munching popcorn, she draws them into a discussion of how the juxtaposition of heat and moisture forces kernels to explode or "pop." In this sheltered scenario, understanding has been enhanced by both demonstration and firsthand experience, two typical sheltered English strategies.

In another Southern California district, in a sheltered World History course at Mark Keppel High School, Janeane Vigliotti asks students to write once a week in learning logs. She poses a question about a current lesson or a recent event and provides ten minutes of class time for writing. The learning logs are commented on by the teacher and then are returned to the students. Students are encouraged to respond to remarks before embarking on a new topic; often a dialogue between the teacher and a student opens new areas to explore. For example, the following exchanges between the teacher and one student occurred when (referring to the civil rights movement of the 1960s) the teacher posed the question, "What shall we overcome?"

3/01

S: We shall overcome the things such as wisdoms, etc., that we struggle to be. To get self confidence and helped connecting, overcome the rights to be free, have a equality treatment, especially, it's meanful to all the world.
Overcome things that does not fair, things that we can't ~~not~~ come up with it, get a successful ~~and~~ purposes.

T: *I am having trouble understanding all of your ideas. I agree that we need equal treatment and that "it's meaningful to all the world." Please tell me what you mean by "overcome the things such as wisdoms, etc." If we overcome wisdom, isn't that a bad outcome?*

3/07

S: ~~Overcome means is that things that we can't get, but we want to get it. Like people say you can not go to school because you can't speak English. And we~~
Overcome means everything that we prefer, we like to have it soon. But people wouldn't allowed you ~~to~~, even get closer to it.
Like people say you can't go attend school because of your English. You surpose to go back to your country. Then we never get hesitate, ~~try everything~~ it doesn't fair, we try our best even people will beat you ~~when~~ if you stand for it to get equality, I mean keep trying until we get successful, and we can't go to school soon.

T: *This is a very powerful answer to my question. Thank you!*

This type of exchange between the teacher and a student struggling to express complex ideas exemplifies several principles of sheltered classrooms in action. The teacher and her student have been collaboratively engaged in constructing meaning. On March 1, when the student struggles to explain the meaning of "overcoming," the teacher does not address the issue as one of a right/wrong answer; she casts it instead as her desire to know more, to understand his labored message. Encouraged by the teacher's response, a week later the student devotes himself to the task of explanation. He brings in an example of injustice from his own experience ("you can't go attend school because of your English") and as he writes, he elaborates his ideas, in the process making them clearer—to the teacher and no doubt to himself as well. Had this been a test, with only one opportunity to get the answer right or wrong, this student would have had no chance to "keep trying until we get successful."

In a required career exploratory course at San Gabriel High School, English language learners learn information-gathering and writing skills by searching for information on a career of interest to them. In preparation for writing an I-Search paper (Macrorie, 1988) in this sheltered course, they role-play job interviews, conduct class discussions to share their interests and dreams, compose resumes, deliver short talks to their classmates, and learn how to locate information on computer databases and CD-ROMs. These activities and the discussions which precede and follow them generate vocabulary which students will use in writing their papers. Because the I-Search format motivates students to choose a personal topic and use other people as a source for information, students feel secure in interviewing counselors, placement officers, and community members as they gather information about their topics. Because they have the freedom to write from their own experience, the relatively abstract research process is demystified. The whole process of career exploration provides students with opportunities for linguistic, academic, and social growth.

Borrowing from strategies once used exclusively in language classrooms, sheltered teachers modify their mode of instruction to better serve English language learners. These teachers not only maintain high expectation levels for content mastery but also make language structures accessible so that English does not obstruct student learning. By employing sheltering techniques and going beyond routine classroom procedures to reach out to English language learners, these teachers send a positive message to students, telling them that they count as learners.

Conveying Concepts

In the above examples, teachers have consistently sought the best vehicle for conveying each concept. Consider what they did to teach content to students with limited English proficiency:

1. *They created a relaxed and welcoming atmosphere.*
   Rationale: An enabling classroom environment acknowledges and respects both linguistic and cultural diversity. In this atmosphere of respect, the tone is set for all that follows. Such an environment frees students to ask questions when a point needs clarification and encourages students to risk answering a question that has been posed to provoke their understanding. Students acknowledge the

teacher's efforts to follow what they say and respond to their ideas with integrity. Students also recognize that in their classroom no one will mock or make fun of them or a classmate. All participants in this classroom community share trust and respect.

2. *They provided firsthand experiences with content materials.*
   Rationale: Sheltered teachers understand that the text is only one of many routes to content learning. These teachers understand that learning modalities vary: Some students are engaged through visual input and others through aural; many students need to touch or manipulate objects and teaching aids to internalize the concepts they represent. As difficult concepts are contextualized, demonstrated, illustrated, and exemplified, students are helped to build a repertoire of learning strategies and are encouraged to demonstrate their understanding in a variety of informal assessments.

3. *They used visual materials to supplement printed text whenever possible.*
   Rationale: In sheltered classrooms, students and teachers use charts, graphs, and other visual organizers for reading and writing activities. When students use a visual organizer in conjunction with a textbook, the organizer assists them in categorizing unfamiliar vocabulary—and simultaneously in demonstrating comprehension. When students explain the data in a chart or graph, they have genuine opportunities to use new vocabulary specific to the content of the sheltered course. When students create a graphic to demonstrate reading comprehension, the assessment process is enhanced—almost at a glance, it is evident what the student understands.

4. *They modeled and demonstrated frequently.*
   Rationale: Because sheltered teachers understand the learning process, their lessons provide both cognitive and linguistic scaffolds or frames for students. Within such frames, the teacher provides the language model of vocabulary and strategies in which the concept or task is embedded. Activities often engage students in interaction with a familiar idea before they move on to a new one; they also tend to provide concrete examples before abstract ones. By exploring what students know before introducing new material, sheltered teachers provide models of the linguistic and cognitive tasks ahead.

5. *They utilized collaborative and cooperative structures.*
   Rationale: Peer group interactions encourage student interaction and provide further scaffolding. Students see how they can use the target language to unlock the meaning of content lessons. Students often benefit from the affective climate of a group; freed from the direct presence of a teacher, some students will risk asking questions which they would never venture in a whole group activity; most students will work hard to clarify the meaning of their own ideas and opinions.

6. *They are able to vary the sizes and purposes of group structures.*
   Rationale: In addition to whole class activities, students in sheltered classrooms are accustomed to tasks designed for pairs, triads, groups of four or five, as well as for individuals.

7. *They modified their speech.*
   Rationale: Just as relatives adjust at family gatherings to fit their speech to each individual member from kindergartner through grandparents, sheltered teachers make similar adjustments. They slow the pace at which they speak. They control their use of slang and idioms and the length of their sentences. In introducing vocabulary, sheltered teachers embed new words in definitions and examples, finding more than one way of using cognates to convey meaning.

8. *They questioned appropriately and made frequent comprehension checks.*
   Rationale: Successful sheltered teachers adjust their wait time after asking a question—the slightly longer pause between question and answer allows students to search for and employ unfamiliar vocabulary and language structures.

9. *They demonstrate a variety of questioning types, modifying difficult, open-ended questions to elicit one-word answers or yes/no responses as needed to assess the demarcation lines between conceptual understanding, misunderstanding, and lack of comprehension.*
   Rationale: In their skillful use of questioning patterns, sheltered teachers can lead students back to confident and successful answers to open-ended questions.

10. *They prepare students by building on and expanding background knowledge.*
    Rationale: It is common for sheltered teachers to open a lesson with a brainstorming activity, a journal entry, or a collaborative structure like a four-corners activity.[2] These attention-gathering strategies help English language learners tap their previous experiences before moving into unfamiliar conceptual territory. At their most effective, sheltered teachers know their students well. They understand the skills and talents which all students bring to class. When effective teachers plan lessons, they consider the varied backgrounds, previous schooling experiences, literacy skills in both first and second languages, and life experiences of their students.

---

[2] A four-corners activity is an adaptation of a forced-choice values clarification exercise. Four visuals (quotations, other stimuli) are placed in four places in the room. After looking at all four stimuli, students select the one they connect with and would like to discuss. After discussion, a spokesperson for each group shares a summary of the conversation with the entire class. Other values clarification exercises may be found in Simon, Howe, and Kirschenbaum (1972).

11. *They focused on key concepts and contextualized them.*
Rationale: These teachers understand that sheltered instruction differs from "just good teaching" in several important ways. Sheltered teachers may not cover as much material as may teachers of native speakers. Because sheltered teachers seek out and make connections between key ideas in their content areas, they may cover some concepts in great depth and others not at all. Consequently, sheltered teachers adjust the pace at which they cover the curriculum.

These classroom modifications immediately serve English language learners, enabling them to demonstrate their understanding in a variety of informal and formal assessments and experiencing a variety of social roles as they interact with partners and small groups. In the process, sheltered lessons provide a host of cultural concepts that would never surface in a traditional lecture/textbook reading scenario.

CONCLUSION

Sheltered classroom tasks or activities also occur within a wider context; each task has been designed to minimize linguistic and conceptual barriers to allow for the free passage of ideas from instructor to students, from students to instructor, and from student to student. Making content and language more accessible to English language learners requires providing a stimulating cognitive and affective environment. Sheltering content lessons is not an easier way of teaching; sheltered lessons demand flexible and creative thinking, skillful application of many instructional strategies, and careful planning. One of the benefits of sheltered instruction is the development of a lively dialogue by teachers who seek out and share approaches that work.

Like the widening ripples from a pebble dropped into a pond, all this occurs within the wider context of the school and its program of instruction for English language learners. Although a classroom may offer shelter from a veritable storm of concepts and language, one classroom alone, without the support of a coherent and articulated program, will struggle to enable students to take their place as members of the greater community and the world. In the best of all possible situations, the contexts work together for true learner empowerment. As Dewey so well expressed this notion, "Education is not preparation for life; education is life itself." For no group are these words more true than for English language learners and their sheltered teachers.

chapter 4

Moving from Comprehensible Input to "Learning to Learn" in Content-Based Instruction

Kate Kinsella

I regularly teach in a program which brings university faculty into inner-city high schools to teach a year-long college preparatory class. The immigrant students who attend my special ESL section are always excited by the novelty of taking a class for college credit from a university instructor. They are equally excited and proud to be the first members of their families to have access to higher education. Most of these motivated bilingual students, however, also share gaps in cognitive, academic, and linguistic skills in English. These gaps impede their successful maneuvering within the high school curriculum and jeopardize their imminent advancement to college.

A recent class was comprised of high school juniors who were all relative newcomers from Central America and Southeast Asia. Most had endured considerable educational disruption prior to immigration, and few had received any formal English language instruction before beginning their secondary studies in California. One particularly earnest Vietnamese student named Kien lingered after every class session to query me about our impending field trip to the university or to ask me about a note he was bringing home from his counselor. His most frequent questions, however, were about homework assignment instructions and vocabulary from lectures and reading in his core classes: "What does it mean *to react to* the film? How do I put these ideas in *chronological order*?" Raised in a bilingual home, Kien was already proficient in both Chinese and Vietnamese, and he was a diligent English language learner whose notebook contained columns of unfamiliar words gleaned from class activities throughout the school day. A few weeks into the term, when his vocabulary inquiry had become an after-class ritual, I asked him to show me his notebook. This particular day he had jotted down several terms from a history chapter on early U.S. immigration during a sustained silent reading period. His vocabulary study sheet contained the items listed in Figure 4.1.

Kien's independent efforts to expand his academic English in this social studies class reflect a very conscientious yet relatively unproductive and uninformed approach to academic vocabulary study. For this U.S. history chapter, for example, it consisted of writing down any new and seemingly important word he encountered in the assigned pages, then stopping to look up the meaning first in his pocket Chinese-English dictionary, and possibly in his English-English dictionary. The seven words Kien had stopped to jot down and investigate during this half-hour in-class reading session were more general vocabulary items (e.g., *opportunity; lack of*) rather than unfamiliar academic and discipline-specific terms, which led me to wonder whether he hadn't missed the higher order lesson concepts. It was also not difficult to see from Kien's self-selected vocabulary list that he had looked up these new words without first examining their original contexts. As a result, he ended up with the word *wave* as a verb meaning "to move one's hand as a signal or greeting" rather than the correct meaning of the noun form in the context, that is, a *wave of immigrants*. In addition, he

FIGURE 4.1 High school ESL students vocabulary study list

<u>**Vocabulary Words to Learn**</u>

Date:	Class:	Word:
3/5/94	U.S History	poverty – 貧窮 lack of – absence wave – to move one's hand as a signal or greeting to search for – to look carefully opportunity – a favorable moment or occasion for doing something immigrant – 僑民 refugee – same as immigrant

understood the definition "absence" for the expression *a lack of* to mean "being absent from school." When he could not explain to me what a "favorable occasion" meant, I told him that an *opportunity* was simply a *chance* to do something. Finally, using the resources available to him, he was unable to distinguish between *immigrant* and *refugee*, failing as well to notice that these two italicized key terms had already been clearly distinguished in definitions within the assigned chapter section.

Like the other immigrant students enrolled in my Step to College class, Kien was well aware that his gaps in academic English proficiency made it difficult and at times impossible for him to comprehend lessons and homework assignments across the high school curriculum. He thus perceived vocabulary acquisition as the key to his educational access and mobility, and he felt insecure about his ability to ever master the seemingly endless barrage of new words he daily entered in his notebook. This frustrated ESL student's columns of arbitrarily selected, randomly organized, and decontextualized terms, coupled with sketchy first language translations and often inappropriate English definitions, were clearly not worth the fruits of his labors. More serious, Kien's insecurity about his rate of second language acquisition and his ability to complete challenging reading, writing, and note-taking tasks in his required subjects had led him to question the prospect of ever truly excelling in high school and being prepared to enter the university.

Unfortunately, after three years of high school ESL and sheltered content instruction, Kien had not yet effectively "learned to learn" vocabulary in various content areas. His teachers had no doubt spent countless class hours explaining focal lesson concepts and defining new terms. However, it appeared that none of his teachers had demonstrated to him how to effectively study and learn within their respective fields. Among the most essential content-area learning tools Kien had not acquired was a vocabulary study system based on sound principles of learning and memory, incorporating word awareness, context analysis, association with prior knowledge, categorization, visualization, and application. He was in critical need of a more viable vocabulary expansion system than his random listing—one that could be adapted to mastery of terminology within distinct disciplines such as social studies or mathematics.

Kien's vocabulary study travails point to a potential shortcoming in content-based instruction (CBI) for second language students, particularly in upper-elementary schooling through higher education. It has become axiomatic to both content-based ESL and sheltered content instruction to make core curricula *accessible* to English language learners who are not yet able to perform adequately in mainstream classes designed for native speakers of English. Support for this emphasis on comprehensibility and accessibility of instructional delivery has in great part been drawn from Krashen's (1982) theory of second language acquisition. Krashen (1985) contends that second language students acquire rather than learn new language and concepts when provided with comprehensible input just beyond their current level of second language competence. With this premise, comprehensibility must therefore be carefully designed and implemented by the instructor to set the stage for simultaneous language acquisition and academic mastery. A major thrust of CBI has thus justifiably been the amount, variety, and quality of contextual support given to second language students in order to promote their interest and involvement in the specific subject area, and the development of their academic language proficiency and conceptual understanding.

The development of academic language proficiency, however, includes much more. Students must master the specialized terminology of various fields of study along with the discourse features characteristic of very different disciplines such as science and literature. Understanding the distinct expectations for performance on assignments which stipulate directions such as *analyze*, *compare*, or *trace* and recognizing the critical shifts in focus when lecturers or writers employ transitional signals such as *moreover* or *nevertheless* are examples of the multiple forms of academic language proficiency necessary for success in secondary and higher education. This proficiency is primarily developed through extensive reading in a variety of academic contexts and through years of repeated exposure to academic terminology during class discussions, lectures, cooperative tasks, and homework assignments. ESL students who have completed less than five years of schooling in English and who do not yet have the skills or inclination to read widely in English are at a decided disadvantage with regard to development of academic language proficiency. They rely on instructors to provide the rich, contextualized environment which will support their dual learning of concepts and language and their ability to perform more ably in traditionally context-reduced formats (Cummins, 1981, 1994).

SHELTERED CONTENT INSTRUCTION

The repertoire of instructional orchestrations and curricular modifications consistently suggested in faculty development sessions and professional literature addressing CBI are all viable means for an instructor to promote greater curricular contextualization and comprehensibility, and thereby greater access to cognitively and linguistically demanding subject matter for ESL students. Nevertheless, I believe that these suggested instructional practices do not in and of themselves foster informed and empowered learning. Many ESL students do not confidently enter the academic mainstream because inadequate time and attention have been devoted to "learning to learn" within and across individual disciplines, that is, to the academic competencies for confident and competent content-area learning that Kien and his college-bound ESL classmates so sorely needed yet lacked. An examination of the common classroom practices in sheltered content instruction might most clearly illustrate how the pedagogical emphasis on comprehensibility and contextualization of instructional delivery in much of CBI has been some-what too "teacher driven" and "curriculum centered," with less careful con-sideration given to the development of effective, self-directed learners.

Students whose English is newly emerging should properly be placed in content classes taught in their primary language until they have reached at least an intermediate level of social interactional English. Before ESL students are transitioned from bilingual classes to the academic mainstream, they are "sheltered" from competition with native speakers of English in specially designed content courses that only enroll ESL students (see Rosen and Sasser, Chapter 3 in this volume). In these sheltered content classrooms, monolingual English-speaking teachers employ principles of successful ESL instruction to teach discipline-specific language and subject matter to students at the level of intermediate fluency in English. At this level, students are presumably ready for the task demands of English-medium instruction in core subjects such as math and science because they have acquired the receptive and productive skills which will allow them to more ably negotiate both spoken and contextual meanings in English.

However, at intermediate stages of second language development, students are still nowhere near ready to successfully follow a half-hour lecture, read an entire textbook chapter, or complete a science lab report without considerable contextual support and scaffolding. The term *scaffolding* was first introduced in language acquisition research by Bruner (1978, 1986) to refer to the special ways in which adults unconsciously expand on a child's early linguistic attempts through natural interactions, thereby encouraging the child toward a com-municative level somewhat beyond her current conversational competence. Scaffolding in the sheltered content classroom takes the form of conscientiously guided instruction which enables students to safely and comfortably take risks and reach beyond their current level of academic and linguistic competence. Walqui-van Lier (1995) points out that scaffolding for second language learners in CBI is intended to support not only the development of concepts and academic skills but also the oral and written discourse characteristic of a given discipline. Learning to read, write, and speak like a scientist or a historian in a second language is a monumental task for a student who is still simultaneously acquiring everyday social and academic language proficiency, one that can only be accomplished with consistent, long-term modeling and coaching.

It seems reasonable to expect that ESL students are acquiring the language and concepts they need to advance in core curricula as well as the active learning and study skills they need to succeed in mainstream classes. Frequently, however, the primary focus in sheltered classes is on providing comprehensible input to merely increase the ESL students' ability to understand the particular lesson of the day. In other words, the majority of class time is dedicated to teacher-driven efforts to help students understand the new language and con-cepts needed to accomplish a specific task.

In this common scenario, the provision of comprehensible input manifests itself most noticeably in vocal and visual enhancements of a traditional lecture-discussion format. These modifications of instructional delivery place the bulk of the responsibility on the teacher, and while facilitating short-term comprehension, they do not necessarily contribute to the ESL students' ability to confidently and competently embark on independent learning endeavors in biology, algebra, world literature, or history. The ESL students are instead frequently assigned to a relatively passive role, listening and observing to glean the main lesson points while the teacher strives to help them comprehend by using visual aids and a "listener-friendly" delivery. Few students, meanwhile, have accurately and adequately recorded for future study the global lesson concepts, supporting examples, and explanations. Indeed, the instructor faced with teaching both language and content to underprepared learners in sheltered classrooms is frequently the only person in the classroom who has actually bothered to write down the main points from the lesson presentation and class discussion or read and understood the assigned homework chapter. ESL students who are not "text-wise" and "text-ready," for example, labor independently over content-area reading assignments, with little payoff in terms of comprehension and retention of subject matter. It does not take many weeks into the school term for frustrated and discouraged readers to deduce that it is much more worthwhile to simply attend class and wait for the ESL or sheltered content teacher to skillfully identify and explain the main points.

This sort of learner passivity and subsequent "learned helplessness" (Coley & Hoffman, 1990; Cummins, 1989) is fostered when students feel daunted by unwieldy academic tasks and insecure about how to proceed. Teachers who conscientiously design lessons for optimal content and language comprehension while neglecting strategic learning integration may unintentionally send ESL students demoralizing messages about their chances for success in various subject areas. Furthermore, students who lack effective academic strategies often develop their own unproductive coping behaviors. Without scaffolding in the form of "sheltered" modeling and incremental practice with vital, discipline-specific learning processes like textbook reading and lecture note-taking, ESL students have a tough road to hoe once they leave the nurturing academic arena of the ESL and sheltered content classroom, even if they have actually acquired a fair amount of prerequisite subject matter knowledge.

Sheltered instruction has been criticized for watering down the curriculum, though skilled and informed instructors in sheltered classes know that by enriching and contextualizing their lessons they can facilitate engagement and interaction with challenging academic language and concepts and provide greater access to core curricula. Many ESL students have been excluded from higher-level classes in core subject areas because of their perceived cognitive and linguistic limitations. Nonetheless, educators who regularly provide CBI for ESL students must examine the extent to which they may inadvertently function as "institutional gatekeepers" (Erikson & Shultz, 1982), denying students social mobility within the school system. This occurs when the majority of class time is spent striving to make lessons more engaging for ESL students, without allocating sufficient time for the development of both the academic language and the active learning processes vital to completion of more complex and common academic tasks within content-area coursework. Instructional formats such as lectures and sustained silent textbook reading have become associated with a "transmission model" of teaching (Cummins, 1989), which views students as passive recipients of predetermined and presequenced knowledge. The current emphasis on developing strategic, empowered learners and critical thinkers has prompted classroom teachers across grade levels and content areas to reconceptualize and retool their traditional instructional approaches. Many teachers nonetheless cling to their comfortable repertoire because they steadfastly believe in the primacy of these techniques or because they have not had adequate or effective professional development and support to confidently venture into new pedagogical frontiers (see Peterson, Chapter 13 in this volume).

Therefore, any student who aspires to genuine secondary school success and an eventual college degree or training for a technological field must have a repertoire of effective strategies for learning within traditional formats (such as lectures) as well as within more progressive formats (such as cooperative structures). Without scaffolding for effective "learning to learn" in both traditional (teacher-fronted and student-centered) collaborative classroom formats, ESL students are not adequately prepared for academic success across the school curriculum. Motivated second language learners may consequently emerge from the week's sheltered biology unit with a deeper understanding of human anatomy and an appreciation for learning with and from peers; however, they may be no better equipped to tackle the next textbook chapter on their own, take effective lecture notes, prepare for an upcoming exam, expand their academic English vocabulary, or competently answer an essay question.

A RATIONALE FOR STRATEGY INSTRUCTION

As advocates of educational equity for linguistically and culturally diverse students and as agents of social change, we must seek and share practices which extend our students' voices and opportunities. Mohan (1986) warns that the integration of language, literacy, subject-area knowledge, critical thinking skills, and discipline-specific study skills requires systematic planning and cannot be left to chance, as is currently the norm in many secondary and postsecondary programs for ESL students. Academic competence can dramatically impede or accelerate an ESL student's performance and progress within the school system. We cannot wait until our students are ready to transfer to the academic mainstream to begin to assist them in developing academic survival skills, or leave them to their own devices to come up with inefficient and ineffective academic coping strategies. We also cannot safely assume that their future mainstream instructors are professionally prepared or willing to assume any responsibility for this critical competency development. The leadership role seems to lie with the ESL and sheltered content instructors who best understand the learning needs and styles of these students.

Although individual teachers are conscientiously integrating strategy instruction into their ongoing curricula, there appear to be few systematic programwide efforts. It is not realistic for the ESL instructor alone to take the initiative and shoulder the responsibility for comprehensively preparing English language learners for the varied demands of mainstream curricula. Students who spend the school day in diverse content classrooms, lacking full English language proficiency as well as subject matter background knowledge, need *every* teacher to demystify learning by sharing the academic secrets of successful students in their respective disciplines. Faculty across the content areas who are genuinely committed to educational access and equity must form a united front in cohesively preparing bilingual-bicultural students with rigorous content, language, and learning tools for academic and social mobility. It is therefore incumbent on us to infuse our bilingual, ESL, and sheltered curricula with more carefully designed and consistent opportunities for students to increase their linguistic and cognitive proficiency, and to better understand how to learn in and across various disciplines.

Adamson (1993) provides some thoughtful direction for academic strategy integration in CBI. His case studies of how graduates of secondary and college-level ESL programs survived in content courses document the great difficulties ESL students can have in adjusting to new classroom expectations and curricula covered in a language they have not fully mastered. All thirty-four research participants found their academic work in English extremely challenging, and those who managed to succeed did so by devoting enormous time and energy to their studies. The best students in these case studies also utilized productive strategies for enhancing their understanding of course material and for completing assignments when necessary with less than a full understanding. In addition, these more effective learners tended to vary their strategies depending on the subject matter and their degree of understanding, whereas students with less academic competence clung to a single method of note taking, reading, or test preparation. Furthermore, the strategies less successful students relied on to complete academic tasks (e.g., writing research papers and participating in discussions) were based on quite different educational expectations from their home culture.

Perhaps the most significant finding of Adamson's study was that when ESL students are faced with course material that is beyond their ability to linguistically and schematically comprehend, they develop ways of completing assignments without truly understanding them, thereby concealing their learning obstacles and confusion from the teacher. An example of one common "coping strategy" employed by underprepared ESL students was to complete textbook assignments by merely scanning for the answers to chapter questions rather than attempting to actually read and study the material. These critical observations led Adamson to recommend that pedagogical priorities in developmental coursework for ESL students include explicit instruction in the academic skills and background knowledge of the content material they will need to master in order to thrive within the academic mainstream.

INTEGRATING STRATEGY INSTRUCTION

Two general categories of problems can impede effective studying and learning for ESL students within academic subject matter instruction: impoverished background knowledge and inefficient or nonexistent academic strategies. In principle, then, CBI should be aimed at overcoming both problems. We can begin to help second language students "learn to learn" across the school curriculum by first critically examining the content areas for which we are preparing our ESL students. After identifying key academic competencies for individual content areas, we must thoughtfully analyze the steps involved in the development of each critical skill. The more we are able to specify strategies and skills employed by effective learners, the more we will be able to successfully instruct and guide novice learners. We should then take our students carefully through the steps involved in each skill and provide them with regular, manageable classroom opportunities to practice, receive feedback, and ultimately master these skills.

I find that the immigrant students who regularly attend my high school and college ESL classes benefit from a predictable set of learning and study tools for CBI. Most have received little or no assistance in developing effective strategies for comprehending and remembering new language and material in required subject areas. They consequently resort to inefficient and unproductive strategies for taking notes, reading and studying textbook assignments, using dictionaries, mastering academic terminology, and preparing for and actually taking different kinds of tests.

In addition, many recent immigrants, like Kien and his Step to College classmates, are still having trouble decoding the overt and covert expectations for student behavior and performance in U.S. high school and college classes. They are not sure exactly what they are supposed to do in various classes or how and when they are supposed to go about doing it, and thus they apply inappropriate scripts for schooling developed in elementary school or in their native countries. Nelson (1977, 1986) describes a script as a generalized scenario of actions that fit a common event such as buying groceries, ordering food in a restaurant, or answering the telephone. The script specifies the roles and props appropriate to a particular goal within a particular context and defines both obligatory and optional actions. In school contexts, knowledge of scripts for recurrent classroom events enables the child or adult learner to accurately predict *who*, *what*, and *when* in familiar teaching and learning situations. As an example of inappropriate script application from prior schooling, many neophyte ESL high school and college students do not regularly take accurate and complete notes in class. They concentrate on following the lesson presentation and discussion, and they only copy down information that is written by the instructor on the chalkboard or on an overhead transparency. Beyond elementary schooling within the United States, however, instructors use a variety of less obvious methods to signal that information is essential and worth noting, such as rhetorical questions, intonation, and gestures. Some ESL students fail to recognize these more subtle cues and leave with an incomplete record of the lesson. Still others may not bother to attempt any note taking whatsoever, having emerged from classrooms where instructors greatly underestimated their abilities and did not even hold them responsible for going through the motions of taking out paper and a pen.

Adolescent and adult ESL learners alike can benefit from direct clarification of expectations for behavior and performance in various classroom contexts. Many of the secondary school travails of my ESL students stem as much from their lack of understanding of the scripts for learning in their high school classes in the United States as from their low general proficiency in academic English. For these adolescent newcomers, I have found it useful to formally decode the "active learner" expectations for my class, and presumably all their remaining high school classes, by distributing and discussing the chart shown in Figure 4.2.

In class, we contrast the expectations for student roles and responsibilities in different cultures with those of the North American classroom, while assigning no value judgment. Students brainstorm additional active learner behaviors they have observed while attending their other classes, and as a group decide on the items that should be added in the blank spaces on the chart. I ask them to keep a two-week record of their daily active learner behaviors in my college preparatory class as well as in their content classes. Keeping such a record of their learning behaviors is a challenging but useful activity for these students.

At the end of the two weeks of data collection, the students are encouraged to evaluate their active learning strengths and challenges, and to establish a few immediate personal goals. The self-assessment worksheet shown in Figure 4.3 is a practical record which, if updated throughout the term, can enrich an ESL student's portfolio. These active learner goals are always student-identified, assessed, and modified over the course of the semester, and I provide ongoing feedback and assistance to students in brief conferences and journal responses.

Another critical component of this introduction to active classroom learning is some familiarization with active and responsible classroom learner language strategies. Students can utilize these strategies within any class to appropriately enter the instructional conversation and have their learning needs met. When adolescent and adult ESL students are transferred to the academic mainstream, they are expected by their various instructors to already possess the sophisticated repertoire of social and academic language functions necessary for participation in the instructional process. Some of the language functions most crucial to confident learning and interaction within content-area instruction include asking for information, requesting clarification, requesting explanations and examples, interrupting, restating, and making suggestions.

However, ESL students in need of immediate clarification of important concepts, vocabulary, or assignment instructions frequently opt to remain passive and silent, then consult with a classmate later, because they lack the linguistic and pragmatic machinery to appropriately disrupt the lesson flow and articulate their learning needs. For this reason, ESL and content teachers can do their students a great service by discussing how and when it is appropriate to voice instructional needs and desires within a class session. The language strategies for active classroom learning featured in Figure 4.4, while by no means exhaustive,

FIGURE 4.2 Active learner progress chart

ACTIVE LEARNER PROGRESS CHART							
Name: Class:		Date:					
ACTIVE LEARNER CLASSROOM BEHAVIORS	M	TU	W	TH	FR	TOTAL	
I arrived to class on time.							
I brought all necessary supplies (binder, paper, pencil, etc.).							
I brought all course material (text, dictionary, handouts, etc.).							
I completed all homework assignments before class.							
I sat up straight and alert throughout the class session.							
I made eye contact with the teacher.							
I listened attentively whenever the teacher was speaking.							
I voluntarily answered a question or made a contribution.							
I listened attentively whenever a classmate was speaking.							
I participated actively in all small-group activities.							
I took careful notes of any information I need to remember.							
I wrote down the homework assignment.							
I understand what I am supposed to do for homework today.							
I let the teacher know if I needed an explanation or help.							
I learned some new things in class today.							
I tried my best to pay attention during class today.							
I helped out a classmate who was in need of assistance.							

ACTIVE LEARNER GOAL SETTING

Name: _____   Class: _____   Date: _____

My Active Learner Strengths:

1. _____

2. _____

3. _____

4. _____

5. _____

My Active Learner Challenges:

1. _____

2. _____

3. _____

4. _____

5. _____

My Active Learner Goals for the Next Two Weeks:

1. _____

2. _____

Teacher's Comments:

FIGURE 4.3 Self-assessment worksheet

do offer a tangible and accessible starting point for ESL students who are eager to assume greater responsibility for their learning in diverse classroom communities and subject areas.

This process familiarizes ESL students in upper-elementary and secondary classes with some of the most fundamental culturally based scripts for classroom learning in their new school system, instead of making it incumbent on them to be astute observers and independently arrive at these understandings. It also delivers a strong message early in the school term about the teacher's positive expectations for each and every student within the class. Once students have a

---

INTERRUPTING

Excuse me, but . . . (e.g., I don't quite understand/I have a point to make).
Sorry for interrupting, but . . . (e.g., I don't understand/I missed that definition).
May I interrupt for a moment?

ASKING FOR CLARIFICATION

I have a question about that.
Could you please repeat that?
In other words, are you saying that . . . ?
Could you please explain what _____ means?
Would you mind repeating that definition?
Could you please say more about that?
I'm not sure I understood that word/term/concept. Could you please give us another
   example?
Would you mind going over the instructions for us again?

REQUESTING INSTRUCTIONAL ASSISTANCE

Could you please help me?
Can you please help me do this?
I am having trouble with this. Would you mind helping me?
Will you please show me how to do this/write this/draw this/solve this?
Could you please write that term/word on the board?
Could you pronounce that word for me again?
Can I talk to you after class for a moment about the assignment?

FIGURE 4.4   Active learner language strategy worksheet

clearer understanding of their educational possibilities and responsibilities within
a particular context, they are generally more receptive to making significant
changes in the ways they approach studying and learning. At the risk of sounding
facetious, there is no point, for example, in introducing a vocabulary expansion
method if the students have not come to class equipped with a dictionary,
binder, paper, and pen, and if they have not completed the assigned reading
and identified important new terms worth studying and remembering. Having a
firmer grasp of the most essential characteristics and language functions of
responsible, active classroom learning in turn helps to relinquish English language
learners from the relatively passive and powerless role frequently ascribed to
linguistically and culturally diverse students within the academic mainstream.

The scripts for responsible and dynamic classroom learning highlighted in
the Active Learner Progress Chart in Figure 4.2 set the stage for the more difficult
work ahead for both the teacher and students in "learning to learn" development.
In order to thrive within CBI, ESL students require powerful tools for studying
in specific subject areas. Some study skills (such as dictionary use) have fairly
general applicability; others (such as lecture note taking) must be modified to
accommodate the learning demands of distinct disciplines. As an example, the

lecture note-taking system which would be most useful in recording focal lesson content in a concept-driven field like history would not necessarily be the most practical for a data- and process-driven field like mathematics.

It would certainly seem more appropriate for content-area learning strategies to be introduced, analyzed, modeled, and practiced in the history, biology, economics, or math class rather than in the ESL class (see Srole, Chapter 8 in this volume). These instructors are more familiar with the subject matter and requisite study skills for their respective fields; such an approach also delivers a more convincing message about the applicability and usefulness of a particular study technique within a specific subject area if it is demonstrated and justified by a content expert rather than by an English teacher. Native and nonnative speakers of English alike at all grade levels can surely benefit from systematic strategy instruction across the curriculum, yet this instructional component is frequently missing. For example, classroom texts are regularly assigned in grades 4 through 12, yet showing students how to "read to learn" from these texts and supplemental expository material infrequently enters into the lesson plans of content area faculty. This phenomenon has been documented at both the elementary level (Hare & Borchardt, 1984) and the secondary level (Bullock, Laine, & Slinger, 1990). Ratekin, Simpson, Alvermann, and Dishner (1985) describe the widespread reluctance on the part of secondary school faculty to assume any responsibility whatsoever for integration of reading instruction in their content areas. This is quite alarming, given the reading development course required nationwide in secondary credential programs and the proliferation of instructional resources for reading development in specific domains. It does nonetheless serve as a reminder of the dire need for effective "learning to learn" strategy integration in ESL and sheltered content instruction.

An ESL student grappling with unfamiliar subject matter and language in several different classes will encounter predictable hurdles throughout the school day, two of the most formidable being textbook reading and vocabulary acquisition. I find that my secondary students and college students are equally underequipped with strategies for effective "reading to learn" and vocabulary expansion. They do not approach content-area reading assignments in a "text-wise" manner; and like Kien and his classmates, they struggle to enlarge their productive English vocabulary with a fairly haphazard and uninformed method. In the following discussion, I will present two illustrations of "learning to learn" strategy development. These process-oriented approaches enable underprepared ESL students in CBI to tackle textbook assignments and vocabulary study more confidently and systematically.

One of the greatest obstacles to curricular access for nonnative English speakers in grades 4 through 12 who have been transitioned to English-medium academic instruction is accomplishing reading tasks in their content classes. In fact, reading has been recognized as probably the single most important competency for second language learners in secondary and postsecondary academic contexts (e.g., Adamson, 1993; Carrel, 1989; Lynch & Hudson, 1991). In middle school, high school, and college classes, students must not only comprehend texts but also be able to integrate and react to that knowledge during class discussions, debates, and cooperative activities. When tested, they are expected to recall main points and details and synthesize information from reading with other related information, such as from lectures and films. Shih (1992) asserts that the critical thinking and study planning skills needed to learn and demonstrate learning in this academic process can be extremely demanding for native English speakers, but even more discouraging for second language students with inapplicable scripts for learning developed in a very different educational system. The relatively short and adapted literary and expository selections carefully covered in ESL classes fail to prepare nonnative English readers for the conceptually and linguistically dense texts they must independently manage in required social studies, science, and literature classes.

Many conscientious ESL instructors, aware of the obstacles their students face when confronted with the majority of their reading assignments, attempt to prepare them for the academic mainstream by infusing their curriculum with sporadic exercises to develop discrete silent reading skills (e.g., identifying main ideas, guessing unfamiliar vocabulary by using content clues). However, Shih (1992) criticizes this traditional skill-building approach, arguing that ESL students may be asked to practice scanning skills with one selection and summarizing skills with the next, yet not complete the school year with genre-specific processes they can apply to distinct content-area reading tasks. Furthermore, Carrell (1989) points out that ESL students are often asked to practice a strategy without really understanding its rationale and utility in a variety of appropriate domains. Without a comprehensive approach to reading and studying from texts and a compelling rationale for this approach, an underprepared reader will no doubt resort to a variety of familiar though unreliable academic coping strategies, such as avoiding reading altogether and depending on the class lecture for coverage of main lesson points.

One academic reading competency crucial to content-area learning and achievement is familiarization with the distinguishing organization and text features of each assigned textbook, in order to use the textbooks appropriately and acquire maximum knowledge. The structure and organizational features of a mathematics textbook, for example, are significantly different from those of a social studies textbook. And the fiction in a literature textbook takes many forms that challenge students' comprehension skills. ESL students in my college preparatory class tend to approach reading assignments in any content area in essentially the same way: slowly and painstakingly, bilingual dictionary in hand, with little comprehension and recall—in part because they do not know how to identify main and supporting ideas, and in part because they rarely synthesize and organize information for study purposes. Having spent relatively few years studying in the United States, and much of this time in ESL classes emphasizing development of language for social purposes, they view any reading selection as a "story" and lack the requisite familiarity with typical English rhetorical devices and organizational structures to accurately perceive and approach reading material in a significantly different manner.

A goal in my content-based ESL class is to help these motivated yet under-prepared college-bound adolescents become more "text-wise." I begin by teaching them how "to get ready to read" and study the kinds of expository and textbook reading material they are already encountering in their high school classes. Through strategy instruction in "prereading," students become familiarized with the distinguishing organizational features and task demands of distinct content-area reading assignments. Again, my high school ESL students generally dive into their content-area assignments as if they were reading a story for pleasure, and rarely complete more than a few of the assigned pages. This is largely because they have not learned where and how to identify the most important information in academic content texts; consequently they wander aimlessly, with no clear sense of purpose or direction. Lacking the necessary knowledge and skills for effectively reading content-area expository texts, they do not understand the role of textual aids such as boldface and italic print, subheadings, and focus questions in margins; similarly, they do not understand the function of an introductory paragraph, a topic sentence, a summary, a conclusion, or a transitional device such as "moreover." It therefore offers little reassurance or comfort to these ESL readers when their teachers encourage them to put down their bilingual dictionaries and simply look for the "main ideas." Everything appears "main" to them because so much of the language and subject matter is unfamiliar, and they have not been shown where to concentrate their reading efforts to locate the more essential information.

Part of being "text-wise" and "text-ready" is knowing how to identify significant information. Unless ESL students are acquainted with the layout, organizational features, and reading aids of a particular text, it will be extremely difficult, for example, to distinguish a thesis from subordinate points, to focus their study reading, and to acquire maximum knowledge from the material. Early in the term I begin to help my students become more "text-wise" by introducing a process for "prereading" a textbook chapter. My students are consistently overwhelmed by reading within social studies and science classes, so I want to equip them from the outset with productive strategies for approaching and managing these unwieldy assignments.

PREREADING A TEXTBOOK CHAPTER

Prereading is a preliminary learning activity that helps students become familiar with the overall content and organization of a selection before they actually read it. Instead of just jumping in and plowing through a selection, as many undirected readers are inclined to do, students are encouraged to first create a mental outline of what they are preparing to read. Readers can form this general outline or set of "mental hooks" by focusing initially on organizational aids such as the chapter introduction, summary, and questions and the other visual and typographical guideposts such as boldface headings, italicized terminology, and diagrams. The portions to look at when comprehensively prereading a textbook

---

HOW TO PREREAD A TEXTBOOK CHAPTER

1. **Read the chapter title.** The title provides the overall topic of the chapter.

2. **Read the chapter subtitle (if included).** The subtitle suggests the specific focus or approach to the topic of the chapter.

3. **Read any focus questions at the beginning of the chapter.** These questions indicate what is very important in the chapter. They are meant to guide your reading and help you be on the lookout for their answers.

4. **Read the chapter introduction or first paragraph.** The introduction, or first paragraph if there is no introduction, serves as a lead-in to the chapter. It gives you an idea of where the material is starting and where it is heading.

5. **Read each boldface subheading.** The boldface subheadings will give you an idea of the major topic of the following chapter sections.

6. **Read the first (topic) sentence of each paragraph.** The first sentence often tells you what the paragraph is about or states the central thought. However, be aware that in some material the first sentence may instead function as an attention getter or transition or lead-in statement. In this case, go on to the second sentence to try to determine the main idea of the paragraph.

7. **Look over any typographical aids.** Notice important chapter terms that are emphasized by being written in slanted *italic* type or in dark **boldface** type; often a definition or an example of a new important term follows.

8. **Look over any other visual aids.** Notice any material that is numbered 1, 2, 3, lettered a, b, c, or presented in list form. Graphs, charts, pictures, diagrams, and maps are other means of emphasis and are usually included to point out what is important in the chapter.

9. **Read the last paragraph or summary.** The last paragraph or summary gives a condensed view of the chapter and helps you identify important ideas. Often the summary outlines the main points of the chapter.

10. **Read quickly any end-of-chapter material.** If there are study questions, read through them quickly since they will indicate what is important in the chapter. If a vocabulary list is included, skim through the list rapidly to identify terms you will need to learn as you read.

FIGURE 4.5   Guidelines for textbook prereading

---

chapter are described in Figure 4.5. Examining the organizational and visual aids gives readers valuable clues to the overall structure and focus of the chapter, as well as a sense of the scope and sequence of ideas. Underprepared and reluctant readers then have a clearer sense of direction and purpose for their follow-up reading. This cursory learning activity in turn helps students analyze their reading task and make realistic, proactive plans for reading and studying the material, depending on the difficulty, length, and importance of the assignment.

There are at least two other compelling reasons for ESL students to learn how to preread content-area assignments. Many put off or avoid difficult reading assignments altogether because of the cognitive, linguistic, concentration, and time demands they present. Having spent one-half hour prereading, a frustrated or exceptionally busy reader can at least come to class somewhat familiar with the material and more conceptually ready for subsequent class activities. Students with weak listening comprehension in English will also be better prepared to successfully follow a related lecture and class discussion if they arrive with an agenda of what to expect developed through prereading.

Although this content-area reading strategy would seem to be fairly straight-forward and manageable, both academically prepared and challenged English language learners initially have trouble prereading on their own and therefore benefit from considerable in-class modeling and practice. I introduce this strategy by making transparency copies of a chapter within the first thematic unit in the course. Using the overhead projector, I start at the beginning of the chapter and ask the students what they would pay attention to if they had limited time and could only do a cursory reading before coming to class. They invariably point out the title and illustrations, but the process breaks down when we get to finer nuances of textbook organization such as subheadings, topic sentences, focus questions in the margins, highlighted terminology, and introductory and con-cluding paragraphs. As we move from one prereading step to the next, I highlight the relevant textbook feature and make sure that the students understand its function, along with the reason why it would help them establish a clearer mental outline of the chapter content. The students also highlight and label the relevant aspects of the chapter as we go along; this tactile involvement provides a visual representation of the process and a written record of some of the critical language they will later need to discuss text. With younger learners, it is also helpful to distribute a short chapter which has been cut and pasted so that the only remaining parts are those they will focus on when prereading. This gives an additional visual representation of the process and helps them internalize the sequence of steps.

After taking a class through the process of prereading a chapter, it is essential to clarify why this is a worthwhile study strategy, one used regularly by successful readers, and not just an additional reading chore. The rationale provided above is a good starting point, but the most convincing proof will be improvement in their reading confidence and competence. Students will not be willing to hazard a strategic change in their content-area reading approach unless they have had adequate scaffolding and feedback. I generally revisit this process in numerous class sessions and help them see just how much they have managed to find out about the chapter content and organization simply by prereading. It really is not worth introducing a learning strategy unless the students are going to have enough guided opportunities to practice and eventually be able to see the academic rewards.

One way to document and assess a class's prereading efforts is to distribute a worksheet like the model shown in Figure 4.6. While this prereading worksheet is fairly generic, it works well with science and social studies chapters assigned at the upper-elementary and secondary levels. However, instructors who assign texts from diverse disciplines and at higher grade levels will need to consider the unique organizational and textual features of their required reading material when demonstrating prereading and designing relevant assessment measures.

I take the class through the process of filling out this worksheet after I have completed the initial prereading demonstration. Later, students can complete this worksheet in cooperative groups or pairs and as an individual homework

CHAPTER PREREADING WORKSHEET

1. Chapter title _____

2. What does the introduction (or first two paragraphs) tell you about what the chapter will cover?
_____
_____
_____

3. What points are covered in the summary (or last paragraph)?
_____
_____
_____

4. Write the major subheadings from the first section of the chapter.
_____
_____

5. What kinds of visual aids are included in the chapter?
_____
_____
_____

6. List vocabulary which is emphasized in italic or boldface type.
_____
_____
_____

7. Are questions included at the beginning of the chapter or in the margins to focus your reading on the main ideas? _____

8. Is there a vocabulary list at the beginning or the end of the chapter? _____

9. What is the difficulty level of the chapter? Very difficult _____ Somewhat difficult _____ Easy _____

10. How many pages are included in the chapter? _____

11. Into how many sections is the chapter divided? _____

12. Estimate the time it will take you to read the entire chapter. Hours _____

13. What is your reading and study plan? Will you read the chapter all at once or will you break it down into two or three study sessions? _____
_____

14. Where and when do you plan to read this chapter? Place _____
      Study session #1 _____   Session #2 _____   Session #3 _____

FIGURE 4.6 Sample chapter prereading worksheet

assignment. Reviewing the completed worksheets allows me to gauge my students' proficiency with this strategy and highlights potential problem areas for the group and for individuals. The worksheet additionally serves to build in learner accountability for experimenting with the strategy, and it yields a useful record for authentic assessment. A prime objective of "learning to learn" strategy development in CBI is to encourage and enable more informed and self-directed learning. ESL students who know how to preread regularly assigned texts in different subject areas are definitely in a more strategic position to take charge of their own learning.

VOCABULARY STUDY CARDS

The second illustration of "learning to learn" strategy development is assisting students with an organized, systematic approach to prioritizing and internalizing new terms. Mastering the countless terms and expressions an ESL student encounters in a comprehensive school curriculum requires both motivation and skills. It is the rare high school or college ESL student who does not perceive vocabulary acquisition as an educational priority. While many ESL students have enough basic dictionary knowledge to find out what a word means, few possess an efficient and effective system for actually *remembering* the definitions. What they do remember the next time they encounter the word is that they looked it up once before, but they can no longer recollect the meaning. Some students like Kien take the additional step of actually recording new words and their definitions, but fail to consider the context in which they first encountered the word and rarely attempt to use the word in a meaningful application of their own. They consequently retain little more than their peers, who do nothing more than consult the dictionary or a more proficient English user. ESL students enrolled in mainstream or sheltered content courses face a tremendous catch-up in terms of both general and course-specific word knowledge. In grade 6 and beyond, an ESL student cannot afford to rely on a random or indirect approach to vocabulary acquisition through outside reading and interacting in natural contexts. Instructors in content-based classrooms can do their English language learners an immeasurable service by introducing them to a systematic and pedagogically sound method of vocabulary expansion.

One of the most successful ways for ESL students to study and learn general and specialized terminology is the vocabulary study card system. Students who have felt demoralized by their prior attempts to increase productive English vocabulary have a concrete method which they can easily adapt to the lexical demands of distinct content areas. Although some students may initially find the process laborious, they soon see the pay-off in terms of a marked increase in vocabulary comprehension and retention. The sample vocabulary card shown in Figure 4.7 graphically illustrates the format for this study system. Once a student has identified new terminology from course readings, lecture notes, and other activities, the next step is to effectively organize information about each word for study and review.

For each new term, the student creates an index card with a specific sequence of information about the word, gleaned primarily from the dictionary. On the blank front side of the card, the student records the new word and its part of speech, along with a pronunciation guide and any related word forms. When possible, instructors should point out to English language learners any high-frequency related word forms when they introduce key terms within a lesson. In many cases, the form that surfaces in a course reading is not even

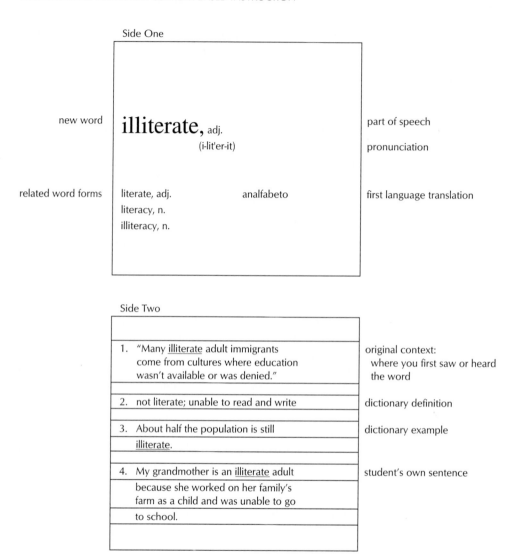

FIGURE 4.7 Sample vocabulary study card

the most widely used word form. It is extremely difficult for students with emergent academic English proficiency to accurately identify important related word forms from a dictionary or glossary. I also encourage students to make note of their primary language translation, since those with disrupted schooling often lack a strong foundation in academic vocabulary in both English and their native language. On the lined back side of the index card, the student first copies the source sentence containing the new word, in order to have an association with the original context and also to be more apt to select the correct dictionary definition. The source sentence is followed by the dictionary definition and example sentence. One advantage to using an advanced learner's dictionary is that it provides accessible example sentences often not included in standard dictionaries. For many of my frustrated readers who have a strong visual component to their learning style, this example sentence proves more helpful than the actual definition in clarifying the word's meaning. The final and perhaps most important step in this process is applying the new word to an original sentence, which demonstrates that the student has understood the word and is able to appropriately use it. I encourage students to write a sentence which incorporates aspects of their personal experiences and interests, rather than to simply modify the example sentence from the dictionary. This takes them one step closer toward internalizing the word's meaning and use and toward making it a vibrant part of their productive English vocabulary.

This vocabulary study system can be easily adapted to accommodate the learning demands of different content areas. For example, to study specialized science terminology, it would be more productive to use the textbook glossary and to include an illustration or diagram instead of the dictionary's example sentence. These manageable and practical vocabulary cards can be used for study, for review, and for self-testing. Students can sort the cards into words they definitely know and those they still are not sure of. This sorting procedure allows them to devote more study and review time to words they have not yet mastered. In order to successfully transfer these new words into long-term memory and productive language status, however, students need to review the entire pack periodically.

As discussed, students enrolled in specially designed content classes and ESL classes have critical gaps in both general and course-specific word knowledge. While a more natural and indirect approach may be suitable for younger learners, secondary and college students need to master a wide range of new lexical items quickly and efficiently to survive in academic study. Instructors who introduce the vocabulary study card system, or other equally viable methods, provide their students with a thorough, organized, and self-conscious means of expanding their English vocabulary within and beyond the classroom.

CONCLUSION

Prereading and vocabulary study cards are only two of a host of academic strategies that ESL students need to enhance their understanding of course material and to complete assignments as well as possible in CBI. They rely on their instructors to demystify academic competence by sharing strategies for successful learning within their respective fields as well as subject matter and terminology. A specially designed content class or ESL class can be either an invaluable gateway to academic competence or merely an academic holding pattern.

Many educational researchers and scholars agree that the focus of both equality and excellence in education is maximum development of the personal talents of all students. By merely providing our ESL students with enough comprehensible input to have access to our lessons, we do not sufficiently develop their talents. When linguistically and culturally diverse students can also "learn to learn" across the content areas, they can have independent access to knowledge without constantly relying on instructional facilitation. We should, therefore, continue to use ESL methodology to enrich and contextualize the content-based curriculum while we also systematically nurture active learner competence. Equipped with sophisticated language, subject matter, and self-directed learning skills, ESL students can see that they have a genuine chance, that they are indeed prepared to succeed in secondary school and higher education.

chapter 5

Teaching Content Knowledge and ESL in Multicultural Classrooms[1]

Gloria M. Tang

How can we help ESL students learn new content knowledge written or spoken in English? How can we enable them to demonstrate their content knowledge in English? How can we assist them in using and expressing their background knowledge in English and linking it to new knowledge? Methods which endeavor to answer these questions can be divided into two categories: those that bring the students' English proficiency to a level at which they can read expository text in content textbooks, or those that bring the language in content textbooks to the level of the students.

Traditionally, the former has involved removing students from the mainstream and giving them intensive courses to develop written and oral English skills until they have acquired adequate proficiency for enrollment in content-area classes. However, marginalized or segregated programs deny students the full benefits of education, that is, full access to content-area subject matter and, possibly, development of thinking skills. The alternative approach involves modifying the text and, perhaps, using ancillary materials to bring the language in classroom texts to students. This process commonly results in watering down the course content and exposing students to language that is not usually found in real textbooks.

A more effective solution is to employ a model which combines the two, systematically integrating language and content. The proposed classroom model shown in Figure 5.1 enables ESL students to access the language of textbooks

---

[1] From "Teaching Content Knowledge and ESOL in Multicultural Classrooms" by Gloria M. Tang, 1992, *TESOL Journal, 2,* pp. 8–12. Reprinted by permission. The author wishes to thank Cathy Humphries of the Burnaby School District, Burnaby, British Columbia, for permission to use her graphic supplements to *Other People, Other Times* (Neering & Grant, 1986).

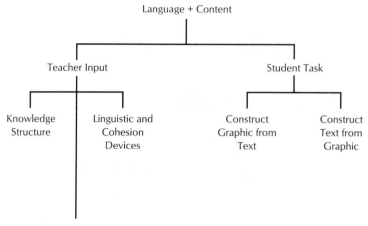

Graphic Representation of Knowledge Structure

FIGURE 5.1   A classroom model

and, at the same time, reach a level at which they can read the language of content classroom texts independently as well as write academic discourse in English. It takes into consideration systematic development of students' thinking skills. It has five components, which can be sequenced in a variety of ways:

1. Explicit teaching of text/knowledge structures of text organization
2. Explicit teaching of graphic representation of text/knowledge structures
3. Explicit teaching of linguistic and cohesion devices of text/knowledge structures
4. Setting student tasks which involve constructing graphics from expository prose
5. Setting tasks which provide opportunities for students to practice constructing expository prose from a graphic.

This chapter explains how the model has been successfully implemented in a seventh-grade social studies class.

IMPLEMENTATION

A teacher from the Burnaby School District (in British Columbia, Canada) introduced some of the components of this model into her seventh-grade social studies class and found the strategies successful. She used the textbook *Other Places, Other Times* (Neering & Grant, 1986), a social studies textbook widely used in public schools in the Vancouver and Burnaby school districts.

The teacher planned her lesson according to Mohan's (1986) knowledge framework. She read each chapter to determine the top-level structure of the text, to organize the content according to knowledge structures in the knowledge framework (see Figure 5.2), and to prepare a structured overview, or graphic organizer, which best summarizes the content of the chapter. Chapter 1, entitled "Early People," looks at the Earth from 1.75 million years ago until the time of the first civilizations. It concentrates on the development of the four major classifications of early humankind: Homo Habilis, Homo Erectus, Neanderthal Man, and Cro-Magnon Man. The top-level structure of the chapter is a temporal sequence of descriptions, so she decided that the structured overview that would best represent it was a time line (see Figure 5.3). The graphic helped her plan the content she was going to present (i.e., early people) as well as linguistic devices associated with the time line (e.g., *lived from . . . to . . .; began in . . . and ended in . . .; inhabited the earth for . . . years; during that period*). In presenting the chapter overview, she explicitly introduced the knowledge structure "sequence" and the language used in chronologically ordered texts.

Having identified the knowledge structure of each section, she decided that the chapter could be divided into four sections according to the four major groups of early people. Each section describes one group of early people, their

FIGURE 5.2 Knowledge structures of Chapter 1, *Other Places, Other Times*

CLASSIFICATION/CONCEPTS	PRINCIPLES	EVALUATION
Homo Habilis—early tool-using ancestors of modern man **Homo Erectus**—first human to walk upright **Neanderthal**—more sophisticated tools and social structure **Cro-Magnon**—most technically advanced of early people	**Homo Erectus** • use of fire allowed migration to colder climates • development of stronger tools and weapons allowed Homo Erectus to kill larger animals **Cro-Magnon Man** • sophistication allowed them to survive the Ice Age • development of farming provided food for long periods of time	
	Homo Habilis • 1.75 million to 800,000 years ago **Homo Erectus** • 1.25 million to 250,000 years ago **Neanderthal Man** • 130,000 to 30,000 years ago **Cro-Magnon Man** • 30,000 to 10,000 years ago	
DESCRIPTION	**SEQUENCE**	**CHOICE**

Early People

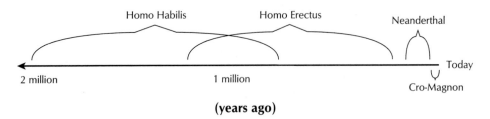

(years ago)

FIGURE 5.3   Time line of Early People to accompany Chapter 1, *Other Places, Other Times*

way of life, the change and development they experienced, and the impact the environment had on them. She put each section's information in a graphic; and because similar information can be extracted from each of the sections, she organized the information in the same weblike graphic form for all the sections (see Figure 5.4). The purpose of recycling the same graphic form was to provide a schema students could access again and again. It also allowed her to use the same linguistic devices repeatedly to reinforce learning. She decided on a web because this graphic was familiar to her students.

The teacher presented the first of the completed graphic organizers, Figure 5.3, on the overhead projector (OHP). She consistently used the language of

FIGURE 5.4   Graphic representation of Homo Habilis to accompany *Other Places, Other Times*

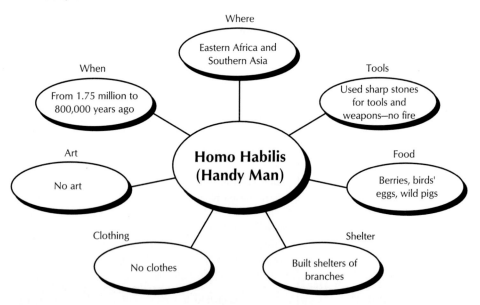

description to answer the questions *When? Where?* and *What?* After the graphic presentation, she referred students to the text and drew their attention to the knowledge structure, description, and linguistic devices specific to that knowledge structure. In presenting the next two major groups of early people, she varied her strategies. She built up one of the graphics on the OHP while presenting the section, and she built up the other cooperatively with the students by assigning the paragraphs to be read and by again asking *When? Where?* and *What?* The linguistic points she focused on were verbs in the past form (e.g., *were; was; lived; ate; hunted*) and adjectives and adverbial phrases of comparison (e.g., *longer than; short; erect; sharp; pointed; different from; the same as; similar to; as large as*). By building the graphic together with students, she helped them to make the link between the graphic and the text and to see that the two give the same information but in different forms. She also exposed students to the real language of description found in textbooks, a step toward managing school knowledge independently. After sufficient exposure to the structure and the language in two similar graphics on Homo Erectus and Neanderthal Man, the students were able to complete the graphic on Cro-Magnon Man (see Figure 5.5) on their own.

To bring the whole chapter together, the teacher prepared a graphic (see Figure 5.6) and required students to complete it using the information in the webs. Using such a graphic serves several purposes: It summarizes the chapter; reinforces the content knowledge students have learned; and enables the students

FIGURE 5.5   Graphic representation of Cro-Magnon Man to accompany *Other Places, Other Times*

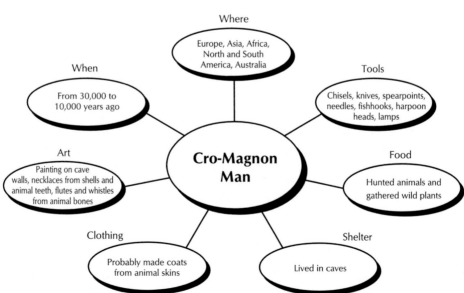

	When	Where	Tools	Food	Shelter	Clothes	Art
Homo Habilis	From 1.75 million to 800,000 years ago	Eastern Africa, Southern Asia	Sharp stones for tools and weapons—no fire	Berries, birds' eggs, wild pigs	Built shelters of branches	No clothes	No art
Homo Erectus	From 1.25 million to 250,000 years ago	Africa, Asia, and Europe	Fire, flint blades, pointed wooden spears	Wild animals • elephant • cooked meat	Probably built shelters of branches	No clothes	No art
Neander-thal Man	From 130,000 years ago to 30,000 years ago	Europe, Middle East	Knives, borers, spear sharpeners made from stone	Wild animals • bear • cooked meat	Lived in caves	Animal hides for clothes	No art
Cro-Magnon Man	From 30,000 to 10,000 years ago	Europe, Asia, Africa, North and South America, Australia	Chisels, knives, spearpoints, needles, fish hooks, harpoon heads, lamps	Hunted animals and gath-ered wild plants	Lived in caves	Probably made coats from animal skins	Painting on cave walls, necklaces from shells and ani-mal teeth, flutes and whistles from animal bones

FIGURE 5.6   Chapter review, *Other Places, Other Times*

to see the relations among the knowledge in the slots, that is, the development of the early peoples. The teacher was moving her students from managing information in isolation to managing the relations among information—a step forward in their cognitive development. The graphic also provides further opportunities for students to use language to compare and classify. Note that whereas the vocabulary inside the cells are terms which show the content schemata of the information as well as the shape of each web and the lines which join them, the headings such as *Where, When*, and *Tools* represent the formal schemata or the linguistic devices specific to that knowledge structure or genre. These terms can be used again and again across topics and curricula.

The students were gradually trained to build similar graphics on their own after working cooperatively with the teacher on a number of occasions. She pointed out linguistic devices and provided opportunities for them to practice constructing graphics from similarly structured text. She introduced the time line in Chapter 1, and she was delighted when all her ESL students could construct a time line on their own when they came to Chapter 5 (see Figure 5.7).

To give students practice in writing a coherent passage from a graphic, the teacher provided familiar graphic representations of familiar knowledge structures and asked students to write an essay based on the graphic. She found that she had to provide linguistic devices and ensure that students knew "how to link sentences together ... and how to present and focus information" (Mohan, 1986, p. 94).

Only by interacting with the graphic after explicit teaching can they truly learn to read and write graphics and to recognize text structure. Constructing a prose passage from a graphic is also a step toward writing expository text. The graphic and the text are semantically comparable (see Mohan, 1989): They convey the same information and have the same knowledge structure. But to convert the graphic into expository prose, students have to translate the lines, arrows, and spatial arrangement (which are graphic representations of linguistic and cohesion devices) into linguistic and cohesion devices in text form. Figure 5.8 is a cause-effect graphic. Its title and headings signal that it is a graphic representation showing a series of causes and effects; its spatial arrangement (i.e., the lines separating the slots) signifies *caused; brought about; resulted in; leading to; so; because; the effect of ... was ...; or as a result of ... , ... occurred.*

FIGURE 5.7   Student-generated time line

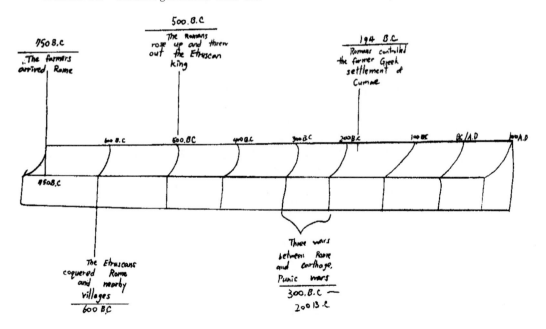

Cause	Effect
The Roman Empire expanded rapidly.	Romans had to spend a lot of time and energy defending their empire from invaders.
Angry Italians wanted the advantages of Roman citizenship. They threatened to rebel and attack Rome.	The Romans granted citizenship to the Italians.
Many internal problems existed: • Poor people were starving • Government officials became corrupt • Consuls were assassinated • Slaves rebelled against rough treatment from masters.	The republican system was weakened.

FIGURE 5.8 A cause-effect table for *Other Places, Other Times:* Events leading to the end of the Roman Republic

The teacher had taught the knowledge structure of cause-effect and exposed the students to cause-effect graphics. She had also repeatedly pointed out the linguistic devices and given the students practice in constructing text passages from graphics. Figure 5.9 shows that the students could write a coherent passage

FIGURE 5.9 Student-generated text

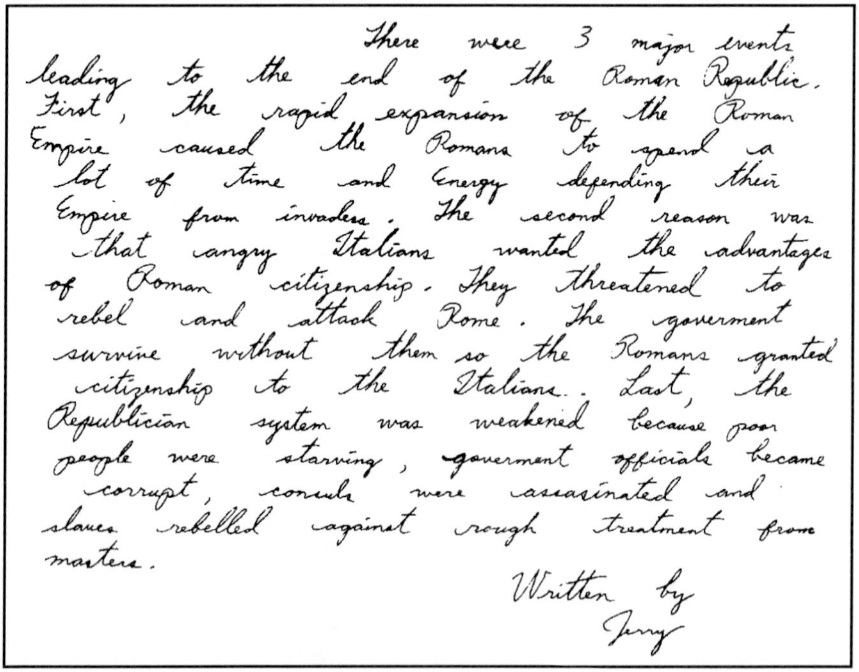

There were 3 major events leading to the end of the Roman Republic. First, the rapid expansion of the Roman Empire caused the Romans to spend a lot of time and energy defending their Empire from invaders. The second reason was that angry Italians wanted the advantages of Roman citizenship. They threatened to rebel and attack Rome. The goverment survive without them so the Romans granted citizenship to the Italians. Last, the Republician system was weakened because poor people were starving, goverment officials became corrupt, consuls were assasinated and slaves rebelled against rough treatment from masters.

Written by
Jerry

about the events leading to the end of the Roman Republic and that they could produce expository prose using devices of cause-effect (e.g., *cause; the reason was; so;* and *because).*

It should be noted that the process takes time. Students cannot be expected to understand a social studies text or to write expository prose using linguistic devices of description, classification, or cause-effect after simply going through the five components once. They need explicit teaching and practice to acquire the skills of understanding and expressing content knowledge with appropriate academic language.

CONCLUSION

Results of research (Early, Mohan, & Hooper, 1989) carried out in schools in Vancouver, Canada, point to the fact that adopting the proposed model in classroom teaching (i.e., explicit teaching of text/knowledge structure and graphic representation of knowledge structures, and providing practice in constructing graphics from text and text from graphics) in intermediate and secondary ESL social studies classes can help increase students' ability to read and write academic discourse. In other words, this classroom model appears to have the potential for bringing classroom texts to a level that students can comprehend, and at the same time bringing students to a level of English proficiency where they can read classroom texts and write academic prose.

chapter **6**

A Six-T's Approach to Content-Based Instruction

Fredricka L. Stoller and William Grabe

Professionals in many instructional settings are developing approaches to content-based instruction (CBI) which emphasize the multiple benefits of integrating language and content instruction for second language (L2) students. The approaches vary, however, representing diverse contexts for instruction, different perspectives on the integration of content and language, and differing assumptions about content, language, and learning strategies. Despite differences in theoretical and practical orientations, these approaches to CBI uniformly view language as a medium for learning content, and content as a resource for learning language. In addition, they endorse purposeful and meaningful language use in the classroom, while assuming a distinction between academic and social language. Most approaches also assume preselected, predetermined content, specified in institutional curriculum guidelines or existing course offerings.

Over the past decade, we have developed a new approach to content-based instruction which seeks to incorporate the criteria stated above. We have labeled our approach a Six-T's Approach; the significance of the label will be easily understood by the second half of the chapter. Our approach has been influenced by a range of other CBI approaches; an overview of these will help to situate our views on CBI. Below we outline eight well-documented approaches to content-based instruction. Although the descriptions are only simple indicators of much richer instructional approaches and educational philosophies, they highlight important issues related to CBI. We then describe the Six T's Approach as another option for the development of CBI.

EIGHT APPROACHES
TO CONTENT-BASED INSTRUCTION

One of the best-known approaches to CBI is one we label the *Center for Applied Linguistics (CAL) approach*. For a number of years, CAL has been carrying out broad-based research on CBI and training K–12 teachers in content-area instruction to make learning tasks more manageable for language–minority students (Burkart & Sheppard, 1994; Crandall, 1987; Kauffman et al., 1994; Sheppard, 1994; Short, 1994; Spanos, 1990; Tucker & Crandall, 1989). CAL's efforts have focused on (a) how to integrate the teaching of content and language (Crandall, 1993; Short, 1991, 1994), (b) how the language used in particular academic content areas may create comprehension problems—not due to the content but to the language itself, and (c) how to assess students' knowledge of language and subject matter (Short, 1993a). Based on CAL's activities across the United States, and its analyses of language demands in different content areas, many instructional recommendations, teaching techniques, and assessment tools have been developed to achieve CBI objectives.

A second well-known set of approaches to CBI follows from discussions of *English for Academic Purposes (EAP) instruction* at North American universities. This work is best represented by studies reported in Adamson (1993), Brinton, Snow, and Wesche (1989), Snow (1993), and Snow, Met, and Genesee (1989). They suggest that content-based EAP instruction may follow one of three prototype models: sheltered instruction, adjunct instruction, and theme-based instruction. In the two former models of instruction (sheltered and adjunct), content is relatively predetermined; in the latter case (theme-based), content is selected by the language teacher (and/or students). Extensions of this framework —from strictly EAP contexts to other instructional contexts—have also been explored (Snow, 1991a; Wesche, 1993).

A third approach, sometimes overlapping with the second one, is that of *university-level foreign language CBI* (Krueger & Ryan, 1993b; Straight, 1994; Wesche, 1993). There are two distinct contexts for this general approach. The first involves foreign language instruction that is organized around cultural, geographic, historical, political, and literary themes. For example, in North America, students might attend a university language course defined by a curriculum that is centered on content themes related to the countries in which the language is spoken (Musumeci, 1993). The second context involves instruction in nonlanguage courses (e.g., philosophy, history, anthropology, political science) that makes extensive use of informational resources in a foreign language (Jurasek, 1993; Sudermann & Cisar, 1992) or in content courses taught in a foreign language (Krueger & Ryan, 1993b). The latter two contexts have, at times, made use of sheltered and adjunct formats to combine language and content (Wesche, 1993).

A fourth distinguishable approach is that developed by Mohan (1986, 1990; Tang, 1992, see also Chapter 5 in this volume). In this approach to K–12 language and content instruction, learning centers around the use of *discoursal knowledge structures* to convey content information. The key to the approach is the assertion that all content information is organized according to six basic types of knowledge structures: description, sequence, choice, classification, principles, and evaluation. The first three types of knowledge structures (description, sequence, and choice) represent more specific ways to organize information; the latter three (classification, principles, and evaluation) represent more general patterns for organizing knowledge, allowing for generalization and theorizing. Regardless of the persuasiveness of Mohan's overall theory of knowledge structures, the approach provides a pedagogical framework for combining content and language instruction, as well as for helping students develop higher-order thinking skills (see Tang, Chapter 5 in this volume).

This approach provides teachers with a natural forum for introducing detailed content information while also helping students see the discourse patterns that support and organize many types of content knowledge. It is assumed that the identification of underlying knowledge structures in one topic area, signaled in various ways through the language used, will transfer to other content areas, thereby providing students with skills for future classroom settings. Mohan and Tang emphasize the importance of using graphic representations to reveal textual knowledge structures and to help students develop competence in academic discourse. The coordination of language and content learning resulting from this approach to CBI reinforces knowledge structures and teaches related language functions and forms.

A fifth approach to CBI is that of researchers in Australia who propose a *genre-based approach to K-12 literacy instruction* with a content emphasis (Christie, 1991, 1992; Collerson, 1988; Martin, 1993). Based on Halliday's functional theory of language use (see Eggins, 1994), this approach proposes that language forms and language uses serve communicative functions; these functions are reflected in basic instructional genres which students can recognize and then use for their own learning purposes. In this respect, the genre-based approach is similar to the Canadian approach presented by Mohan (1986, 1990).

A sixth approach is that of *language immersion programs* in K-12 contexts in North America. In these instructional contexts, content which is normally taught to first language students is taught to students in their second language. Extensive research documents the relative success of this approach (Met, 1993; Swain, 1988, 1991; Wesche, 1993). However, little attention has been given to *how* to teach content in a way that is appropriate for L2 learners, and little discussion is reported of ways that instruction is specifically designed to focus on and enhance language learning (Swain & Lapkin, 1989).

A seventh approach is the *Cognitive Academic Language Learning Approach,* or *CALLA* (Chamot & O'Malley, 1994; O'Malley & Chamot, 1990). Initially developed for L2 students in North American secondary education contexts, this approach combines emphases on language development, content-area instruction, and explicit strategy training. Its goal is to prepare language minority students to handle advanced academic skills and content knowledge in mainstream classrooms. In CALLA lessons, content drives decisions about academic language objectives and the types of learning strategies that are appropriate. Just as

Mohan's model reinforces the importance of graphic organizers, the CALLA approach relies heavily on scaffolding, that is, "the provision of extensive instructional supports when concepts and skills are being first introduced and the gradual removal of supports when students begin to develop greater proficiency, skills, or knowledge" (Chamot & O'Malley, 1994, p. 10).

An eighth approach combining language and content instruction is a version of *whole language instruction* explored by Enright and McCloskey (1988) and others in elementary school contexts (e.g., Manning, Manning, & Long, 1994; Meinbach, Rothlein, & Fredericks, 1995; Roberts, 1993). In this approach, instruction centers on thematic units or theme cycles which integrate language-skills instruction and content information from social studies, natural science, arts, math, and so on. The emphasis is on purposeful language use to communicate personally important and motivating content. Thematic units are developed by brainstorming possible topics within a theme, transitioning between topics to provide thematic coherence, and developing a culminating task to complete the cycle (see also Faltis, 1993; Peregoy & Boyle, 1993; Walmsley, 1994).

An examination of these eight approaches to CBI leads us to believe that there is, in fact, much more overlap among them than the preceding classificatory discussion would indicate. These approaches (and perhaps a few others) share a number of common features which any good CBI program would want to incorporate and which we have tried to incorporate into our Six-T's Approach. In general, these approaches promote student involvement in content learning, provide opportunities for student negotiation of language and content tasks, allow for cooperative learning, focus on the development of discourse-based abilities, and use content materials that should motivate students.

CONTENT-BASED INSTRUCTION IS THEME-BASED INSTRUCTION

A further commonality (at least implicitly) among many of the approaches discussed above, and a central curricular notion in the Six-T's Approach, is that all CBI is fundamentally theme-based (cf. Brinton, Snow, & Wesche, 1989). This assertion is perhaps best introduced by considering two quite different content-based instructional contexts.

In applied linguistics graduate programs, courses such as Introduction to Linguistics, Psycholinguistics, Sociolinguistics, and TESOL Methodology (or virtually any other course) are essentially theme-based. That is, each course is a sequence of topics tied together by the assumption of a coherent overall theme. For example, Psycholinguistics can address topics such as language comprehension, language production, language acquisition, and applied issues in psycholinguistics (e.g., bilingual processing, development of reading skills). In this case, the course covers four topics that are held together by an overarching theme captured by the course title and a general interest in language and the mind. An Introduction to Linguistics course generally amounts to a different topic per week, as do introductory courses in sociolinguistics and TESOL methodology.

Similar interpretations can be given for almost any university-level course (except, perhaps, performance courses which stress repetition and skills practice, e.g., piano or sculpting). The challenge for any university instructor is to create a sense of seamless coherence among the various topics which combine to create a theme for a given course.

Similarly, at the other end of the educational spectrum, elementary school classrooms are organized around thematic units as the basic structure of the curriculum. As Walmsley (1994) states, the elementary curriculum consists of content-area themes (e.g., themes drawn from social studies, math, health, music), calendar-related themes (e.g., seasons, national holidays, anniversaries of specific events), conceptual themes (e.g., themes that are organized around abstract concepts such as "courage" or "growing up"), biographical themes (e.g., a famous person), current event themes (e.g., local or national issues), and form themes (e.g., genres such as myths, legends, science fiction). In elementary school contexts, themes are central ideas which (a) help teachers define and plan appropriate classroom activities; (b) suggest more specific topics for exploration; (c) allow for the learning of appropriate content, language structures, and learning strategies; and (d) lead to significant culminating projects.

An examination of other educational settings would further illustrate how CBI instruction is fundamentally theme-based. Theme-based curricula are prevalent at the secondary level in science, math, social studies, and literature classrooms as well as in vocational programs (Chamot & O'Malley, 1994; O'Malley & Chamot, 1990; Richard-Amato & Snow, 1992a; Tchudi, 1993). Theme-based instruction is also becoming more common in intensive English programs housed in institutions of higher education (Benesch, 1988).

In most educational contexts, thematic instruction is basic; that is, practically all instruction is theme-based. In the CBI literature, there are common references to other models of content-based instruction (e.g., adjunct or sheltered instruction models). These models are not alternatives to theme-based instruction; rather, they represent two different organizational structures for carrying out theme-based instruction. For this reason we see the two terms, *content-based instruction* and *theme-based instruction,* as interchangeable.

In the next section we outline the Six-T's Approach, a new approach to theme-based instruction that is applicable to a wide range of CBI contexts and that does not presuppose institutional preselection of content-area knowledge; it has applications both when the teacher controls content and when content is controlled by a central curriculum plan. Moreover, the theme-based nature of the approach can be incorporated into a sheltered curriculum and within certain adjunct programs.

DESIGN CRITERIA FOR THE SIX-T'S APPROACH

Given the broad interpretation of theme-based instruction presented above, we outline the *Six-T's Approach to language and content instruction.* The approach has three basic goals:

1. the specification of theme-based instruction as central to all CBI
2. the extension of CBI to support any language-learning context, including those in which teachers and program supervisors have the freedom to make major curriculum (and content) decisions
3. the organization of coherent content resources for instruction and the selection of appropriate language learning activities.

With the Six-T's Approach, as with any curricular approach, it is also assumed that first consideration must be given to an array of student needs, student goals, institutional expectations, available resources, teacher abilities, and expected final performance outcomes. When these criteria are specified, informed decisions can be made about the six curricular components which define the Six-T's Approach: Themes, Texts, Topics, Threads, Tasks, and Transitions.

Themes are the central ideas that organize major curricular units; they are chosen to be appropriate to student needs and interests, institutional expectations, program resources, and teacher abilities and interests. Normally a class explores more than one theme in a given term or semester. (See Figure 6.1 for a brief list of sample themes from different instructional settings.)

Texts, defined in a broad sense, are content resources (written and aural) which drive the basic planning of theme units. Text selection will depend on a number of criteria: Student interest, relevance, and instructional appropriateness provide a first set of guidelines for determining text selection; format appeal, length, coherence, connection to other materials, accessibility, availability, and cost represent secondary criteria. Four basic types of texts, as specified in Figure 6.2, are used in theme units.

Topics are the subunits of content which explore more specific aspects of the theme. They are selected to complement student interests, content resources, teacher preferences, and larger curricular objectives. In general, topics should be organized to generate maximum coherence for the theme unit and to provide opportunities to explore both content and language. A given theme unit will evolve differently depending on the specific topics selected for exploration. For example, a teacher could choose to develop a theme unit on Native Americans by exploring the Navajo, the Hopi, and the Apache (each tribe representing a

FIGURE 6.1 Sample themes from different instructional settings

Sample themes	Possible instructional setting
Insects	Elementary school classroom
The solar system	Middle school or high school classroom(s)
Demography	University intensive English program
Austrian historic monuments	High school foreign language class (German)

Types of texts	Examples of content resources
Instructor-compiled content resources	Readings of various genres, videos, audiotapes, maps, tables, graphs, software
Instructor-generated content resources	Lectures, worksheets, graphic representations, bulletin board displays
Task-generated content resources	Student freewrites, discussions, problem-solving activities, graphic representations, library searches, debates, surveys/questionnaires
External content resources	Guest speakers, field trips

FIGURE 6.2 Four basic types of texts used in theme units

different topic for the theme unit); conversely, the same theme unit could be developed to examine the tensions that exist in contemporary Native American communities by means of three different topics: rural versus urban living, traditional versus contemporary religious practices, and the values of young and older generations. These examples, as well as those outlined in Figure 6.3, illustrate how theme units can be developed in different ways, depending on the topics designated (or negotiated) for exploration.

Threads are linkages across themes which create greater curricular coherence. They are, in general, not directly tied to the central idea controlling each theme unit. Rather, they are relatively abstract concepts (e.g., responsibility, ethics, contrasts, power) that provide natural means for linking themes, for reviewing and recycling important content and language across themes, and for revisiting

FIGURE 6.3 Different sets of topics which can define a theme unit

Theme	One set of sample topics	Another set of sample topics
Insects	a. Insects which are helpful b. Insects which are harmful c. Insects which eat other insects d. Insects which eat vegetation	a. Ants b. Bees c. Caterpillars
Solar system	a. Humans in space b. Technology in space c. Research in space	a. Earth b. Venus c. Mercury d. Pluto
Demography	Impact of population on a. air b. water c. natural resources	Population trends a. in developing countries b. in developed countries c. and their impact on the environment

Thread that links various theme units	Themes
Responsibility to	
uphold civil rights for citizens	Civil Rights
control pollution	Pollution
regulate family size	Demography
conduct ethical research	Solar System
protect endangered cultures	Native Americans

FIGURE 6.4 Thread that provides linkages among different themes

selected learning strategies. Threads can bridge themes that appear quite disparate on the surface (e.g., American education, demography, and toxic wastes), thereby fostering a more cohesive curriculum. There can be a number of threads linking thematically different content, providing opportunities to integrate information and view both language and content from new perspectives. Figure 6.4 illustrates how one thread could be used to link five different theme units.

Tasks, the basic units of instruction through which the Six-T's Approach is realized day-to-day, are the instructional activities and techniques utilized for content, language, and strategy instruction in language classrooms (e.g., activities for teaching vocabulary, language structure, discourse organization, communicative interaction, study skills, academic language skills). In the Six-T's Approach, tasks are planned in response to the texts being used. That is, content resources drive task decisions and planning. Major tasks, sequenced within and across themes to realize curricular goals, are recycled with higher levels of complexity as students move from one theme unit to the next and as students progress through the academic year. Devising a series of tasks which leads toward a final culminating activity or project—one which incorporates the learning from various tasks in the theme unit—is particularly effective; culminating activities which require the synthesis of content information help students develop the skills they will need in regular content-area courses, and provide a sense of successful completion for students as well. Specific examples of tasks are given in the following section and are discussed at greater length in Brinton, Goodwin, and Ranks (1994); Brinton, Snow, and Wesche (1989); Chamot and O'Malley (1994); and Mohan (1986).

Transitions are explicitly planned actions which provide coherence *across* topics in a theme unit and *across* tasks within topics. Transitions create links across topics and provide constructive entrees for new tasks and topics within a theme unit. Two major types of transitions are particularly effective: topical and task transitions. (See Figure 6.5 for sample transition activities.)

The six T's provide the means for developing a coherent content-based curriculum. In this approach, the *themes* become the primary source for curriculum planning. A variety of relevant and interesting *texts* leads to *topic* selection. A coherent set of topics is expected to stimulate student interest,

Transition types	Sample transition activities in a theme unit on demography
Topical transitions	A deliberate shift in emphasis from global population trends, to trends in developing countries, to trends in developed countries, to trends in students' home countries. Students are explicitly made aware of these transitions.
Task transitions	Students are asked to (a) interpret a graph depicting population trends; (b) create a new graph with raw data obtained from a classroom survey; (c) write an interpretation of the new graph; (d) reconstruct the graph on the computer; (e) incorporate the graph into a research paper, bulletin board display, or oral presentation.

FIGURE 6.5   Sample transitions that provide coherence across topics and tasks

create connections that maintain student involvement, and allow for the completion of a meaningful final project. Specific *tasks* are designed to teach the language knowledge and content information central to the texts for a given theme unit, thereby meeting student needs and achieving curricular priorities. *Transitions* and *threads* create additional linkages throughout the curriculum, creating a sense of coherence and seamlessness.

Unlike structural, communicative, or task-based approaches to language teaching, the Six-T's Approach views content (in essence, defined by the theme, texts, and topics) as driving all curricular decisions. That is, a content-based course, following a Six-T's framework, must initially be defined by specifying themes, assembling appropriate texts which will support the themes, and designing/negotiating a coherent set of supporting topics. Varied and plentiful content resources (i.e., texts) provide opportunities for relevant language learning activities and strategy instruction. They also provide opportunities to use language and content for meaningful communicative purposes. The language, strategy, and content learning activities that are an integral part of this approach should be generalizable to a wide range of text resources.

The primacy accorded to text resources reflects the assumption that specific content materials can also constrain possible language tasks, language structure awareness, and communicative uses. Language learning and learning strategy tasks should not be artificially imposed on any available set of content resources; that is, sequences of tasks should not be decided on without determining whether specific content resources—written and/or aural—are compatible with the sequences.

A BRIEF EXAMPLE

A relatively brief example, taken from a higher education intensive English program setting with an English for Academic Purposes (EAP) emphasis, will demonstrate how the Six-T's Approach operates. Note that despite the setting for which the example was designed, the issues that arise in planning and implementing the theme unit are applicable to other instructional settings that endorse a content-based approach to language instruction (e.g., elementary, secondary, adult, and other university settings).

To frame the example, we first outline the core objectives for the EAP curriculum being illustrated. The curriculum will

1. prepare students to learn subject material through their L2,
2. introduce students to academic language and study skills needed in mainstream classes,
3. simulate the rigors and expectations of regular university courses in a sheltered environment,
4. promote students' self-reliance and positive engagement with learning,
5. motivate students to use language to learn something new about topics of interest and of relevance to their situation.

One theme that is generally appropriate for EAP students in the United States is that of *civil rights*; the theme not only is intriguing to students but also serves as a window to understanding the new U.S. environment in which they are living. Fortunately, there are extensive content resources available, a wide range of topics worth exploring, and many opportunities for student contributions to support such a theme unit. A civil rights theme unit could easily be a semester-long university course or a brief unit in an L2 textbook. In our example, it is a three-week unit comprising ten hours of classroom instruction per week, for a total of thirty hours (equal in time to a two-credit university course).

Following the preliminary decision to use civil rights as a *theme*, various *texts* were assembled and examined. Interesting and appropriate materials from a number of sources were selected (e.g., videos, readings, newspaper clippings, charts and graphs, guest speakers, radio program excerpts).[1] Based on text selections, related *topics* were considered and then a set of topics was designated for the unit. Topics for the civil rights theme included, on this occasion, the history of African Americans in the United States, the civil rights movement in the United States, and civil rights leaders in the United States (with an emphasis on African Americans).[2]

After texts were assembled and topics determined, the material was examined for *threads* which could easily link the civil rights unit to other themes in the

---

[1] The primary text materials selected for this unit were entitled *America's Civil Rights Movement*, a complete teaching packet with a text (*Free at last: A history of the civil rights movement and those who died in the struggle*) and a video (*A time for justice: America's civil rights movement*), available from Teaching Tolerance, Southern Poverty Law Center, 400 Washington Ave., Montgomery, AL 36104.

[2] Topics that were rejected for this three-week unit but that could be used in future units—with a different set of texts but the same theme—include civil rights for different ethnic minorities in the United States; discrimination based on gender, age, and disability; and civil rights and discrimination in other countries.

fifteen-week course (e.g., Native Americans, demography, pollution, American education). Among the possibilities for threads were the notions of responsibility, collaboration, and ethics.[3] These concepts form natural bridges between civil rights issues and issues raised in other theme units, creating a sense of curricular coherence and giving students opportunities to review and reconsider previous learning in relation to current material.

As an example, the thread of "ethics" could easily link the themes specified above if students were asked to consider (a) the ethics of civil and human rights movements (civil rights unit), (b) the ethics of the imposition of "Western ways" on Native American peoples in North America (Native American unit), (c) the ethics of governmental intervention in family planning (demography unit), (d) the ethics of clean water regulations (pollution unit), and (e) the ethics of honest research and reporting in academia (American education unit).

Text materials were then evaluated in terms of the language and learning strategy needs of EAP students. In general terms, *tasks* typical of an EAP context[4] were designated as important for students and as complementary to text resources; the two constraints governing decisions were that the tasks be keyed to the theme being explored, and that they be natural extensions of the content resources (i.e., texts) being used to develop the theme.

At this point, the curriculum planners began thinking about a significant culminating task that would provide a sense of closure to the unit and give students an opportunity to synthesize and/or apply content and language learned throughout the unit. Final projects considered were as follows: a group report on current civil rights activities; poster displays exploring different topics covered in the theme unit (Esposito, Marshall, & Stoller, 1997); a debate on some aspect of civil rights; a research paper and corresponding oral presentation on a civil rights topic of individual student interest; a media presentation reporting on civil rights violations in designated parts of the world.

Transitions were contemplated after topics were selected and learning tasks developed. Although it is difficult to actually finalize transitions before a theme unit begins, it is important for teachers/curriculum planners to view transitions as crucial components of this approach to CBI. With properly orchestrated transitions, students sense the logical progression from one topic to the next and from one task to the next. Efforts to bridge topics and tasks provide

---

[3] Many other abstract notions could serve as threads to link this theme unit with others: for example, respect, human rights, collaboration, cooperation, social structures, power, conflict, authority, law, truth, innovation, and change.

[4] Tasks typical of an EAP curriculum include listening to lectures and taking notes, using notes for reading and writing tasks, small group discussions and problem solving, learning and using key vocabulary, associating and brainstorming key concepts with graphic organizers, finding and incorporating relevant information from outside sources, reading and writing activities across various genres, writing activities focusing on synthesis and argumentation, and practicing test-taking strategies. More in-depth discussions of tasks relevant to CBI instruction are found in Brinton, Goodwin, & Ranks (1994); Brinton, Snow, & Wesche (1989); Chamot & O'Malley (1994); Mohan (1986); and Short (1994).

coherence within and across topics and contribute to the overall coherence of the theme unit. Transitions should not be overspecified in advance, since teachers should take advantage of emerging classroom situations to create meaningful transitions.

Transitional activities can take up but a minute of class time or involve a complex set of problem-solving activities to create meaningful linkages. In the case of the civil rights unit, purposeful transitions occurred when students (a) chose a U.S. discrimination case and related it to a similar incident in their own countries; (b) examined how the history of African Americans in the United States led to the modern civil rights movement; (c) nominated three notable figures in the civil rights movement and analyzed their leadership qualities. Other transitions occurred when students were asked to predict new topics, discuss the importance of prior tasks, consider issues that prior tasks did not address, brainstorm additional concepts and associations, engage in guided speed writings, discuss the relationship between the latest reading and a prior reading, and relate personal experiences to past and upcoming tasks.

IMPLEMENTING A SIX-T'S APPROACH

The civil rights unit described above illustrates the means by which the Six-T's Approach is implemented and the ways in which the six T's create coherent and meaningful instructional units for content and language learning objectives. We recognize, however, that any brief example is incomplete and likely to raise as many questions as it answers. Thus, in this section we anticipate a number of these questions by considering initial planning issues and outlining step-by-step procedures for implementing the Six-T's Approach. It is important to keep in mind, however, that each instructional context will impose its own constraints on, and opportunities for, adaptation and variation.

Initial Planning Considerations

Before actually planning a theme-based curriculum that uses a Six-T's Approach, curriculum designers need to evaluate five important preplanning considerations. First, they must review students' needs (based on critical needs analyses), institutional expectations and corresponding objectives, resource possibilities, and teacher preparation. The results of such a review will determine (and constrain) the content, language, and learning skills which students will need to, and be expected to, develop. These considerations should lead to straightforward taxonomies of important language skills, learning strategies, and task options for language practice and content exploration. Such lists, however, should not be viewed as rigid specifications of required tasks or necessary sequences of activities; rather, they should be seen as additional resources for planners to reflect on, and consider, when implementing a specific theme unit.

Second, planners need to ascertain the extent to which the curriculum is institutionally predetermined or shaped by teacher and/or student choices. While *theme* choices may be constrained by the institution, teachers, and/or content resources, specific *topics* may be open to student selection and/or negotiation. Student choice may also play a role in determining learning tasks and culminating projects.

Third, designers need to decide on the degree of "tension" a theme is permitted to generate. Tension arises when students consider complex and/or controversial issues associated with varying perspectives and alternative viewpoints on topics defining a theme unit (see also Williams & Reynolds, 1993). In EAP contexts, for example, it is our view that themes which highlight and/or create some amount of tension promote student involvement and engagement with the content. Finding the delicate balance between sufficient and excessive tension is important and highly variable. Clearly, too much tension should be avoided because it will create a classroom atmosphere that obstructs rather than enhances language and content learning.

Fourth, planners need to determine the number of theme units to be explored and designate the amount of time devoted to each theme unit (and topics within theme units). The number of theme units incorporated into a curriculum (and their duration) is highly variable and largely dependent on institutional constraints. Theme units may last intensely for one to three weeks or less intensively for four to ten weeks. It is also possible for multiple themes to run simultaneously over the course of a year, with student work on any given theme only occurring on an intermittent basis.

Fifth, planners must consider their own commitment to CBI and its objectives. Themes may be viewed as little more than convenient shells for language improvement activities or as a means for serious engagement with important concepts. We believe that the need for serious engagement is a requirement of CBI. Themes that serve as convenient opportunities for unimportant and incoherently linked language and content activities do not engage students in meaningful and long-lasting language and content learning.

Steps for Implementing a Six-T's Approach

Once preliminary issues are considered, language educators can actually begin planning and then implementing theme units following the Six-T's framework. Below we sketch out the general steps one would take to implement the Six-T's Approach. We present the steps in a sequential manner, though in fact the process is quite fluid and requires planners to revisit and reconsider earlier steps as the planning process progresses.

Step One.   The first step requires establishing the content to be used through theme determination, text selection, and topic designation. Defining the content of theme units at the outset—as determined by themes, texts, and topics— follows from the argument that curricular decisions need to be content-driven rather than task- or language-driven as a first priority. Although the determination of themes, selection of texts, and designation of topics could be seen as following a sequenced order, in practice they tend to be decided on interactively.

In some settings, themes, texts, and/or topics are decided on by a centralized group of curriculum planners, leaving few decision-making responsibilities at this level to teachers and local curriculum planners. In other settings, teachers and curriculum planners have more significant decision-making powers. When in a position to make theme, text, and/or topic decisions, teachers/planners need to anticipate student interests, look for engaging content materials that can lead to a strong culminating task, and outline opportunities for coherent sequencing. In addition, they should keep the following in mind:

1. *Themes* should be based on conceptually important and relevant ideas for one's particular students and instructional setting; themes that are relevant to the local context are particularly effective. For example, in the context of a southwestern U.S. classroom, a theme on Native Americans can be considered locally relevant and of great interest to students at all instructional levels. Other considerations for initial theme selection will depend on (a) the types and extent of interesting and appropriate texts that are available, and (b) the number of options for captivating topics within the theme unit.

2. A range of *texts* that complements core institutional objectives and includes a variety of genres and formats at the appropriate level of difficulty must be assembled in order to determine (a) which content material will be motivating, (b) which material will provide an engaging lead-in to the theme, (c) which topics are best in light of the content resources available, (d) which threads surface to create additional linkages across themes, and (e) which culminating tasks or projects are natural extensions of the content. Including texts that introduce varying perspectives on the theme and/or topics under consideration is crucial; the tasks that spring forth from texts with alternative perspectives can lead to important critical thinking skills and strategy training.

3. In most settings, *topics* are determined by core content resources. Additional topics can be selected by students—individually, in groups, or as a class—to give students greater involvement in curriculum decisions. What is particularly important in terms of topic selection is the need to select a coherent set of topics, rather than a disparate set of superficially linked topics, that fit under the broader theme.

Step Two.   The second step involves selecting possible threads that emerge from final theme, text, and topic designations. Related tasks can be developed later at appropriate times during theme exploration to encourage students to consider these threads, which will naturally connect themes and add coherence to the overall curriculum.

Step Three.   Step three involves making decisions about the sequencing of content (themes, topics, and texts) and the length of theme units. Sequencing decisions will largely be based on (a) the availability of content (e.g., guest speakers, field trips, special events), (b) the relative ease or difficulty of tasks likely to follow from the content, and (c) the cognitive demands made on students as they manipulate the content and carry out culminating activities. As a culminating task, for example, a theme that lends itself easily to a research paper should be sequenced after a theme that lends itself to a descriptive paper. A theme that lends itself to a debate on abstract issues should follow a theme that lends itself to a straightforward oral presentation of facts and figures. When making sequencing decisions, planners must also consider the evolving nature of each theme unit as the instructional orientation evolves from more teacher-centered to more student-centered during the term.

Step Four.   An additional consideration at this point is the extent of teacher involvement, knowledge of thematic content, and willingness to learn additional information with the students. Walmsley (1994) refers to the need for teachers to "bump up their knowledge," arguing that teachers need to read additional information on designated topics. Such a commitment builds teacher motivation and enthusiasm, provides teachers with expanded expertise that students can call on, allows teachers to introduce multiple perspectives on the content under consideration, and provides teachers with additional options for classroom tasks. The extent to which such "bumping up" is necessary is a question we leave open, but some form of teacher investment is necessary.

Step Five.   Step five requires the specification of core objectives for each theme unit in terms of language, content, and strategy learning. This also involves the planning of selected tasks and task sequences to open and close the unit.

Step Six.   The sixth step involves the initial design of tasks to carry out the content and language goals of each theme unit. Selected tasks should emerge from content resources rather than be arbitrarily imposed on them; they should develop students' language learning, facilitate the learning of content, and model strategies for language and content learning. Tasks, viewed as integral parts of a coherent content framework, should serve larger content-learning and language-use purposes.

Step Seven.   The seventh step involves the initial determination of transitions across topics and across tasks. These should be explicit but kept flexible so that teachers can take advantage of student-generated resources and other unexpected variations that typically arise in any complex teaching situation. Transitions will facilitate a natural and systematic flow of content and tasks from one day to the next.

Step Eight.   The final stage involves the fine-tuning of theme units while they are being implemented. When theme units are taught, it is expected that plans will change and vary as teachers take advantage of students' interests and ongoing input. As each theme evolves, new topics will emerge that are of interest to students, requiring teachers (and motivating students) to locate and/or create additional support materials and tasks. Supplementary resources can give students additional opportunities to "bump up" their own knowledge and, in many cases, to engage in a certain amount of individualized learning, thereby increasing student interest in and engagement with the theme unit. Supplementary resources can also provide teachers with opportunities to integrate new tasks and transitions into the unit, and to exploit additional threads as these resources connect the current theme to other themes in new conceptual ways.

CAVEATS

Content-based instruction, in its various configurations, entails some potential difficulties. It is important to point them out so that teachers and curriculum planners can avoid them and design more effective instructional units for content and language learning.

First, planners need to keep language and content learning in balance. It is easy for teachers to become excited about interesting and appealing content and overlook the language exploitation aspects of instruction. CBI should not overemphasize content nor underemphasize language learning activities.

Second, it is important that those implementing theme units not lose sight of content and language learning objectives, and the time allotted to meet those objectives. Achieving planned objectives, pacing the activities appropriately, and providing a sense of closure are important components of CBI if interest and motivation are to develop and remain high. There is often the temptation to allow "well-received" themes, topics, and/or tasks to "run too long." The key is to know when to move on to the next stage of the curriculum so that students maintain a level of excitement and engagement in content and language learning.

Third, it is important not to overwhelm students with too much content. There are usually many ways to exploit interesting content for language learning purposes without moving through large sets of resources too quickly. Sometimes teachers become so involved in their own content learning that they want to share all their new insights (and content resources) with students. Despite the fact that students are often motivated by teacher enthusiasm, they also need sufficient time to work with and reflect on the content and language of the assigned texts. It is better to examine the same set of content sources from a range of perspectives and for a variety of purposes than to cursorily examine excessively large amounts of content.

Fourth, teachers and curriculum planners have spent far more time exploring issues related to the design and implementation of CBI than on procedures for the *evaluation* of content and language learning in CBI classrooms. Once again, we run into the problem of balance. How much content learning do we evaluate and how much language learning do we evaluate? Evaluation of content and language is an important part of CBI. Excluding the assessment of one area, in order to focus on the other, does not serve the students well. Teachers and planners must keep in mind the need to evaluate both content and language on a regular basis. (See Turner, Chapter 15, and Weigle and Jensen, Chapter 16, in this volume.) (See also Brinton, Snow, & Wesche, 1989; Chamot & O'Malley, 1994; Meinbach, Rothlein, & Fredericks, 1995; Roberts, 1993; Short, 1993.)

CONCLUSION

In this chapter, we have set out to examine current perspectives on content-based instruction and describe an approach which is adaptable to many instructional contexts. Even though our discussion of the Six-T's Approach drew on examples from an EAP pre-university curriculum, the general goals and planning procedures are applicable to K–12 contexts for English as a second dialect students, language minority students, and immigrant students. In addition, the principles organizing the Six-T's Approach can be used to reorganize foreign language curricula and assist in adapting EFL instruction into more coherent and interesting formats.

The Six-T's Approach is exploratory in nature, and there are a number of issues which still need to be addressed in greater depth. Important among these are more detailed investigations of (a) task taxonomies as they relate to theme units and transitions across topics; (b) the concept of threads and their contributions to curricular coherence; (c) the connections between topics and themes as the former support and extend the latter; (d) assessment of student language and content development, and curricular success overall; and (e) principles of text selection.

Despite the need for further refinement of the Six-T's Approach, it offers language educators means for devising coherent curricula that will facilitate both content and language learning. The motivation and student engagement with learning that result from this approach can provide students with more successful classroom experiences and prepare them for the rigors of mainstream classes.

chapter 7

The Challenge of Language and History Terminology from the Student Optic[1]

Anthony Bernier

As demographic shifts gradually transform our student populations, one hears frequent discussion of institutional needs and methods for improving persistence and retention of these diverse populations at the academy: offering in-depth orientations, increasing "bridge" programs, beefing up tutorial staffs, and enlarging learning center capacities. Clearly, all these measures play vital parts in fulfilling the university's larger social goals of educational equity. Yet these designs overlook the pivotal responsibilities of faculty and the role of pedagogy.

Because demographics continue to transform our student profiles, faculty must keep their audience in tight focus.[2] While historians and other teaching faculty routinely revise course content to incorporate new scholarship, they should revise their pedagogical approaches to reflect changes in the *linguistic* and *social class diversity* of their students as well. In other words, now that we have finally achieved some ethnic, racial, and class diversity on campus, we must update our teaching methods to minimize academic alienation and marginalization of these diverse students.[3]

---

[1] This article is reprinted with permission from *The History Teacher, 28*(1), November 1994.

[2] Thanks to Carole Srole, Francisco Balderrama, Eugene Fingerhut, and their lower division History 202a and 202b classes; to California State University, Los Angeles' Study Group Program Coordinator, Steve Teixeira, for generous guidance and assistance in profitably exploiting study groups for this research. Also, thanks to Lillian Taiz, Lawrence Guillow, Nancy Fitch, Edward Berenson, Nancy Page Fernandez, and especially Carole Srole, for their readings and comments on an earlier version of this essay entitled "Language and History Pedagogy from the Student Optic," presented at the 86h Annual Meeting of the Organization of American Historians, Anaheim, CA, 1993.

[3] At CSULA, for example, a recent census reveals that 69 percent of the campus's incoming 1991 fall freshmen were *not* "native English speakers." Secondly, 52 percent reported parental income below $20,000 (only 19 percent over $40,000). "Fall 1991 Freshmen," *Cal State L.A. Facts* 10 (March 1993), 1.

This chapter reports on my experiences as a graduate student study group leader for Project LEAP (Learning English for Academic Purposes) at California State University, Los Angeles (CSULA). Our team, consisting of Learning Resource Center study group leaders, general education history faculty, and language specialists, examined language and content issues surfacing in the department's United States history survey courses. The LEAP team focused on the pedagogical implications of these issues particularly as they impact two student groups: first, language minority students whose primary language was not English but whose diligence gained them sufficient English competency to participate in mainstream courses. The second group of students (referred to as "working-class students") come from socioeconomic backgrounds that, by definition, represent the first generation in their families to enter academia. Indeed, many of our lower division history students come from both non-English speaking and working-class backgrounds. All these students face many language and class barriers to academic culture and curriculum that other students do not. These barriers inhibit history content acquisition.

As a study group leader, I facilitated small discussion groups consisting exclusively of the students described above. The groups ran in tandem with their United States history survey courses. During our bi-weekly meetings, I recorded long lists of content vocabulary words these at-risk students identified as unfamiliar and confusing. In fact, students frequently spent more time trying to decode vocabulary than discussing themes, theses, or their own thoughts about the content material itself. From these student-generated lists emerged the typology presented below.

Much of the difficulty these student audiences found with the language in lectures, textbooks, and in examinations arises from the use of terms, phrases, and references the mainstream would deem "common knowledge." For today's complex and diverse audiences of second language and working-class students, much of the classroom's academic (and non-academic) lexicon presents a double challenge: They must learn the content of United States history, just like all the other students, and they must do so against a linguistic backdrop in large measure unfamiliar to them. This is one of the great undiscussed challenges before today's university faculty.

Even the best history lecturer, armed with the most recent scholarship and fascinating assignments, inadvertently holds students accountable for much more than United States history. They also hold students responsible for "common knowledge" well outside the cultural, disciplinary, social class, chronological, and linguistic experiences of their students. While these circumstances risk estranging insecure first and second year students, they ultimately also frustrate our expectations for academic performance. If faculty become more conscious of their use of language (and the language in their assigned readings), all students stand to benefit.

A TYPOLOGY OF TERMINOLOGY

The typology consists of three broad categories: (1) **Content Terms**, which routinely occur in lectures and textbooks as "common knowledge" references to course material *within the discipline of history.* These are jargon for historians, but not common knowledge for many students. The second category in the typology, (2) **Language Terms**, refers to vocabulary technically *outside* the boundaries of history content, but that frequently finds its way into course lectures, readings, and assignments. Faculty may consider these references common knowledge as well, irrespective of the audience's linguistic or social class background. The last category in the typology which obstructs second language and working-class student comprehension of history content is (3) **Language Masking Content**. This category encompasses the fluid boundaries created by the first two: terminology appropriated by historians and other scholars frequently masking content due to variant and multiple meanings and unfamiliar metaphors and oxymorons.

These problematic terms, however, should not be simply discarded from lectures or avoided in textbooks. When faculty begin to recognize that these language typologies impede student access to content material, they can develop strategies and techniques to address them. (See also Srole, Chapter 8 in this volume.) Furthermore, as faculty incorporate these strategies into normal lecture revision, assignments, and examinations, they improve persistence and performance not only for the two groups under present consideration, but for all students.

Content Terms

"Content Terms" properly appear in lecture and text material because they directly label discrete historical concepts, ideas, and personalities. These are the historian's professional jargon, terms faculty most likely invest at least nominal effort to define, even though they may feel students ought to already know some of them. While all faculty define terms, they also assume students know words they do not. In my observations of history survey course discussion groups, five groups of "Content Terms" surfaced: (1) "regular" history terms, (2) archaic language, (3) non-history terms, (4) obscure acronyms, and (5) non-English vocabulary.

"Regular" history terms label discrete concepts, ideas, and phenomena which faculty recognize as historian's jargon. But they also may assume a term is "common knowledge" or, conversely, that the phrase lies too far from the lecture's thesis or theme to warrant lecture time to explain it. For an audience of second language and working-class students, however, faculty need to increase their sensitivity to what they consider obvious or common knowledge. Another example is the use of *archaic language*. Faculty and textbook authors frequently try to vary their prose with language or quotations from a particular era under study. Yet this practice not only assumes knowledge unfamiliar to second language and working-class students, but is inaccessible to them as well. Professors also employ archaic words when drawing comparisons across time, such as "the 'New Woman' of the 1890s was not a 'flapper.'" But students studying the 1890s may have not yet encountered "flappers" in their course reading.

While such textbook terms like "artisanal," "mercantile," and "yeoman," for instance, refer to easily understood historical occupational titles, the references draw upon terms no longer in currency. Students, then, find themselves trying to unravel archaic vocabulary rather than connecting relationships and ideas to history. A few other dated examples are "gilded age," "dowry," and "draft animals" along with more recent terms such as "Contragate," "Negro," "Cracker Jack," even "tramp."

The third group of terms, *non-history vocabulary,* impacts all history students. Faculty frequently borrow terms and concepts from across academic and disciplinary borders. However important to course content, such border crossings confound uninitiated students as well as penalize them, irrespective of student attempts to keep up. "Overproduction," "inflation," "recession," and "stagflation," for instance, all come from economics. And while we need these terms in history, the assumption that survey students possess an adequate background in economics automatically disadvantages them. A "free market," then, understandably evokes a barter system. Likewise, "cattle prod," "plowed under," and "stubborn as a mule" come from a rural and agricultural past. And "taking a different tack," appearing so frequently in parenthetical comments, is, after all, a nautical term. "Assimilation," "upward mobility," and "socialization" come from sociology. "Intelligence" refers to the "information gathering community," probably from military studies.

A fourth group of problematic terms are *obscure acronyms.* While "F.B.I.," "C.I.A.," and "WASP" may appear in the popular media, students seldom maintain more than sight recognition of them. Yet faculty assume students know much more. Other historically important acronyms present problems as well: "FDIC," "IMF," "WPA," "V-J Day" and "V-E Day," "GI," "FOB," "PFC," "CSO," and "GOP" represent only a few. While these initials bounce around in casual faculty banter, they often provide pivotal illustrations for larger concepts and yet students cannot merely "look them up."

The last group of examples illustrating the "Content Terms" typology, *non-English vocabulary,* refers to a variety of phrases important for history content material but troublesome to second language and working-class students. Admittedly, some of these terms may even appear familiar to students. But they quickly become hard-pressed when questioned directly for definitions. Other *non-English vocabulary* remains disconnected throughout the entire term and thus interferes with learning content. Terms such as "elite," "suffrage," "bourgeoisie" and "proletariat," "bureaucracy," and "coup" may garner serviceable recognition; a student may offer the definition "'elite' means rich people," for instance. Other terms simply go unconnected and ignored, such as "laissez-faire," "de jure" and "de facto," "antebellum," and "bracero." If faculty inadvertently blend *non-English vocabulary* into their lectures without somehow flagging or defining them as non-English words, they cause added problems for their students because foreign spellings preclude "looking words up."

A common faculty refrain—"Well, why don't students just raise their hands and ask questions?"—reveals the degree to which these pedagogical issues are not well understood. First, the student who writes "steak dinner" (rather than "state dinner") into her class notes feels confident that she *did* understand the term. Second, the sheer number of problematic terms *from each lecture* (even by sensitive faculty) far and away precludes constant student interruptions. More important, however, second language and working-class students number among the least confident students in general survey courses, the least likely to ask any questions at all, even in comfortable classroom settings. Their written and verbal skills need the most development. They tend to believe that asking clarification questions (especially on material just covered in class) reveals their stupidity. And for second language students, asking questions aloud in class also exposes a most sensitive aspect of their identities to public scrutiny, their imperfect oral language skills. Must students risk social exposure of personal insecurities to succeed in United States history classes? These are the "silent minority" of our classroom audiences. And they are the most at risk from our inattention to language and pedagogy.

Language Terms

While "Content Terms" refers to actual content vocabulary that faculty inaccurately assume as "common knowledge," the second problematic language category, "Language Terms," illuminates words constantly borrowed from *outside* history's disciplinary borders to illustrate content material. These terms bear no explicit or literal relationship to history content material. Nevertheless they appear in lecture and textbook narratives, ostensibly to heighten student comprehension or to enliven prose.

Yet even enterprising students cannot find many of these terms in reference sources because they may have never heard the term before, making spelling especially difficult as well. Many of these terms do not appear in dictionaries. For the idiosyncratic terms and phrases fitting this typology, reference sources provide no help at all. Four groups of "Language Terms" highlight the problem: (1) metaphors, (2) colloquial usages, (3) class-based constructions, and (4) cultural idioms.

Metaphors surface particularly frequently in lectures (but in texts as well) and can easily derail understanding among second language and working-class students when unwittingly introduced. The term "bread and butter issue," for example, confounds students understandably groping for literal meaning. Assuming that these students even knew the expression "which side your bread is buttered on," they would still be hard pressed to understand what bread and butter had to do with United States history.

If faculty were more attuned to their diverse student audience, then the phrase "to light a fire under the Senate" might be used without confusing it with an act of arson. "Offering an olive branch" illuminates meaning only to those on nodding terms with biblical verse and symbolism. "Taking a girl home to Mother" and "I wouldn't write home to Mother about it" evoke literal domestic and gendered imagery to these students. Is "to whitewash" akin to "laundering the colors separately"? If not, what then is to "blackwash"? Even common phrases such as "paving the way for" and "laying the groundwork for" do not necessarily transmit intended meaning. Last, "on the floor of the Senate" likewise understandably obstructs a student's understanding about a matter discussed in Congress.

"Language Terms" also encompass *colloquial* terms. Colloquial terms, phrases, references, and allusions (that is, ordinary or familiar conversational speech interspersed throughout an otherwise formal lecture) obstruct student access to the content material of the history survey course. The term "nose to the grindstone," for example, joins other very common bodily references, such as "looking down one's nose at," "facing prejudice," "fell on deaf ears," and "taken at face value," all of which confound students removed from colloquial familiarity.

Such assumedly familiar phrases as "in cahoots with," "down South" (as opposed to "up North" or "out West" or "back East," perhaps?),"old world" (as opposed to "new world" or "old planet"?), "passing muster" (which shows up in students' notes as "passing mustard"), and many like them all conspire against students trying to gain insight and understanding of the course content we work so hard to teach. Further, when faculty shift from the formal speech pattern of college professors to informal registers of a grammatically familiar and common vocabulary and then back to formal lecture references, they may send working-class and second language students confusing signals, taking them even further away from content.

A third group of "Language Terms," *class-based constructions,*[4] describes vocabulary unfamiliar to many, if not most, first and second year students, but especially to first generation college students. Some of these terms come directly from an unfamiliar academic culture itself: "syllabus," "office hours," and "Department Chair," for example, pose problems for many students particularly during the important, transitional, and difficult first few weeks of the fall term. To the academically uninitiated, "office hours" understandably collides with the conventional times during which offices are open, 9 A.M. to 5 P.M. Further, students frequently do not know that professors keep office hours for them. Few of the students I worked with could properly describe what actually happens during office hours. (See Kamhi-Stein, Koch & Snow [1977] for a suggested teaching strategy.)

While "syllabus," "ivory tower," "credentials," "M.A.," "Master's degree," "MBA," "Ph.D.," "doctorate," "grant," and "provost" may not often appear during lectures, working-class and second language students do not know these terms because they are new to university culture. How often is "ivory tower" defined? Many other terms come from a decidedly middle-class experience where familiarity comes from long years of socialization: "mortgage," "stocks and bonds," "title" (either one of land or profession), "Wall Street" (as in "Was that before or after the crash of Wall Street?"). When faculty casually include such class-based terminology and references in history lectures or assignments, they block the understanding of first generation college students.

---

[4] While second language students must struggle to overcome the unenviable task of hurriedly becoming bilingual in English, working-class students struggle against social class alienation. For an especially cogent and useful discussion of working-class student assimilation into the academy, see Bell, 1985).

Cultural idioms illustrate the last group of the "Language Terms." Cultural idioms consist of peculiar terms and references that make sense only to those students initiated or already familiar with American (and frequently, middle-class) cultural icons, symbols, and experiences. They exclude first generation students almost by definition. Even good faith attempts by sensitive faculty who con-sciously refer to popular culture also may fail in attempting to connect with contemporary student experiences. While students may know many of our popular culture's current icons and idioms, "Rambo" and "Jaws" haven't held currency for years. And, unfortunately, students have not seen fifteen-year-old *Saturday Night Live* sketches. Such casual references to popular cultural icons hearken back to an older cohort's descriptors that no longer speak to a student audience born in the mid 1970s. Other, once-popular terms, like "preppie," "powertrip," and "soap opera," may receive offhand references in lecture, but still elude student experiences and connections. Nevertheless, faculty and textbook authors press on through lecture and narrative with faulty assumptions about student familiarity.

Faculty also frequently refer to "classic" works of fiction. *Alice in Wonderland,* for example, may well peg a surreal image for a professor. For students raised on tales from other languages and cultures, however, this classic English language work of children's fiction not only presents an unconnected image, but more important, risks obstructing comprehension of a central idea. Some terms come from middle-class exposure to the arts; for instance, a striving student writes "Mac Beth and Mrs. Beth" into his notes for a Shakespearean allusion to Macbeth. Similarly, references to classical Western literature and culture—"American Caesar," "Romance language," and "reaching Olympian heights"—can transmit very con-fusing meanings when heard by a Mexican national student in the United States only a few years. The same may be said for allusions to film celebrities—for example, a reference to "a real John Wayne type."

Thus, while faculty may try a variety of methods to spruce up their lectures and "keep students interested" with "common" metaphors, informal speech, class-based vocabulary, and cultural references, they run a high risk of obstructing content for working-class and second language students whose experiences preclude access to the intended meaning and who rely especially heavily upon literal translations and explicit definitions.

Language Masking Content Terms

Unlike the two previous categories, "Content Terms" and "Language Terms" (which employ vocabularies clearly either in or out of history's disciplinary boundaries), the last one, "Language Masking Content Terms," encompasses both language and content vocabulary. These terms have meaning among historians but also have colloquial, literal, or alternative meanings for second language or working-class students relying on clear, literal interpretations and not yet familiar with eclectic scholarly jargon. Hence, these terms mask meaning even for simple material. Two groups of terms illustrate pedagogical problems associated with this last category: (1) double or variant meanings, and (2) historically specific metaphors and oxymorons.

The first group, *double or variant meanings,* frequently comes from a general knowledge vocabulary but contains terms with multiple or alternative meanings that send even the most attentive student off on unintended tangents. Even if students do straighten out the difference, they are distracted for a time. Common words or phrases (like "class," for example) carry multiple meanings that confuse students. Does the term mean "high" social breeding, a socio-economic category (as in "all classes lived in the same neighborhood"), a group of people due to graduate from an institution during the same year (as in "the class of 1997"), or merely the next science course one enrolls in after passing "Chemistry 101"? Another example, "left," evolved from eighteenth century French politics, and, among other uses, literally doubles as a directional indicator. While faculty may wish to evoke this term as shorthand for a more liberal political environment (vis-à-vis "the right"), they can easily confuse students with this seemingly simple term. Similarly, "occupation" in lecture can mean political or military take-over, but it also means the job one does to earn a living. In lecture, "labor" usually refers to organized efforts to press workers' rights instead of the physical or mental exertion of work itself, or even the last stages of a new mother's delivery. And wouldn't the term "laborer," then, imply a union member? Other examples of multiple meanings include: "hearing," "movement," "state," "gang," "kickback," "intelligence," "party."

Some masking terms relate to each other in odd ways. Faculty, for instance, may even explain Truman's "Fair Deal" policy with reference to Roosevelt's previous "New Deal" domestic programs, but the literal term remains dangling and unconnected to content. Doesn't the term "deal" actually speak to card playing and the relationship between life chances, mobility through hard work, and luck? Still other masking terms make literal reference to a name. "Jim Crow" (even few faculty know the origins of this term), "Uncle Tom," and "Roe" (as in *Roe vs. Wade*) provide examples of personal or fictive names with symbolic meanings; yet lectureres or textbooks typically do little more than make passing references to these terms. To students, Jim Crow could reasonably refer to just another historical personality.

Names of wars illustrate how terms can mask meaning because they frequently confuse the name of the war with the name of a place, and recent military actions omit countries entirely. "Vietnam," mentioned in a class, more than likely refers to the American war in Vietnam, rather than to the country itself. The same obviously holds true for "Korea," "Grenada," "Panama." And "the Gulf War" does not mention any country at all! But the student only seven years removed from Southeast Asia or Latin America could lose the thread of an entire argument trying to figure out the differences. Chicano students, for example, trying to unravel the "Mexican American War," might easily be thrown "off track." After all, "Mexican Americans" never declared their own war.

Many faculty consider these variations, spins, or complexities "standard" or "self-evident." But by the time a student unravels the contextual meaning, if ever, a central concept is lost and the professor has moved on to new topics. One student actually began research on the "Iron Curtain" by searching for its photograph in a reference book. Yet what may appear as standard in academic and scholarly milieus, or even in casual conversation among those with shared backgrounds, occludes the comprehension of United States history content for many students.

The second group of terms qualifying as "Language Masking Content Terms" comprises *historically specific metaphors and oxymorons.* This vocabulary creates confusion precisely because its literal meaning appears self-contradictory, incon-gruous, or idiosyncratic to still-acculturating students. American intellectuals constantly send up complex linguistic codes that spin off secondary or variant meanings. We make fun and play with many of them—"military intelligence" and "American foreign policy" (how can something be American *and* foreign at the same time?). The "arms race," for example, conjures a comical and strange image, and "labor pool" left unconnected to the course's content reasonably suggests a place of recreation for working people. Similarly, an "eight-hour day" literally challenges students' concept of a "twenty-four-hour day."

CONCLUSION

I have presented samples of problematic vocabulary extracted ethnographically from a year's worth of history survey course lectures and student discussion groups. A large percentage of these terms slip invisibly in and out of everyday conversation between scholarly colleagues, graduate students, and others already assimilated into academia. But a daily barrage of such terms alienates second language and working-class students from lectures and readings. It also wastes valuable energy that we would prefer them to expend grappling with the history material itself. Now that the academy has begun to successfully attract a somewhat more diverse student audience, faculty need to take these audience changes into account as they review and revise their pedagogical approaches. Much of what we assume as "obvious" is, in fact, not obvious to second language and working-class students. As a consequence, much of our language holds them accountable for more than the content we teach. These students are unable because the problem is so frequent, and unwilling because of social and aca-demic insecurities, to risk interrupting a lecture each time unknown words or phrases arise. And to whom can they turn for clarification while completing a reading assignment? If faculty take different student audiences into considera-tion as they update their course preparations and materials, they can avoid academically estranging these students and improve learning for all students.

chapter 8

Pedagogical Responses from Content Faculty: Teaching Content and Language in History[1]

Carole Srole

Language and content blend in the academic discourse of the history class. We historians borrow the tools of one to probe the meaning of the other; our interpretations of history influence the type of language employed. History professors use a broad range of terminology, from archaic words and labels (like *mercantilism*) to academic jargon (like *agency* and *family economy*). Some terms come from other disciplines; others are acronyms. We also employ metaphors, colloquial terms, cultural idioms, and sophisticated vocabulary to enliven our analysis of history.[2]

This fusion of language and content requires students to understand non-history content and cultural references that linguistically and culturally diverse students do not yet possess. Compounding the problem is the fact that they typically do not have time, in the midst of a lecture or exam, to look up vocabulary words beyond their understanding, nor can they find the relevant meanings of the terms later in the dictionary. Thus, these hidden language requirements for achievement undermine student comprehension of history.[3] Students often fail to perform to our expectations because they do not understand what we think we teach. So, what do we do?

---

[1] This chapter is an expanded version of an article published in *The History Teacher.* "Pedagogical Responses to Student Diversity: History and Language," appeared in November 1994 (vol. 28), pp. 49–55. Adapted and reprinted with permission.

[2] Without the encouragement of Ann Snow and Janet Tricamo, principal investigators of Project LEAP, the discussion presented in this chapter would not have taken its present form. Thanks also to Edward Berenson, Nancy Fitch, Larry Guillow, Lillian Taiz, and especially Anthony Bernier for their comments on an earlier version of this paper delivered at the Annual Meeting of the Organization of American Historians, April 1993.

[3] See also Bernier, Chapter 7 in this volume, for a more in-depth discussion of the challenges of academic vocabulary development.

Neither trained nor interested in teaching remedial skills, faculty blame the high schools, lament our own lack of suitable training, shun "handholding," and sneer that "mumbo jumbo" educational theory conspires to eclipse content. Ultimately, university professors fear that confronting the educational demands of these new student populations sacrifices course content and lowers university standards. Class time is too precious to devote to remedial education, they feel. "We teach history. This is not high school," instructors insist.

However, if students do not understand our content, then we teach nothing at all.[4] All good teachers know that they must reach their audience. If we can successfully reach more of our students, university standards will rise and faculty can expect, demand, and receive more from everyone. Ultimately, instruction can be pitched at a higher level, producing better-skilled students.

The linguistically and culturally diverse nature of today's university population demands that faculty continue to improve classroom preparation and presentation. This chapter, however, does not propose to redirect our teaching from course content to language. It seeks, rather, to surmount the barriers to communication precisely so instructors can better teach their content. We can eliminate language blocks to student learning of course content, raise expectations and standards, and retain at-risk students with specific pedagogical responses.

Two teaching techniques, *building vocabulary* and *disclosing rhetorical structures,* are described in this chapter. Building vocabulary involves techniques that supply new vocabulary within the context of course material; disclosing rhetorical structures exposes academic frameworks which help students master course material independent of the vocabulary. These two approaches apply to all faculty and student interactions: oral communication (lectures, class discussions, and office hours), written communication (essay and objective exams, syllabi, handouts, chalkboard writing, and readings), and pictorial representations (from films to photo captions). All these forms of communication demand adjustment to our new audiences. Although well-prepared students benefit as well from these two teaching techniques (especially disclosing rhetorical structures), language minority and working-class students often require such assistance to persist at the university.

BUILDING VOCABULARY

Some people assume that teaching to students from diverse linguistic and cultural backgrounds means "dumbing down" a course—instructing at a lower level, assigning less reading, or speaking with less sophisticated vocabulary. This approach, however, does not challenge students to broaden their language skills, think at higher analytical levels, or prepare for advanced reading. Instead, faculty can enhance students' understanding and increase their vocabulary simultaneously.

---

[4] Filene (1993) notes that students may remember so little because they do not connect what they learn to their own lives.

Building vocabulary extends two techniques that most faculty already execute: *defining* (supplying specific meanings) and *embedding* (situating the context).

Faculty typically define and embed historical terms, such as *indentured servitude, feudalism, capitalism, Enlightenment,* or *family economy,* while lecturing on topics hinging on these words. When lecturing about *the left* in the 1930s, for example, we would, of course, include a definition of the term. However, the problem occurs more frequently when the term is not central to the lecture. In a lecture about abolitionists, for example, we might refer to the Garrisonians as *the left of their day,* without defining *left.* We need to remember to define and embed in all problem categories, not just the obvious historical content terms: so, referring to *Garrisonians, the left of their day—or political radicals who wished to open up the system,* for example, would provide additional cues to meaning.

At other times, however, an instructor might define a word but not go far enough. For instance, before discussing the origins, reasons, and implications of the U.S./Soviet arms race, we might define *arms race* as competition for military dominance between two countries, specifically the United States and the former Soviet Union (a name that already needs defining) and connect the term to something students already know to elucidate its meaning. For example, one might suggest the scenario where two athletes vie to be the strongest on a team, progressing from three- to six-hour workouts, to ingesting muscle-building steroids (drugs). Competition hurts both of them (and possibly others as well). Revealing the root of a word further clarifies terms with dual meanings and aids retention. In this case, *arms* from armaments (weapons) avoids confusion with *arms* as limbs. By defining and embedding in this fashion, faculty can lead students to understand the difference between arms-as-weapons and arms-as-limbs and to the ultimate realization of how a race can impair its participants.

Content faculty have the best opportunities to build vocabulary in those domains where they construct the language for their courses. These include oral communication settings such as lectures and office-hour encounters and written documents prepared for the course such as essay exams and writing assignments, objective exams, and syllabi.

Lectures and Office Hours

Two avenues of oral communication, lectures and office-hour encounters, provide excellent occasions for defining and embedding because faculty control much of the content, structure, and time; furthermore, immediate student feedback supplies clues to language problems. One useful technique when preparing course lectures is to mark both content and language words that need attention in course lecture notes. During the lecture, these terms can be highlighted and definitions or synonyms already familiar to the students can be embedded to help clarify meaning.

We can also use "quotation marks" (with our fingers) to denote archaic or colloquial language. Vocabulary words can be defined in parenthetical phrases.

For example, "Immigrants reconstituted or *remade/re-established* patterns from their homeland, their original country, in the United States." Another technique is to embed by verbally describing or acting out a common scenario (such as *gang labor* among American slaves to distinguish work teams from street gangs) or to elucidate by showing a visual representation or playing music. Many of these same techniques apply to office-hour encounters, where easily intimidated language minority and working-class college students can receive more exposure to extended definitions and embedded terms.

Essay Exams and Written Assignments

On essay exams and written assignments, we should either eliminate or define problem language. Imprecise words—such as *discuss, explore, examine, describe, evaluate, interpret, analyze, compare and contrast, be specific, be thorough*—should be avoided unless specifically defined or contextualized.[5] On an exam, we might ask students to: "Evaluate this statement: The American Revolution was truly a revolution, not merely a war of independence." To avoid being vague, however, the question could be rewritten as: "Was the American Revolution a revolution or a war of independence?" along with a definition of *evaluate:* "Provide evidence to support and oppose the statement; decide which you think is correct, and support your opinion by giving examples."

For take-home exams, term papers, or exams where students receive the questions in advance, step-by-step instructions can be provided:

1. *Define* both "Revolution" and its other name, "War of Independence."
2. *Compile* (gather) two lists of information from course materials:
   - one that supports the idea that the conflict was a revolution
   - the other, that it was *not* a revolution, but a war of independence.
3. *Identify the criteria* you used to decide whether the American Revolution was more a revolution or a war of independence.
   - Do you think the longer list is correct?
   - Do you think the list with the more important items (such as affecting the most people) is correct?
   - Did a revolution lead to a war of independence? Or did a war of independence lead to a revolution?

Even instructions such as the preceding can be confusing; as such, students need many opportunities to practice these steps in class long before exam time.

Objective Exams

Unlike essay exams or term papers (where faculty can provide instructions), restricted space in objective exams (multiple-choice, fill-in-the-blank, short-answer, or identification) limits sufficient definitions and embedding. Students mistakenly

---

[5] See Blackey (1981) for further ideas on essay construction in history.

think they have more options with objective exams; but all too often they are tested on language such as the following test bank question, which tests vocabulary that many second language students do not possess: "The individual prospectors who discovered veins of precious metal usually . . ." (Roe & Warren, 1988). Because we test students on content, there is only one solution—to stay clearly focused on content, eliminating vague, misleading, archaic, nonhistory content and obscure language. Because of time constraints, sometimes difficult vocabulary should be eliminated. In the example above, replace *precious metals* with *valuable gold and silver* and substitute *miners* for *prospectors;* better still, embed "individual prospectors *who mined for gold* usually . . ." or define the term, "the individual prospectors (*miners*)."

Syllabi

Other forms of written communication require defining or embedding as well. All too often, for instance, syllabi are written for experts in the field, not for students. We tend to use the language of our discipline to describe a course to undergraduates, exposing students to undefined content words. If the purpose is achieving clarity and precision, rather than impressing students with historians' jargon (or assuming students understand esoteric and complex words such as *discourse, class formation,* and *agency*), we should use synonyms, define, embed, or place in "quotes" terms that need further explanation. Handouts and writing on the chalkboard can also include alternative definitions, such as "similarities/same" or "agenda/schedule," and abbreviations should be avoided or explained.

Readings

When we do not have control over the language in our classes, we face limited opportunities to build vocabulary and thereby improve students' content understanding. Readings and films present the most notable problems. Of course, we can refuse to order texts or show films whose language blocks course content. We can also pressure textbook authors, editors, and documentary filmmakers to adopt more stringent language criteria, or we can provide glossaries or reading guides that assist language minority students with unfamiliar terminology.

We can also give students practice in distinguishing between language and content words found in readings and lectures. In discussion groups of four to five people, students can be asked to make two lists of words from readings and/or lectures: one of content words, the other, of general vocabulary.[6] Each group should have two record keepers, one for each list, who hand the lists to the professor after the activities have been completed. Such an exercise helps students recognize that their classmates do not understand everything either;

---

[6] Thanks to Anthony Bernier for this technique. Language and content words will overlap, but that in itself is a good lesson.

as such, they feel more confident in addressing what they collectively do not know. Professors, too, gain understanding of what their students do or do not understand. Handouts of content terms can flag words for students to look up in the textbook.

It is also helpful to develop assignments for reading primary sources that encourage students to think about language. Give them practice in defining content words with conflicting meanings, such as *equality, freedom, lady, middle class, power, victim,* and *love.* For example, students can be asked to list as many definitions of *equality* as they can, then compare their definitions with the one(s) in the reading for the particular historical era.

Films

Pictorial representations, like films, display the same problems as readings, except that professors are usually present. Define any essential terms before showing a film, and write problem words on the board during the film.

The key techniques for building vocabulary and addressing language obstacles merely extend common pedagogical practices of defining and embedding to more language categories and to contexts beyond lectures. In oral communication (lectures and office hours) we, as faculty, exercise the most control—we speak the words and are present to intervene. In written communication (exams, written assignments, syllabi, handouts, and writing on the chalkboard) faculty generate the language—thus, we can define and embed. In other cases where we do not have control over language choices, we must endeavor to choose texts and films carefully and be prepared to attack directly the differing vocabulary problems.

DISCLOSING RHETORICAL STRUCTURES

When we assume that students understand what we say in lectures or assign for course reading, we also presume that they recognize the rhetorical structures we often take for granted as academics—that they read what we read and absorb what we say. Of course, we know from experience that many do not. When students read, they often get lost in the details and fail to see the connections between ideas. Having spent years focusing on facts for tests further leads them astray within a sea of isolated terms and concepts. For second language learners and working-class students, this labyrinth of words frustrates even the most conscientious individuals. Such students flounder as they wade through a maze of unfamiliar terms, vocabulary, analogies, and cultural references steeped in middle-class academic culture. They are even less likely to have grasped the relevant rhetorical structures, remaining oblivious to the very frameworks that could guide their reading, listening, and writing, as they do ours.

By teaching rhetorical structures, faculty can bridge the chasm between our expectations and student performance, thereby assisting students to improve their reading, listening, and even writing. By observing rhetorical forms through modeling and disclosure, students can more easily transfer these necessary but often obscured skills to their own writing. Enhanced understanding and recall of lecture material will also be reflected on exams.

The main objective of disclosing rhetorical structures is to teach explicitly the patterns of academic rhetoric necessary for the tasks faculty require. To teach patterns of academic rhetoric, we must disclose rhetorical forms, sometimes by manipulating and exaggerating them. But we ought to do more than merely reveal structures; we can devise new forms as beacons where none exist. By identifying, manipulating, and giving students practice with the rhetorical structures of reading texts, pictorial representations, lectures, written assignments and exams, and even syllabi, we chip away at obstructions to faculty-student communication and student success.

Readings

One critical technique in this approach is to teach students to find the thesis and rhetorical structures of course readings. Faculty should disclose and label American academic discourse conventions which present the thesis in the introduction (often at the end of the introduction after an anecdote) and in the conclusion. Next, they should model the process of finding the thesis in written sources and provide ample practice by encouraging students to go through the following steps:

1. Read the introduction and conclusion looking for possible theses.
2. Consider the following clues to confirm a possible thesis:
   - Titles and subdivision titles and topics: Does the thesis explain them?
   - Subtheses: Find the subtheses by reading the beginning and ending of each section. Do they support the thesis? Does the body of a section aid in reconstructing a chapter or article's thesis?

Students must also be taught to find supporting sections, distinguishing between parallel, superior, and subordinant constructions, and to recognize "signal" words that expose transitions and ranking, such as *first, second,* and *finally.*

It is also useful for students to analyze the structure of the table of contents to gain insight into the organization of a textbook and its chapters. Survey texts often include the sections of a chapter in the table of contents. Better texts divide chapters into only a few subsections. Faculty can point out that the subsections support the larger sections and that the major divisions support the thesis. If the text breaks down the chapter into too many parts, show students how to group the topics together, as the authors of the text should have done. For example, point out that *walking city, urbanization,* and *geography of the city* all fit under the category *cities* and probably support the same subthesis;

this helps students to see the thesis and supporting topics and connect the details. It also helps to lessen the importance of particular vocabulary terms.

Pictorial Representations

Delineating conventional forms of pictorial representations also helps to remove language barriers. When showing a film, for example, prepare students beforehand to distinguish between the thesis and supporting evidence and to notice beginnings, endings, transitions, music, and camera angles. Give them practice in looking for perspectives and formulating alternative interpretations. Photographs and paintings themselves do not introduce language problems, but captions in texts do. Encourage students to disclose, label, model, and practice locating the topic and form of a picture: Who or what is in the center, foreground, and so on?

Because the teaching of rhetorical structures requires clear and consistent forms, we should try whenever possible to choose course materials that more explicitly expose their own structures. Does the author follow standard conventions of American academic discourse, stating the thesis near the beginning, connecting subordinant points and details to that thesis, and restating it in the conclusion?[7] Does the filmmaker present a clear point of view or merely a jumble of unconnected facts? When we cannot find materials that meet these criteria, we must point out how weak or vague theses and transitions cloud understanding, a typical problem in survey texts.[8]

Lectures

Lectures offer the best opportunity to expose skeletal frameworks. If they cannot recognize a lecture's rhetorical structure, students may have difficulty following even a well-constructed lecture. The instructor can easily reveal this structure by using a simple outline on the chalkboard to distinguish main points from details. Gesturing to the outline's parts at transitions further connects the segments of the lecture. Writing an outline on the chalkboard, however, is not enough. Weaker students tend to copy the outline, then disregard it as they take notes. Faculty need to provide written guidelines of note-taking tips and give students practice early in the term in critiquing model notes and evaluating their own lecture notes.[9]

---

[7] In more advanced classes the instructor can discuss the varieties of discourse forms, such as presenting an anecdote and then moving to the thesis or introducing the historical debate and then the thesis.

[8] Because text authors often try to appease many of their peer evaluators, they include information that does not connect to their thesis, resulting in digressions or very weak and bland theses that sound more like topic sentences than interpretations.

[9] For specific suggestions on the teaching of note taking, see Benjamin (1991, pp. 30–35) and Srole (1993).

The subordinant elements of a lecture make little sense without the glue: the thesis. A thesis links the sections of an outline. Faculty should also disclose, label, and model theses, explain their importance, and show students where to find them in lecture (introduction, transitions, and conclusion). They should point out the relationship between subordinant material and the thesis, and advise students to write transitional phrases or sentences connecting each major section of the outline as an aid to reconstructing the thesis. Furthermore, faculty can (a) develop assignments which summarize lecture theses, and (b) provide practice in reconstructing the thesis from the lecture outline and differentiating the thesis (interpretation) from a nebulous "main idea" or topic. When students receive guidance in thesis identification, their enhanced understanding of lectures and readings is reflected on exams.

Written Assignments and Exams

To provide guidance for written assignments and essay exams that also adhere to discipline-based rhetorical patterns, demonstrate the similarity of structures found in assigned readings and in good written models. Again, disclose signal words and standard writing conventions, but also provide specific steps for students to follow in preparing assignments, thereby enabling them to organize, control, and communicate their ideas better.

In preparation for written assignments, show students how language cues guide a reader through an essay. Attach a list of signal words to assignment instructions or provide a modified outline supplying phrases, such as *on the one hand . . . on the other hand,* for compare-and-contrast questions. To present conflicting interpretations or evidence, teach expressions such as *Some scholars think . . . but in reality . . .* or *on the surface . . . but actually . . . .* Introduce words—such as *the first, the second,* or *the most important* and *the least important*—to help students connect supporting evidence in writing. Providing lots of practice in writing with logical connectors enhances students' ability to organize content material more clearly in written assignments.

Require that all essays and papers contain a thesis that is stated in the introduction, conclusion, and in each major transition. Initially, phrase exam questions in such a way as to force students to answer in the form of a thesis: "Was the railroad or the city a better symbol of the Gilded Age?" or "Was nineteenth-century middle-class identity a reaction to the working class?" are examples of such questions. Teach students that topic sentences organize thoughts and communicate them effectively in history and all disciplines, not only in English course assignments. Encourage them to read "A" exams that follow these academic conventions, such as having theses in the appropriate places, having subtheses that tie to the theses, and using signal words. Explicitly label these features on the model exam or paper, and consider distributing a check-off sheet to serve as a useful guideline.

For take-home exams or paper assignments, provide a matrix of specific skills and steps showing the execution of tasks necessary for analysis or evaluation, and give students practice in following these steps. In history courses, for example, point out that they should go through the steps below when categorizing and prioritizing:

1. Gather evidence in *lists.*
2. *Group/categorize* listed items (into historical eras, for example, or groups of people or topics).
3. Prioritize *criteria* for evaluating: quantity of evidence; groups of people involved or affected; differing definitions for key words in the question, or others.
4. Write a *possible thesis* for each side of the question. For example, write a thesis that explains why the railroad is a better symbol of the Gilded Age. Write a second thesis that explains why the city is a better symbol of the Gilded Age.
5. Decide which *thesis* your categories support.
6. *Outline.*
7. *Write* the paper.
8. *Edit* (topic sentence, transitions, avoid verb "to be" and passives, redundant language).

For identification exams, disclose and review the parts of an appropriate answer. Supply instructions like these:

Part 1: Define the subject—who, what, when, and where.
Part 2: Contextualize the subject—How does it fit? Why is it important? Explain its relationship to other political, social, economic, or intellectual trends. Use mapping to show how this particular subject connects to others.

In sum, signal words, writing conventions, scaffolded steps (which show the step-by-step procedures to follow), and segmentations of assignments expose structures for written assignments and for essay and identification exams.

Syllabi

The course syllabus also tends to conform to a standard form, which, like lectures, can be exaggerated to reveal course structures. Construct syllabi with distinct parts. On the first day of class, disclose and define the different sections of the syllabus: Explain that an introduction often announces many themes for a given course and can help in preparation for essay questions on the final exam. Groupings of lectures and assignments reveal a course's structure. Compare these divisions with those in the readings to help students understand different ways to organize similar subject matter.

Faculty can also extend the notion of disclosing structures to those arenas where they do not inherently exist. Disclosing and exaggerating rhetorical structures in readings, pictorial representations, lectures, written assignments and exams, and syllabi expose extant structures. Instructors can devise structures to serve the same function for other components of a course such as primary source readings, class discussions, and office-hour encounters where the inherent structures might not be very obvious.

Primary Sources

Primary sources call out for guiding frameworks. When assigning a document for its evidence rather than its thesis (as with many autobiographies, diaries, and even fiction), devise an external structure to give coherence to the reading, such as a handout which organizes note taking by categories. For example, instruct students to list the categories discussed in a lecture on immigration (e.g., family, work, and culture) and then have them employ the same topics to organize notes for a reading assignment based on an immigrant autobiography (Koch, Krilowicz, Srole, Galanti, Kamhi-Stein, & Snow, 1997).

Class Discussions

Faculty can also impose frameworks on class discussions[10] to facilitate note taking and help disclose connections across course material. For example, students can be assigned to cooperative learning groups to answer a "yes/no" question, such as "Was the Civil War a 'watershed' (major transition/change) for African Americans?" In their groups students can be instructed to make two lists to gather the conflicting evidence: one to support the "yes" position, the other the "no." To teach students to compare and contrast, provide the groups with criteria/categories such as "sex ratio," "family," "class," and "religious beliefs" and ask them to compare, for instance, the New England and Chesapeake colonies in the seventeenth century.

Groups are also a useful forum for teaching students mapping techniques for brainstorming and finding interconnections among conceptual material. For instance, by mapping related social, economic, and political issues surrounding and leading to the Supreme Court case *Brown v. Board of Education of Topeka, Kansas,* students can realize its significance and prepare to answer identification exam questions. After discussing and listing all the related topics, such as "African-American protest in the 1940s," "the Warren Court," "the NAACP's court strategy," and "World War II urbanization," students must consolidate the information on their lists, combining "African-American protest" and "the NAACP's court strategy," for example, or "the Warren Court" and "the NAACP's court strategy" together, depending on the students' interpretations or faculty questions. A culminating activity might be to have students construct a graphic representation, such as

---

[10] The word *discussion* describes a range of classroom interactions from professors asking questions to student-centered cooperative learning groups. See Carson, Chase, Gibson, and Hargrove (1992) for a description of typical discussion formats found in undergraduate university courses.

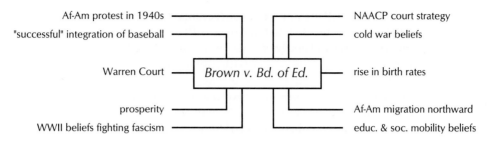

FIGURE 8.1 Social, economic, and political issues leading to *Brown v. Board of Education of Topeka, Kansas*

the one shown in Figure 8.1, which reflects the key social, economic, and political issues identified during the group discussion.

Finally, to introduce the notion of perspectives, students can work in groups with the task of shifting a topic from the margins to the center. For example, if readings or lectures focused on European immigrants, shift Asian immigrants—Chinese, Japanese, or Koreans—to the center and ask students to answer the question, "What characterized immigrant experiences?" In the course of the discussion, have students shift again—from men to women, or from first to second generation—and answer the questions from these different perspectives.

Office Hours

Visits to faculty during office hours offer yet another opportunity to disclose and reinforce structures. Because many students do not know to seek help, the purpose of office hours must be clearly explained several times during the term. One especially productive use of office hours is to invite students to the office to read sample "A" exams and term papers. Inform them in advance that they do not have to discuss their own papers but can say, "I've come to read the 'A' papers." And if the professor asks to see their paper, they can respond, "I left my paper at home," a code for "I don't want to talk about my own paper right now." Another strategy is to assign students to develop two questions before an office-hours meeting: a content and a language question (Kamhi-Stein, Koch, & Snow, 1997), or a content and a professional question, such as, "Where did you attend college?" "Why did you become a history professor?" "What do professors do besides meet their classes?"[11]

By disclosing and exaggerating rhetorical structures in all arenas of faculty-student communication, faculty can teach rarely stated (but assumed and required) standard practices of academic rhetorical culture. And by devising structures, we can impart the benefits of focused guidance. Through disclosing and exaggerating

---

[11] Thanks to Anthony Bernier for this suggestion.

rhetorical structures in readings, lectures, written assignments and exams, syllabi, primary sources, discussions, and office-hour encounters, faculty can communicate clearly to students what is expected of them. Students connect details, experience less frustration with unfamiliar vocabulary, enhance their critical reading and writing skills, and learn content better. Even "A" students benefit by mastering structures that govern academic discourse. With a solid understanding of rhetorical structures, students will increasingly possess the confidence and skills to engage course material more successfully, both in the current course and in their other classes down the road.

CONCLUSION

The two approaches described in this chapter, building vocabulary and disclosing rhetorical structures, enable faculty across the disciplines to help their students surmount language and cultural barriers that distract from content acquisition. Through defining and embedding, we help students increase their vocabulary as they learn content better. By teaching rhetorical structures, we help students recognize conceptual themes and organize them appropriately. They learn what we expect of them and perform better, acquiring the skills necessary to remain at the university. To teach these skills, we must *disclose* the goals and techniques of each task, *label* strategies so students can recall and then use again, *model* the steps, and give students extensive *practice* over time. Such guidance demonstrates our commitment to educating linguistically and culturally diverse students.

chapter **9**

Content-Based Instruction in an EFL Setting: Issues and Strategies[1]

Tim Murphey

Even though content-based instruction (CBI) is gaining popularity and research support in the ESL setting, it is still relatively new in much of the EFL world. Thus, several issues may require special attention when implementing CBI courses in EFL contexts. First, there may be few content-area specialists who also speak, or are willing to teach in, the target language; and there may be few language teachers who have experience in content teaching. Designing curricula and relevant courses is another issue. Finally, traditionally oriented administrators may be reluctant, and students themselves may need to be persuaded that they can in fact learn language while concentrating on meaning. These issues are ongoing concerns for anyone attempting to pursue CBI in an EFL context. In this chapter, I first give some background about the development of CBI workshop courses at Nanzan University in Japan, then I look more closely at issues related to implementing CBI in an EFL setting. Finally, I outline strategies used to deal with these issues at Nanzan University.

BACKGROUND

Nanzan University is a private Catholic university founded in 1949 in Nagoya, Japan, the third largest metropolis in Japan with 2.5 million inhabitants. The 6,000 students are all Japanese except for about 180 foreign students, mostly studying at the Center for Japanese Studies. In 1991 our department began

---

[1] Thanks to Uichi Kondo for help with the data on the surveys, and to Masataki Arimoto and Mark Wright for clarifying elements of administrative detail. I alone am responsible for any inaccuracies.

reorganizing the English program and incrementally implementing small changes. The first CBI workshop courses were part of this larger reorganization.

In 1992 I was invited to create "something different" for native English-speaking teachers with the course hours originally devoted to "translation" courses taught by Japanese instructors. I opted for a content-based approach in the form of six-week-long sheltered courses. I called them "workshop" courses to imply that students would be interactively and experientially involved with the content. These courses can be considered "sheltered" to distinguish them from upper-level classes offered at Nanzan in which natives and nonnatives are mixed in the same class.

PROGRAM DESCRIPTION

First-year students in the Nanzan University English department's Intensive English Program take a total of seven 90-minute classes, or *koma,* in their language concentration; second-year students take six such classes (see Figure 9.1). One 90-minute class each week is a CBI workshop. Thus, all first- and second-year students have a native English-speaking teacher for at least one class a day, five days a week, in the Intensive English Program.

In designing the workshop courses, one of the goals was to give students as much variety in content as possible to complement their more form-focused language course. As a result of the workshop format, students are also exposed to different topics and to a variety of native speakers with different teaching styles and accents. The short length of the courses and their interactive lecture style keeps motivation and interest high and allows students to concentrate on meaning.

FIGURE 9.1   Course offerings in the Intensive English Program

90-minute native speaker courses: FIRST YEAR				
Monday	**Tuesday**	**Wednesday**	**Thursday**	**Friday**
Conversation	Reading	Conversation	Workshops	Conversation
Language Lab		Language Lab	CBI (4 topics)	Language Lab
+2 *koma* of Writing taught by a Japanese teacher				
90-minute native speaker courses: SECOND YEAR				
Monday	**Tuesday**	**Wednesday**	**Thursday**	**Friday**
Conversation	Writing	Conversation	Workshops	Conversation
Language Lab		Language Lab	CBI (4 topics)	Language Lab
+1 *koma* of Reading taught by a Japanese teacher				

In the first year, 1992, we started with five sections of workshop courses and five teachers (simply because there had been five sections of the previous translation course that we replaced), offered in approximately five-week courses. For financial and administrative reasons, in 1993 we reduced the number to four teachers and lengthened the courses to six or seven weeks each (depending on the school calendar). This has remained the case for the past four years. Each teacher now presents the same course four times a year to rotating groups of about forty-four students.

Titles of courses have been Alternative Learning Forms; TV Commercials; Environmental Concerns; Journalism; English Idioms; Computer Literacy; Rock 'n Roll History; Health and Fitness Awareness; and English in Japan. Because of the workshops' popularity and the planned incremental increase in number of contact hours with native English-speaking teachers, we recently expanded the program into the second year with courses in Women's Studies; South Africa and the World; The Origins of American Music; and Japanese/American Education. All first-year workshops are scheduled at the same time, on the same day; this is true for all second-year workshops as well. Thus, each time students rotate teachers, they simply change classrooms. In their first class at the beginning of the school year, students are given a schedule of which classes and teachers they will have during the year and on what dates they will be changing classes.

STUDENT POPULATION

Participants are Japanese students ages eighteen to twenty-one. Because workshops are part of the required program of English contact hours during their first two years, all students in the department take them and receive one credit per semester for two years. The courses are especially effective for students who are planning to study abroad and those choosing to take more semester- or year-long content courses in English during their third and fourth years of study.

Student language levels in English span the proficiency continuum. They range from fluent speakers of English who have had extended stays abroad (about 10%) to those who have never been abroad and have had little contact with English, especially listening to English (about 50%). Students in this group do have quite a bit of passive knowledge about English after six years of grammar translation courses (taught almost totally in Japanese) in junior and senior high school. However, their listening skills are quite low. The rest of the students (40%) have had varying degrees of experience with travel abroad and teachers who use English in their classes.

ISSUES AND STRATEGIES IN AN EFL SETTING

At least five important issues warrant attention by those in EFL teaching situations wishing to implement CBI: (1) choosing an approach and methodology (which will guide other decisions); (2) selecting and orienting teachers;

(3) selecting courses; (4) convincing students, staff, and administrators of the value of CBI; and (5) encouraging the continuation of CBI in upper-level courses to provide continuity. These issues are closely interrelated, but for the sake of discussion I will treat them separately.

Issue 1: What Approach and Methodology?

Being conscious of the values and goals inherent in any approach and the procedures of the methodology chosen provides vision and congruence to a program as a whole. Teachers, administrators, and students have the right, and desire, to know why things are done in a certain way; they also deserve to know the connection between various program components. Thus, users of CBI in the EFL context must carefully think through the goals for their students. Clarifying goals first for themselves and then negotiating the rationale with those involved can help things go much more smoothly. This doesn't mean, however, that all the details must be worked out or that the program shouldn't change and adapt as it continues. Instead, an action research cycle (see Nunan, 1990) should be in place at the program level to allow the program administrator and others to clarify what they intend to do and how they will implement their plan. There should also be enough time to reflect, restate goals, plan, and implement again. All participants need to be aware of the consequences of the approach selected and the rationale for their decision, so that they can flexibly adjust as the program is implemented.

Strategies at Nanzan.   Our goals were to appeal to the students' interests through program diversity and to create meaningful interaction with subject matter material. Realizing that for most of the students this would be the first exposure to a subject in English over an extended period of time, we wanted to give them more than just one chance to succeed. Thus, by having four short courses in a year, we increased the likelihood that they would get excited about learning content through English and see its usefulness.

At the same time, we felt the need for unity in the program. Diversity just for diversity's sake can be disorienting. A congruent understanding among teachers of why diversity is desirable and a few common operational features in all the courses can lend coherence to what otherwise could be seen as a disconnected group of courses. This is all the more important when CBI is a new approach to the staff and when four teachers must evaluate each student for a cumulative grade.

Workshop teachers are all given a brief orientation handout (see Appendix 1 for excerpts) which outlines the program and suggests a variety of instructional strategies to enhance student learning. These include using fun and interactive activities (e.g., pair work, questionnaires), rotating partners by numbering off students in the class each week, lecturing for only ten- to fifteen-minute segments at most, and then allowing students to reformulate (i.e., tell partners what they have understood or not understood and ask for clarification). Assigning a minimum amount of homework reading (approximately 1,000 words a week) and using action logs—journals describing the content and activities in each class (Murphey, 1992, 1993)—are also suggested.

The repetition of six-week courses allows teachers to test small amounts of material and adjust the courses for later groups. So that teachers can adjust even more during each course, students write action logs. These are handed in to teachers either weekly or biweekly. This regular feedback from students allows teachers insights into students' comprehension of and interest in the material. It allows teachers to adjust their instructional goals in an ongoing fashion while also getting students more involved as they perceive their impact on the courses. Since each student uses the same action log notebook for all four courses, students may feel the courses are somewhat connected (in form, if not in content), and teachers can also see what the students' previous teachers did in class as well as get an idea of the students' past work. Inside the front cover of each action log is an information form that students fill out about themselves and to which they attach a photo. This helps the teachers get to know the students' names more quickly. Figure 9.2 shows a sample action log entry.

Teachers are also given orientation letters to distribute to students which outline the courses, the action log procedures, and their schedules. They are also asked to briefly explain the rationale behind the courses. Finally, teachers explain the grading criteria at the beginning of each six-week term (e.g., 25% class participation; 25% homework; 25% action logs; 25% final test, quizzes, or project).

Each teacher gives tests, quizzes, or projects to evaluate student work and involvement with the content. The action logs are also used to evaluate the students' grasp of what is going on in class. We are working on new ways to measure students' language development, but over the past four years teachers

FIGURE 9.2 Sample student action log entry

Fun scale: 1 = not much,   2 = OK,   3 = lots of fun
Useful scale: A+ = great,   A = good,   B = somewhat,   C = passing,
               F = trying something else

April 30, 21:00

DID	FUN	USEFUL
1. listened to a story	2	B
2. read a passage	2	A+
3. discussion of passage	3	A
4. teacher lecture	1	B
5. had a quiz	1	C

Comment: I didn't understand some of the points in the reading: What is chunking? Sometimes Mr. Murphy spoke too fast. Please speak slower. My partner today was Yuki and it was fun to get to know her. We got a lot of homework, but it looks like fun. I'm looking forward to the next classes. I will prepare more for the quizzes.

and students have become convinced that the worshops are indeed extremely valuable and exciting additions to the program.

Issue 2: Which Teachers? How Can They Adjust?

One critical issue in the EFL context is the lack of content teachers, native and nonnative, who can teach in the target language. Three central questions emerge: To what extent can we choose language teachers and have them adapt to content teaching? To what extent can content teachers adapt their language and teaching to make it comprehensible? How can all teachers adjust what they do to be more effective?

Strategies at Nanzan.   Teacher and content selection has basically been left up to the coordinator, with recommendations offered by the faculty and approval received through private discussion and consensus. At first the regular staff was surveyed regarding content areas they were excited about; we reasoned that when language teachers are given a chance to teach content they are interested in, they will communicate this enthusiasm to the students.

In recent years I have tended to look for enthusiastic teachers first and then ask what topic areas they are knowledgeable about and willing to share with the students. Finding enthusiastic teachers seems to be the most essential ingredient, since there are many topic areas that could be addressed. Students are also regularly asked what kind of courses they would like and which ones they appreciate. Presently the teachers include three full-time professors, two full-time lecturers on two-year contracts, and three part-time teachers, all teaching topics in which they have practical and academic expertise.

Because of the relatively stable teacher population at Nanzan University, program administration demands were minimal once the workshop curriculum was in place and the teachers oriented. Over the first four years, only one or two teachers had to be replaced owing to teacher turnover. However, in 1996 there were four new teachers to select and orient owing to the expansion of the workshop classes into the second-year curriculum. Since approximately 85 percent of the department's students are female and there is only one woman in the twenty-eight-member department, more women teachers were sought for the program to add balance, variety, and role models. This effort resulted in the hiring of two part-time female instructors and the inclusion of a Women's Studies workshop course in 1996.

Most of the English teachers have jumped at the opportunity to do what they have been doing covertly in their language classes for a long time: teaching through their favorite content. Still, some teachers may occasionally drift unconsciously into traditional language teaching simply from habit. I have tried to persuade them to stay away from too much straight language teaching and to concentrate more on simply making the content understandable. Most of them find this exciting when they see that content teaching, when it is comprehensible to the students, is effective language teaching at the same time. They also often realize that much of their most effective language teaching in their regular (non-CBI) classes is actually CBI-oriented.

Content teachers, on the other hand, have been more reluctant to adapt their content level and teach introductory courses in a six-week time frame. The action logs, however, have been very beneficial in helping the content teachers adjust to the students' language levels and content desires. In a way, the open and regular communication between students and teachers created by the action logs allows the students themselves to train the teachers.

The hardest task for most teachers seems to be in making their content area comprehensible and in avoiding the two extremes. If they get sidelined into thinking students cannot understand the content until they understand the language, they may end up teaching too much isolated language. If they think the content is "almighty" and "if students can't understand, then too bad," they are in danger of becoming nonadjusting, noncommunicative subject specialists. However, if they really want their students to understand what they themselves are fascinated about and if they adjust their messages so that students can grasp the concepts, they can become effective communicators of both content and language. When this occurs, students realize that the language is actually being used and understood, and that they are learning something important to them and their teachers. This is the "ah-ha!" experience that often escapes description and for which I feel CBI is striving. This is the experience that gives meaning to language and allows acquisition to occur. CBI doesn't work when teachers fail to grasp this methodological concept and drift toward the extremes of decontextualized language learning or unadjusted content overload; teachers must instead continually and dynamically strive for a meaningful balance between language and content. These types of adjustments facilitate learning in all teaching contexts, but they are absolutely essential in CBI where the goals are to teach both language and content simultaneously.

Issue 3: Which Content Courses?

What courses should be chosen? Which course mix provides a good variety? Which courses would be acceptable to your administration and exciting to your students? What is available? What can be created?

Strategies at Nanzan. It is clear that any course in practice can be more or less form- or content-focused and that the title often has little to do with the actual teaching. However, most administrators see only titles and course descriptions; and in many EFL situations, CBI courses and course titles (such as those of Nanzan University's workshop courses) arouse the suspicion that they are not language courses per se.

Thus, although the concept of theme-focused or CBI instruction may be widely accepted and may very well guide pedagogical decisions for many native English-speaking teachers abroad, this is far from the case for most nonnative teachers. In my experience, we still need more evidence and gentle, culturally appropriate persuasion if CBI is to be accepted and implemented in EFL curricula. We need as well to be open to adapting our agendas to the EFL context as we increase our own cultural sensitivity (see Holiday, 1994).

EFL language curriculum planners wishing to convince administrators of the benefits of CBI might consider starting with CBI courses that bear a closer surface resemblance to traditional courses and only later present those that seem to have less of a language focus. The courses we have offered at Nanzan could fall into three categories as seen from the eye of the administration:

Language-Focused Courses
English in Japan

English Idioms

Courses Related to Language Education
Alternative Learning Forms (Psychology)

Computer Literacy

Japanese/American Education

Journalism

Language Use in Communication

Rock 'n Roll History

The Origins of American Music

TV Commercials

Non-Language-Focused Content Courses
Environmental Concerns

South Africa and the World

Women's Studies

Health and Fitness Awareness

Teachers might have more success initially convincing administrators to give CBI a try if they choose courses like those in the first two categories. In fact, it might be advisable to not even call it content-based instruction—just keep the old course titles, implement CBI, monitor and document its success, and then post hoc provide the administration with new ways to view what you have already done. In the first three years that the workshops operated at Nanzan University, they retained the name *yakudoku,* or "reading/translation," even though the content was obviously very different and they were being taught by native speakers of English whose levels of Japanese were in fact quite low. After several years, the department's administration was reasonably enough impressed to officially recognize them and plan for their expansion into the second-year curriculum. (However, the administration was not pleased with the label "work-shop." "Workshop" does not sound very serious to Japanese teachers, whereas for native English-speaking teachers and students it has a positive connotation in that it implies interaction.)

Issue 4: How Do We Convince Students, Teachers, and Administrators of the Value of CBI?

When students, teachers, and administrators see the value in CBI, it can be much more effective and less problematic to implement. However, as Brinton, Snow, and Wesche (1989) observed from the implementation of CBI in The People's Republic of China (PRC) in the 1980s, "it is not an easy task to convince students (or all teachers, for that matter) used to English being taught through a very traditional methodology that taking content courses can improve English language skills" (p. 81).

One North American university administrator organizing a small meeting on CBI in Japan recently wrote to me, "We are trying to make the . . . [Japanese] administration more comfortable with the idea that this is the 'state of the art' in terms of the language instruction/education their students are receiving." Obviously, acceptance of CBI will take time, much hands-on experience, and systematic documentation of its efficacy.

Strategies at Nanzan.   The workshop courses are a required part of the Intensive English Program, so no additional publicity is necessary to attract students. However, convincing students and staff that the courses are serious and valuable did help toward their eventual expansion. More important, when students embrace the method it enhances their own learning. As in any self-fulfilling prophecy, when students believe in the method they invest more of themselves in the course, and that produces even better results. We have found, for example, that telling students how much previous students have learned from and enjoyed the courses goes a long way toward getting them to invest themselves.

To inform the other teaching staff members who are not involved in the workshops, we distributed the orientation materials and survey results along with reports in all departmental mailboxes. However, since reports in mailboxes often go unread, I suspect there remains a wide gap between what the workshop teachers are actually doing and what others think they are doing. As with all the previous issues, this one needs ongoing attention.

The most convincing evidence of the workshops' value is provided by the formal (questionnaires) and informal evaluations (action logs). Although action logs were principally used for the teachers' evaluation of day-to-day activities, they have been used at times for evaluation of the program as a whole. The more official student feedback surveys, conducted in the first and the fourth years of the program (see Appendix 2 for a sample evaluation instrument), provided another vehicle for collecting information with which to evaluate the program statistically. Furthermore, they were a method of program evaluation that was more acceptable to administrators and other staff members. The surveys revealed that students were generally very positive about the workshop courses and were glad when the classes were extended to the second year. Results of the surveys were shared with the teachers concerned, so they could get a better grasp of how students felt about their classes and then could improve their teaching. The questionnaires specifically asked about the usefulness of the things students were learning as well as about their engagement in and enjoyment of the course. In 1993 students responded that they wished that about 40 percent of their classes were taught as the workshops were (with four different teachers and over six-week intervals). In 1996 most students thought that the workshop classes demanded too much homework, but most also said they would take other workshops if they had the opportunity.

It was also clear from the surveys that some students could have benefited more from a clearer understanding of the rationale behind CBI. This in turn would have made teaching easier. Especially in EFL environments, teachers of non-language related content courses may sometimes need to convince students that the content classes are good for their English acquisition in order to decrease their initial reluctance. This might also be achieved by providing more language-specific tasks at the beginning and end of the course (e.g., providing content-specific vocabulary lists).

As the coordinator, I am aware of only a handful of complaints from teachers about how the workshops are organized. Workshop length was one cause of concern. When first beginning to teach the workshop courses, several teachers thought that six weeks was much too short. However, after teaching several groups and streamlining their material to have a better impact, they found the short time period more attractive. The short workshop courses seem to function as a useful bridge between theme-based language courses and the semester- and year-long content courses. Other complaints related to workshop length are the fact that teachers must assign grades more frequently and that it is hard to really get to know forty students in just six weeks. However, these issues can be reframed in the positive light of more variety; greater stimulation of learning through frequent testing, quizzes, and projects; and the better-organized lesson planning that comes along with the need to conform to the short course design.

Issue 5: CBI in the Upper Levels

The workshop courses described in this chapter offer one way of infusing content into language teaching programs in the EFL context. However, we also need to be aware of the enormous potential for CBI in upper-level courses that are typically conducted in the students' L1. When courses (e.g., advanced English literature and linguistics) continue to be taught in the L1, teachers are not only failing to promote further meaningful language use but are also discouraging it in the lower levels by not providing an incentive, that is, a goal for language use later in a student's academic development.

Strategies at Nanzan.   In describing the CBI experiment in the PRC, Brinton, Snow, and Wesche (1989) state:

Although the majority of the Chinese teachers have had well-developed English language skills, even the more proficient ones tended to lack confidence in their English—especially when they (and their students) compared it with that of their American colleagues. (p. 80)

In Japan, too, many Japanese teachers could well teach content courses in English; however, most do not. In probing their beliefs, we found that some teachers lack confidence; some find it uncomfortable and unnatural to speak in English when they can get their messages across more easily in Japanese and some do not think the students' language ability is high enough to understand the content in English (Murphey & Purcell, 1996). Others (often unjustifiably) say they make too many mistakes and would be poor models for their students (Murphey, Deacon, & Murakami, 1996). When university teachers hold these beliefs and teach in the L1, CBI in the lower levels may not seem especially warranted because it does not lead to increased content instruction in the L2 later. Were it not for the few professors who do teach their courses in English and for our study-abroad programs, there would be little progression. Of course, one could also argue that the workshop courses are even more necessary because students have limited exposure to content in English later in their coursework. I fear, however, that until more advanced-level nonnative teachers are convinced that they themselves could provide a richer education to their students through content instruction in the L2, CBI in the lower levels will not be seen by the students in as valuable a light as it could be.

In places like Holland, Switzerland, Germany, Finland, and Israel, upper-level courses in language departments are usually taught in the target language; thus, whether to deliver instruction in the L2 has become a moot issue. In a setting like Japan, the professors are probably right in saying that the L1 is more efficient for teaching their content because the English proficiency level of the majority of their students would not allow them to follow at the professors' pace. Yet their lack of willingness to try creates an unending cycle. Students at lower levels may see no need to become more proficient in English because their courses are all taught in Japanese later on, and junior and senior high school teachers will continue to teach English in Japanese because the future uses of English remain very limited.

The university teachers' reluctance is also due to tradition and the ease of explaining things in Japanese. Although most are more than capable of conducting their classes in English, the switch would undoubtedly add more work and preparation to their already overloaded schedules. In EFL situations similar to Japan, teachers returning from graduate studies abroad are often the most eager to lecture in English and may be the best hope for change.

Support for CBI itself, on the other hand, is on the increase in Japan. Within the last year alone three articles (Campbell, 1996; Lewitt, 1995; Volker, 1995) were published in the Japanese Association of Language Teachers' journal. The plethora of sample content-related publications coming into the staff room tells me that a lot of Japanese English teachers are indeed using content for their English instruction (if not actually using English in the classroom).

In addition, my current classroom-based research reveals a variety of ways in which high school Japanese teachers can incrementally increase the amount of English they speak in their classes (Murphey, 1996). Periodic increases of even a few words more of English for classroom management, use of Total Physical Response (Asher, 1982), or the telling of short personal stories (with a lot of nonverbal aids to ensure understanding) have not only increased student motivation but have made teachers more confident as effective teachers and English speakers. Obviously, more research on the use of English as the medium of instruction in the EFL context is needed. These are serious concerns, and we need to mount convincing arguments to encourage nonnative teachers to increase the amount of time spent teaching in the target language.

It would also be helpful to dethrone the myth that native speakers are necessarily the "best models" for students to learn from. Many nonnative teachers may unconsciously believe that all native speakers are like Chomsky's hypothesized "ideal speaker." This belief not only keeps them from using more English in their own classes, but it keeps them from hiring Japanese teachers who do use English in class and who could be excellent role models for the students. These practices continue despite recent research in Japan showing that when Japanese students hear Japanese people using English, they are much more impressed than when they hear a foreigner (Murphey, 1995). Thus, one of the goals of our program in the next few years is to include native Japanese teachers willing to teach in English among the group that teaches workshop classes.

In the meantime, however, we must contend with an administration that wants to promote the program by saying, "Students have a native speaker teacher for one class a day, five days a week, for two years." But wouldn't it also be impressive to hear students say, "Even the Japanese English teachers teach in English at my university!"

CONCLUSION

The fact that the Nanzan University workshops were allowed to continue and expand shows that they now have the endorsement of the Japanese administration and faculty. Feedback in the action logs, as well as survey data, are very positive. The administrators are not only convinced of the instructional effectiveness of the workshops but have begun to believe in the underlying rationale for CBI. In gathering information for this chapter, I asked one administrator in our department why we chose to implement CBI five years ago. He responded, "We decided that through doing something with language, students could learn more." This indicates that some Japanese decisionmakers have joined the "community of explanation" supported by CBI successes (Freeman, 1995).

The five issues raised in this chapter will, no doubt, remain a challenge as we attempt to implement the content-based approach in Japan. The specifics of each EFL situation will be different as will the variety of ways to address them. For now, we are convinced from this experience that CBI in the EFL context is an exciting endeavor well worth the doing, and well worth improving.

APPENDIX 1

Excerpts from the Orientation Packet for Workshop Teachers

MEMO

From: Tim Murphey, March 1996

To: Workshop Teachers

General goals of the workshop classes: to have students operationalize their English knowledge in dealing with interesting content, to encourage them to take charge of their learning beyond the classroom with new options, to give lecture courses in small doses adjusted to their level, to have them actually DO something with English, to have them hear a variety of lectures and styles, and to start dealing with academic English in context. These are content-based courses, an approach based on the idea that when students are really interested in the subject they learn the language automatically, especially when the teacher concentrates on making sure they understand the material.

Suggested syllabi and procedures: Teachers will teach adaptations of the same short course four times to four different groups. The first group will meet for 7 weeks, with some of the first class devoted to orientation; then groups will have 6 weeks for the rest of the year, with one class left over in January to solicit feedback and have a short cumulative test of all four classes. In each year, there will be 4 sections of 40–45 students. After the first session, you will have another teacher's students for the next three sessions. Please give a copy of your grades to that teacher within one week after the end of the session.

Student orientation information: A few things to think over (and revise as you go along):

1. Weekly homework readings (suggested around 1,000 words at their approximate level), assignments, and topics.
2. A description of what is expected of students and how grades are given. I suggest equal parts of homework, participation (includes speaking English in class), action log, and project/test (25% each).
3. A description of how you want them to do an Action Log for your particular course. The action log can contain "HW" (homework) but is essentially the students' reactions to each class, what they did, liked, and thought about it.
4. Let them know if you have a project, paper, or test.

Of course individual teachers are free to organize their classes however they wish—with group and project work, etc. However, we should agree on minimum and maximum amounts of work so that we can average all the scores together at the end of each semester (the students you have at the beginning of the year are "yours" for the whole year, and other teachers will give you their grades to average together to give to the administration).

Suggested methodology (mixed with goals): Active and intensive interaction is my goal. For me this means three things: insearch, interaction, and independence. Insearch: It's nice if we can already use what is inside the students, their experiences with our content, what they think about it. Initial questionnaires and opinion surveys are helpful to use at the beginning of a course and then at the end again to show them how their thoughts and information may have changed. This becomes the material for Interaction: Activities can be organized in which they have to interact with each other and the material so that experiential learning takes place. And finally, Independence: Training can allow students to continue learning on their own. What things will you give them, spark in them, that they can continue to use after your classes? It is recommended not to lecture for more than 10 or 15 minutes at a time and then allow students to reformulate with their partners and tell their own opinions. We ask that they try to do all this in English as much as possible. Lots of pair and small group work is usually used to interact with the material.

APPENDIX 2

Sample Workshop Year-End Survey Instrument

COURSE EVALUATION

A. Journalism
B. English Idioms
C. Environmental Concerns
D. Video Commercials and Production
E. Alternative Learning Forms

The two classes I have had were _____ and _____ (A, B, C, D, or E).

In the space under each letter of the course you took, write the number that gives your opinion (1 = disagree strongly   2 = disagree   3 = agree   4 = agree strongly).

	A	B	C	D	E
1. I learned a lot of English in this class.	___	___	___	___	___
2. I learned a lot of other useful things in this class.	___	___	___	___	___
3. This class was enjoyable.	___	___	___	___	___
4. The teaching was helpful.	___	___	___	___	___
5. The teaching was understandable.	___	___	___	___	___
6. There was too much homework in this class.	___	___	___	___	___
7. I was willing to do more homework for this class.	___	___	___	___	___
8. I would take another class like this if I had the chance.	___	___	___	___	___
9. This class was too easy.	___	___	___	___	___
10. This class was irrelevant to what I wanted to study.	___	___	___	___	___
11. I had a chance to interact with the teacher more in this class than in other classes.	___	___	___	___	___
12. I had more time to interact with other students in this class than in other classes.	___	___	___	___	___

Do you have any suggestions and recommendations for improving the program? Are there any other courses you think should be taught? Please add general comments below or on the back.

chapter **10**

Syllabus Design in Content-Based Instruction[1]

David E. Eskey

COMMUNICATIVE LANGUAGE TEACHING, CONTENT-BASED INSTRUCTION, AND SYLLABUS DESIGN

In a brilliant, if somewhat neglected, paper the late H. H. Stern (1981) identified and discussed two major and largely unreconciled versions of what had become (and still remains) the dominant approach to second language teaching, that is, "communicative" language teaching (CLT). One version—mainly European, and especially British—he dubbed the L- (for linguistics) approach, because it derived from new kinds of linguistic analyses: not analyses based on linguistic forms like phonemes, morphemes, and syntactic structures, but analyses based on such semantic elements as notions and functions and particular speech acts. The other version—mainly American—he dubbed the P- (for psychology and pedagogy) approach, because it derived not from any kind of linguistic analysis but from studies of learners and the language learning process. This approach is mainly concerned with establishing the kinds of conditions under which learners learn second languages best and the kinds of activities most likely to facilitate second language learning.

Because the L-approach generated a new kind of content for language courses, it led to work on syllabus design, to what Munby (1978) called *communicative syllabus design,* and to the work of Wilkins (1976), Van Ek (1975), and many others on so-called *notional* syllabuses. Since the P-approach was based

[1] This article originally appeared in *The CATESOL Journal, 1992, 5*(1). Reprinted with permission. Parts of this chapter appeared in much earlier form in D. E. Eskey (1984), Content: The missing third dimension in syllabus design. In J. A. S. Reid (Ed.), Case studies in syllabus and course design. *RELC Occasional Papers 31,* 66–77.

on process studies, it led to work on methodology, to such new ways of teaching as Total Physical Response (Asher, 1969) and the Natural Approach (Krashen & Terrell, 1983). It is interesting that each of these approaches was weakest where the other was strong; the L-approach had little to say about how semantic units should be taught, and the P-approach had little to say about what the content of a language course should be.

Content-based instruction (CBI) is clearly a descendant of the P-approach, in the sense that it rejects the commonsense notion that the content of a language course should be language. A basic premise of CBI is that people do not learn languages and then use them, but that people learn languages *by* using them. Thus, in the list of works on CBI (e.g., Brinton, Snow, & Wesche, 1989; Cantoni-Harvey, 1987; Crandall, 1987, to name just three of the book-length treatments), there is very little detailed discussion of syllabus design for content-based courses. By "detailed" I mean providing discussion of how a content-based syllabus for a class of second language learners would differ from one for a class of native English speakers. The best work addressing this particular problem is that of Mohan and his colleagues (e.g., Early, 1990; Mohan, 1986), but most of those promoting CBI seem to assume that in this area (as opposed to methodology, an area in which differences are widely recognized and discussed) content-based courses for second language learners are no different from other subject-matter courses (an assumption I believe to be false, for reasons which I will discuss in the third section of this chapter).

On the other hand, CBI does provide content for courses in a natural way—the subject matter to be studied—and although I will argue that this kind of content does not (in the form that courses for native speakers employ) constitute the proper content for content-based *second* language courses, I will also argue that it does constitute the proper place to begin. And I will argue, more broadly, that CBI represents a very promising way of redefining CLT in a more comprehensive and unified manner.

THE CASE FOR THE CONTENT-BASED SYLLABUS

The 1970s and the Advent of Syllabus Design

It would hardly be revolutionary to say that the advent of the notional syllabus in the 1970s (Wilkins, 1976, provides a convenient starting point) was the beginning of serious discussion of the syllabus in modern ESL (or British ELT) circles. It might, in fact, be more accurate to say that the subject of syllabus design for language courses barely existed as an issue in the field before the notional syllabus was offered, about twenty years ago, as a more enlightened approach to the problem of designing second language courses than what came to be known as the *structural* or *grammatical* syllabus, a type of syllabus so well established among the course designers of the day that few of them had considered the possibility of organizing a course in any other way. Since that time, however, it has become a commonplace of the field that the older structural syllabus is based on some set of the grammatical forms of a language, as identified by the typical linguistic analysis of forms (phonological, lexical, and morpho-syntactic); whereas the newer notional syllabus is based on some set of the notions and functions of a language, as identified by some kind of semantically based text or discourse analysis (see Yalden, 1983, for an excellent summary of the history, to the early 1980s, of syllabus design in second language teaching).

The 1980s and the Notional or Communicative Syllabus

From that major premise, the substantial body of work that was published in the 1970s on syllabus design for second language courses developed around two major arguments: first, that the notional syllabus, or some form of communicative syllabus, was superior to the structural syllabus (a literature devoted to explaining what this newer type of syllabus was and why it was better than earlier types, e.g., Wilkins, 1976); and second, within a few years, that the notional syllabus was not as wonderful as its proponents thought it was (a kind of backlash literature devoted to exploring some of the limitations of this kind of syllabus, e.g., Brumfit, Paulston, & Wilkins, 1981). In the 1980s a more descriptive tradition developed. Most recent work on syllabus design takes one of three tacks—historical (there now being some history to record, e.g., Yalden, 1983); how-to (syllabus design having been recognized as an integral part of course and program design, e.g., Dubin & Olshtain, 1986; Yalden, 1987); and survey of types (e.g., Krahnke, 1987, which includes some discussion of CBI)—or some combination of these (e.g., Prabhu, 1987, which introduces the *procedural* syllabus, in my opinion one kind of content-based syllabus; it is virtually identical to Krahnke's *task-based* syllabus). The current feeling seems to be that just as there is no one best method for teaching a second language, so there is no one best syllabus type. This may be literally true but can be pushed too far. I will argue that the best syllabus for a second language course, though it may differ from others in detail, will always meet certain criteria (Krashen, 1982, advances a similar argument for methods).

Problems with the Structural and Notional-Functional Syllabus

In any case, the controversy provoked in the 1970s by claims for the notional syllabus was never really resolved. It simply petered out. It soon became apparent that the so-called *notional-functional approach* had almost nothing to contribute to many of the questions (e.g., method and materials) that second language teachers are most concerned with answering. From a purely theoretical point of view, however, the trouble with both sides of this controversy was that they based their positions on a concept of competition between two major syllabus types (with a third, minor type—the so-called *situational* syllabus—having some limited usefulness), but this view of the issue is misleading. These two approaches to syllabus design are not contradictory but complementary. Both the notional syllabus then in vogue and the structural syllabus of an older period can best be understood not as simple alternative approaches to syllabus design but as direct applications of the major theoretical work of their times on the subjects of language and second language learning and, therefore, as part of a larger, ongoing developmental process. As the scope of linguistic inquiry has increased, so has the scope of syllabus design, from a one-dimensional concern with grammatical form to a broader, two-dimensional concern with both grammatical form and communicative function. Since this increase in scope has breached the old wall between the study of language as a formal system and the study of systems of communication, it constitutes a major breakthrough in second language teaching. But I would argue for still another level of development embodied in the content-based syllabus, which represents a still broader conception of language and second language learning and attempts to apply insights from newer research on these subjects. Just as the notional syllabus is best viewed as an extension and development of the structural syllabus (not, as noted, a mere alternative to it), so the content-based syllabus is best viewed as an even newer attempt to extend and develop our conception of what a syllabus for a second language course should comprise, including a concern with language form and language function, as well as a crucial third dimension—the factual and conceptual content of such courses.

More specifically, the structural syllabus is best viewed as a direct application of the notion of *competence*—a speaker's largely unconscious knowledge of the grammar of any language he or she can speak (as opposed to *performance,* the speaker's real language behavior, which must be based on competence and perhaps additional sets of sociolinguistic and pragmatic rules). This notion also includes most of the pre-Chomsky work in descriptive linguistics, both in the United States and elsewhere, the controversies that raged over Chomsky's (1957, 1965) transformational-generative model having to do little with the scope of linguistics but more with the nature of the systems of rules that constitute the grammars of human languages. For most of the competing approaches to linguistics, grammar remained the proper object of inquiry until a few scholars (mainly sociolinguists) began to argue for a broader conception of language as a system for generating not only grammatical sentences but also genuine communicative acts. For a few applied linguists, these ideas led to the notion of the notional syllabus, which I believe is best viewed as a direct application of the notion of *communicative competence*—a speaker's knowledge of what is not only possible (i.e., grammatical) in a language but also appropriate in particular contexts where people use language for real communicative purposes. It is important to note that this conception of language includes the earlier conception but expands on it, just as the notional syllabus includes some description of the grammar of the language to be learned (in the form of *exponents* for the notions and functions) but treats it as just one subsystem of rules for realizing a speaker's ideas, feelings, and intentions, which in turn involve another sub-system of different kinds of rules (i.e., the rules of discourse).

Widdowson (1979) has proposed a model of language incorporating both these systems of rules, which he calls *rules of usage* (i.e., grammatical rules of the kind on which the structural syllabus is based) and *rules of use* (i.e., discourse rules of the kind on which, together with grammatical rules, the notional syllabus is based). But Widdowson's system is even more inclusive. He also argues that a speaker must master what he calls *procedures* for negotiating meaning in specific real-world contexts, and these correspond more closely to Chomsky's unspecified *rules of performance,* which neither of the syllabus types just referred to deals with in any serious way. In fact, these procedures are not rules at all. In reality, as Widdowson (1981) notes, human language behavior is not so much rule-governed as merely rule-referenced. And if Widdowson is right, something more than rules is required for learning how to use a new language in the real world, where the forms that are needed and the precise language acts that must be performed are, nearly always, to some extent unpredictable.

Content: The Missing Third Dimension in Syllabus Design

The problem is that learning rules is not enough, even if the rules of discourse are included. Rules are abstractions which normally apply only in token or typical situations. They cannot tell learners exactly what to say in particular cases, in which they must often make a judgment as to what should be said or how to interpret what someone else has said. Real language learning is most likely to occur when the context of that learning is not only typical, but real; when the learners are not merely acting out roles, but trying to use their new language to fulfill genuine communicative purposes. In real language use, speakers do not begin with a list of either forms or functions that they wish to produce, but with a subject that they happen to be interested in and would like to learn more, or say something, about. Language syllabus designers, however, have not been much concerned with the purposes of learners, other than linguistic purposes, nor with subjects, so much as with the language of subjects, which most learners do not find especially interesting. Thus, the missing third dimension in syllabus design is, I would argue, subject matter or content; and a real concern for subject matter is what most distinguishes the content-based syllabus from other syllabus types.

Content, in this kind of syllabus, is not merely something to practice language with; rather, language is something to explore content with. Such a syllabus does not begin with a list, or any selection from a list, of either forms or functions, but with a topic (or topics) of interest—a network of issues, concepts, and facts which a skillful instructor can bring to life for some particular group of students—an approach that coincides with what we know about human learning in general and second language learning in particular.

As a number of psycholinguists have noted (e.g., Rumelhart, 1980), people do not acquire or store knowledge in the form of random lists of facts but in what is known as cognitive structure, a kind of picture of the world (Smith, 1975) that each of us carries around in his or her head and to which everything we know is related. Thus, acquiring new knowledge always entails relating new information to what the learners already know, to the networks of knowledge (now often called *schemata*) of which their cognitive structures are composed. Before learners can begin to make such sense of a subject (before it can, for them, become a subject of interest), they must therefore acquire what Grabe (1986) has called a *critical mass* of information on that subject (i.e., sufficient information to give that subject a shape of the kind I have just referred to as a network of issues, concepts, and facts). If, for example, I were to say, "It takes good outside shooting to beat a zone defense," some readers would be hard-pressed to say what I was talking about (although there are no words in this sentence that an educated reader could not define), whereas others would instantly recognize my remark as a common observation about the game of basketball. Moreover, as a number of scholars in our field have noted, language learning is essentially a natural process in which students learn or acquire the language by using it, not by memorizing rules or doing meaningless drills, and by using it to fulfill real communicative needs. Widdowson (1981) says, simply, "acquisition and use are essentially the same phenomenon" (p. 21); but, as I have tried to show, normal use cannot take place in the absence of a genuine subject of interest.

Form and Function in the Content-Based Syllabus

Given these insights into the way that people learn, and the way that they learn second languages, the crucial role of content in the language learning process can be defined in relation to two basic learning problems.

There is, first of all, the problem of knowledge (for researchers, the *cognitive* variables). For learners to make normal use of a language—the usual condition for successful acquisition—they must apply it to subjects they know something about (for which they have acquired the relevant schemata) and subjects they know something about in that language. They must develop some skill in the use of the language forms and routines needed for dealing with those subjects in whatever ways they may have to deal with them. But in the process of acquiring the key knowledge and skills, it is content which, when a course is built around it, will eventually provide that critical mass of information on the subject that will make it increasingly comprehensible. And in using the language to make sense of that subject, it is content, not form or function, that the learner will attend to. But it is just that kind of use, and that kind of attention, which results in the real acquisition of language.

Almost equally important is the problem of feeling (for researchers, the *affective* variables)—the learners' feelings that a subject really matters in some way that relates to their personal values and beliefs. The learners need to not only know about subjects but care about them, if their study of those subjects is to evoke a normal learning experience. This point is very closely related to Stevick's (1976) notion of *depth,* and what some colleagues of mine call *engagement*—the personal involvement of the learner in the learning, at a level which guarantees real interest in it. There is, after all, no better motivation for learning a language than a burning desire to express an opinion in that language on a subject that one really cares about. In fact, only when that happens do most learners begin to take a serious interest in the problems of language forms and language functions, that is, in the problem of how to say it right.

I hope I have made it plain that like the notional syllabus, the content-based syllabus should not be considered a mere alternative to earlier types but a logical extension and development of them. At its best, this kind of syllabus incorporates all three dimensions of the good language course—the dimensions of content, function, and form.

Such a syllabus must be concerned with language form and function wherever they constitute problems for a learner, as they frequently do. To understand a lecture on any subject of interest, a learner must comprehend most of the words and structures that the speaker employs. To write a paper on that subject, he or she must have some understanding of what it means to compose written discourse in that language. But in the format provided by a content-based syllabus, these linguistic forms and functions are never ends in themselves but simply means of achieving communicative ends—of comprehending or producing information on a subject that the learners are exploring because they are interested in it. The structural syllabus tends to treat its content as mere tokens of various grammatical structures; and even the notional syllabus, concerned as it is with teaching for communicative purposes, approaches content mainly as a sampling of key discourse types—which, I think, is why both kinds of courses have a way of breaking down into a disjointed series of old familiar language lessons that do not have the feel of the normal learning process. By contrast, in focusing on real subject matter, the content-based syllabus provides a kind of natural continuity, creates genuine occasions for the use of those procedures for negotiating meaning that Widdowson identified, and tends to pull all three dimensions of language learning together around a particular communicative goal.

PROBLEMS AND PROSPECTS

During its brief ten to fifteen years of existence, content-based instruction has clearly prospered. From K–12 immersion programs to the adjunct courses offered at colleges and universities (see Brinton, Snow, & Wesche, 1989, for discussion of the various kinds of content-based courses), this approach has attracted widespread interest and support. In American university ESL programs, it may in fact have become, in one form or another, the most popular method currently employed (Casey, 1991). At my own university, probably the first to implement what Brinton, Snow, and Wesche call *theme-based language instruction,* we are more convinced than ever that this approach to language teaching is the best one that has been developed so far, at least for the kind of populations we serve. Student reaction has been consistently good, the first sign of which was a massive increase in the quantity of comments on our evaluation forms. In the main, students seem to find such courses interesting, challenging, and relevant to their experience in the American university system. Faculty, too, seem to favor these courses, finding them (as do students) far more interesting, if more difficult to teach, than our more traditional language skills courses. Finally, many others who have tried such courses have reported a considerable measure of success (e.g., Hauptman, Wesche, & Ready, 1988).

Problems and Limitations of the Content-Based Syllabus

But we have also discovered that our courses—and by extension, any courses built around a content-based syllabus—have limitations and generate certain problems. Two are especially troublesome.

The first is the problem of relating language form to language function and content in this kind of syllabus. This is the old accuracy/fluency problem, and content-based courses tend to come down hard on the side of fluency. Content and function flow rather smoothly together, being complementary aspects of language as a system for communication, but attending to grammar in any systematic way is difficult within communicative paradigms. One major reason may be the absence of insightful theoretical work on the relationship between grammatical form and discourse function (discourse studies are expanding dramatically but are still relatively underdeveloped; see also Zuengler and Brinton, Chapter 20 in this volume); but there are also those who would argue that grammar cannot be taught (although it can be learned), and that the notion of somehow attending to it directly is simply misguided. As students learn to communicate in a language, so this argument runs, they will acquire whatever grammar they need. But those of us who work with real students in the real world have seen too many apparent counter-examples—speakers and writers of a fluent but ungrammatical English, a kind of pidginized ESL—to find this very convincing (see Eskey, 1983, for further discussion). It seems to me that on the issue of how to teach linguistic forms, or how to ensure that they will be learned, we don't really even know the right questions to ask.

A second important (and perhaps related) problem is the student who does not make normal progress in the course. One reservation I have about learning by doing is that those who don't do well don't learn. Content-based instruction can provide students with genuine opportunities for learning, but it is far from clear to me what should be done for a student who cannot seem to exploit these opportunities. I am speaking of a small minority, and the answer may be "nothing": It may be that a certain percentage of students are, for any number of a wide range of reasons, incapable of learning a second language well. If that is true, then no kind or amount of teacher intervention could make very much difference; but the trouble is, we don't really know that it is true. For some students, a more structured approach might be better.

The real source of both these problems, I suspect, is that we have never come to terms with the fact that what we teach in any kind of content-based course is not the content itself but some form of the discourse of that content—not, for example, "literature" itself (which can only be experienced) but how to analyze literature; not "language" (in the sense of de Saussure's *langue*) but how to do linguistics. For every body of content that we recognize as such—like the physical world or human cultural behavior—there is a discourse community—like physics or anthropology—which provides us with the means to analyze, talk about, and write about that content; but these are culture-specific communities to which students must be acculturated.

Thus, for teachers the problem is how to acculturate students to the relevant discourse communities, and for students the problem is how to become acculturated to those communities. Since each of these specialized communities grows out of, and remains embedded in, the larger discourse community of the speakers of the language being learned, the content of courses for nonnative speakers (by definition members of another culture, another major discourse community) cannot be exactly the same as the content of courses for native-speaking learners, who are normally much better attuned to the assumptions, conventions, and procedures of their own discourse communities. With respect to all of these, courses for second language learners should be far more explicit than those for native speakers; but this principle assumes that the designers of such courses know (in the sense of having conscious knowledge of) what these assumptions, conventions, and procedures are—an assumption that is largely unjustified at this time. In this area, the best work is being done by scholars specializing in English for Specific Purposes, often in relation to academic writing (e.g., Johns, 1986, 1991b; Swales, 1990; see also Campbell, 1990), but we have a long, long way to go.

CONCLUSION

I think we have arrived at what I would call Phase 2 in the design of content-based courses, a phase of what I hope will be extensive fine-tuning of this fundamentally sound approach, especially in the area of syllabus design. The first step will be to recognize the problem, to discard the false assumption that content-based courses for nonnative speakers should differ from courses for native English speakers in methodology but not in content. The second step will be to develop, through research, much more explicit knowledge of what the kinds of discourse we want to teach consist of—an especially challenging research agenda because it entails our achieving a better understanding of ourselves and some of our most basic (and normally unexamined) assumptions and values. The final step will be to build this new knowledge into content-based syllabuses for our students. Such work might even have implications for subject-matter courses for native-speaking students in a society as diverse as our own, which is (at least in principle) committed to providing every student with the maximum opportunity to develop his or her academic potential. There is currently substantial evidence that many children—minority children, in particular—enter our schools improperly prepared to deal with the culture they encounter there (e.g., Gee, 1990; Heath, 1986a). A more explicit understanding of what these children need to know in order to perform more successfully in school might provide us with the means to alleviate this problem.

Even if we were to succeed in developing more explicit versions of CBI for second language learners (and other culturally different populations), there would still be a certain irony in the fact that the best syllabus for a second language course might end up looking a good deal like a syllabus for any other kind of course. Have we come around at last to organizing our teaching in the way that our brains have always organized learning in our day-to-day lives? That would seem to confirm both the scientist Einstein's observation that if we could see far enough, what we would see—space being curved—is the backs of our own heads; and the poet Eliot's (1962) observation that "the end of all our exploring will be to arrive where we started and know the place for the first time" (p. 145). But perhaps that should merely reassure us. Innovative ideas have a way of turning out to be reasoned explanations of what our intuitions tell us; and I suspect that the content-based syllabus, with its stress on our culture's normal use of language to explore issues of real interest to students, may turn out to be what we have been looking for all along.

chapter 11

Thematic Units: Creating an Environment for Learning[1]

Marge C. Gianelli

How do teachers decide what to teach every day? Do we follow the curriculum guide? Do we use the sequence of the textbook(s)? Do we analyze the deficiencies of each student and individualize lessons? Is coverage of the content of a discipline the best way for our students to become knowledgeable, competent students, or should we focus on language?

Answers to these questions are essential for teachers of English as a second language (ESL). Especially in an elementary or secondary school setting, we teachers find it tremendously difficult to balance the demands of the school curriculum and the students' need to learn English. There must be a way to ensure that neither need is neglected while children are learning both language and content.

Although I am no longer in the classroom, I struggled for years with these questions. For the past five years, as director of bilingual and ESL programs, I have been working with teachers to implement a thematic approach to curriculum organization in Canutillo Elementary and Canutillo Middle School in Texas. Together we began the process at the kindergarten level five years ago and have now progressed through grade 6.

A drastic change like organizing the curriculum around themes requires a tremendous amount of effort, but the results have been worth the effort. Previously, classes were set up so that students spent set amounts of time in the different disciplines: an hour for reading, an hour for ESL-Spanish, thirty minutes for spelling, twenty minutes for social studies, and so on. The lesson concluded at the proper time no matter what was going on. I observed many

---

[1] From "Thematic Units: Creating an Environment for Learning" by Marge C. Gianelli, 1991, *TESOL Journal*, (1) pp. 13–15. Reprinted by permission.

fine lessons cut short because "time was up." Reading, writing, study of grammar rules, and spelling were never connected; each was self-contained. In addition, the bilingual teachers were frustrated because there was never enough time to teach in both languages. Other teachers also complained about the lack of time.

But worst of all, students weren't learning. They couldn't remember from one day to the next what they had been taught, the spelling words were never spelled correctly in actual writing situations, and more than one-third of the first-grade students were being retained because they were unable to read. Students counted their successes by the number of papers they had to turn in, and were kept after school only for not turning in a paper (never for inability to read); thus, the object of the day was to turn in papers. No students I ever asked knew what they were learning in science, or what story they had read in reading. When asked, "What is science?" a student responded, "It's right after lunch." To remedy this fragmented approach to learning, the teachers (who were as discouraged as I) and I decided to try focusing on themes.

The thematic approach can be defined as application of "a methodology and language from more than one discipline in examining a central theme" (Jacobs, 1990, p. 8). An example from our second-grade curriculum guide is the theme of weather. Weather can be studied from the point of view of science (formation of clouds), social studies (rain or lack of rain's effect on crops), health (effects of weather on well-being), art (graphic depiction of weather concepts in a mural), music (weather songs and sounds), and language arts (poetry about rain). We decided to make the themes one week long for kindergarten and first grade and in the second, third, and fourth grades to extend them to two and three weeks. The themes we chose were basically broad concepts that would have been studied in the context of one of the disciplines but that in reality were multidimensional. Each theme was developed to include all appropriate subject areas. Students studied the seasons in kindergarten, the concept of living and nonliving in first grade, the ocean in second grade, and dinosaurs and fossils in third grade. We decided in fourth, fifth, and sixth grades to combine only two or three disciplines instead of all of them. Language arts, music, and art are studied in conjunction with the social studies theme of Asia, for example; and health and math are integrated into a thematic unit on heredity. These units are six weeks long, and two units are studied at the same time, a half-day each.

The results have been dramatic. No longer do students forget what they're studying. For example, kindergartners who study giants in mythology for a whole week become experts on the subject. No longer is the number of papers turned in the goal. Students in first grade voluntarily take their books on farm animals home to read to their families, because the object is to be able to read! Now only about 8 percent of our bilingual students fail first grade, and they are usually new arrivals during the year, not products of our year-long program.

Research on how the brain works gives us insight into why thematic units facilitate learning. In an article on a brain-based approach to learning and teaching, O'Keefe and Nadel state:

> The search for meaning (making sense of our experiences) is survival-oriented and basic to the human brain. The brain needs and automatically registers the familiar while simultaneously searching for and responding to novel stimuli. (cited in Caine & Caine, 1990, p. 67)

The authors conclude that the learning environment must provide stability and familiarity yet "satisfy the brain's enormous curiosity and hunger for novelty, discovery and challenge" (p. 67). Because students learning through thematic units become quite familiar with the general context, new information is easy to introduce. It relates directly to the familiar, making it more meaningful.

In addition, the brain seems to search for meaning through patterning.

> The brain resists having meaningless patterns imposed upon it.
> . . . When the brain's natural capacity to integrate information is acknowledged and invoked in teaching, vast amounts of initial unrelated information and activities can be presented and assimilated. (Caine & Caine, 1990, p. 67)

By organizing material thematically for the students, we create a powerful integrated learning environment where students have little problem assimilating new information. Language learning is also facilitated because theme-related language and vocabulary are used and reused in new contexts, all of which are meaningfully related.

CREATING THEMATIC UNITS

Planning is important in utilizing thematic units to avoid what Hirsh calls a "potpourri problem"—a unit being only "a sampling of knowledge from each discipline" (cited in Jacobs, 1990, p. 2). Ackerman (1990) proposes four criteria to use as guidelines for adopting a thematic approach.

1. "Verify that the concepts identified are not merely related to the subjects but are important to them" (p. 27).
2. Verify that the thematic approach "actually enhances the learning of discipline-based concepts" (p. 27).
3. Verify that the unit has "the power to develop a sensibility incorporating and transcending those of the component subjects" (p. 29).
4. Verify that the unit will develop "desirable intellectual dispositions" (p. 30).

The particular details of the lesson plan to be included in the curriculum guide depend on the needs of the teachers of that grade level. For kindergarten and first-grade units, we find that a general framework is sufficient. In the remainder of the grades, the teachers have requested more detailed guides describing how to use suggested materials and strategies to develop the concepts and skills in each subject area. As much as possible, the teachers of the target grade level participate in the writing of the curriculum document. The procedure we followed is described below.

1. Selection of themes. We make lists of possible themes by poring over the state-mandated curriculum, textbooks, and previous curriculum guides, and choose only those themes we deem most worthy according to the criteria described above. For example, at one level *dinosaurs* was one topic suggested. With reference to the above criteria, we found this topic to be limited in the area of enhancing the learning of discipline-based concepts. We then added *fossils* to the unit, and together they formed a very complete integrated theme.

2. Identification of the most important content area concepts. It is impossible to teach everything about a topic. To choose the critical concepts of a theme, we brainstorm ideas, discuss them, and add and eliminate topics. We then divide each chosen concept into subtopics. We follow the same procedure for each thematic unit we write. For example, we asked ourselves, If we were to study dinosaurs, which concepts would be absolutely critical? We decided that their place in evolution, their characteristics, their habitats, and their extinction were important concepts, but that most important were both the scientific methods used to discover and study them and the application of those methods to learn about other extinct (and nonextinct) species. We decided that memorization of the names of the dinosaurs did little to enhance the development of the important concepts, although children could do that if they wanted to (and did). We develop subtopics for each of the main concepts and evaluate these subtopics according to the same procedure we use for the main topics.

3. Identification of the skills to be emphasized. The development of skills calls for a different procedure. We write objectives by content, grade level, and English language proficiency. For each grade level we develop language skill objectives for beginners, intermediates, and advanced learners, in oral language, speaking, reading, and writing. Because this task was gigantic for a small district such as ours, we worked off the bilingual immersion program curriculum guides developed by the El Paso Independent School District. Their bilingual department had spent considerable effort in developing language arts objectives for second language learners based on the state-mandated essential elements.

By incorporating content, basic skills, and language arts objectives into our thematic units, we give a definitive scope and sequence to our curriculum. At this point in the development of the curriculum guides, we have a hierarchy of concepts related to a theme and a list of objectives to be taught and reinforced throughout the year.

4. Identification of strategies. Strategies must be appropriate. My district had a lock-step skill-based reading program and a text-dependent curriculum. Again we asked for assistance from the El Paso Independent School District. The philosophical basis of the bilingual immersion program was whole language, and we needed training. One of their master teachers trained a core group of our teachers. This group then identified the learning strategies we wanted to use and wrote (or borrowed) descriptions for each one so they could be incorporated into the lessons. Of course, all the teachers needed in-service training in both the Whole Language Approach and the teaching of themes.

5. Gathering of materials. At this point we determine which discipline and what materials best teach each concept. We review the available textbooks and supplementary materials as well as books and audiovisual materials in the school library to locate materials supporting the teaching of the concepts we have delineated. Because we found no materials available to teach some of the critical concepts, certain materials had to be purchased or developed. We synthesized the results on a chart that lists the days across the top and the disciplines on the left side (see Figure 11.1).

Because purchasing thematic support materials for each teacher was too costly, we assembled a resource box for each thematic unit. The teachers sign up for a thematic unit on a calendar and receive the guide, which contains references for all available materials, and the resource box when no other teacher is using it. This procedure is possible because the thematic units do not have to be taught in any specific order. The librarian coordinates the materials exchange process for us.

As an example, a third-grade teacher reserving the dinosaur-fossil thematic unit for the first two weeks in October receives the resource box, which includes the curriculum guide, filmstrips, models, posters, stories with tapes, resource

FIGURE 11.1 Overview of week one of Dinosaur-Fossil thematic unit

Week One:

	Monday	Tuesday	Wednesday	Thursday	Friday
Native Language	Introduction to Dinosaurs	Dinosaur Vocabulary	Dinosaur LEA	How Dinosaurs Died	Fossil Hunt
English Language	Flow Chart Digging up Dinosaurs	Dinosaur Vocabulary	Dinosaur Story	Fossil Hunting	Four Great Eras
Social Studies	Digging up Dinosaurs	Fossils and Minerals	Life in Prehistoric Times	Life in Prehistoric Times	Four Great Eras
Science	Way Fossils Are Made	Paleontology	Minerals/ Products	Formation of Fossils	Dinosaur Eggs
Health			Going on a Dig Preparations		Going on a Dig
Art	Making Imprints			Geological Time Mural	Geological Time Mural
Music		Dinosaur Rap	Dinosaur Rap		

information for the teacher, plaster of paris, and games. The teacher reads the guide, looks over the resources, finds references to the basals and state-adopted textbooks (which are located in the classroom), checks out suggested library books, and then plans the unit to fit the needs of the students. Generally first-time teachers follow the guide closely and improve on it in their own way in subsequent uses.

Incorporating the concept of a resource box has been our most critical step toward success. Kindergarten and first-grade teachers already have access to most of the materials, but the teachers of the second and third grades have more difficulty finding related materials because of the large quantity and variety of resources needed to develop the themes adequately. With a resource box and a detailed curriculum guide, everyone has equal access to materials.

For the kindergarten and first-grade teachers, the work ends here. Each thematic framework they receive includes a description of the teaching strategies, a list of the objectives, a list of suggested themes and the materials available at their campus for each theme, and a sample lesson plan. Teachers make their own daily lesson plans. The remaining grade levels require an additional step.

6. Writing of model lesson plans. Because the expanded length and variety of materials increase the complexity of lesson planning for each subject area within a thematic topic in the second through sixth grades, we decided to help the first-time teacher by writing model lesson plans that incorporate all the elements (important concepts, skills, materials, teaching strategies, and evaluation).

Jacobs (1990) recommends following a model of cognition like Bloom's Taxonomy. We follow the lesson-cycle model in writing a suggested daily lesson plan and encourage the curriculum designers to incorporate strategies associated with whole language and a variety of grouping patterns into the lessons they write. The detailed model lesson plan uses the format shown in Figure 11.2. One of these pages is filled out for each day and each discipline. This model includes

FIGURE 11.2 Model lesson plan format

THEME: _____

FOCUS: _____

DAY: _____ DISCIPLINE: _____

TEACHING OBJECTIVE: _____

MATERIALS: _____

STUDENT EXPECTATIONS: _____

PRESENTATION: _____

GUIDED PRACTICE: _____

INDEPENDENT PRACTICE: _____

RETEACHING: _____

ENRICHMENT: _____

ASSESSMENT: _____

more learning activities than can be accomplished in the time allotted; thus, the thematic unit can easily be extended if the students and teachers so desire.

The thematic units were developed over a period of five years by many people. The units are versatile. Individual teachers can create them to teach a specific theme, or a district can take on a large operation such as the one described here. In either case, the procedure is the same.

CONCLUSION

The teachers I work with enjoy using thematic units, but more important, students are excited about school and are never bored. The teachers are impressed with the length of time students remember concepts and with how easy it is to teach vocabulary. Parents know what their children are learning because they talk at home about what they do in school. Caine and Caine (1990) state that "emotions are critical to patterning. . . . Teachers must understand that students' feelings and attitudes will be involved in learning and will determine future learning" (p. 67). The atmosphere in a thematically based classroom is positive and fun when students are involved. "When literacy skills are developed in an integrated fashion through themed units and literacy activities serving a realistic function, then children see a reason and purpose for becoming literate" (Strickland & Morrow, 1990, p. 604). Thematic units give our students intensive, in-depth experience and exposure to a tremendous amount of meaningful language and a context in which to understand difficult concepts.

chapter 12

Adapting the Adjunct Model: A Case Study[1]

Martha Iancu

Language educators seek to provide meaningful content and opportunities for real communication to facilitate language learning. One approach to this goal is content-based ESL, in which students build their language skills as they interact with academic content, whether in ESL topic-centered modules or minicourses, sheltered subject-matter courses, or ESL adjunct courses (Brinton, Snow, & Wesche, 1989; Shih, 1986).

In the adjunct model of content-based ESL at the college level, ESL students attend an academic content course that is paired with an adjunct ESL skills course. ESL students are expected to fulfill all content course requirements. In the adjunct ESL course, students develop their academic English skills using content from the regular course. The adjunct model can and should be adapted to suit the unique and changing conditions of any particular program.

When content instruction was integrated with ESL skills instruction at a small liberal arts college in Oregon, tensions arose for both students and instructor. Many students focused on mastering content and neglected their language skills, while the ESL instructor struggled to balance the roles of language and content specialist. After presenting the reasons for adopting and maintaining the adjunct model in this setting, I will detail how efforts to resolve tensions involving content and language skills have gradually transformed an adjunct *course* into an adjunct *program*.

---

[1] From "Adapting the Adjunct Model: A Case Study" by Martha Iancu, 1993, *TESOL Journal*, 2(4), pp. 20–24. Reprinted by permission.

BACKGROUND

The English Language Institute (ELI) at George Fox University in Newberg, Oregon, adopted the adjunct model of content-based ESL in an attempt to raise student morale by providing a different context for learning English. We also hoped that adjunct courses would motivate students, help to integrate them into the university community, and facilitate their transition into regular academic courses.

The ELI prepares native Spanish-speaking Puerto Rican students, immigrant students from Mexico, and students from Japan, Korea, Hong Kong, Taiwan, and other countries to pursue an undergraduate academic degree at a U.S. college or university. A few students, however, do not plan to continue their education in the United States but come to learn some English and enjoy an American experience.

The ELI's early struggles to provide effective, culturally sensitive, multilevel instruction to a small number of students fell short of the mark. In its second year, the ELI suffered a crisis in terms of student morale. Sensing that drastic change was needed to keep the program alive, the faculty decided to abandon the skills-based program structure, and ESL students attended a U.S. history course along with an ESL adjunct course. Later, we reintroduced a skills-based curriculum that included paired content and ESL courses for higher-level students. As the program has evolved over a three-year period, the adjunct model has fulfilled our expectations and brought other benefits as well.

First, students are highly motivated to succeed in a credit-bearing academic course. Most recognize that ESL adjunct courses help them to develop skills essential for success in college coursework. Many students express appreciation for ESL courses rather than frustration about having to "stay in ESL."

Second, enrollment in a regular academic course helps ESL students feel more a part of college life and helps them develop relationships with English-speaking peers. Relationships may not occur spontaneously but can be cultivated through specific assignments, such as peer dialogue journals.

Third, the adjunct model greatly eases the transition between ESL status and regular student status. It helps students realize what challenges they will face as regular students and motivates them to develop language and academic skills. It requires students to perform academically, yet provides a support system to enhance their ability to do so. Finally, because it generates invaluable information about each student's ability to manage the demands of regular courses, it helps teachers decide when a student is ready to advance.

Besides these anticipated effects, the adjunct model has produced other benefits for our faculty and curriculum. First, it has helped to integrate ESL faculty into the college faculty. Collaboration with other faculty members has enhanced mutual understanding, appreciation, and respect for the activity of preparing nonnative English speakers for U.S. college courses. Cooperation between the ESL and history faculties has also facilitated the restructuring of one history course—which now offers modified examinations and includes frequent small-group discussions, a teaching style that Benesch (1992) encourages ESL faculty to foster in other disciplines.

Finally, the adjunct model has profoundly affected ELI curriculum by enhancing ESL faculty familiarity with how students in regular courses are expected to perform. As we identify specific academic skills, we incorporate them systematically into the ELI curriculum at appropriate levels. As a result, expectations of student performance are becoming more rigorous and focused at every level.

The adjunct model has brought distinct benefits, but it has not been without problems. The evolution of the adjunct model at the ELI has been shaped by attempts to resolve these issues.

THE EVOLUTION OF THE ADJUNCT PROGRAM

Phase 1

Three key tasks involved in attempting the adjunct model of content-based ESL were to (a) select a content course, (b) establish an English proficiency range for the group, and (c) define how the paired courses would fit into the ESL program.

We selected a general education course in U.S. history for several reasons. First, the professor was interested in working with ESL students. Next, along with lectures, this professor used a variety of media and learning activities both in and out of class. We felt that this variety would allow ESL students to develop a greater range of academic and language skills, and enhance their chances for success. In addition, a course fulfilling a general education requirement would be of interest to every ESL student who planned to pursue degree studies. Finally, we considered the subject matter, the history of the United States, to be especially pertinent to help students interpret their American experiences.

Twenty students with intermediate to advanced English proficiency, with TOEFL scores ranging from 387 to 520, enrolled in the U.S. history course. Both the number and language abilities of the students caused problems. First, the ESL students comprised about a third of the students in the history class, significantly altering classroom dynamics. Second, most students' English skills were too low for them to do the reading and grasp important lecture points without help. They sought assistance from the ESL instructor in understanding the material. If they perceived, however, that an activity did not lead directly to the limited goal of passing the history course, they viewed it as "extra" and resisted it. For example, when students realized that they would receive study keys for their multiple-choice exams a week ahead of time, they did not want to complete the assigned readings from the history course syllabus, preferring instead to wait for the study key—as did many of their U.S. classmates—and then merely scan a few pages for answers. Likewise, students considered as super-fluous other assignments related to the reading, such as outlining or summarizing main ideas.

In terms of its relationship to the program, we viewed the history course with its ESL adjunct course simply as another component, independent of other courses. These two three-hour courses replaced the reading course and the

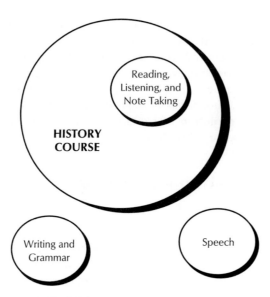

FIGURE 12.1 Initial relationship of content course to ESL courses

listening and note-taking course. The writing and grammar course and the speech course remained unchanged (see Figure 12.1).

Students were taking elective ESL courses as well, so that some were enrolled in as many as twenty-one hours. For many of the students, one three-hour adjunct course was not adequate. Also, the use of unrelated materials in the other ESL courses generated a feeling of fragmentation and overload.

We found that there was a significant mismatch between the history course requirements, the ESL students' abilities, and the time allotted for development of academic English skills. It produced a situation in which highly motivated but inadequately prepared students regarded the ESL instructor as their key to passing the content course, that is, as their content tutor. As ESL instructor, I considered the role of content tutor inappropriate, believing I would become a crutch for the students, perhaps enabling them to pass one course but not necessarily helping them develop skills that they would be able to apply independently in future courses. Nevertheless, I recognized that the students' need for content support was real.

Phase 2

To better help the students improve their academic English skills using the adjunct model, we made some significant adjustments. The following year, we raised the minimum required English proficiency of students in the paired courses and increased the number of ESL adjunct course hours. Through these and other changes, the ESL adjunct course began to evolve into an ESL adjunct program.

To challenge repeaters with a fresh content course, we selected an introductory sociology course in the fall semester to alternate with the spring semester U.S. history course. Like the history professor, the sociology professor was interested in working with international students and offered course activities that allowed for differences in students' learning styles. The course fulfilled general education requirements and international students trying to make sense of American culture considered its content helpful. In contrast to the history course, the sociology course required the students to write a research paper. Therefore, the fall semester ESL writing course was refocused to guide the students through the process of writing a research paper.

To ensure that the students possessed most of the fundamental English skills necessary to function in a regular content course with ESL support, we increased the minimum English proficiency for new students to TOEFL 440–450. This level of proficiency might be considered low for students who are expected to perform satisfactorily in a college course; nevertheless, a threshold score of 450 for the advanced level is consistent with the program's four-level structure. Raising the minimum required English proficiency of the adjunct courses to TOEFL 480 or 500 (as, for example, at St. Michael's College in Colchester, Vermont [Duffy, 1991]), was not possible given budgetary and curricular constraints. However, students who felt that they were not yet ready to attend a regular course could request placement in a lower level in the ELI.

One result of increasing the minimum proficiency was a reduction in class size; the ESL students constituted 10 to 20 percent of the students in the regular class. Higher proficiency and lower numbers of ESL students in their classes enabled the professors to view the ESL students more as a source of enrichment through diversity than as an impediment to classroom interaction. In addition, the smaller class size allowed the ESL instructor to provide greater amounts of timely, specific feedback on student assignments.

We began a process of integrating content and skills from the content courses into the Level 4 curriculum (see Figure 12.2), imparting a new sense of coherence. This process occurred on several fronts. First, we added a second three-hour ESL adjunct course so that the curriculum included Adjunct Reading and Adjunct Listening and Note Taking. At the same time, we reduced student access to elective courses from a maximum of seven hours to two hours. In addition, the writing and grammar course began to incorporate content and skills from the content course, as students wrote essays in response to study questions from the content course. These changes addressed the most salient problems and did not constitute a comprehensive effort to connect the entire Level 4 curriculum to the content course. Thus, at this point, we made no changes in the speech course, which focused on public speaking.

During Phase 2, the adjunct program's success increased. Seventy to 90 percent of the students were promoted during Phase 2, compared to 35 percent of the Phase 1 group.

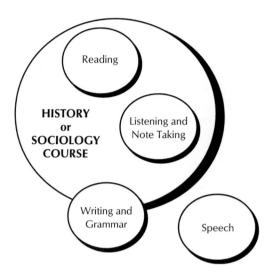

FIGURE 12.2   Early relationship of content course to ESL courses

The changes made during Phase 2 ameliorated but did not completely resolve the problem of student dependence on the ESL instructor for content support. In fact, with one ESL instructor teaching both adjunct ESL courses and, the writing and grammar course as well, the program itself was structured so that the students' primary resource for coping with the sociology or history content was the ESL instructor.

The rationale for having one ESL instructor teach this group of adjunct courses was that it would be easier for one ESL instructor to coordinate the adjunct courses with the content of the regular course. One ESL instructor would be able to monitor syllabus changes, keep track of the relationship between readings and lectures, and consult with the content-area professor about the course itself and each student's needs and accomplishments. These advantages are real, but there are also drawbacks. In addition to their tendency to look to the ESL instructor for content support, the students do not gain the benefits of working with diverse instructors, and the adjunct program itself does not benefit from the insights of various instructors. Thus, faculty—and the program itself— are deprived of the potential benefits of collaboration between different ESL and content course faculty.

Phase 3

During Phase 3, we made three significant modifications in the way the content course fit into the program. First, we integrated content and skills from the sociology and history courses more systematically into the writing and grammar course. Second, three different instructors taught the adjunct listening and note

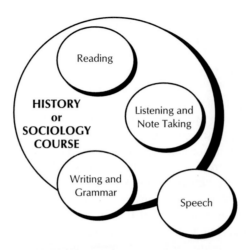

FIGURE 12.3   Present relationship of content course to ESL courses

taking, adjunct reading, and writing and grammar courses. Finally, a tutor helped students with content.

Figure 12.3 illustrates how the process of integrating content and skills from the content courses into the Level 4 curriculum progressed.

The writing and grammar course linked most assignments to the sociology and history course content. To bring consistency to the fall and spring semester writing courses, we added a research paper to the spring semester course. (The history professor agreed to evaluate the content of these papers, even though a research paper was not a requirement of this history course. The ESL instructor evaluated technical aspects of process and form.) Students interacted with content on a less formal plane in peer dialogue journals. Other assignments involved various types of academic writing, including essay tests and reaction papers. In their writing activities, students reflected on content from their sociology or history course in a way similar to that proposed by Benesch (1992).

In contrast, the speech course during fall semester remained completely independent of the sociology course. Because ESL students tended to experience great difficulty participating in small-group discussions, we added to the spring semester speech course a component aimed at improving small-group discussion skills. To minimize the outside preparation time of U.S. students who assisted with small-group discussion activities, we based this component on general topics rather than content from the history course.

Two different instructors taught the adjunct listening and note taking and reading courses, and a third taught the writing and speech courses. For such a division of labor to succeed, it was crucial to have frequent communication among the three ESL instructors and the content course professor. The adjunct listening instructor, who attended every lecture, relayed routine information to the other two ESL instructors. On specific issues, each ESL instructor worked directly with the content course professor. The ESL faculty reported that teaching in the adjunct program required more preparation time than did teaching independent ESL courses, but improved student attitudes and progress made the additional effort worthwhile.

To provide further support, a U.S. student who had previously taken the sociology or history course tutored the ESL students. The tutor attended the course with the students and met with them for three hours per week to discuss the ideas covered in the lectures and readings.

These three changes improved the effectiveness of the program. Integrating the content of the sociology or history course into the ESL writing course gave the students another opportunity to interact with the content more thoroughly because they knew that the writing assignments would help them to deepen their understanding of key concepts and directly enhance their performance in the course.

Interaction with three ESL instructors and a tutor, rather than one ESL instructor, had the desired effect of changing the students' attitudes toward the ESL instructor and the ESL courses. Students no longer considered the ESL instructor their one great hope for passing the regular course. They realized that no single ESL instructor had all the answers and that they themselves were responsible for their learning, using many resources—including the ESL instructors, but also their tutor, their dialogue journal partners, other students, and the sociology or history professor—in the process. Student and faculty satisfaction improved significantly. All of the students were promoted during Phase 3.

FIGURE 12.4   Target relationship of content course to ESL courses

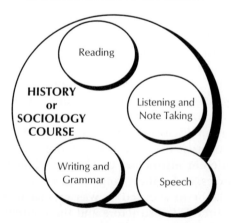

Phase 4

One of our goals for Phase 4 has been to continue the process of integrating content from the sociology and history courses into the ESL writing and speech courses (see Figure 12.4). We also want to increase emphasis in the speech course on boosting the students' confidence and ability to participate in small-group discussion and other classroom interaction. To this end, we plan to replace general public speaking topics with subjects related to the content and link small-group discussion activities to the content course syllabus.

CONCLUSION

Even in the best circumstances, "[p]aired arrangements can easily turn the ESL class into a tutoring service" (Benesch, 1992, p. 8), a clear cause for concern. Our experience shows that the lower the English proficiency of the students enrolled in an adjunct program, the more language instruction they need, the greater the challenge for them to understand and learn the course content, and the more likely they are to look to the ESL instructor for assistance with content. A major consideration in implementing the adjunct model for students whose English proficiency is about TOEFL 450 is to provide them adequate instruction and support without compromising the integrity of ESL faculty. As a result, over the span of three years, we have expanded an adjunct course into an adjunct program in which every ESL course offered at the advanced level—reading, writing, listening, and speech—gives students opportunities to grapple with concepts from the sociology or history course. Results have been most satisfactory when several different instructors teach the ESL courses and when students have access to content tutoring.

The ongoing process of improving the delivery of content-based ESL will lead the ESL community to explore new variations on the adjunct model theme. Our experience is that incorporating a content course into the advanced level of an intensive English program benefits not only that level, but the program as a whole. This account is offered in the spirit of sharing experiences and insights, as Brinton, Snow, and Wesche (1989) encourage.

chapter **13**

Knowledge, Skills, and Attitudes in Teacher Preparation for Content-Based Instruction

Pat Wilcox Peterson

In preparing teachers for content-based language instruction (CBI), teacher educators might regard the teaching act alternately with a wide and a narrow view, as if wearing a set of bifocal lenses.

The wide angle lens is necessary because when we adopt a CBI approach to teaching, we effect a change in the ESL teacher's relationship to the whole school curriculum. ESL, which has previously existed as an add-on to the curriculum, is no longer isolated in a pullout program apart from the regular classroom. Language is now inserted into the mainstream classroom, and the language curriculum must correspondingly respond to the communicative requirements of the content area. Understanding the ESL teacher's role in this setting requires a wide view.

Yet, content-based language instruction is *language* instruction and as such follows the peculiar demands of good second language methodology. We place the subject matter and the expectations of the content teacher under our closeup lens to discover what forms and functions students need to learn for academic success. In so doing, we retain certain principles of language instruction that require careful attention to detail: the simplification of input, the contextualization of new language, the sequencing and recycling of forms, and the reteaching of concepts in new formats and at new levels of abstraction. As ESL teachers learn to work with mainstream content teachers, their collaborative success is partly a result of each being able to see the teaching venture through the other's lens.

Successful CBI programs are clearly situated in a social, political, and cultural context. This chapter refers directly to K–12 classrooms as the context of instruction, but the reader should find it possible to apply the points about teacher education for CBI to the postsecondary context as well.

In response to great growth in numbers of second language learners in the schools, local districts are establishing programs of content-based language instruction; in a 1994 survey the Center for Applied Linguistics (CAL) found that 15 percent of U.S. elementary and high schools support some form of content-ESL for language minority students (see Sheppard, Chapter 2 in this volume). Half of these programs have been established in the last five years. Teacher preparation for CBI involves more than simply adapting language to the content area or inserting content material into the language lesson. In addition, it involves recognizing that ESL is situated in the school and community and therefore must provide teachers with skills for collaboration and program planning.

As the ESL teacher emerges from the isolation of the pullout program, she[1] must be prepared to participate in and even to lead discussions concerning program models, student assessment and placement, heterogeneous proficiency grouping, team teaching, cooperative learning, and promotion of the first language and home culture in the school curriculum. Reports on the language/content collaboration remind us that concern for language minority students is the job of the whole school, not just the concern of the ESL teacher (Early, Mohan, & Hooper, 1989; Genesee, 1994a; Handscombe, 1989; Milk, 1985; Penfield, 1987).

Despite the trend of the last few years to implement various forms of content-ESL in mainstream programs, there has not been a similar shift in teacher preparation programs to add special courses on CBI or to restructure the shape of the teacher preparation curriculum.[2] Instead, in teacher preparation programs which emphasize CBI, exposure to the requisite knowledge base and teaching skills is woven throughout the program in methods and materials courses, second language acquisition courses, and practica. Of the teachers in the CAL study, 72 percent reported that their preparation for content-based ESL teaching had come as inservice training after the completion of their undergraduate degree or teaching credential; only 31 percent had taken preservice courses in CBI.

The adoption of CBI both in teacher preparation programs and in schools belongs to a wider trend in student-centered, communicative language teaching and so shares many features with progressive ESL teaching in general. While it is possible to present academic content in language classes with a structural syllabus and a teacher-centered methodology, such is not the picture given by handbooks that introduce CBI to teachers (Hamayan & Perlaman, 1990; Peitzman & Gadda, 1994; Richard-Amato & Snow, 1992a; Short, 1991). The pedagogy of student empowerment to which CBI typically belongs also includes the whole language approach, experiential learning, process writing, cooperative learning,

---

[1] In this chapter, the ESL teacher will be referred to as a female and the content-area teacher will be referred to as a male. The situation could of course be reversed.

[2] A count of course offerings listed for 171 teacher preparation programs for TESOL in the United States (Kornblum, 1992) shows only ten programs (5.8%) listing separate courses on the teaching of content and language. An additional eleven programs (6.4%) offered a course in English for Specific Purposes and six (3.5%) offered a course in reading in the content areas.

heterogeneous grouping, active teaching, alternate assessment techniques, use of both L1 and L2 in the classroom, and, of course, the integration of language and content. (See Part III in this volume.)

Advocates of CBI have called for teacher preparation institutions to write principles and techniques of CBI into existing TESL/TESOL programs (Clair, 1994; Handscombe, 1989; Milk, 1985); and in some states, mainstream teachers are already required to take coursework in multiculturalism, language, and linguistics (Genesee, 1994a; Sheppard, 1994). Inclusion of special courses on CBI may become more common in preservice teacher preparation programs and inservice workshops in the future, but it is important for this innovation to be viewed as more than an add-on to the curriculum. Teacher educators should look at the certification or graduate degree program as a whole to determine what competencies are needed to support CBI.

This chapter presents an inventory of the knowledge, skills, and attitudes that ESL teachers need to bring to the job for successful content-ESL teaching, and it recommends some tasks and activities for acquisition of those competencies in a professional preparation program.

DEMANDS OF THE JOB: ESL TEACHERS IN SCHOOLS

A description of the target competencies needed by an ESL teacher might begin with consideration of the kinds of demands placed on her by a typical school. Clearly, the nature of the job requires unusual personal and professional flexibility and the broadest possible academic preparation.

The need for great numbers of certified ESL teachers grows dramatically each year, and the new ESL teacher is often hired at a school where ESL is the only program option available to language minority students.[3] In the absence of strong bilingual programs and effective first language instruction, the ESL teacher must devise a program to bring the K–12 second language learner child into the mainstream of English-only instruction. In a report on standards for teacher preparation programs in California, the Commission on Teacher Credentialing

---

[3] First language instruction is more effective than any other program in helping students attain academic competence (Collier, 1989, 1994; Cummins, 1994). However, relatively few maintenance bilingual or two-way bilingual programs have persisted in the United States, and the lack is particularly great at the secondary level (Short, 1993a.) Proponents of bilingual education see a place for content-based ESL instruction at the advanced stages of language learning as a transition to academic work in English (Cummins, 1989) or at the intermediate level in situations where limited resources or small, heterogeneous language groups make bilingual programs logistically unfeasible (Short, 1993a.) Use of the students' first language in instruction is a major tenet of successful content-based programs; use of the students' home language as part of content-ESL was reported by 50 percent of the schools studied in the CAL report (Sheppard, 1994). Inclusion of the home language and culture need not be an all-or-nothing matter, and the home language seems to help learning whenever and to whatever extent it is used (Auerbach, 1993; Lucas & Katz, 1994; Sasser & Winningham, 1994; Saville-Troike, 1984).

(1992) notes that demographic changes in the student population have shifted the position of the ESL and bilingual teacher from peripheral to central importance:

> Their expertise is needed in the classroom and as key agents in school and community collaboration. . . . Bilingual and [ESL] teachers are in a unique position to be a major resource to the total school environment. (pp. 4–5)

In fact, the normal timetable for professional development is compressed in the case of ESL teachers, so that they barely have finished their own education when they are called on to perform functions—such as needs assessment of the school situation, collaboration with colleagues in the subject area, and extensive materials development—which are usually reserved for teachers with some years of experience. If there is only one ESL teacher in the school, as is often the case in small rural districts, she is also consulted on matters of testing and assessing new students, grouping them, and planning individualized schedules for their ESL and mainstream classes. Finally, she is called on to act as consultant to the mainstream teachers, workshop leader, community liaison, and (all too often) subject-matter tutor.

Clearly, a teacher preparation program that aims to give the necessary competence for such a job must plan carefully so as to identify the knowledge base needed and the most effective set of experiences to build the confidence and understandings which the job requires. In order for a novice teacher to face all these demands, she must be able to enlist the help of the administration and other personnel in the school and not attempt to do everything herself. One of the most critical skills that an ESL teacher needs is the ability to convince her colleagues that the effective instruction of ESL students is not her job alone, but the responsibility of all the teachers who see the children. The teacher preparation program must include opportunities to build the candidate's personal attributes in communication skills, collaboration, and respect for herself and her colleagues.

TRAINING OR EDUCATION? PHILOSOPHIES OF TEACHER PREPARATION

What type of teacher preparation program is capable of empowering teachers to perform capably in such demanding contexts? The field of teacher preparation for TESOL reflects the debates of the last decade as to the underlying philosophy of teacher education.

Recent writings in the area of a second language education have outlined contrasting assumptions regarding the basic nature of the teaching act. Larsen-Freeman (1983), Britten (1985), Richards (1987), and Lange (1990) point to the differences between teacher preparation as *training* and as *education.* A critical distinction between the two concepts, according to Larsen-Freeman, is that one type of program *trains* teachers to perform in a specific type of situation whereas the other *educates* teachers to be effective in any situation they encounter. In ESL, each group of students brings different needs and challenges, so the profession is better served by educating teachers with great flexibility, creativity, and understanding.

Similarly, Richards (1987) distinguishes between a *microapproach* and a *macro-approach* to the study of teaching, wherein a microapproach resembles training and a macroapproach resembles education or development. The micro-approach looks at teaching behaviors which can be directly observed and evaluated in quantitative terms, such as drills, pacing, questioning, and use of wait time, repetitions, and restatement. Some of these techniques (such as drills) have questionable value in the communicative classroom; others (such as wait time and restatement) are absolutely essential for a teacher to master in order to provide comprehensible input to the student. The macroapproach looks at teaching behaviors which reflect thinking and reasoning that cannot be directly observed or measured and must be considered in the context of the class over time. These behaviors include decision making, planning, and use of variety in choosing teaching styles to suit the situation.

Since the micro- and macroapproaches look at different levels of behavior, they should not be regarded as mutually exclusive. In fact, as Larsen-Freeman (1983) points out, teacher education subsumes both training and education (and thus, both macro- and microskills). Any consideration of teacher competence for CBI should include both kinds of skills.

KNOWLEDGE, SKILLS, AND ATTITUDES FOR CBI

An institution may opt to add special courses in CBI or may tend toward inclusion of such material throughout the curriculum; in either case, there is a need for an inventory of the target competencies which enable teachers to plan and implement CBI. The theoretical base for these competencies should follow the design in Freeman (1989), which specifies the constituents of knowledge, skills, and attitudes, with a superordinate component of awareness (see Figure 13.1). Awareness acts as a kind of metaconstituent that allows teachers to be conscious of the other three constituents. Freeman explains that "awareness is the capacity to recognize and monitor the attention one is giving or has given to something" (p. 33). This component integrates the other factors and so drives the process of change.

Each constituent of the model is defined in the following discussion, with suggestions for modes of presentation in teacher education programs.

Knowledge

Freeman defines knowledge as: (a) subject matter (the *what* of teaching); (b) student factors (cultural backgrounds, learning styles, language levels—the *who* of teaching); and (c) the sociocultural, institutional, and situational context

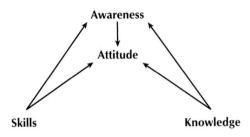

FIGURE 13.1 Descriptive model of teaching (adapted by permission from Freeman, 1989)

(the *where* of teaching). Thus, teachers need knowledge of the students and their place in society as well as knowledge of the English language itself. Sociopolitical awareness is particularly crucial, as it informs the choice of the appropriate program model (the *how* and the *why* of teaching).

The most common modes of delivering content in teacher education are still the lecture and the textbook, seen as sources of expert knowledge. The context for acquiring knowledge can also include more interactive modes such as seminars, workshops, or discovery procedures structured by the faculty (Britten, 1985). Students can learn from each other in problem solving, case studies, simulations, role plays, and observation of classroom teaching. To help close the gap between theory and practice, Celce-Murcia (1983) recommends a problem-solving approach to every phase of teacher preparation, noting that theoretical knowledge should be applied to the familiar world of teaching and tested in the reality of the classroom.

In keeping with Celce-Murcia's recommendation, Freeman cautions against an overreliance on the transmission model in teacher education programs, citing two common misconceptions in English language teacher education. First, he notes that teacher educators often wrongly assume an exaggerated importance for the place of knowledge and skills. Second, he warns against the misconception that knowledge and skills automatically translate into effective practice. Teaching itself is a process separate from (but informed by) the knowledge base. Accordingly, much of good teaching depends on longer-term development of attitudes and awareness.

Skills

The second half of the knowledge base comprises performance skills (here, both macro and micro) which are developed via the teacher education program. Appropriate contexts for acquiring these skills may be through classroom observation, microteaching or peer teaching in methods classes, or ESL practica.

One very important microskill for all teachers of ESL students is the ability to adapt one's speech to make it more comprehensible for nonnative learners. Teachers need to see models of successful adaptation, analyze what the speakers are doing, and then practice their own delivery before students. Some excellent work has been done in this area on videotape with teacher preparation for foreign language immersion programs. The Foreign Language Immersion Series (Montgomery County, Maryland) includes clear analyses of techniques used to simplify teacher talk and to make input comprehensible (Met, 1988). The same series models the use of visual context, discovery learning, and negotiation of meaning in content-area teaching (Lorenz & Met, 1988; Snow, 1989). Some language samples are in English; others are in Spanish, Farsi, and French.

Macroskills include needs assessment, lesson planning, preparation and evaluation of materials, student assessment, and giving/accepting feedback; these skills can be developed through group activities in methods courses and in prepractice teaching experiences. They can be further rehearsed during practice teaching.

Attitudes

Freeman emphasizes the importance of teacher attitudes, which "can begin to account for the differential successes, strengths, and weaknesses of individual teachers" (1989, p. 32). He defines attitude as

> the stance one adopts toward oneself, the activity of teaching, and the learners . . . [it is] an interplay of *externally* oriented behavior, actions, perceptions, on the one hand, and *internal* intrapersonal dynamics, feelings, and reactions, on the other. (p. 32)

Freeman notes the differences among the four constituents of his model by stating that whereas knowledge and skills may be changed by strategies of direct intervention, attitudes and awareness may not. Knowledge and skills can be divided into discrete chunks; they can be "isolated, practiced, and ultimately mastered." The concept of teacher preparation as training is evident here. On the other hand, attitudes and awareness are "complex, integrated, idiosyncratic, individual aspects of teaching" and can only be changed through "increasing or shifting awareness" (p. 39). This is the process of teacher development over time.

Teacher educators cannot, and probably should not even want to, transmit attitudes directly (Ganeles & Darcy, 1977). However, experience shows that some attitudes are more productive in teachers than others, and some attitudes facilitate work with diverse communities and large institutions better than others do. It may be quite effective to provide a simple consciousness-raising experience so that teachers become aware of attitudes they hold implicitly but do not recognize. Pennington (1990) offers examples of group exercises in the pre-practicum course which make candidates aware of their attitudes toward their own language learning, toward different types of students, and toward real and ideal teaching situations.

> There is no right or wrong answer to any question, nor is a uniform outcome expected among candidates. . . . The point of the exercises is to put candidates in touch with their own experiences and attitudes

that will be shaping their future teaching and to increase their awareness and acceptance of other behavior and responses in the same contexts, thus opening them up to potential modification by experience. (p. 142)

Types of intervention that help to raise teacher awareness are role plays, simulations, problem solving, and observation of one's self and others in microteaching (Britten, 1985). A critical time to test awareness and probe attitudes is during the practice teaching experience; at that time it is especially valuable to have periodic meetings with one's peers and supervisor to discuss the events of the week and their meaning, or to be able to write reactions in a dialogue journal to a supervisor (Brinton & Holten, 1989; Brinton, Holten, & Goodwin, 1993; Holten & Brinton, 1995; Porter, Goldstein, Leatherman, & Conrad, 1990).

EFFECTING CHANGE IN KNOWLEDGE, SKILLS, AND ATTITUDES

Teacher education is a process whose purpose is to effect change in the teacher. The change may not be immediate, complete, observable, or quantifiable, but it should eventually result in a difference of knowledge, skill, or attitude over time (Freeman, 1989). Changes may occur during coursework for prospective teachers in preservice programs or during inservice workshops throughout one's teaching career. This section contains scenarios with both real and imagined situations, for both language and content-area teachers.

Scenario 1: Knowledge—Awareness—Change in Attitude

One popular approach to raising teacher awareness is to highlight certain popular myths about language learning and second language learners which lead to negative attitudes. In this approach, the educator attempts to counter the adverse effects of widely accepted misinformation. The hope is that the element of surprise which the teacher feels in discovering the errors in her knowledge base will propel her to examine her attitudes and come to new conclusions about language learning. McLaughlin's (1992) report rests on this strategy. Entitled *Myths and Misconceptions about Second Language Learning: What Every Teacher Needs to Unlearn,* the booklet attempts to repair a faulty knowledge base and goes on to suggest the implications of the revised information for teaching practice.

Certain myths are so widely held and so intuitively appealing that people are generally shocked to hear solid evidence against them. Two such myths (which McLaughlin also treats in his work) are the benefit of English-only instruction and the harmful effects of first-language literacy instruction. We commonly encounter well-meaning ESL teacher candidates and practicing content-area teachers who hold these myths in all good conscience. Their point of view is often heard as follows:

Students need to *learn English as soon as possible, certainly within a year.* It is a mistake to give content instruction in L1 because *using the first language retards the learning of English.* It is wrong for newcomers to continue to speak their L1 in and out of school, on the playground, and at home, for *L1 use will separate them from the majority, harm their self-image, and impede their chance of success at school.*

The italicized sections represent misinformation common to the American myth of the melting pot. This misinformation leads many teachers to reject first language instruction as found in bilingual education programs, and may also influence teachers to prohibit all forms of first language use during content-based ESL instruction.

In countering the effects of this misinformation on teacher attitudes, the teacher educator can draw on solid findings from second language acquisition research. The fact is that it takes much longer than one year to learn English; it takes five to seven years to achieve academic proficiency in a second language under the best of conditions (Collier, 1989). It is also a fact that the programs which bring students to the highest levels of academic achievement are those with the greatest percentage of L1 instruction and L1 development (Collier, 1994).

Teachers are often surprised to learn that spending the maximum possible amount of time in L2 instruction actually does not yield the maximum level of L2 proficiency; rather, literacy instruction in the primary language facilitates both the learning of content material and the acquisition of English. Use of the students' home language in the school context is also a powerful tool for building positive self-image, family solidarity, maintenance of the home culture, and student retention in school. However, knowledge by itself can be cold comfort. The danger of presenting knowledge in isolation from skills, attitudes, and experience is that the teacher may not be able to accommodate the new information into her action system. Instead, she may be quite discouraged at the discrepancy between the ideal program model and the realities of her teaching situation.

Often when teachers learn about the limitations of ESL-only instruction, they immediately question the appropriateness of their own local programs. Doing the math themselves, they calculate that a high school student will not have enough time to become academically competent in English while he is still of school age. Further, the demographics of the school situation may make primary language instruction for all students very difficult. Why, then, should teachers bother to pursue certification for programs which the research dooms to failure?

At this point it may be helpful to remind teachers that they need not be forced into a closed system of choice between complete L1 content instruction and no L1 intervention at all. The teacher educator can provide teachers with a broader spectrum of alternatives for primary language instruction. For example: inclusion of parent volunteers, peer tutors, community aides, acquisition of L1 books in the library, and frequent opportunities for recognizing the various languages and cultures in the school. All these activities contribute to the comfort and the pride of the language minority student, and teachers who understand the range of options are more effective in their efforts to advocate for a balanced inclusion of L1 and content-based ESL in the school day.

The next step in the dialogue might be to move to simulations and role plays in which teachers practice sharing the information about language acquisition with parents, counselors, and administrators who make programmatic decisions for ESL students. Simulated practice in advocating for better language programs is valuable preparation for being an advocate out in the field. ESL teachers can also develop workshop materials for content-area teachers and the general community in which these issues are discussed.

Scenario 2: New Skill—Awareness—Change in Attitude

It is also possible that by helping teachers gain new instructional skills, educators can enable them to see the teaching situation or their students in a different light. Over time, as teachers master new skills appropriate to the needs of the ESL population, the success they achieve can cause them to think in new ways. It is not the skill itself which brings about the change in attitude, but rather their awareness of the changed situation. The following two examples demonstrate how new skills in student assessment (a macroskill) and in error correction techniques (a microskill) can lead to more positive attitudes toward language learners.

Adopting New Assessment Tools. Imagine a group of content-area teachers who suspect that CBI for ESL students in the mainstream will lower the academic excellence of the school by setting a different standard for ESL student achievement in content areas. They resist alternate assessment tools as being less valid and yielding less reliable information. (This stand may be fairly common in schools that have adopted outcome-based education.) Their point of view might be expressed as follows:

Attitude before the workshop: Fairness in public education requires that standards be set and evaluation of achievement be measured in the same way for all students. The best way to achieve fair assessment is to administer standardized tests, which are easiest to use and give comparable measurements across groups of people. For advancement to the next grade, all students should reach the same criteria of achievement on these tests.

In order to effect a change in these teachers' attitudes, the inservice director might plan a workshop with both knowledge and skills components. Below are some of the objectives of such a workshop.

Knowledge Objectives. Participants will come to understand that:

- the language used to explain the items in a standardized test may be much more difficult than the content that is being tested; for a nonnative speaker, every test written in English is partly a test of English.

- tests normed on one cultural group cannot be culturally fair for a different group.
- discrete item tests which sample only a portion of the knowledge base show what a student does not know, rather than what he or she does know.

Skills Objectives.   Participants will have hands-on experience in:

- developing a performance-based test for a social studies class in which the student may choose to draw a map, construct a time line, follow an outline to write a short summary, or participate in a simulation game.
- setting up a system for science students to practice new vocabulary in a word bank, to draw the steps used in an experiment for growing plants, to chart the growth of various plants over time, and to write conclusions about the plants' requirements for growth.

It is unlikely that attitudes would be changed over the long run by simply becoming aware of the knowledge objectives about testing in the example above. However, if teachers develop concrete skills that allow them to replace their current practice with more useful alternatives, they might recognize the utility of the new skill. Their attitudes about alternate assessment may generalize not only to ESL students but to all the students they teach. The new attitude is hypothesized below:

Attitude after some experience: Within any group, there is diversity in learning styles. Assessment that is multifaceted gives everyone a chance. By considering more open-ended assessment devices, we are able to get at competencies that were not observable using the previous assessment tools. The new tests are actually more accurate because they show more. Besides, they are much more fun.

Learning How to Handle Error Correction

In the next example, imagine a CBI program that has been in operation for some time in a middle school or a high school. The particular problem area is in how to handle ESL students' emergent aural understanding and speech. When language and content teachers begin to work together in a team effort, the content teacher might define her new task as teaching grammar prescriptively, in an effort to elicit correct English from the student. This practice shows a lack of understanding of the nature of language learning, an understandable gap for a person who has never studied language acquisition. The content teacher's misunderstanding might be stated thus:

Attitude before discussion of the topic: Whenever ESL students in my class make grammar mistakes, I should correct their language. This practice will help them learn English and I will be providing support for the ESL staff.

The ESL teacher might want to share her knowledge about second language acquisition with the content-area teacher and may model some skills for handling student speech.

Knowledge Objectives.   The content teacher will come to understand that:

- Students can either focus on fluency (which supports communication and content learning) or on accuracy (which raises anxiety and diverts attention from the content)—but they cannot focus on both at once.

Skills Objectives.   The content teacher will practice:

- Separating the message from the form of the language and responding to the accuracy of the message. For the time being, he will ignore errors of form and give feedback that serves to reinforce the student's ideas, while modeling extended and elaborated versions of the student's utterance.

Again, the knowledge about language learning alone would probably not be effective in convincing the content-area teacher to change his behavior with the student. What is more helpful is a concrete suggestion on how to interact with the student. (Actually, this advice might be quite liberating for the content-area teacher, who might have been devoting a great deal of energy to correction practices and losing time for content-area instruction!) The change in attitude over time, as the content teacher notices the progress of the student's natural language acquisition, might be summarized as follows:

Attitude after some discussion and experience: Grammar mistakes are not a big problem; as fluency increases, over time, the student's accuracy improves as well. My job is to teach content and to act as a language coach, encouraging the student to express himself/herself.

Scenario 3: Experience—Awareness—Attitude—Skills

The third case is an interesting example reported in the literature concerning the development of language teaching skills in a content-area teacher (Enright, 1986). Molly, an experienced mainstream kindergarten teacher, was working for the first time in a lab situation with ESL children and was surprised to discover how much trouble they were having with the content language necessary to practice the skills of counting and categorization. In a very short period of time, after a single day of teaching, she had gained increased awareness of the need for explicit teaching of the "thinking language" children use to perform academic functions. Accordingly, she began to adjust downward the amount of content she planned to present each day.

Molly's attitude toward her own teaching role shifted from a cognitive, content-oriented perspective to a communicative, language-oriented perspective. As the weeks went by, she practiced the teaching skills necessary to implement her new vision of her role: modeling language, setting up interesting activities, using simplified language, and planning for communication. In a parallel development, Molly also became aware of the need to let students practice extended sentences of their own, so she began to build in more opportunities for student output. Her attitude toward her own role changed again, from language giver to language facilitator, and she became skillful at eliciting longer sentences from her students.

This case study is particularly useful because it illustrates two rather common tendencies in mainstream teachers: a primary concern for content (over language), and a preference for lecturing (rather than teacher-student dialogue). The case also shows how Molly's teaching style was transformed by her classroom experience, owing to changes in awareness, attitude, and skills.

PROBLEM-SOLVING AND EXPERIENTIAL ACTIVITIES

The example of Molly emphasizes the effectiveness of supported practical experience in teacher preparation, and of the richness possible in collaboration between language and content teachers. One goal of teacher preparation programs might be to give a wide variety of hands-on experiences and to begin language/content collaboration as early as possible. An informal survey of syllabi for CBI courses yielded techniques for practical activities[4] which can be included in a course preparing teachers for CBI.

---

[4] In the fall of 1994, a request for information on content-based language instruction went out to all the professional preparation programs in TESOL listed in the 1992–1994 directory. The list of activities in Figure 13.2 is a composite of suggestions from materials sent in by a number of sources; because a given activity may have been mentioned by a number of programs, ideas are not credited individually. Acknowledgment and thanks go to the following persons and institutions for contributing information and/or syllabi from their teacher preparation programs:

Paul Angelis, University of Illinois; Anonymous respondent, University of Puget Sound; Donna Brinton, University of California, Los Angeles; Angela Carrasquillo, Fordham University; Steve Chandler, University of Idaho; Mark Clarke, University of Colorado, Denver; Rebecca Freeman, University of Pennsylvania; Jia Frydenberg, University of California, Irvine; Alexandra Rowe Henry, University of South Carolina; Dorit Kaufman, State University of New York, Stony Brook; Carolyn Kessler, University of Texas, San Antonio; Natalie Kuhlman, San Diego State University; Marguerite MacDonald, Wright State University; Kathleen Mahnke, St. Michael's College; M. O'Donnell, University of South Maine; Shirley Ostler, Bowling Green State University; Adelaide Parsons, Southeast Missouri State University; Kitty Purgason, Biola University; Steve Ross, California State University, Long Beach; Virginia Samuda, Sonoma State University; Ann Snow, California State University, Los Angeles; Elaine Tarone, University of Minnesota; Dovie Wylie, San Jose State University; Richard Young, University of Wisconsin, Madison.

- Meet with content teachers

- Analyze content area texts and other materials

- Listen in on content lectures

- Create an original Big Book

- Present and discuss model theme-based units

- Select a relevant content area and design a unit

- Collect a picture file of at least twenty pictures relating to a content area and demonstrate an activity in using those pictures

- Demonstrate a lesson with context-embedded, cognitively demanding language

- Teach a lesson in a classroom with ESL students; videotape the lesson and conduct a self-analysis of the lesson on tape

- Develop a lesson plan or activity to teach a strategy of writing to learn from text

- Develop a prereading activity for a content-area text

- Develop a plan for a needs analysis for a specific group of learners

- Interview a CBI teacher on issues of program model, course development, materials design, assessment, and feedback

- Observe a content-based ESL class

- Conduct a case study of one language learner in the mainstream and draw implications for integrating language and content

- Aid in a content-based ESL classroom for two hours/week and reflect on the experience in a dialogue journal (via e-mail or hard copy)

- Prepare a general curriculum for a theme-based, sheltered, or adjunct course as a group project

- Role play the part of an ESL consultant

- Practice problem solving and how to set up an ESL program in a school with scarce resources

FIGURE 13.2   Problem-solving and experiential activities

Several features of the certification program at SUNY Stony Brook are interesting in the degree of teacher collaboration they present (see Kaufman, Chapter 14 in this volume). For example, all students who are preparing for TESOL certification must take an interdepartmental course ("Language and Science: A Multicultural Perspective"); preservice math and science teachers also enroll. The fieldwork for the course brings students into contact with ESL children for mentoring in science and with parents for language enrichment workshops. In another example, in the student teaching seminar, math, science, and ESL student teachers join to create teaching projects in the content areas.

At the University of South Carolina, TESOL interns have had the opportunity to teach in a K–8 summer camp with a content-based curriculum. Although various programs exist for content-based foreign language immersion or content-enriched Foreign Language in the Elementary School (FLES) (Curtain & Pesola, 1994), the application of a summer camp concept for ESL children is unusual and interesting.

COMPETENCIES FOR CONTENT-AREA TEACHERS

A content-area teacher working with ESL children would benefit from having any of the competencies listed for ESL teachers. In fact, an increasing number of subject-area teachers have developed an interest in working with language minority children and returned to the university to add an ESL endorsement to their license or credential. The situation is ideal in many respects: The teacher with double or triple certification is well equipped to give sheltered English classes in her content area; she brings a knowledge of the school system and some years of teaching experience to the field; and she has already acquired a position of respect in the school from which she can speak as an advocate for ESL students.

Content teachers who take up a second specialty in ESL are exempt from the discomfort that ESL teachers often feel and that Master (1992) labels "fear of subject matter." They do not have to worry, as ESL teachers often do, that they are diluting the content or giving a somewhat false picture of the academic discipline. On the other hand, certain competencies on the ESL teacher's list may not come so easily to subject-area teachers, who have developed a very different emphasis in regard to content and the ways to deliver it (Master, 1992).

In her ethnographic study of ESL students in mainstream classes, Harklau (1994) found that content classes were largely dominated by teacher-led discussions, where the input was not adjusted for comprehensibility. Of particular difficulty was teacher discourse containing puns, sarcasm, irony, asides, fast speech, and digressions. There was little group work, and opportunities for student output were few. In both the spoken and the written mode, student answers were mostly limited to single words or phrases. Mainstream teachers never corrected ESL student speech for fear of causing the students embarrassment; they did not correct grammar mistakes in written work because they lacked the linguistic training to do so. Nor did they encourage teacher-student or student-student interaction; accordingly, ESL students did not mix with language majority students but remained isolated in small ESL groups in the mainstream classroom.

In contrast, ESL classes were adjusted for comprehensible input and there were more opportunities for interaction and student speaking. Students participated actively in class discussions and received implicit instruction in pronunciation and speaking skills. A variety of extended writing assignments were given, and the teacher monitored students closely to ensure that they really understood what they wrote. The ESL class provided a safe haven for ESL students and served as the center of their social life. The ESL teacher provided tutoring during lunchtime and assisted her students through various personal crises, including "course placement changes, college application counseling, and coping with family (and legal) problems" (Harklau, 1994, p. 266).

Teacher education in the content areas predisposes teachers to think of their subject matter as the product, to be concerned with the quality and completeness of the product, and to be less concerned with the delivery system or the personal characteristics of the recipients. Content-area teachers in the Harklau study talked for most of the class period. In contrast, TESOL has a long tradition of interactive methodologies. Language teachers, whether audiolingual or communicative in approach, are not trained to lecture; moreover, their teacher education programs predispose them to think of learning as a process, with focus on a variety of activities for active student engagement. The choice of subject matter has always been somewhat arbitrary at lower levels of language teaching. Teachers may as easily substitute a newspaper article as follow the textbook, as long as the article interests the students and accomplishes the language objective.

This disparity in approach to subject matter can create discomfort in an ESL/content-area collaboration: Subject-area teachers may regard the ESL teacher as somewhat cavalier in her stance on the lesson, and the ESL teacher may urge the subject-area teacher to lighten up on content and involve students in more active learning.

Fortunately, recent curricular reforms in math and science are closing the gap between process and product views. Standards for student achievement in math and science consider the delivery systems and characteristics of the recipients on the same level as the product (National Council of Teachers of Mathematics, 1989; National Science Teachers Association, 1991). Subject-area specialists are urging a more student-centered pedagogy that should coincidentally ease the process of collaboration for ESL and content-area teachers.

In the interest of providing a holistic education for ESL students, ESL and content-area teachers need each other. The content teacher benefits from second language pedagogy in making the lesson accessible. ESL lessons gain in interest and relevance when the focus shifts from language disassociated from the academic life of the student to the study of content-based language. To bridge these differences in perspective and training, workshops for content-area teachers might include the following topics:

- Second language acquisition theory (conversational competence and academic competence, and strategies for developing them)
- Activation of ESL students' prior knowledge (and how to take advantage of it)
- The importance of comprehensible input for language learning (with practice in contextualization and modifying teacher talk)
- Approaches to integrating content and language (with practice in providing active learning experiences, presenting content visually, giving opportunities for students to speak and write)
- Alternate assessment procedures for ESL students (portfolio development, modified objectives, grading on progress)
- Ways to encourage interaction between native speakers and language minority students (changing the social climate in class, peer teaching, cross-language tutoring)

CONCLUSION

Owing to the great increase in ESL students, institutions are opting at all levels for programs of content-based language instruction. In K–12 schools at the intermediate language level and above, the ESL pullout model is yielding to collaborative models of content and language in the classroom. In university programs, language and content are being combined in special sheltered classes, through the adoption of adjunct courses, or by other models of teacher collaboration.

Some teacher preparation programs are responding to the need for CBI by including information on it throughout the curriculum, but there is a need for total program planning and specification of necessary teacher competencies.[5] This chapter has suggested a range of competencies and some modes of delivery. In the future, teacher educators may contribute successful program ideas which offer experiential learning activities and foster collaboration between the content teacher and the ESL teacher.

---

[5] For a basic inventory of ESL teacher competencies, see the *TESOL Statement of Core Standards for Language and Professional Preparation Programs* (Teachers of English to Speakers of Other Languages, 1985).

chapter 14

Collaborative Approaches in Preparing Teachers for Content-Based and Language-Enhanced Settings[1]

Dorit Kaufman

The increasingly diverse student population in schools across the country has dramatically altered the demographics of educational institutions (National Clearinghouse for Bilingual Education, 1991; Waggoner, 1992) and has left many mainstream teachers unprepared (McKeon, 1994; Penfield, 1987; Stewart, 1993). While literature advocating a language-enhanced curriculum and content-rich teaching is abundant (e.g., Brinton, Snow, & Wesche, 1989; Crandall, 1993; Short, 1993a), documentation on new ways to prepare teachers for operating within interdisciplinary paradigms is sparse.

The implementation of interdisciplinary approaches in teacher education programs requires a shift from familiar models to a major reorganization of the curriculum. Current instructional practices reflect the tendency of teachers' behavior to be modeled on their own prior educational experiences and for their beliefs and instructional practices to remain relatively fixed (Hollingsworth, 1989; Pajares, 1992; Pennington, 1995; Richardson, 1990; Shavelson & Stern, 1981). In fact, prevalent models of teacher education generally do not cross disciplinary boundaries or include collaboration across disciplines. It is therefore hardly surprising that few preservice teacher education programs include models for interdisciplinary collaboration which provide mainstream teacher candidates with

[1] I would like to thank Jacqueline Grennon Brooks, Discover Lab Director, and Wallace Nelson from the Center for Science, Mathematics and Technology Education; Marie Fitzgerald from the Social Sciences Interdisciplinary Department; and participating teacher candidates for contributing to the success of the collaborative endeavor. Project MORE (Mentors for Richer Education) has been supported in part by grants from the U.S. Department of Education (No. P219A30164) and from the Office of Undergraduate Studies, State University of New York at Stony Brook. Discover Lab has been supported in part by a grant from the National Science Foundation (No. DUE9353460).

alternative approaches to educating linguistically diverse populations or immerse TESOL teacher candidates in exploration across the content areas.

CREATING CONSTRUCTIVIST-BASED COLLABORATIVE CONTEXTS

> *"Meaning is not given to us in our encounters, but it is given by us— constructed by us each in our own way, according to how our understanding is currently organized."*
>
> *(Duckworth, 1987, p. 112)*

Constructivist educators have drawn inspiration and ideas about the processes of teaching and learning from the work of Piaget (1954, 1967, 1970) and Vygotsky (1962). As a result, constructivist environments engage learners in acquiring knowledge through active participation in learning events, including experiential hands-on activities, concrete manipulatives, and guided discovery. Such environments also include opportunities for partnerships and collaboration and time for reflection and reevaluation (Grennon Brooks, 1990; Kamii, 1985; Kaufman & Grennon Brooks, 1996; Sigel, Brozinsky, & Golinkoff, 1981; Tobin, Tippins, & Gallard, 1994).

Constructivist-based learning environments also take into account the readiness levels and multiple experiences, interests, and backgrounds which learners bring to the classroom. Because the construction of knowledge is idiosyncratic and evolves from prior experiences and beliefs, learners' perceptions of external events are influenced by their prior experiences in affective, academic, and social domains. Newly acquired knowledge often conflicts with existing knowledge, and it is the resolution of such conflicts that contributes to new learning, the internalization of new approaches, and professional growth.

Constructivist teachers offer their students opportunities to acquire concepts and understand real phenomena through discovery learning. The teacher's role is not to teach from textbooks, to lecture, or to explain phenomena; rather, it is to engage students in open-ended tasks that enhance observation and problem solving and engage them in a journey of inquiry. In their classroom settings, constructivist teachers carefully balance between enhancing learners' acquisition of new skills, encouraging information gathering, and promoting independent thinking and guided discovery. Constructivist teachers are both researchers and learners as they observe and reflect on their own experiences and the phenomena they encounter. Input from their students offers them insight into how their students construct new knowledge and generate new understandings (Duckworth, 1987; Grennon Brooks & Brooks, 1993). Such insight guides teachers in designing new learning activities for their students.

The benefits of constructivist educational environments for students' academic, social, and affective growth have been widely documented (Driver, 1983; Forman & Kuschner, 1977; Russel, 1993; Sigel, Brozinsky, & Golinkoff, 1981). These approaches have been most prevalent in science, mathematics, and early education programs (DeVries & Kohlberg, 1987; Fosnot, 1993; Kamii, 1981, 1985; Resnick, 1987; Tobin, Tippins, & Gallard, 1994) but relatively infrequent in secondary, higher education, and teacher education programs. For constructivist contexts to proliferate at all levels of education, preservice teacher education programs must actively engage teacher candidates from all disciplines in creating inquiry-based learning environments (i.e., environments where peer interaction and reflection outlets abound and where the construction of new knowledge occurs through hands-on activities, fieldwork opportunities, problem solving, and discovery).

APPLYING A CONSTRUCTIVIST APPROACH TO TEACHER EDUCATION

If constructivist paradigms are to emerge, teacher educators ought to be willing to reach out across disciplines, to form new partnerships, and to reorganize their curricula. This chapter describes a collaborative endeavor among TESOL, science, and social studies teacher candidates that has generated multiple collaborations across disciplines and created richly diverse educational settings for teacher candidates' professional growth. The following sections elaborate on the constructivist perspectives that undergird the collaborative endeavor and highlight a sample of collaborative events that this endeavor generated with peers across disciplines and in fieldwork opportunities with children.

The constructivist contexts described here have provided experiential learning and interdisciplinary activities among TESOL, science, and social studies teacher candidates. The interdisciplinary collaborative endeavor has involved four teacher educators in three disciplines located in two colleges at the State University of New York at Stony Brook and has included twelve graduate and undergraduate courses (see Table 14.1).

This approach adopts a university-wide perspective to teacher education, locating all teacher preparation programs within their respective academic departments. There, students complete the requirements for the departmental major along with their teacher certification requirements. The TESOL teacher preparation program (located in the Department of Linguistics) and the social studies teacher preparation program (based in the Social Sciences Interdisciplinary Department) are located in the College of Arts and Sciences, whereas the science teacher preparation program is located in the College of Engineering and Applied Sciences. Science teacher candidates complete their requirements for the major in departments such as biology, chemistry, earth and space, or physics and take their education courses in the science education center. A central educational

TABLE 14.1 Graduate and undergraduate courses included in the interdisciplinary collaboration

Course	Discipline	Students	Fieldwork Setting	Total Hours
Student Teaching in TESOL	Linguistics	U/G	K–12	450
Student Teaching in Science	Science	U/G	7–12	450
Student Teaching in Social Studies	Social Studies	G	7–12	450
Language and Science: A Multicultural Perspective	Linguistics + Science	U	K–12	30–60
Methods and Materials of TESOL II	Linguistics	U/G	K–12	30
Introduction to Science Teaching	Science	U/G	K–12	50
Science Instructional Strategies and Techniques	Science	U/G	K–12	50

unit coordinates all the teacher education programs on campus. In any given semester there are approximately 50 teacher candidates taking courses in pedagogy with approximately 12 to 20 more students in each of the disciplines participating in student teaching in schools with cooperating teachers. TESOL teacher candidates take general and applied linguistics courses and have extensive fieldwork opportunities in classroom settings. These include teaching semester-long three-credit ESL courses to undergraduate and graduate foreign students, a semester of full-time student teaching in elementary and secondary schools, and a variety of additional interdisciplinary fieldwork opportunities integrated in the academic courses listed in Table 14.1.

The disciplinary rigor, diverse interests, and contrasting perspectives of the teacher candidates and teacher educators from the three disciplines greatly enhance this endeavor. As they interact, participants from the respective disciplines become increasingly aware of the unique needs of ESL learners in linguistically diverse mainstream classrooms. They also engage in the joint exploration of new pedagogical orientations, effective instructional practices, and interactive activities for teaching science, mathematics, and social studies.

PARTNERSHIPS ACROSS DISCIPLINES

The teacher educators at Stony Brook play a significant role in developing constructivist contexts and in planning collaborative activities across disciplines. Extensive preplanning is a prerequisite to the success of these collaborative experiences. The list below illustrates the goals that have guided the planning and implementation of the interdisciplinary educational partnership and have served as the basis for its periodic evaluation:

Objectives in Planning Interdisciplinary Collaboration

- Create interdisciplinary learning opportunities for teacher candidates and teacher educators
- Maximize and diversify fieldwork opportunities across disciplines
- Integrate fieldwork and experiential components into course curricula
- Maximize interdisciplinary problem solving and collaboration through open-ended and learner-generated tasks
- Maximize hands-on participation for richer interdisciplinary experiences
- Relate tasks to learners' emerging academic and professional needs in each of the disciplines
- Open channels of communication for peer mentoring and support within and across disciplines
- Provide time and offer multiple outlets for communication and reflection
- Create opportunities for self-evaluation and peer evaluation within and across disciplines

By exposing teacher candidates not only to theory and hypothetical contexts but also to real-life collaborative experiences, fieldwork promotes the candidates' overall professional development. For the TESOL teacher candidates, this development has entailed the exploration of real settings, and the reflection and evaluation of practices that result from this exposure. For the science and social studies candidates, this development has taken the form of a heightened awareness of the needs of ESL students.

The collaborative fieldwork experiences vary slightly depending on the participants. The science teacher candidates typically focus on designing interactive tasks that target the complementary development of language and science concepts; the social studies candidates typically focus on developing tasks that are experiential and rich in graphic support. These tasks (see Figure 14.1) enhance peer collaboration and contribute to the teacher candidates' autonomy as teachers.

FIGURE 14.1 Open-ended tasks for increased learner autonomy and peer collaboration

Task	Disciplines Involved
Sensitizing mainstream teachers	Linguistics/Science/Social Studies
Developing interactive activities	Science and Linguistics
Conducting fieldwork with children in Discover Lab	Science and Linguistics
Creating social studies and science lessons	Linguistics/Science/Social Studies
Creating a database of interdisciplinary activities	Linguistics/Science/Social Studies

The sections that follow focus on the sensitization process and the design and implementation of hands-on activities for elementary school children in the on-campus teaching laboratory and in local school districts.

SENSITIZING MAINSTREAM TEACHER CANDIDATES

> *I must admit that I went into the project with a skeptical attitude; it was not something that I was excited about or expected to get much out of. I was delightfully surprised. I was made to understand the special needs of ESL students in a very "in your face" way by being put in the very circumstances these students are faced with.*
>
> *Participating teacher candidate*

In the Stony Brook model of collaborative teacher education, science and social studies teacher candidates become sensitized to the ESL experience through immersion in simulated contexts designed for them by TESOL teacher candidates. Through this process, as ideas are transformed into simulated experiences, both groups arrive at new understandings. One open-ended sensitization task, for example, invites TESOL teacher candidates to design five-minute activities that increase the awareness of their mainstream peers to the kaleidoscope of linguistic, cultural, and social communication patterns of ESL students. TESOL teacher candidates initially discuss their individual ideas for these activities with their TESOL peers in small groups. The discussions focus on creating experiential activities that involve the mainstream candidates both cognitively and affectively and communicate the social, cultural, affective, linguistic, and academic needs of the ESL student. These simulations initially trigger feelings of frustration, irritation, and confusion but then mitigate them by giving the teacher candidates the experience of addressing the unique needs of ESL students. In planning these activities, the TESOL candidates focus on various aspects of the ESL experience and model supportive learning environments that can be emulated by mainstream teacher candidates in their own classrooms in the future to ease the acculturation of ESL students.

Designing sensitization activities and models for emulation provides TESOL teacher candidates with a powerful pedagogical tool that allows them to explore effective instructional practices for an authentic purpose and a real audience. Setting aside class time for deliberation and sharing validates the importance of the task, thus giving the candidates opportunities to appreciate the full range of issues. The activity invites teacher candidates to integrate what they have learned about pedagogy—for example, the incorporation of visual aids, the sequencing of activities, time management, and modes of presentation. It further invites them to explore the impact of such practices in instructional settings and, in the process of group deliberation, to discover the dynamics of group work, decision making, and interpersonal interactions.

After deliberation, the groups each present the selected activities to their peers in the TESOL class for additional feedback. Teacher candidates then meet in their respective groups outside class time to refine their activities and develop the visuals that will accompany their presentations. Examples of sensitization activities that were designed in a recent semester have included a demonstration of teacher-learner dynamics through a hands-on DNA analysis activity conducted first by a "renowned yet impatient professor" and then subsequently by a teacher who is "sensitive to the learners' lack of background knowledge and discipline-specific vocabulary." Other examples included mini-lessons taught in a foreign language to demonstrate multiple modalities and diverse instructional practices such as: (a) how to teach body parts through song (Chinese); (b) how to decipher written and pictorial clues (Chinese); (c) how to teach counting through dance (Greek); (d) how body language aids student comprehension (Turkish), and (e) how visual aids enhance student learning (Japanese).[2] The richness and diversity of approaches used in these simulated activities have illustrated the impact of constructivist contexts that invite students to engage in open-ended tasks and explore such issues as teacher-student relations and instructional practices.

Teacher candidates across the three disciplines have reflected on these activities, demonstrating the positive value of the collaborative experience and their awareness of the professional growth that has occurred. The following samples of TESOL teacher candidates' reflections include their thoughts on the challenges involved in creating effective activities and the impact of the pedagogical approaches selected on both the "teachers" and the "learners."

TESOL Teacher Candidates' Reflections on the Collaborative Experience

- Before this collaboration, I had never consciously thought about my future ESL students "on the other side" in their other classes. This whole experience has opened my eyes to the necessity of working hand-in-hand with the other subject teachers.
- This collaboration taught me many things both expected and unexpected. Initially, I was filled with frustration in trying to create (an activity); then exuberance when my idea struck.
- In the sensitization activity there was participation on both sides—the "teachers," meaning the students of "Methods," and the "students," meaning the mainstream students; thus both groups were learning through doing something that is much more memorable and has a significantly longer-lasting effect than passive reception of information.
- Some of the lessons, though 100 percent in another language, were very interesting and motivating . . . there was a lot of movement

---

[2] Similar activities have been demonstrated in Arabic, French, German, Haitian Creole, Hebrew, Hindi, Italian, Korean, Polish, Russian, and American Sign Language.

. . . hand gesture and body talk . . . dance and song. . . . I was able to see more participation in these activities.

- Each activity excited the senses and evoked emotions. These short sessions had so much power within them (I mean deep insights) . . . I think that all of us will remember them for a long time.
- I have never participated in anything like that. Preparing and presenting the activities was a challenging and a creative task for us. By sensitizing teacher candidates, we sensitized ourselves as well and gained an even deeper understanding.

Mainstream teacher candidates have also evaluated these activities as extremely valuable. The experiential activities helped them to develop insights into ESL learners and effective pedagogical practices and, as a consequence, alter their teaching practices. A sample of their reflections is included in the following list.

Science and Social Studies Teacher Candidates' Reflections on the Collaborative Experience

Insights into ESL Learners
- All the groups giving lessons were very patient, caring, and repetitive when necessary, but the fact was that I could not perform to the level at which I was used to performing. This could have devastating effects on an ESL student, especially one used to doing well at school. This will help me be more patient and caring toward any ESL students I may have.
- It is often thought of people who have trouble with a certain language that they are stupid or incapable of learning. . . . It was educational for me in that it illustrated the fact that it is often the case of misunderstood vocabulary and language comprehension that is the biggest deterrent to learning for most ESL students and not an inherent inability to learn.
- This leads me to the understanding that ESL students need to be reaffirmed in their ability to learn. Some may need to break out of a pattern and a burden of successive failures brought about by incorrect teaching methods.

Insights into Effective Pedagogy
- The sensitivity exercises we experienced were very valuable learning. First, I was able to experience firsthand something that ESL students who I may someday be teaching will be experiencing on a daily basis. . . . The second thing that I learned was that it must be very difficult to put together lesson plans that can effectively teach content to ESL students. . . . The last thing I learned was that it is possible to teach creatively in a nonverbal environment.

Several of the activities we participated in showed that language is not necessary to teach and that physical activities and visual stimulation can be used to effectively teach in an ESL environment.

- I learned firsthand the difference of a lesson presented via diagrams on an overhead projector and a lesson which incorporated hands-on demonstrations which invited the student to physically participate. . . . I was motivated to be involved and got the feeling that I could learn about this topic and would research it further on my own outside of class.

- Content must be broken down, basic terms must be defined, and concepts reinforced to insure the necessary level of understanding. I am surprised how well I learned these lessons and so enjoyably. Their effectiveness has had a strong impact upon me.

In addition to these reflections, mainstream teacher candidates responded to questionnaires on how they would modify their lessons as a result of the sensitization experience. In their responses, they indicated they would make abundant use of visual and tactile modes to enhance their lessons. For example, they said they would use more diagrams, pictures, models, hands-on activities, special signs, and body language. They would also repeat more often, provide wait time and individualized attention, and exhibit a positive attitude and patience. Mainstream teacher candidates stated that their students would learn about ESL students' culture and that they would pair up students to foster peer support and greater understanding. Science teacher candidates underscored the importance of giving clear instructions and translating materials for ESL students regarding safety and proper use of equipment.

DEVELOPING INTERACTIVE SCIENCE ACTIVITIES

In the Stony Brook project, the collaboration with science teacher candidates includes the design of hands-on science activities for elementary school children. The experience offers teacher candidates fieldwork opportunities to implement these activities off-campus in ESL and bilingual programs in local elementary schools.

A constructivist approach for creating new activities is modeled for the teacher candidates. For example, a recent activity entitled "Bread Bread Everywhere" was co-designed by teacher educators from both programs for TESOL and science teacher candidates who worked collaboratively in small groups. Each group was given a basket of assorted bread types: Italian, French, pumpernickel, wheat, rye, walnut raisin, multi-grain, as well as bagels and challah. Some of the bread was sliced into square, round, triangular, and oval slices. To stimulate exploration and hands-on inquiry, a toaster, balance scales, a magnifying glass, and measuring tapes were also provided. The task required the teacher candidates to design an interdisciplinary activity using bread as their organizing theme. The lively discussions initially explored ESL and mainstream curriculum issues and the needs of ESL students in mainstream classrooms. Group deliberation subsequently focused on developing activities that included: (a) exploring measurements of diameter and circumference using the bread; (b) having fun with fractions by cutting the bread into halves and quarters and recombining the resulting shapes into new wholes; (c) measuring the amount of water in bread through weighing the bread, toasting it, and weighing it again; (d) measuring the volume by water displacement; (e) calculating the bread's density; and (f) using iodine to test for starch. Teacher candidates also explored the role of bread as a dietary staple in different parts of the globe and studied its use in religious and cultural rituals. They experimented with different methods of bread preparation, such as cooking, baking, and boiling, and graphed the edibility of each kind of bread in relation to the preparation method used.

As they engaged in these activities, the teacher candidates explored ways to enhance the students' language development while advancing scientific knowledge. In order to increase vocabulary enrichment and promote comprehension and production skills, listening, speaking, reading, and writing activities were integrated during all phases—data gathering, sharing observations, making classifications, formulating ideas and hypotheses, making generalizations, making critical judgments and evaluations, drawing conclusions, and presenting results. Oral versus written modes of presenting information were investigated from a variety of perspectives. Students experimented with lists, outlines, recipes, reports, journals, graphic presentation of the data, tables, figures, and charts, and the design of three-dimensional models. Using this collaborative exploration as a model, teacher candidates next developed additional activities for use on campus in the university's elementary teacher lab, Discover Lab.

EXPLORING SCIENCE WITH CHILDREN

> *I discovered . . . that you don't have to be a scientist to make discoveries and inventions. But if you do, I guess you are a scientist.*
>
> *Fifth grade student*

Discover Lab was originally established to bring elementary school children and their teachers to the university to explore science through hands-on activities. Today, Discover Lab is an experiential learning environment where teacher candidates across the disciplines participate in developing learning activities to help children explore scientific phenomena.

The activities for Discover Lab are developed around central themes such as "the interaction of world populations," "machines in our lives," "food for different life forms," and "human physiology." The theme "keeping our planet in balance," for example, has engaged children in a variety of activities such as the exploration of environmentally friendly agents like sand, chalk, oil, vinegar, lemon, toothpaste, and baking soda in search of a recipe for a new cleanser. The children "invent" the new product and test its effectiveness for cleaning brass, iron, and copper and for removing crayon and chocolate stains. The theme has also engaged children in the production of recycled paper, the exploration of erosion and the technology involved in constructing jetties, and the investigation of how polar bears can survive in cold climates and how humans can keep themselves warm.

The lab setting provides new challenges for the teacher candidates as well as for the children. Teacher candidates explore their own role as teachers while they examine how the children discover new scientific phenomena and generate new understandings. They learn to refrain from making explanations while facilitating discovery, observation, note taking, and reflection. Interaction with the children offers teacher candidates a unique opportunity to gain insight into the children's construction of knowledge as they make sense of the new phenomena. In this environment, both teacher candidates and children are researchers making observations, collecting data, and formulating and testing new hypotheses.

The children's experience is extended as they are empowered to become guides and co-planners of future Discover Lab activities. They summarize their thoughts in post–Discover Lab questionnaires compiled jointly by the teacher educators and teacher candidates. The children's written reflections, their choice of language and metaphors to describe the experience, and their suggestions for future activities offer teacher candidates a window into the children's perception of the experience, the questions it generated in their minds, the new knowledge they have constructed, and the quest for further learning that it has stimulated. Such input is invaluable for teacher candidates as they further explore the processes of integrated language and content instruction and search for new ideas for language-enhanced, content-rich, child-friendly activities. Figure 14.2 on page 186 includes a sample of the children's responses to the post-lab questionnaires.

CONCLUSION

> *What I have learned is that working in such a manner has allowed this sort of dynamic synthesis to take place. This class is light-years away from the standard way of teaching we are all (at least myself) used to. This collaboration forced us to bring together all the elements from readings, lectures, group brainstorming, and thinking, and this is what is so energizing.*
> *TESOL teacher candidate*

The collaborative learning environment at Stony Brook has engaged teacher candidates from TESOL, science, and social studies in interdisciplinary exploration, generating new paradigms for them to emulate. The simulations the TESOL

We hope that you enjoyed your visit to the Discover Lab. Other groups will be visiting us too, and we would like your help to make their visit most memorable. Thank you.

1. **What have you discovered from the activities you did today? How did you make this discovery?**
   - I discovered that you can make paper without cutting down trees. You can take a piece of paper that is also drawn on, then wet it, mix it in a blender then squize the water out, put it in a bottle with a screen then iron it. (third-grader)
   - I discovered that a polar bear blubber is like vasoline. (fifth-grader)
   - I discovered how to make a new detergent. I discovered it by experimenting. (fifth-grader)

2. **Choose one activity that you particularly enjoyed. Describe it for the next group.**
   - The houses on the beach: you take popcicle stics and blocks of wood and try to keep the houses on the sand bars from sinking into the water. (third-grader)
   - I chose the activity where you had to get crayon out of the cloth. It was cool how you could try anything you wanted and nobody can stop you. (fifth-grader)
   - I enjoyed every station but I particularly liked the polar bear activity. You first learn how humans and polar bears keep warm and cold. The best part was stepping on the "stepper." (fifth-grader)

3. **What three questions do you think students in the next group will ask while doing the activity?**
   - Will the currents go to the ocean or the same direction? Will the water soak through the sand and slowly sink the houses? Will the water clog up into an area and flood over the wood? (third-grader)
   - How does the polar bear get so much blubber? If polar bears have blubber why don't humans have blubber? why can't polar bears live in the desert or jungle? (fifth-grader)
   - How can sand be a good cleaner? Can you write on the paper we made? How come producers of toxic chemicals cannot change them to safe products as an eleven-year-old can make? (fifth grader)

4. **If you were to design another activity for the exhibit on Keeping Our Planet in Balance, what would it be?**
   - You could take some water, add some food coloring then freeze it a little so it turns hard to make paints. (third-grader)
   - Dump oil into a pan of water and ask the students to use different supplies to try to clean up the spill. (fifth-grader)
   - If I could I might design a mini recycling center sort of like the size of a dollhouse. then you would supply different materials. The kids would try to recycle them and the materials would either be taken or rejected. (fifth-grader)

FIGURE 14.2 Insights into children's discoveries

(Note: The children's writing samples are unedited.)

teacher candidates create to sensitize their mainstream peers, the hands-on activities and lessons all teacher candidates develop collaboratively for the learning of language and disciplinary concepts, and the fieldwork both parties experience greatly contribute to their professional growth in ways that are unique to each individual. The teacher candidates' reflections engage them in a synthesis of experiences and in the construction of new knowledge on their journey to becoming teachers. At the same time, these reflections provide a window for teacher educators into the construction of new understandings by novice teachers and their acceptance of new collaborative paradigms to integrate language and disciplinary content for linguistically diverse classrooms.

chapter **15**

Creating Content-Based Language Tests: Guidelines for Teachers[1]

Jean Turner

The responsibility for developing tests to measure students' progress in their ESL classes usually falls to their teachers. Commercial tests, such as those that accompany textbooks, are occasionally available and appropriate, but often ESL teachers find themselves alone on a dark and dreary night, writing tests to be given the following day. This is a frustrating task; the other demands of teaching often seem much more urgent, and few teachers have received training in writing tests. In content-based language instruction (CBI), where the characteristics of the content and the content instruction determine to some extent the nature of the language instruction, developing suitable tests of student progress can be even more frustrating and complex. For example, teachers doing theme-based language instruction find that they must create a new test for each topic. The tests a teacher creates for a class centered on a particular current event, such as the reunification of Germany, are not going to work for classes that are centered on different issues. In sheltered and adjunct language programs, in which the content is taught by a content expert rather than by the language teacher, there are even greater demands on the teacher developing the language tests.

The test-development guidelines presented here serve several purposes. Their most immediate purpose is to outline the relatively simple steps that test writers should follow to create consistent tests that truly measure the extent to which students learned what they were taught. However, careful execution of the outlined steps produces more than consistent, appropriate tests; the test-development process also promotes more integrated, effective instruction because the guideline activities require the language teacher to consider both language and content objectives, or—in the case in which language and content

---

[1] This article originally appeared in *The CATESOL Journal, 1992, 5*(1). Reprinted with permission.

teachers work together—they require the cooperation of the team members to clarify the purposes of their CBI program. A broader benefit is that the results of tests developed for different classes or programs can be compared with reference to how the guideline activities were executed. This allows language educators to begin to form answers to important questions such as which content areas and classes lend themselves most effectively to CBI programs. It also allows teachers to make judgments regarding the effectiveness of a particular CBI program compared with other CBI programs or other types of language instruction.

OVERVIEW OF THE GUIDELINES

The guidelines are a condensed version of the context-adaptive model for developing language achievement tests for CBI language programs (Turner, 1991). The model and the guidelines are adaptive in that the manner in which the stages are completed and the nature of the tests that are written are determined by

FIGURE 15.1   Context-adaptive model for developing measures of language achievement

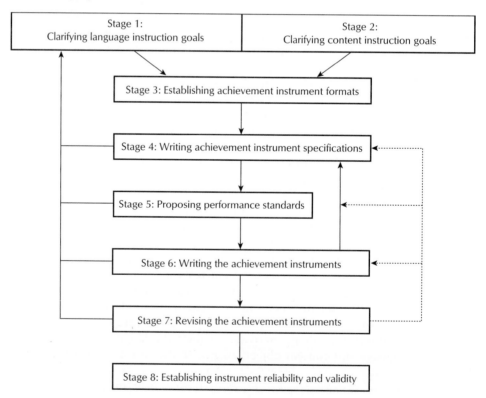

the characteristics of the class or program for which the tests are developed. The guidelines reflect sheltered- and adjunct-model CBI designs but can be used in the development of tests for theme-based programs as well.

The eight stages and the iterative nature of the test-writing process are summarized in Figure 15.1. The proximity of Stages 1 and 2 in the figure represent the high degree of cooperation that is required in CBI programs in which there are both language and content experts. The solid lines and arrows connecting Stages 3, 4, 5, 6, and 7 allow, if necessary, a return to Stage 1 for clarification of the instructional purposes of a program and repetition of stages which follow. The dotted lines and arrows indicate that revision of a test includes revision of the specifications and, possibly, revision of the performance standards. A detailed, illustrative discussion of each stage follows.

THE EIGHT TEST-DEVELOPMENT STAGES

Because tests created through this process are based on specifications derived from the instructional purposes of a particular class, it is critical that the purposes of the language and content components be clear. It is also critical that the purposes be understood and agreed on by all participants. Stages 1 and 2, summarized in Figure 15.2, guide clarification of the instructional purposes. These stages may initially seem unnecessary to teachers/test writers—they already know what they want their students to learn. However, other participants in the program might have different notions of the instructional purposes. The procedures included in these two stages provide an important check of these various perspectives, revealing misunderstandings or ambiguities that should be resolved. The procedures also establish a channel of communication among the

FIGURE 15.2 Diagram of Stages 1 and 2 procedures for clarifying instructional purposes

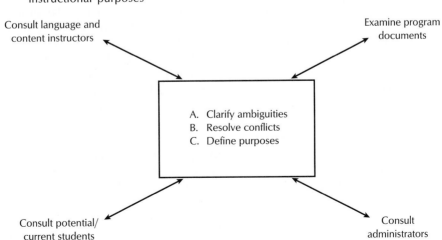

Consult language and content instructors

Examine program documents

A. Clarify ambiguities
B. Resolve conflicts
C. Define purposes

Consult potential/current students

Consult administrators

information sources, allowing negotiation of a consensus regarding the instructional goals. The two-directional arrows in Figure 15.2 represent this interactional quality of the guidelines.

The teachers in a CBI program are perhaps the most important source of information regarding the instructional purposes of a program and should certainly be consulted to resolve any discrepancies among the information sources. As shown in Figure 15.2, other sources include program documentation, such as the curriculum, class descriptions, instructional materials, and existing tests. Program administrators are consulted to confirm their understanding of the purpose of the program. Students' impressions of the instructional purposes also represent an integral component in the process of clarifying the purposes and negotiating a consensus. When students' understanding of the purpose of a CBI program is different from that of the teachers, problems arise. Consider the frustration and confusion that would develop among students who believed they were studying to improve their conversational skills when the course tests reflected their teachers' belief that the purpose was to improve academic reading and writing. Reaching a consensus regarding the instructional purposes requires an exchange of information among the various sources and often results in some sort of adjustment in one or more of them. On a program level, this might involve teacher training, student orientation, or modification of program documents.

Stage 3 guidelines direct the teacher/test writer's decisions regarding what the tests will look like; for example, they might involve multiple-choice items, writing an essay, or less traditional tasks such as structured story telling or problem solving. To complete Stage 3, the teacher/test writer compares the clarified instructional purposes for the language and content components and reviews any content tests. (This process is simpler in theme-based CBI programs in which the content is usually taught by the language teacher.) Stage 3 is especially important in sheltered- and adjunct-model programs because the premises on which these CBI approaches are based include the notion that language instruction should reflect the learner's eventual uses for the language. Students in these kinds of classes have immediate use for language; thus, it makes sense for the language tests to mirror, to whatever extent possible, the format of the tests used in the content class.

The teacher/test writer must keep in mind, however, that the format of the content class tests cannot simply be copied over into tests for the language class. For example, if the focus of instruction for a particular adjunct language class is improvement of expository writing and the exams for the adjunct content class are multiple-choice, it makes no sense to write multiple-choice language tests. Instead, the situation calls for language tests which require the students to demonstrate their improved ability to produce expository writing. Figure 15.3 summarizes the procedures that teacher/test writers perform to define the best formats for their CBI language tests.

At Stage 4, test plans (specifications) for the language tests are prepared. Writing specifications involves a little more work for the teacher/test writer than simply writing tests, but having specifications to serve as a guide can help a

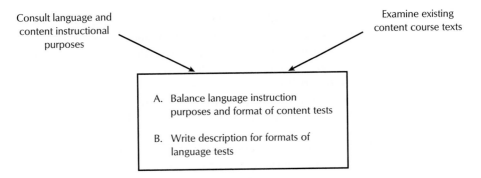

FIGURE 15.3   Diagram of Stage 3 procedures for establishing the test formats

test writer stay on track. Specifications act as blueprints; having them means that the teacher/test writer does not have to invent or reinvent each test activity, but can simply refer to the carefully developed, clearly articulated plan. Specifications also can be used more than once; for example, they might be used to guide the development of additional forms of a particular test.

Specifications have four components (Popham, 1978, 1981):

1. a *general description* of the skill(s) that the test will measure
2. a *passage description* that shows what the text or passage the questions are based on will look like
3. an *example question* or *example task* that shows what the test questions will look like and how the students will answer
4. a *scoring procedure description* that specifies the characteristics of acceptable and unacceptable responses.

The test specifications developed by Macdonald (1991) to determine whether ESL students were ready to participate in a sheltered high school science class are presented next to demonstrate what these four components might actually look like. (See the Appendix at the end of the chapter for the complete test developed by Macdonald.)

1. *General description:* The purpose of this test is diagnostic, that is, to determine if students are capable of participating in the sheltered science class. It measures the students' ability to read and write. It is based on observation of activities that are conducted in the sheltered science class.

- The student should be able to read the passage and demonstrate recognition of the main ideas.
- The student should demonstrate the ability to apply the main ideas to information not specifically given in the text.
- The student should be able to understand vocabulary from the context.

- The student should be able to write a one-paragraph essay that is organized, addresses the topic given, and follows basic rules of capitalization and punctuation, and, although it may contain some errors, they should not interfere with meaning.

2. *Passage description:* (The source for the test passage is a science lesson presented by the science teacher.) The criteria for the passage are as follows:

- The passage should contain all the information that the student needs in order to complete the test, even if the student has no previous knowledge of the topic of the passage.
- The topic of the passage should be a topic that ESL students actually study in the sheltered science class.
- The passage may contain detailed, scientific information, but this information should be explained and paraphrased using terms that the students are likely to understand.

3. *Questions and tasks:* There are four types of items on the test: labeling, matching, vocabulary, and essay. (See the Appendix at the end of this chapter. Test questions 1 through 4, respectively, represent labeling, matching, vocabulary, and essay.)

4. *Scoring procedure descriptions:*

- *Type 1 (labeling) items:* Objectively scored (right or wrong) based on an answer key.
- *Type 2 (matching) items:* Objectively scored (right or wrong) based on an answer key.
- *Type 3 (vocabulary) items:* Objectively scored (right or wrong) based on an answer key. Spelling and word form must be accurate to be considered correct.
- *Type 4 (essay) items:* Subjectively scored using a holistic approach. The essays should be read twice and rated holistically for: grammar (5 points); vocabulary (5 points); mechanics (5 points); and content (5 points). Students receive one point for following the instructions and attempting to respond to the essay.

Like all tests, careful review might reveal areas that could be improved; thus, Macdonald's test specifications (and test) are included here not as a model for developing CBI tests, but as an example of how an individual teacher/test writer applied the test-development methodology presented here to create an appropriate, context-specific test. A teacher/test writer developing tests for a different type of content-based class or a different purpose (e.g., an achievement test versus a diagnostic test) might create tests quite different from the one developed

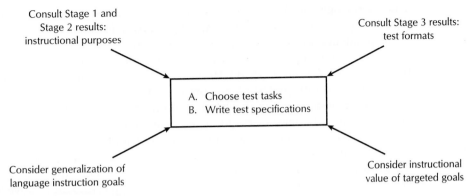

FIGURE 15.4 Diagram of Stage 4 procedures for writing the test specifications

by Macdonald. Figure 15.4 summarizes the main steps a teacher/test writer should follow in writing specifications for a test.

As indicated in Figure 15.4, the clarified instructional purposes for the language and content components of a given program should be held in mind when writing test specifications. In addition, the teacher/test writer must consider the generalizability of potential test tasks. For example, if a teacher wanted to measure students' improvement in expository writing, measuring their ability to write isolated sentences would be inadequate. Although the formation of individual sentences is a component of expository writing, it cannot be assumed that students who write acceptable sentences can also write acceptable paragraphs.

In addition to the generalizability of tasks, the teacher/test writer must consider the instructional value of tasks (Popham, 1981). Test plans should specify tasks that both the teacher and the students understand and perceive to be important. It is also critical that the teacher and students understand and agree on the characteristics of successful accomplishment of the tasks. The students should know what successful completion of the tasks looks like (or sounds like) even if they are not yet able to produce acceptable renditions. When writing test specifications, both the generalizability and instructional value of potential tasks are weighed with the results of Stage 3 in mind, in which the format of the tests is determined.

At Stage 5, how students' test performance will be interpreted is decided. This is known as proposing or setting a performance standard. The procedures at Stage 5 help the teacher/test writer answer questions such as:

1. When tests yield numerical scores, what do particular scores mean? For example, is 85% correct a passing grade?
2. When letter grades are awarded, what is the correspondence between numerical scores and the letter grades that are given? For example, is 85% an A, a B, or a C?

When tests yield profiles or other nonnumerical assessments and translation into letter grades is necessary, Stage 5 activities also help the teacher determine the correspondence between the profiles and letter grades.

Many teachers postpone setting a performance standard for a test until after they see how their students do. However, if one waits until after tests are given to plan how to interpret students' performance, the purpose for giving the test might be subverted. Using the labeling section of Macdonald's test to illustrate (see Appendix), the teacher might decide that students must answer all four items correctly to demonstrate an acceptable level of understanding of the main idea of the passage. That is, the students should be able to perform this task perfectly if they are to be considered able to read and understand the main idea of the class texts. If the teacher finds that not one of her students answers all four correctly, it may be that none is ready for the sheltered science class. Lowering performance standards after giving the test would not change the science teacher's expectations for the students, but would give the false impression that the students have the ability to understand the main idea of science texts.

Figure 15.5 displays the procedures that should be used to determine performance standards. Deciding what performance characteristics or numerical score indicates an acceptable performance depends not only on the instructional goals of a particular language class, but also on what students are expected to be able to do in subsequent language classes or language-use situations. This is true from the entry-level perspective as well. When defining what students should be able to do as they progress through a course, it is important to have a clear understanding of what they can do as they enter it. Consequently, important steps in defining the performance standard for a test include determination of students' skills as they enter the class (usually through examining students' scores on whatever screening or placement test is used) and consideration of the language instruction goals and of students' language needs in situations for which the language class prepares them. Of course, the performance

FIGURE 15.5   Diagram of Stage 5 procedures for proposing performance standards

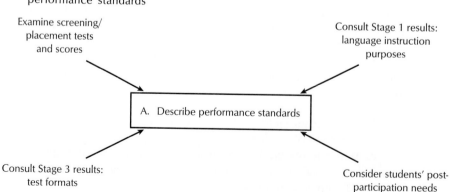

standard should reflect the format that was determined in earlier stages to be most appropriate for the particular CBI context in which the tests will be used.

The sixth stage of the guidelines (Figure 15.6) includes not only writing the test but also revising it. The results of either pilot testing or a critical review can guide revision. Pilot testing is the best way to collect information for revising a test. This procedure provides evidence to determine if the test instructions and tasks are clear enough, if the administration time is adequate, and if students actually interpret the items and tasks as the test writers intended. On objectively scored tests, item statistics such as *item difficulty* and *item discrimination* can easily be calculated. Finding a suitable group of subjects may be difficult, but the information the process supplies makes the effort worthwhile.

Sometimes, however, pilot testing is simply not feasible. In these situations, the teacher/test writer should conduct especially thorough pre-administration test review and revision. Ideally, a test should be reviewed by a language teacher (other than the test writer) who is familiar with the particular situation for which the test is developed. Very often, colleagues are willing to exchange review responsibilities. When this is not possible, the test writer should review the test after allowing several days of objective distance to transpire. The reviewer should examine the items or tasks, making sure they are appropriate and clear. The directions should be reviewed to be certain that they accurately delineate what the students have to do. Obviously, both pilot testing and test review require that the dark and dreary test-writing nights occur several days before the test administration date.

Stage 7, revising the tests, is performed after the tests are given and before scores are calculated or performance reports prepared. Despite the careful development procedures and the review process, there might be items or tasks which simply do not work—items or tasks that are confusing, ambiguous, or flawed in some other way. If problematic items or tasks are identified, they should be eliminated. The results of those items or tasks should not contribute to students' scores or performance profiles. Although this means that the number of items or points might be changed from the original plan, it is only fair that students' test performance be assessed on the basis of good items rather than

FIGURE 15.6 Diagram of Stage 6 procedures for writing the tests

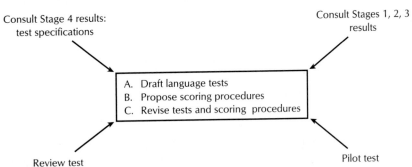

Consult Stage 4 results:
test specifications

Consult Stages 1, 2, 3
results

A. Draft language tests
B. Propose scoring procedures
C. Revise tests and scoring procedures

Review test

Pilot test

poor ones. Sometimes this results in an unexpected number of items—for example, a test that was intended to have 100 points might end up with 99 or 98. However, teachers who are troubled by a feeling of lost symmetry should be consoled by the fact that they have actually created more accurate measures of their students' abilities by eliminating poor items before calculating test scores.

Stage 8, the final stage of the guidelines, directs the teacher/test writer's efforts to determine the reliability and validity of the new test. An important consideration in this process is whether the test or test sections are objectively or subjectively scored. Objectively scored items are those which have only one correct response. In the matching section of Macdonald's test, for example, "dancing" can only be matched with "cerebellum," so one can say that this section is objectively scored. The essay, on the other hand, is subjectively scored. There is more than one correct answer—in fact, any individual's essay might be awarded the full 20 points even though each essay might be quite different. Both approaches to scoring are equally valuable although they are useful for different types of tasks.

Establishing the reliability of the scoring procedure is especially important for tests that are subjectively scored. One way to do this might be to ask the colleague who reviewed the test before it was given to score the tests as well. A correlation between the teacher/test writer's scores and the reviewer's scores establishes *interrater reliability,* an estimate of the consistency of scoring procedure across different scores. Another way that consistency can be examined is to estimate *intrarater reliability.* To do this, the teacher/test writer scores the entire set of tests once, then scores them again perhaps the next day without consulting the first rating. While the teacher/test writer might not find perfect agreement between the first and second ratings (a correlation of 1.00), the scoring procedure should be clear enough to yield a high degree of consistency. Intrarater reliability lower than approximately .80 indicates that there is a serious problem with the consistency of the teacher/test writer's scores. The scoring procedure should therefore be modified to improve the consistency before reporting the students' scores.

Stage 8 also outlines steps to ensure the *validity* of a test; that is, whether it measures what it is intended to measure and measures it comprehensively. Expert review is one manner in which the validity of a test is estimated. The same reviewer who examined the test directions and content can be asked to make judgments regarding the appropriateness of the test content and the extent to which the test measures enough of whatever concept or skill it is designed to assess. For example, Macdonald indicates in her specifications that the test is intended to measure students' recognition of the main ideas in a reading passage. Does the first section of the test, the labeling task, require students to have understood the main idea of the passage (the name, position, and function of the four main parts of the central nervous system)? Not really, since the students do not need to understand the function of the parts to find and label them correctly. If this were the only task on the test, the test's validity would be weak. Even though the labeling task might require recognition of these four important parts and their location in the central nervous system, in terms of comprehensiveness the test would fall short because it does not measure the students' understanding of the function of these parts. Inclusion of the second (matching) and fourth (essay) tasks increases the validity of the test with regard to its comprehensiveness. These tasks require the students to demonstrate their understanding of the function of the various parts of the brain as well as their location and labels.

CONCLUSION

Writing appropriate content-based language tests that are reliable and valid demands a commitment of time and care. The guidelines outlined in this chapter are not a shortcut to test writing—they do not produce instant tests. Teachers who follow the guidelines will devote long hours to creating their tests, just as they did before using the guidelines. However, they will feel a greater sense of confidence in their tests' appropriateness, reliability, and validity as well as in the extent to which the tests measure their students' progress in both language and content mastery.

Appendix

Sample Content-Based Language Test

Instructions: Read the following passage carefully. As you read, you may want to make notes or circle important information. When you have finished reading, you may begin the test. During the test, you should feel free to go back and reread the passage. Most of the information that you will need to answer the questions is in the passage itself.

THE CENTRAL NERVOUS SYSTEM

The central nervous system controls the human body. It's like the captain of a ship. Our brain is part of the central nervous system. It directs and controls everything that the human body does. There are four parts of the central nervous system: (a) the cerebrum, (b) the cerebellum, (c) the medulla, and (d) the spinal cord. The cerebrum, the cerebellum, and the medulla are all located in the brain. The spinal cord goes from the base of the brain down one's back. All of the different parts of the central nervous system have different functions.

The cerebrum is the largest part of the brain. It is the part of the brain that controls the senses, that is, seeing, hearing, feeling, tasting, and touching. It controls thinking and memory. People with good memories can remember many things. It also controls voluntary movement. Voluntary movement is movement that you choose to make. It is movement that you can control. Walking and talking are examples of voluntary movement.

The cerebellum is located at the base of the cerebrum. It controls our sense of balance. If we didn't have balance, we would fall down. The cerebellum also controls coordination. Coordination is the ability to have all the different parts of one's body move and work together. Dancers and athletes, for example, must have good coordination.

The medulla controls involuntary movement. It is found in between the cerebellum and the spinal cord. It controls things that your body does without thinking. For example, it controls how you breathe, how your heart beats, and when you blink your eyes.

The spinal cord is the part of the central nervous system which carries information and messages to and from the brain. The spinal cord goes from the base of the neck, down the back. It is like a telephone wire. The messages and information that it carries are called impulses. These impulses must go through the spinal cord in order to get to the brain. The brain is able to send messages back to the body. These messages from the brain also must go through the spinal cord. If messages cannot go through the spinal cord, then the person is paralyzed. Often people who are paralyzed cannot move or talk.

INSTRUCTIONS:

1. Using the diagram below, label the four major parts of the central nervous system.

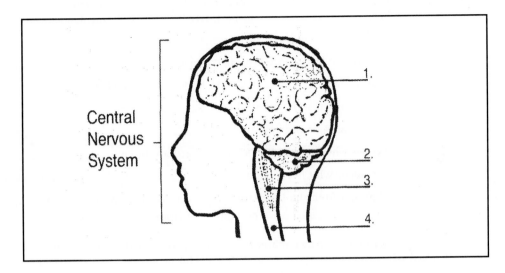

2. Draw a line from each part of the central nervous system to the activities that it controls.

Central Nervous System Part	*Activity*
Example:	Walking
	a. Talking
Cerebrum	b. Feeling cold
	c. Breathing
Cerebellum	d. Dancing
	e. Solving a math problem
Medulla	f. Sweating
	g. Telling a story
Spinal cord	h. Carrying impulses

3. Complete the following sentences using the most correct vocabulary word (and form) from the list.

voluntary	to control	memory
coordination	to be located	involuntary
paralyzed		

a. In order to play sports, you need good _____.

b. The medulla _____ in between the cerebellum and the spinal cord.

c. Movements that you control are _____.

d. Coughing is an example of _____ movement.

e. People whose spinal cords are damaged are often _____.

f. A student who has a good _____ usually gets good grades.

g. Messages from the brain are carried through the spinal cord and _____ _____ the body's activities.

4. Write a one-paragraph essay explaining what parts of the brain are most important when you are playing a sport. You may choose any sport—soccer, tennis, swimming, basketball, football, and so forth.

chapter **16**

Issues in Assessment for Content-Based Instruction[1]

Sara Cushing Weigle and Linda Jensen

Assessment is an integral component of any instructional program; in content-based instruction (CBI), assessment plays an essential role both for making decisions about individual students and for evaluating the effectiveness of the program. Brinton, Snow, and Wesche (1989) present an overview of issues in content-based assessment (CBA), especially regarding the relationship between language and content, and Turner (Chapter 15 in this volume) describes a process of test development that is particularly suited to CBA. In this chapter, we expand on the ideas presented in these two works by considering test development from the perspective of test usefulness, a framework developed by Bachman and Palmer (1996) that considers usefulness as the optimum combination of six different qualities (reliability, construct validity, authenticity, interactiveness, impact, and practicality) for a given situation. As a concrete application of this framework, we then present a sample content-based achievement test designed for the university setting.

GENERAL CONSIDERATIONS OF CBA: LANGUAGE AND CONTENT ISSUES

While the various models of CBI are all based on the premise that language is best learned through active involvement with content, they differ in their primary focus and in the relative importance of language versus content mastery. The most frequently used model of CBI is theme-based language courses, in which language input is organized around a single topic or theme (e.g., marriage and the family, computers, or advertising). In this model, which is common at all

---

[1] We would like to thank James Purpura for his assistance in the conceptual stages of this chapter.

levels of language instruction, language acquisition is the primary focus of instruction and the content serves as a vehicle for the language rather than as a learning objective in its own right. The focus of evaluation in theme-based courses is language skills and functions rather than mastery of the content material.

In sheltered content instruction, which is most common at the primary and secondary levels, the predominant focus of instruction is content, and teachers adapt their language to the needs of the second language students. Language learning is seen as an important by-product of instruction but is not the main goal. Evaluation in this model generally focuses on content, with little emphasis on accurate language.

In adjunct courses, students attend both a content course intended for native speakers and a language course intended to assist nonnative speakers in mastering the academic language and study skills necessary for success in the content course. This model has mainly been used at the university level (see Wegrzecka-Kowalewski, Chapter 24 in this volume, for an example at the high school level). In the adjunct model both language acquisition and content mastery are objectives, and assessment often focuses equally on language and content.

The different emphases on language and content in the three models of CBI, summarized in Figure 16.1, have important implications for the design and selection of appropriate testing procedures. The primary consideration is, of course, that the instructional emphasis be reflected in the focus of assessment, so that, for example, a course whose primary goal is language acquisition should not test mainly content knowledge. Beyond this basic premise, however, it is important to consider the interaction of language and content in all three models of CBI and to avoid testing procedures that are biased because of content or language issues. Assessment methods intended to focus on language should not require specific content knowledge, and assessment methods focusing on content should avoid penalizing students whose language abilities prevent them from displaying their full knowledge of content.

In CBA, the relationship between language and content must be clearly defined beforehand and kept in mind while the test tasks are being designed. For a theme-based course where assessment focuses on language rather than content, any content knowledge required by test items must be accessible to test takers either in the test itself or via an open-book format. In a sheltered program, test tasks should be designed to allow students to display their knowledge of the content even if their language skills are limited. In adjunct courses, if it is not feasible to test language and content separately, different scoring criteria can be used for assessing language and content using the same test tasks.

	Language	Content
Theme-based	✔	
Sheltered		✔
Adjunct	✔	✔

FIGURE 16.1 Primary focus of instruction in three models of CBI

TEST USEFULNESS

We now turn to a discussion of the qualities of test usefulness according to the Bachman and Palmer framework: reliability, construct validity, authenticity, interactiveness, impact, and practicality. Bachman and Palmer (1996, p. 18) present three guiding principles for considering the qualities of usefulness in test construction and selection:

> *Principle 1:* It is the overall usefulness of the test that is to be maximized, rather than the individual qualities that affect usefulness.
>
> *Principle 2:* The individual test qualities cannot be evaluated independently, but must be evaluated in terms of their combined effect on the overall usefulness of the test.
>
> *Principle 3:* Test usefulness and the appropriate balance among the different qualities cannot be prescribed in general, but must be determined for each specific testing situation.

In Bachman and Palmer's view, since every assessment context is different, the relative importance of each of the six qualities of test usefulness will vary from situation to situation. Furthermore, these qualities must be determined for every context in relationship with each other and not as separate factors.

We will discuss each of these qualities and the role they play in developing content-based assessments, focusing primarily on the qualities of authenticity and interactiveness, as these qualities are of particular importance in CBA.

Reliability

Reliability refers to consistency of measurement across different occasions or forms of a test. A test is said to be reliable if individuals receive approximately the same score from one administration of the test to the next, and if a group of examinees is rank-ordered in the same way on different occasions or on different versions of the test.[2] Assessment procedures should be as reliable as possible so that the decisions based on test scores are a true reflection of student ability and not a result of inconsistencies in the testing process.

It is important to be aware of threats to reliability at all stages of test development—from defining the skills to be tested, to item writing and scoring procedures. Some of the most common causes of inconsistency are faulty item construction (i.e., confusing or ambiguous items) and/or items that do not measure the skill being assessed.

Another factor leading to unreliability in testing is inconsistency in scoring procedures. In scoring short-answer items, it is important to create a clear scoring key with examples of both appropriate and inappropriate responses and to make sure criteria for correctness are explicit. Specifically

---

[2] See Bachman (1990) for a more thorough discussion of reliability in language tests.

for CBA, the extent to which correctness is based on content or language must be clearly indicated.

When essays are used in assessment, reliability can be increased by using two raters, a detailed scoring rubric, and adequate training and practice in using the scoring rubric.

Construct Validity

Construct validity refers to "the meaningfulness and appropriateness of the *interpretations* that we make on the basis of test scores" (Bachman & Palmer, 1996, p. 21). If the test does not measure what it is intended to measure, decisions based on the test scores may not be accurate or fair.

The term *construct* is used to refer to the attribute or skill being measured by a given instrument; *construct validation,* then, refers to the process of determining whether the test is actually measuring what it is intended to measure. The process of construct validation involves considering numerous types of evidence, two of which are content coverage (the match of test content to the goals of instruction and assessment) and criterion relatedness (the match between test scores and other indicators of the ability being tested).[3] The test content should be derived from a detailed description of the ways in which language is used both in the classroom and in the real-life situations for which the class is preparing students. This description should be operationalized in detailed test specifications that describe the test content in terms of topic, language, and task (Lynch & Davidson, 1994). After the test has been administered, the criterion relatedness of the test can be investigated by comparing students' scores with other measures of the same ability: for example, teacher judgments of language ability and/or content mastery, depending on the situation.

In CBA, the balance of language/content is critical in assessing the validity of interpretations based on test scores. As discussed above, the focus of instruction must be reflected in the focus of evaluation for decisions to be fair and accurate. In particular, if the primary focus of instruction is language rather than content, the same should be true of assessment, and vice versa.

Impact

An important factor in test usefulness is the *impact* that testing procedures have, both at an individual level and at an institutional level. At the individual level, there are several categories of people who are affected by assessment, including students, teachers, and test scorers. For students, the most important effect of any assessment is the decision that is made on the basis of the test score; clearly, this decision must be as fair and accurate as possible. In addition, students' attitudes are an important consideration: The use of test tasks that are appropriate in terms of both content and level of difficulty should lead to more positive

---

[3] Bachman (1990) provides a more detailed introduction to the process of construct validation.

attitudes toward the learning and testing situation. This in turn may lower students' anxiety levels, facilitating more accurate assessment of their abilities. For teachers, tests should provide useful information for helping to make decisions about individual students and about the curriculum. Finally, the individuals involved in administering and scoring tests must be taken into account when designing test tasks. To this end, administration and scoring procedures must be clear and efficient to ensure standardization and to minimize any possible negative effects on scorers' attitudes.

At the institutional level, testing procedures can have both negative and positive effects on program and curriculum design and implementation, a phenomenon known as *washback*. Negative washback occurs when there is a mismatch between the stated goals of instruction and the focus of assessment, which leads to the abandonment of instructional goals in favor of test preparation (i.e., teaching to the test). To promote beneficial washback in CBI, test tasks should require the same authentic, interactive language use promoted in the classroom so that there is a match between what is taught and what is tested. In other words, there is no difference between teaching the curriculum and teaching to the test.

Practicality

Practicality is defined as the ratio of required resources to available resources (Bachman & Palmer, 1996). Required resources include such factors as the time and personnel required for developing, administering, and scoring tests; any duplication of test materials; space requirements for test administration; and any necessary audiovisual support. These must be balanced against the constraints of the available resources; thus, practicality can be a major limiting factor in creating an instrument that incorporates all the other aspects of test usefulness.

Practicality affects item formats in terms of both development and scoring. Multiple-choice and true/false items are easy to score but require extensive effort to develop. Conversely, short-answer or essay items are easier to develop but time-consuming to score. Generally, a test given repeatedly to large numbers of students will be more practical in the long run if it includes items that are easy to score, whereas the effort to write good multiple-choice or true/false items on classroom tests given only once to a small number of students may make that format impractical. In this case, essay or short-answer items are more efficient. Since most CBI programs are locally developed and curricula are geared to the immediate needs of the local population, practicality considerations usually favor the latter type of test item for content-based assessments.

Authenticity

Bachman and Palmer (1996) define *authenticity* as "the degree of correspondence of the characteristics of a given language test task to the features of a TLU (target language use) task" (p. 23). In other words, according to Bachman and Palmer, a task is authentic to the extent that it simulates a real-world language task. This definition is broader than traditional considerations of authenticity in terms of text (i.e., unedited texts intended for native speakers).

Traditional language tests often contain tasks that are particular to the language classroom but are inauthentic in terms of language use outside of the classroom. In CBA, authentic tasks require students to process and produce language associated with content that has been dealt with in class. This might mean (a) using a previously read passage as input for a timed composition on the exam, or (b) listening and taking notes on a lecture in class and writing a summary of the lecture from the lecture notes during the exam. These tasks simulate typical academic testing situations in which the test requires students to synthesize information from lectures or reading in a response to an essay question.

Interactiveness

Interactiveness is defined by Bachman and Palmer (1996) as "the extent and type of involvement of the test taker's individual characteristics in accomplishing a test task" (p. 25). The most relevant of these characteristics for a language test are language ability, topical knowledge, and affective or emotional responses to test tasks. Language ability, in Bachman and Palmer's framework, includes both language knowledge (knowledge of various aspects of the linguistic code) and metacognitive strategies (ability to set goals, self-assess, and plan language use). An interactive test task is one that requires test takers to use these metacognitive strategies as well as display their language knowledge. An example of such a task is writing an essay response to a reading or listening passage.

Because communicative language use always takes place within a context (i.e., it is always *about something*), tasks that are interactive must also deal with topical knowledge to some degree. For example, single-sentence grammar items are not as interactive as comprehension questions on a reading passage, since the test taker has to integrate the information from the passage with his or her background knowledge to understand the reading. Finally, a test task that engages test takers' emotions in a positive way (e.g., a reading passage that is intrinsically interesting) will be more interactive than one that has either a negative or a neutral effect on test takers. Interactiveness thus refers to the interaction between test-taker characteristics and the test tasks; the better the match, the more interactive the task.

FOCUS ON AUTHENTICITY/INTERACTIVENESS

Although all six qualities of test usefulness are important to consider in any test development effort, we believe that special consideration should be given to authenticity and interactiveness in CBA. The rationale for this emphasis is that the goal of CBI is to foster language use through purposeful engagement with content, and this goal should be reflected in assessment as well. Assessments should be authentic in that they simulate as closely as possible the actual language use situations that students will engage in outside of the language classroom. Assessments should also be interactive in that they draw on test takers' metacognitive strategies as well as their language knowledge, require test takers to integrate test content with their existing topical knowledge, and take into account test takers' emotional responses to the test tasks.

Bachman and Palmer (1996) provide illustrations of how test tasks can be categorized as high or low in terms of authenticity, and high or low in terms of interactiveness. Figure 16.2 presents a framework for analyzing tasks, depending on their degree of authenticity (high vs. low) and interactiveness (high vs. low). Included in the figure are four sample test tasks for CBA that represent the four possible combinations of authenticity/interactiveness.

As Figure 16.2 suggests, test tasks can vary in both dimensions of authenticity and interactiveness, and a grid such as this can be used to gauge the levels of each of these features for different tasks. We believe that the most appropriate test tasks for CBA are those that are high in both authenticity and interactiveness. However, these qualities must be balanced with considerations of reliability, construct validity, practicality, and impact for the test to be maximally useful for its intended purpose.

In the following section we describe a university-level assessment instrument which exemplifies both authenticity and interactiveness. This instrument is used as a final examination in an ESL program at the University of California, Los Angeles (UCLA).

FIGURE 16.2 Authenticity/interactiveness in test tasks (adapted from Bachman & Palmer, 1996, p. 27)

	Interactiveness	
Authenticity	High	Low
High	Task 1	Task 2
Low	Task 3	Task 4

Task 1:   *High authenticity/high interactiveness:* watching a videotaped lecture; taking notes; using notes to write a summary of the lecture, which will be used to study for an exam

Task 2:   *High authenticity/low interactiveness:* copying definitions from a textbook

Task 3:   *Low authenticity/high interactiveness:* oral interview on non-academic topics

Task 4:   *Low authenticity/low interactiveness:* discrete-point grammar test

A UNIVERSITY-LEVEL CONTENT-BASED
FINAL EXAM: AN EXAMPLE

The ESL Service Courses at UCLA provide language instruction for matriculated university students who are held for an ESL requirement based on their scores on the university's placement examination. There are four required ESL levels; ESL 33A, 33B, and 33C are multi-skills courses, and ESL 35 is a developmental composition course. Students may "place in" at any given level or be exempt by examination. ESL 33A, 33B, and 33C are designed as simulated adjunct courses; that is, videotapes of actual lectures and assigned readings from undergraduate courses provide the content for the ESL classes.

The final exam for ESL 33C at UCLA was designed specifically to meet the requirements of authenticity and interactiveness. Taking authenticity into account, it was decided to create a final exam that was an extension of the content of the course rather than creating a final exam on a topic that was not contextualized or that had not been studied previously in class.

The content focus for the final exam comes from the second half of the course: a unit on the First Amendment of the U.S. Constitution. Students view segments of a videotaped lecture, read related articles, and do library research for an argumentation paper.

The first step in developing the final exam was to identify a suitable listening passage. A ten-minute segment, previously unviewed, of the same videotaped lecture that the students had seen in class was identified as appropriate for the specific content of the final exam. The segment deals with the limits of free speech and the implementation of speech codes on college campuses.

Once the content was determined, a reading passage that developed the topic had to be identified. A reading from a legal journal was chosen; however, as it was extremely lengthy, a shorter excerpt of the article was edited down to approximately four pages—a length appropriate for this level and similar to other readings for the course.

After identifying the listening and reading sources (i.e., the content), the next step was to determine the language and study skills which would be assessed at the end of the course. Numerous listening comprehension, reading comprehension, and argumentative writing skills had been the focus of the previous ten weeks. Since it was impossible to test all these skills, skills were selected from the list of skill objectives taught at this level (see Figure 16.3) based on (a) their relevance to academic success, and (b) the feasibility of assessing them in a two-hour time frame. The skills tested on the ESL 33C final exam are marked with an asterisk (*) in Figure 16.3.

The ESL 33C final exam consists of three sections: listening, reading, and composition. During the last week of the term, students view a videotaped lecture segment in class, take notes, and write a brief summary of the segment. The notes and summaries are then collected and kept by the teacher until the day of the final exam. In addition, students are given the reading passage for the final to read at home and to discuss in study groups during class time. Unlike

Reading Skills

* previewing academic texts
* skimming texts to find main ideas
* scanning texts to locate specific information
  inferencing to recognize implicit information
* recognizing author's opinion/bias
* analyzing author's argument
  increasing rate and improving comprehension
  expanding vocabulary through context clues/word forms
* synthesizing reading information in writing assignments

Writing Skills

  practicing brief and extended definitions for essay questions based on readings and lectures
* writing comparison/contrast essays, cause/effect essays, and argumentation essays synthesizing information from readings and lectures
  writing a brief research paper using citations in three drafts
* editing grammar errors
* writing summaries of selections from readings and lectures

Listening Skills

  improving comprehension of academic lectures
* note taking, outlining, and summarizing of academic lectures
* synthesizing lecture information in writing assignments recognizing lecturer's register/opinion/bias

FIGURE 16.3   ESL 33C skill objectives

other reading passages encountered during the term, however, the teacher does not discuss the reading passage with the students, so that students take responsibility for understanding and synthesizing the material on their own.

On the day of the exam, the listening notes and summaries are returned to the students, who use them to answer multiple-choice comprehension questions dealing with main ideas and important details of the lecture. The purpose of this section of the exam is to evaluate students' abilities to take and use notes from a lecture. Since the exam takes place several days after the lecture is viewed in class, students must rely on their notes and summaries rather than their short-term memory to answer the comprehension questions.

For the reading comprehension section of the exam, students are given a clean copy of the reading passage and are asked to complete several open-ended comprehension tasks. These involve locating main ideas, defining the main points of view and the author's argument, defining key terms, identifying opposing points of view, and identifying solutions. These are scored for content only, without regard to language, since the focus is on reading comprehension and not language issues such as grammar and spelling.

Finally, the writing portion of the test consists of the following essay prompt, which requires students to take a position on the issue of speech codes on college campuses:

> Currently, a topic of discussion across the country among college administrators, professors, and students is the issue of speech codes on college campuses. On one side, there are those who feel that speech codes protect minorities from "fighting words" or racist and bigoted language; on the other side, there are those who feel that any type of speech code is a restriction of freedom of speech, which is protected under the First Amendment. Do colleges and universities have the right to create speech codes or does the First Amendment prohibit campuses from censuring any type of speech? Using information from the lecture, reading, and personal experience, take a position on this issue.

Students are encouraged to consult the reading passage and lecture notes in preparing their response and are allowed to use dictionaries. In many respects, therefore, the composition reflects a type of writing expected of university students, in that they must synthesize information from a variety of sources and use this information to develop and support an argument. Authenticity is also derived from the fact that students are allowed to use their dictionaries as they would in a writing assignment for any content course.

Compositions are graded on a three-part scale focusing on content, organization, and language (see Appendix). Two instructors read each essay; ideally, instructors do not read their own students' essays. In the case of discrepancies, the course supervisor reads the essay and decides which score to assign.

The weighting of the three skill areas of the ESL 33C final exam indicates that half of the final exam score (50%) comes from the writing section, with less weight placed on reading (30%) and still less on listening (20%); this reflects the relative emphasis placed on these skills in the course curriculum. We feel it is important for both teachers and students to see that the examination is consistent with the curriculum in terms of skill area focus.

Our experience with this format of the examination has been quite successful, especially in terms of the quality of the compositions. Because students have become familiar with the content in class over several weeks, their ideas are more developed than if the final exam dealt with new and unfamiliar content. In addition, the content of the essays tends to be more substantial and sophisticated than it otherwise might be, since students must synthesize and incorporate information from the listening and reading passages into their compositions. Finally, the topic itself is engaging and personally interesting to most of the students because it deals with issues relevant to their lives as university students.

While the exam described above is specific to an achievement test in one instructional context, key features of the exam can be adapted to other content-based instructional settings and to other testing situations, such as placement or diagnostic tests. These features can contribute to the authenticity and interactiveness of a content-based test. In terms of authenticity, the following recommendations[4] can be made:

- both receptive and productive skills should be tested;
- listening and reading (receptive skills) should precede writing and/or speaking (productive skills);
- composition or speaking tasks should synthesize information from the listening and reading passages;
- for an achievement test, the content of the exam should be directly connected to content that has been covered in class.

In terms of interactiveness, the following guidelines are suggested:

- test tasks should engage students' metacognitive strategies by involving higher-order thinking skills such as analyzing main ideas and supporting details, recognizing the author's point of view, synthesizing information from multiple sources, and planning and developing a well-supported argument;
- test tasks should require students to integrate test content with their background knowledge on the topic;
- the test should deal with personally engaging material that is relevant to students' lives;
- the test should include multiple tasks so that students with different strengths have a better opportunity to demonstrate their competence and knowledge of the topic without feeling disadvantaged by a single format or skill area focus.

CONCLUSION

Assessment is an essential component of a content-based curriculum, and issues of assessment must be given the same careful consideration that is afforded curriculum planning. One important issue that must be addressed in test development is the balance between language and content, which should reflect the goals and purposes of the curriculum. Additionally, the Bachman and Palmer framework provides helpful guidelines for developing fair and accurate assessment procedures by considering six important qualities of test usefulness. Finding an appropriate balance among these six qualities can be a demanding task for test developers because this balance cannot be specified in advance but must be determined independently for each situation. We believe, however, that while all six qualities of test usefulness are important in content-based assessment, considerations of authenticity and interactiveness are paramount if assessment is to match the goals of content-based instruction.

---

[4] The recommendations made here are not necessarily specific to CBA; some pertain to good testing practice in general.

Appendix

ESL 33C Composition Scoring Rubric

CONTENT _____ */6 points*

_____ Paper clearly addresses the content of *all* parts of the task.

_____ It is on topic with little or no irrelevant or off-topic material.

_____ Evidence (examples, illustrations, and details) is well chosen, clearly explained, and sufficient enough to support main idea.

_____ Evidence from the unit reading and/or listening passages is synthesized clearly or used appropriately to support arguments.

_____ Personal experiences and ideas are used appropriately for support.

_____ Ideas from the readings and listening passages are incorporated as support—*without plagiarism*.

_____ The paper engages the reader's interest.

ORGANIZATION/ RHETORIC _____ */6 points*

_____ There is a clear organizational plan evident throughout the paper which is appropriate to the task.

_____ The thesis statement is clearly formulated to express the main idea of the paper.

_____ The topic sentence of each paragraph is clearly formulated.

_____ Examples and details develop the main idea of each paragraph logically and completely.

_____ A variety of transitions (either words, phrases, or entire sentences) is used effectively to connect sentences and paragraphs.

_____ The conclusion ties the paper together by clearly and concisely restating the thesis and summarizing the main ideas.

LANGUAGE _____ */6 points*

_____ Ideas from assigned readings and/or listening passages are cited correctly and paraphrased using a variety of techniques.

_____ Vocabulary is varied/accurate, academically appropriate, and integrates terms from the unit.

_____ Sentences are well formed with a variety of simple and complex sentences.

_____ There is evidence of careful editing for mechanics.

_____ There is evidence of careful editing for grammatical features.

chapter **17**

Reading and 'Riting and . . . Social Studies: Research on Integrated Language and Content in Secondary Classrooms

Deborah J. Short

Imagine you are a seventh-grade social studies teacher in a middle school in a metropolitan district in the eastern United States. It is August and the new school year is about to begin. On the teacher workdays before students arrive, you receive incoming students' portfolios, collected by sixth-grade social studies and ESL social studies teachers the previous June and housed in the guidance office over the summer. These portfolios contain samples of written work, some artwork, some homework assignments, a few quiz and test entries, a skills checklist completed by the teacher, some anecdotal notes about individual students written by the teacher and classmates, and student-written letters justifying the inclusion of several items. As you skim through the material on this first day back in your classroom, you pull out the following essay written in April of the past year:

Sybil Ludington and Paul Revere

During the Revolution, there were two great people who helped save the nation. their names are Paul Revere and Sybil Ludington. Alone the line Paul and Sybil did the same things. One, they were both riding horses. I think in the olden days that was the fastest way to travel. Furthermore, they were both dressed like men, although Sybil was a Teenager girl and she didn't want the British troops to see her so she decided to dress like a man. Inddition [In addition], they were both sending messages at night. I think they were both sending message at night because the people who tell Paul and Sybil, their messages always told them the messages at night.

On the other hand, Paul and Sybil were different in some ways too. One, they both weren't riding at the same years. Paul's ride was before Sybil's ride. For example Paul's ride was in 1775 and Sybils ride was in 1777. Furthermore, Sybil's day of the ride was'nt as good as Paul Revere's. For example, when Paul went to send his message the moon was out and it was shining. When Sybil when to send her message it was moonless and it was also raining. It was dark for Sybil and she didn't have any lights to guide her but Paul did. Inddition, Paul Revere was seen by the British troops but Sybil wasn't even seen. I think Paul was seen because he had all this lights helping him finid [find] his ways that is why the British troops saw him. Sybil wasn't seen because it was raining and she didn't have any lights helping her finid her way and she was also dressed like a man.

Now that I have talked about these people. I'm going to choose one of them and that is Sybil Ludington as a hero because she is a girl, she was als 16 year old, she was a brave girl who wanted to helpe her nation and she does things that men does that is why I think she is a hero. I think these two people did great thing to helpe their nation.

Intrigued by the subject matter and the writing style, you look at this student's background on your class profile. Monique[1] was an ESL student, having arrived in the United States in May of her fifth-grade year. The past year, her first in middle school, she was placed in the intermediate level of an integrated language and content program (called High Intensity Language Training at her school) and received all instruction in English, none in her native language, Fante, or her other languages, Ga, Twi, or French. The program in the school offers content-ESL classes in language arts, social studies, and science. As a result, Monique studied the regular curriculum in a modified manner that could scaffold her developing English language skills while she learned the curricular objectives for each subject area. Her teachers have been specially trained and—in the case of social studies, at least—use some specially designed materials to facilitate this integration of language and content instruction. Having exited from the High Intensity program, she is now in your class.

Wanting to know more about the preparation of students from this program, you check the sixth-grade teacher's name and then pull out the portfolio of another of her students who has been placed in your class. This student had been in the United States for less than two years when he took the class. His home country is Peru and his first language is Spanish. For this portfolio the student also selected the essay assignment about Paul Revere and Sybil Ludington. As you read it you notice certain similarities, for Jorge wrote:

---

[1] All student names are aliases.

The Story of Paul Revere and Syvil Ludington

When the British soldiers were attacking Massachusetts and Connecticut in the Revolution, there were two people who help their nation, their names were Paul Revere and Syvil Ludington. I will tell you'll three ways that Paul and Syvil were the same and using the trandiction [transition] words. The first way that they were the same is that they both save their people like these [this] they both were shouting to there people like these [this] the Red coat are coming, the red coat are here and that's how they save their people. Furthermore they both were valiant or brave to ride their horses and to notify or let know their people. They knew if the British soldiers catch they will be dead, but they were very valient or have [brave] anyway. In addition they both rode their horses at night because if they rode their horses in the day the British will kill them. And that's how Paul and Sybil were

On the other hand I will tell you'll three nice ways that Paul and Sybil were different. The first way the [that] they were different is the [that] Paul sound the alarm in Massachussetts and Sybil she sound the alarm in Connecticut. Furthermore when Paul was saving lives with his horse he got a fullmoon and a nice weather in fact, he did have a lanter [lantern], but Sybil she didn't have a really bad weather she's weather was really modly with a thunderstorm and guess what, she didn't have any lanter. In addition Paul rode his horse above 17 miles and I think he when [went] to 2 or 3 places, but Sybil she rode hers horse above 40 and she when to 10 or 11 places, which is alot for a girl who has 17 years old. And that's how Paul and Sybil were different.

No [Now] it comes the big part. Now I will tell you'll what I think was the biggest hero. Guess who was the biggest hero Paul or Sybil. Sybil. you are right Sybil was the biggest hero because she did all the things the no men couln't do in Connecticut. The first thing the [that] Sybil did to be the biggest hero is that she was the only person and the only women to be a voluntary to help hers nation for example to tell their people that the [British] were coming. Furthermore she rode 40 miles and that's mean the no women couldn't support all those miles and shouting in fact she rode 40 miles that Paul couldn't dued [do]. In addition she rode hers horse in that night which was terrible with rain, and very very dark, I think if other girl shout be riding hers horse in that night she will shouting like these [this] dad, dad, mom, mom. And that's how she was the super hero.

This student, however, had more attached to his essay than the first. Jorge included a Venn diagram that compared Revere and Ludington, his first draft of the essay, and a checklist (see Figure 17.1) that was apparently completed by a peer in the class. Clearly, a process writing approach had taken place during the class assignment.

Checklist

Did he or she   Circle

Write an introduction?   (yes)   no

Write three paragraphs?   (yes)   no

Use furthermore? In addition?   (yes)   no

Begin second paragraph with "On the other hand"?   (yes)   no

Explain the details?   (yes)   no

Write a conclusion?   (yes)   no

Who did he/she think was the
biggest hero? _Sybil Ludington_

Your Name: _Emma_

Author's Name: _Jorge_

Your Comments: _good_

FIGURE 17.1   Peer checklist

In looking at these items, you realize that much more than learning the historical context and achievements of Revere and Ludington were at stake in this American history task. Rather, the teacher took a more comprehensive approach to learning, combining practice in rhetorical style (comparison essays), in cohesive writing (use of transition words), and in persuasive speech (justification of heroism) with factual information about the historical figures and their impact on the course of the American Revolution. Although you certainly noticed some spelling and grammatical errors in the two students' writings, you found the essays compelling as they mixed information with personal opinion and some speculation. The students synthesized the information and communicated their impressions through this comparison task in a manner not often encountered in sixth-grade social studies classes.

What you will not learn until later, when you have a chance to talk with the sixth-grade ESL social studies teacher, is that students gleaned the information for their essays not from the textbook but from two poems, the well-known one about Paul Revere's midnight ride by Henry Wadsworth Longfellow and a stylistically similar one about Sybil Ludington by Cindy Mahrer. In this way, the teacher relied on authentic material (literature) to supplement the traditional instruction in social studies. Further, you will discover that the products in the students' portfolios were part of a larger thematic unit, each lesson replete with language, social studies, and thinking objectives. The ESL social studies teacher will explain to you that she finds the thematic unit a very effective instructional format for her ESL students.

INTEGRATING LANGUAGE AND SOCIAL STUDIES: RESEARCH BACKGROUND

This chapter will focus on a specific content area, social studies, and the academic language associated with it. In particular, the reading and writing tasks prevalent in social studies will be discussed in light of the language development of ESL students. Drawn from research conducted since 1991 by the National Center for Research on Cultural Diversity and Second Language Learning (NCRCDSLL),[2] the chapter will highlight the instructional strategies and materials development techniques used by social studies teachers with English language learners that help them achieve success in the subject area and strengthen their English language skills.

Language teachers (ESL and bilingual) have begun to recognize that social studies is academically more challenging for English language learners than many other subjects because it demands a high level of literacy skills and is predicated on students' familiarity with extensive background knowledge. Many immigrant and refugee students in the United States, however, have not had the benefit of prior years of social studies instruction during which time they could acquire the requisite background knowledge. Moreover, much social studies instruction is still delivered through the teacher lecture–textbook reading mode (Thornton, 1994), a style of pedagogy not very effective with many English language learners. In the National Council for the Social Studies Task Force report (Jarolimek, 1989) that identified essential skills for social studies, many higher-order thinking skills (e.g., interpreting information, drawing inferences, representing print information visually, and identifying alternative courses of action and their consequences) begin to be emphasized in the scope and sequences

---

[2] This center was sponsored by the U.S. Department of Education, Office of Educational Research and Improvement, and housed at the University of California, Santa Cruz. In 1996, it received a second five-year award and was renamed the Center for Research on Education, Diversity and Excellence (CREDE) to reflect a new scope of work.

at the middle school level. Given this, middle school social studies instruction can be characterized, in terms of Cummins's framework (1994), as cognitively demanding and context-reduced.

The project reported on in this chapter has conducted research in middle school classrooms around the United States. Some of these have been sheltered classes with all nonnative English-speaking students; some have been heterogeneous, with a mix of native and nonnative English-speakers; some have been bilingual classes. Social studies, ESL, and bilingual teachers have worked closely with the researchers in designing instructional units, observing student participation, monitoring achievement, and modifying lessons to fit their local needs. The first phase of the research examined American history courses; the second, world studies. The second phase was more diffuse because although all middle schools offer an American history course, world studies courses vary across schools: nonwestern studies, world geography, world cultures, world history to the sixteenth century, and more.

Within these classrooms, we investigated the use of social studies language in academic settings. We used observation protocols and audiotaped many sessions. We also analyzed the academic language of popular commercial textbooks. Participating teachers kept teaching logs and gathered samples of student work and assessment measures. Using discourse analysis techniques, we examined transcription data from the classroom audiotapes, student written assignments, and textbook chapters in order to identify and typologize the academic language features of social studies. During this process, we considered both language associated with classroom routines and general academic directions, and language and activities specifically targeted to the social studies objectives. We also distinguished between language used by the teachers, the students, and the materials.

SOCIAL STUDIES LANGUAGE: RESEARCH FINDINGS

Our findings from this component of the research study have been described elsewhere (Short, 1994, 1996), but a summary will be provided here. Our research has shown that certain key vocabulary terms, concepts, and tasks that are specific to social studies (e.g., the Stamp Act and Francisco Pizarro; patriotism and trade negotiations; reading time lines and interpreting maps) need to be mastered as part of a social studies course. This result is consistent with the content-obligatory language described by Snow, Met, and Genesee (1989). Other aspects of social studies language are not exclusive to social studies (e.g., defining vocabulary, using verbs and other parts of speech to delineate sequence, comparing information) but are, nonetheless, required for successful participation in social studies classes. Once mastered by students, however, many of the processes involved in performing social studies language tasks and functions, as described below, could be transferred to other subject-area demands.

We discovered that several language functions occur regularly in both student and teacher discourse, whereas other functions are more common in the teacher domain. For instance, both teachers and students define terms, retell a series of related events, compare historical outcomes, and request information. Teachers, however, are more likely than students to ask questions, rephrase student responses, conduct reviews of information, and give directions. In social studies classes, student tasks included reading expository text, preparing research reports, giving oral presentations, role playing, forming opinions, writing summaries, and more. All these tasks serve as training for activities found in many other academic courses.

In terms of the language features of social studies textbooks, we began our analyses with the macrostructural component, which we found to be primarily chronological. Some texts, and certainly some chapters or sections within, also organized the information around cause-effect, problem-solution, or descriptive structures. However, with regard to how the information was presented within those structures, we found the coherence and cohesion among text paragraphs and passages to be poor, often failing to connect information in one section with information in the next, lacking transition markers, and/or using inappropriate headings. Textbooks also fail to treat vocabulary adequately: Usually ten words or fewer are explained per chapter, and the glossaries only contain words highlighted in the chapters. These findings are consistent with work by several reading researchers who have also studied social studies textbooks (Beck & McKeown, 1991; Beck, McKeown, & Gromoll, 1989; Brophy & Alleman, 1991; Tyson-Bernstein, 1988). We found further that recent textbooks, intent on increasing their presentation of "diversity issues," have added sidebars and special sections that break up the main narrative. This layout feature increases the difficulty for English language learners who are not sure where to read next. In contrast, though, one interesting finding about the syntax in recent textbooks was that most of the text was written in the active voice and the most frequent verb tenses were simple past or historical present. This finding offers slight reassurance for English language learners. Although they will still have to struggle with the dense presentation of information in textbooks, the additional burden of analyzing the passive voice, complex verb tenses, and sentences with many embedded clauses has been reduced.

In preparing students for these varieties of social studies language, project teachers employed several strategies that seem to be effective. For key vocabulary terms and concepts, teachers alternated among explicit vocabulary instruction, dictionary practice, and defining vocabulary through context. Much of the explicit instruction involved developing word webs as a class, eliciting relation-ships among key words and associations with other known words. Several teachers made use of cognates or words with Latin derivations for students with Romance language backgrounds. The use of demonstrations, illustrations, and mini–role plays were other effective ways to help students associate the written word with its meaning. Because teaching the abstract concepts was more difficult, many teachers relied on examples from the students' personal experiences, school-based activities, and current events to facilitate comprehension. Vocabulary as well as the major historical events were also reinforced through artwork, hands-on activities (e.g., sentence strips, games), drama, and writing projects. When less important vocabulary items were involved, teachers showed students how to determine the general meaning of a sentence without knowing all the words.

For functional language use, teachers relied on a variety of strategies. In some instances they modeled appropriate social studies language through paraphrasing; in others, they probed and encouraged students to add to or clarify their own responses. Teachers also provided opportunities for extended classroom discourse by increasing wait time, creating small groups where students spoke with one another, and having students give mini-presentations and respond to questions. A few teachers enjoyed using a fish-bowl technique. They would gather a small group of students to the center of the room while the classmates stood around watching. The group in the fishbowl would generate a dialogue or act out a historical scene, such as the treaty negotiations between Commodore Perry and the Tokugawa government. The teacher would help students, when needed, with appropriate expressions and also point out where one "turn of phrase" might be more effective than another.

To help students succeed with lesson tasks, teachers frequently used modeling. They would demonstrate a portion of a task (e.g., writing a sample "similarity" in the appropriate section of a Venn diagram and a corresponding "difference" in the other) before asking students to work individually or in small groups to finish. Or, if a task involved creating a time line, such as the actions that led Martin Luther to establish a new religion, teachers first worked with the class to make a personalized time line (e.g., capturing the dates for the wins and losses of a school sports team) before having students do the lesson assignment.

For reading and writing assignments, both at the micro-level (sentences) and macro-level (paragraphs and essays), teachers needed to be explicit and teach the linguistic cues to the students. These signals included verb tenses and conditions, expressions of time, and rhetorical markers such as temporal phrases, conjunctions, and causative words (e.g., "as a result"). Drawing from research by Coelho (1982), we trained the teachers to provide this direct instruction to signal readers and writers to time references, cause and effect, comparison and contrast, and generalization and example frameworks. As will be discussed in more detail below, graphic organizers were critical tools for teaching these aspects of academic language. For many social studies–trained teachers, these explicit language learning practices were new techniques and required adjust-ments in their traditional teaching style. Moreover, whereas Coelho had recom-mended that students be taught to recognize these cues to help improve their reading comprehension, we found that those cues also transferred to student writing, as evidenced in the student essays presented earlier in this chapter.

SOCIAL STUDIES UNITS

Another component of the research project was the development and field-testing of thematic units for the courses. First, ESL and social studies teachers worked with project staff to create, field-test, and revise an American history unit, *Protest and the American Revolution* (Short, Mahrer, Elfin, Liten-Tejada, & Montone, 1994), which is grounded in the theme of protest with subthemes of symbolism and societal diversity in prerevolutionary America. Covering the time frame from 1763 to 1781, the lessons expose students to the assorted protest actions that occurred and relate the information to historical events in the students' home countries and to current affairs. Students also examine the prerevolutionary period through the eyes of diverse parties such as Native Americans, Patriot women, and African-American slaves. This multiple perspective aspect is important, not only because it matches recommendations issued from national groups (Crabtree, Nash, Gagnon, & Waugh, 1992; National Council for the Social Studies, 1992) but also because it focuses student attention on the population diversity that has been present in the United States since colonial times and on the resultant diversity of opinions, values, and beliefs among its peoples.

We then developed a series of mini-units to harness the various world studies offerings at the middle school level, *Conflicts in World Cultures* (Short, Montone, Frekot, & Elfin, 1996). This unit focuses on the themes of conflict and conflict resolution, with a subtheme of how culture shapes perceptions. It includes lessons on the Incas and the Spanish conquistadors, the Reformation, the opening of Japan to trade with the United States in the mid-1800s, and Ethiopia's struggle to maintain independence in the late 1880s and early 1900s. These units span different continents and time frames and also reflect various conflicts (cultural, economic, political, religious) and resolutions (peaceful separation, resistance, negotiation, war). Findings from our classroom observations and discourse analyses, along with information collected from literature reviews of effective social studies and ESL instruction, laid the groundwork for the objectives and activities included in the units.

In designing these lessons we consulted state and national curriculum guidelines for middle school social studies as well as ESL guidelines and skill objectives lists.[3] We recognized that checklists of language skills and social studies objectives afford only a narrow perspective on learning. Therefore, we wove language tasks within social studies tasks as we wrote lessons that included art, literature, hands-on activities, structured and creative writing opportunities, reading scaffolds for text passages, and activities that promote discussion and debate. The connections to art and literature and the inclusion of hands-on tasks were essential so that students could practice and reinforce information through different learning modalities and genres. It was important for us to broaden the context of the students' learning environments and help them see connections

---

[3] For more information about the materials development process, see Short, 1993b.

between their own lives and history. We wanted the material to encourage them to think critically, form and justify opinions, be persuasive, and examine multiple perspectives.

Finally, we chose to provide both authentic and adapted readings in the units as well as lessons that were directly linked to the regular class textbook. The authentic readings gave students a chance to examine the original words of historical figures and historians. The adapted readings solved the problem of information gaps in the textbooks and allowed us to design reading passages that present multiple perspectives and information about diverse members of the societies studied. The adapted readings were also written to accommodate the students' developing English skills. The directed practice with commercial textbooks was necessary to help prepare English language learners for the real demands of the mainstream classroom, where textbooks will be ever-present in their educational futures.

APPLYING THE RESEARCH KNOWLEDGE

The curricular units described above demonstrate our best efforts at present to apply knowledge about learning academic language with successful instructional strategies for English language learners in integrated language and content classes. The remainder of this chapter will describe effective reading and writing activities that have been tested and refined during the research project, explaining the rationale for each and demonstrating them through samples of student work.

Reading

We begin with reading strategies, particularly the use of graphic organizers to accompany social studies reading tasks. We incorporated these organizers extensively in the lessons for several purposes. First, they act as tools for comprehending text, through prereading, concurrent, and postreading activities. Students learning English need support in recognizing and understanding the complex concepts found in text passages as well as help in separating the important information from extraneous details. Representing information visually helps language learners by highlighting key points and reducing dependence on written words. Second, the graphic organizers provide a means to familiarize students with the structures of text. As Drum (1984) recommends, difficult content should be framed within text structures known to students. Venn diagrams, for instance, indicate to students that the text will discuss issues of comparison and contrast, whereas flow charts represent sequence or cause-effect structures. Some of our efforts were guided by the work of Mohan (1990) and Early and Tang (1991), who have developed a framework for graphically representing text according to its embedded knowledge structure (see also Tang, Chapter 5 in this volume). In conjunction with these structural organizers,

SOCIAL STRUCTURES

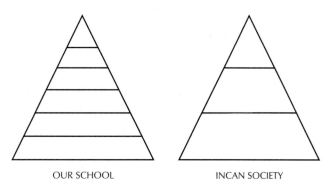

FIGURE 17.2   Sample graphic organizer used in prereading

project teachers were encouraged to explore the rhetorical markers—words signaling comparison, sequence, and so forth—with the students.

By activating either background knowledge or personal experience, we know students comprehend written work more successfully because they can interact with the material (Barnitz, 1986; Carrell, 1987) and can attach new information to stored knowledge. For certain topics, students may have limited knowledge or experience, so prereading organizers, like the one shown in Figure 17.2, provide foundational schema.

In this case, the students are preparing to read about Incan society and learn about the social classes and their interrelations. In preparation, students reflect on the social hierarchy of the school. Most students in our field-test sites placed the principal at the top of the pyramid and themselves at the bottom, yet teachers pointed out that without students the school structure would topple. Students then realized that they, as well as groups at the bottom of other hierarchical societies, have substantial power; namely, that the society could not exist as it does without their presence. The lesson continues with the teacher describing the classes among Incas and having students complete the second pyramid. Students are divided into four groups to read about the different Incan social classes: emperor, nobles and professionals, overseers, and craftsmen and farmers—one reading per small group. Afterwards they share their information with the whole class in order to complete a postreading chart that summarizes and organizes the information.

Figure 17.3 depicts a graphic organizer that students use concurrently while reading a passage from their regular textbook. As stated earlier, it is a critical skill for students to learn how to read and understand textbooks because they will be using them in mainstream classes. By providing an accompanying organizer like the one shown in Figure 17.3, teachers assist and train students in comprehension skills.

FLOW CHART

Directions: Complete the flow chart by listing and describing the British action and the colonial reaction on the lines below. You can draw a picture to illustrate your description in the boxes.

British Action: _____   Colonial Reaction: _____

FIGURE 17.3   Sample graphic organizer used during reading

While reading in their textbook about the events leading to the American Revolution, students use this graphic organizer to focus on the British actions and colonial reactions. Small groups are assigned an event connected to a protest response, such as the Stamp Act, the Boston Massacre, or the Tea Act. Each group completes a mini-flow chart (Figure 17.3) for its event, using pictures and written descriptions. By offering drawing and writing aspects, the activity accommodates multilevel learners. Students in the small groups who lack strong literacy skills may be assigned the illustrating job; better writers may craft the description; good readers may find the information in the text passage. The groups then present their charts and as a class create a larger chain by organizing the individual flow charts sequentially: either by holding them in their hands and standing in order, or by taping them on a chalkboard or wall. As the students describe their charts orally, the teachers encourage them and/or teach them to use appropriate causal and sequential words to connect their discourse. To synthesize the information given by all the groups, the lesson continues with the same small groups reconvening to make a three-dimensional cube, illustrating the sides with scenes of different colonial protests. To review, students roll the cubes and must explain the picture that comes up.

The third use of graphic organizers, as a postreading activity, is shown in Figure 17.4. For this particular lesson the students had read about the life and achievements of Menelik II, king and emperor of Ethiopia. The reading passage was written by project staff because commercial textbooks rarely, if at all, discuss

FIGURE 17.4   Sample graphic organizer used after reading

OUTLINE

I.   **CHILDHOOD**

    A. Birth

        1. _____ (place)

        2. _____ (date)

    B. Family

        1. _____ (father)

        2. _____ (guardian)

    C. Education

        _____

II. **LEADERSHIP POSITIONS**

    A. _____

    B. _____

III. **CONTRIBUTIONS TO ETHIOPIAN SOCIETY**

    A. Improvements to the lives of Ethiopians

        1. _____

        2. _____

        3. _____

    B. Modernizations to society

        1. _____

        2. _____

        3. _____

        4. _____

Ethiopia and its successful resistance to European colonization during the last quarter of the nineteenth century.

The highly structured nature of the outline shown in Figure 17.4 suggests it is a training tool for students. Because generating an outline is a common study technique in social studies and other subjects, we sought to introduce English language learners to it. Quite a bit of information is already given; the students need to reread the passage to complete the remaining items. The outline follows the text structure which describes the life of Menelik II and enumerates his accomplishments.

The reader may have surmised from this discussion so far that classes in our project frequently relied on small, cooperative group work to complete tasks and present information to the whole class. It is often the case that social studies classes are full of events, dates, and historical activities; when such a wealth of information is presented to English language learners, and those learners are not at the advanced level of English proficiency, they are often overwhelmed. Rather than expecting *all* students to read *all* the material and process the information individually, successful teachers in our study divvied up the workload. These teachers were always cognizant that their students were doing at least two things at any one time in the social studies class: They were learning English and studying social studies. Because of the heavy cognitive demands in this area, teachers would assign sections of a chapter or topics to small groups. These groups would be responsible for learning their material and then conveying that knowledge to the rest of the class. In effect, these teachers generated more manageable tasks for the students to accomplish. The students took responsibility for their topics and assumed the role of peer tutors. In addition, several teachers trained students to field questions from classmates as they presented their information, making the question-and-answer sessions a regular part of the classroom routine.

Besides the use of graphic organizers, teachers employed a variety of other reading strategies with their students, many locally designed to serve the needs of the individual classes. As mentioned earlier, all the teachers used an assortment of prereading and vocabulary activities: brainstorming, webbing, dictionary practice, mini–role plays, and so on. To strengthen student comprehension as a result of a reading activity, however, the following two examples reflect strategies of two of the project teachers.

One of the teachers, whose class of thirty-three included a mix of students in the ESL program (beginning and intermediate levels), students who had exited the ESL program, and native English-speaking students with learning disabilities and attention deficit disorder, found that he often needed to have "whole class reading" to keep the students on task. He would select one student at a time to read a paragraph or two aloud while the others were to follow along. Certainly in a class that size several students' attention would stray, but the teacher managed to keep most students focused by progressively pausing as the class moved through the passage and nominating a student to summarize the paragraph or two that had been read aloud.

Another teacher of a sheltered history class found some readings in the Inca lessons too lengthy for her advanced beginner class. Insightfully, she created a drama activity around one reading passage that described the initial encounter between the Incas and Spanish conquistadors and their perceptions of each other. She arranged her class into teams of three and cut the passage into one- or two-sentence chunks. She distributed the sentences to the groups and had each prepare a mime presentation to reflect the historical account. The students were very excited and practiced their sentences for one period in preparation for the "show" the next day. That following day, several students arrived with props they had prepared at home (e.g., costume jewelry, a vest made out of a brown paper bag, a hat from construction paper). Other students, inspired, asked the teacher for additional time to use classroom art materials to construct their own props. The groups then took turns presenting their mimes, but out of sequence with the passage. This variation on the sequential nature of the "show" posed a challenge to nonperforming students who had to pay attention and then find the representative sentence(s) in the text. Points were given to groups that located the correct sentences and justified their selections appropriately. As a wrap-up to ensure the students understood the whole text—not only their piece of it—she asked the students to draw a series of pictures about the events and then explain them.

Writing

Certain traditional and nontraditional activities in our lessons provide students with opportunities for both creative and expository writing practice. Participation in ESL and bilingual programs is intended to be a temporary situation for English language learners in most educational settings. As a result, it is essential that students be trained to succeed in the rigors of mainstream classes. Expository writing tasks help them do so. However, in the lessons we designed, scaffolds were developed to support the students' efforts. In particular, a process writing approach was promoted with substantial use of graphic organizers as tools for gathering information and harnessing ideas before drafting an essay, report, or letter.

An examination of the process that led to Jorge's essay (presented in the first part of this chapter) will demonstrate how the teaching of language skills and content knowledge can be woven into practice. Jorge relied on a graphic organizer as his bridge between reading and writing. After analyzing the two poems, he prepared a Venn diagram listing the similarities and differences between Paul Revere and Sybil Ludington. In this manner, Jorge not only demonstrated comprehension of the text he read, he also organized the information in a way that would lead to his writing task. Because the teacher had explicitly instructed the class in temporal (*when*), comparative (*both*), enumerative (*in addition, furthermore, the first way*) and causative/conditional words (*because, if-then*), Jorge was able to incorporate them as he drafted and revised his work.

By looking closely at Jorge's essay, we see many sophisticated sentences. Very few are simple sentences; most are complex or even compound-complex. He uses a variety of subordinate clauses (e.g., temporal, relative), embedded sentences (introduced by *that*), and phrases to provide details and connect ideas. Although he still needs additional instruction in some of the mechanics of writing, such as punctuation, spelling, and capitalization, he has clearly communicated information in a satisfactory and compelling manner. He even uses topic and concluding sentences in his paragraphs, and his linguistic signals cue the reader to his comparative and enumerative frameworks. Moreover, concerning the social studies objectives, he uses key vocabulary (e.g., *British soldiers, attacking, valiant, sound the alarm, Red coat*) and demonstrates understanding of important concepts (e.g., use of messengers in wartime, saving people in a nation, heroism and bravery). The only instance where his communication breaks down is when he reports "she didn't have a really bad weather." He is confused in describing the bad weather Sybil did have during her journey, but he later explains there was "a thunderstorm."

Other social studies writing tasks in the units ranged from writing a summary paragraph to preparing biographical research reports on famous historical figures. The following "Letter to the editor" written by a beginning ESL student from Haiti in a sheltered history class in metropolitan New York represents an activity that allows for some creativity but also asks for an opinion and highlights important civics objectives—the value of free speech, communicating with public officials, and participating in a political process:

Dear Editor,

   While I was in Boston in 1770 the soldiers were shooting the citizens of Boston. Those citizens were not doing anything wrong. One of the man was black man is [his] name was Crispus Attucks he got shot too. I feel bad about what happened because the soldiers didn't have to shot the people. I hope that the soldiers be punish for what they did. I hope that those thing would solves [would be solved].

                                                         Sincerely
                                                         Josephine

---

In preparation for this task, the teacher had his students examine letters to the editor from their local newspaper. Josephine clearly has the right tone for her letter, expressing her opinion and basing it on a factual situation. She offers a solution to the problem she perceives. Like Jorge, she uses complex sentences yet needs further instruction in writing mechanics.

We believed that by incorporating creative writing tasks in our lessons we could be more responsive to the needs of English language learners and also engage them more fully in the learning process. As we know from research on learning styles and multiple intelligences (Gardner, 1993; Kolb, 1984; Oxford,

1990), students respond to academic material in different ways and learn well through different modalities. One genre that is generally lacking from traditional social studies classes is creative writing. Expressive students, nonetheless, can demonstrate their knowledge through creative activities, such as those we have included. Furthermore, creative activities have the benefit of energizing a class; and for English language learners who may not function well in a lecture/ textbook-based class, such activities can ease the stress of studying content through the second language. Through creative writing assignments, students are able to be reflective, use their own words, and craft their own sentences without needing to follow the rigid structures of English very closely. Overall, these tasks represent a departure from the traditional social studies fare while reinforcing historical information through a different genre.

One creative writing task our lessons have explored is student-produced poetry. One type of poem, the diamante, relies on parts of speech for its structure but knowledge of contrasts and characteristics for its essence. Students in a sheltered social studies class in a middle school in Los Angeles (mostly from Mexican-American backgrounds) created the following poems after studying the Incan social classes:

Priests
respected, faithfull
praying, sacrificing, advising
loyally, religiously; poorly, faithfully
tilling, growing, working stealing:
common, poor
Farmers

by Mindy

Farmers
humble, poor
enjoying; growing; hardworking
faithfully: noisely: selfishly: powerfully
stealing: imposing: counting
royal: amazed
Emperor

by Sofia

Corn
tortillas, grain
grinding, cooking, tasting
delicately, deliciously; cheerfully, painfully
burning, glowing, rising
bright, yellow
Sun

by Altagracía

A diamante, named for its shape, compares or relates two things and uses nouns, adjectives, present participles, and adverbs to do so. While showing students how to construct these poems, teachers can review or teach these grammatical items. A diamante begins by describing one object and halfway through, after the second adverb in the fourth line, switches to describing the compared object. In these poems, students used their knowledge of life among the Incas to create their work. The first two poems shown here describe members of different social classes in Incan society and represent the student authors' interpretations of the Incas' activities and feelings. In the third poem, the student author perhaps projects an aspect of her own culture in assuming the Incas ground corn into tortillas. Nonetheless, she captures beautifully the relationship between corn and the sun.

The following acrostic poem from the same class integrates the subtheme of cultural perceptions with the historical information regarding the first encounter between Incas and Spanish conquistadors.

THE INCAS CONFLICTING INTEREST

Pizzaro went back to Spain to ask permision to queen of Spain to conquer the Incas.

Every Inca thought Spanierds were Gods because the qualities like having beard, horses, ect.

Reception for the Spanierds from the Incas was great.

Cajamarca was the home of the Incas and Emperor Atahualpa

Emperor Altahualpa did not now about the bible and Christianity because he was the god of the sun and because he couldn't understand the bibble.

Pizarro held the Emperor Altahualpa captive.

The Emperor Altahualpa thought that the Spaniards were not immortal.

Incas at first thought the Spanierds were nice people but then changed the percepition.

Offerd Altahualpa his help with his enemies this was said by Pizarro

New perception was thought by the Incas after the Emperor held was prisoner.

by Altagracía

Altagracía incorporates a good deal of information that she learned through the mini-unit in this poem: the Incan legend about the god Virococha (gods with beards), religious influence on Spanish explorations and conquests (bible and Christianity) and on Incan society (god of the sun), where the emperor lived (Cajamarca), the trickery that occurred (Pizarro captured Atahualpa), Pizarro's awareness of civil war among the Incas (help with his enemies), and reasons that perceptions changed (emperor was held prisoner). She uses key vocabulary terms as well as a variety of sentence types. Although, like the other students, she needs to improve her writing mechanics, her teacher has an excellent passage on which to base grammatical instruction.

A third poetic form, haiku, was taught in the mini-unit on Japan to reflect part of the Japanese culture. In order to model the activity and discuss syllabication, the teacher elicited key words from the class, a heterogeneous mix in metropolitan Washington, D.C., and together they generated the first stanza. Individual students then wrote the following haiku stanzas.

CLASS:

> Matthew Perry sailed.
> He came to Japan to trade.
> He brought them presents.

STUDENTS:

		Tokugawa
Foreigners arrived	His mission was hard	Beheaded farmers
The Japanes were angery	He feared Japanese attack	Crusified all criminals
They feared to much trade	He might have been shot	Yet they wanted peace
by Oscar	*by Gabrielle*	*by Ramon*

Again, although errors in mechanics appear, the social studies content is accurate. These students not only generated haiku with the required syllables per line but also created a cohesive message, indicating their vocabulary and conceptual comprehension. The first student writes from the Japanese perspective; the second, from Commodore Perry's. The third student describes the type of government present at the time of Perry's arrival and demonstrates an understanding of the rationale behind the Tokugawa's strict laws: They wanted peace.

In general, our lessons have successfully used poetry as a reinforcement activity. Students have enjoyed writing poetry, and more structured varieties, like those described here, have given students a framework to organize their thoughts. One teacher involved with the project said, "Students who never do their homework got turned on by this. Some wrote the best poems in the class."

CONCLUSION

The integration of languge and content teaching does not happen without a great deal of effort. First, there must be systematic alignment of the language and content objectives during curriculum development (see Genesee, 1994b). Second, both language and content teachers need training outside their areas of expertise: language teachers in content information and teaching strategies, content teachers in language learning strategies and SLA theory. Third, in order to implement this approach effectively, teachers and administrators must be dedicated and willing to try, revise, and try again, as they design lessons and activities that not only suit the needs of their students but also engage them in the learning process. Fourth, because there is a limited supply of commercial materials in this area, teachers must expect to spend many hours preparing materials themselves to ensure that both language and content objectives are included. Fifth, as a corollary to the fourth point, lesson and curriculum design work best when language and content teachers collaborate, as they have done in this research—writing lessons, testing them, discussing what went well and what needed work, sharing ideas for revision, and relishing success.

And so, as the new school year dawns, you have an exciting ten months ahead. Your seventh-grade history class will be filled with students who, you hope, will be determined to learn and eager to participate. You need to channel their enthusiasm productively, and the tips you have learned from your ESL colleague should steer you in the right direction. You now have ideas that can help all students, native and nonnative English speakers alike. By teaching reading and writing processes more explicitly, by using graphic organizers to understand text meaning through its structure, by cueing students to linguistic signals, by reinforcing vocabulary and supplementing the textbook, by setting high expectations, and by making connections between the social studies material and student experiences, you can foster the students' comprehension and production. Knowing the types of language tasks inherent in social studies classes, you will be able to set up an academic learning environment that begins the year by accommodating the proficiency levels of students but systematically moves the students forward to the higher levels required in mainstream classes. Further, although using thematic units may require curriculum flexibility on your part, the effort will be worthwhile because students will have more opportunities to acquire a depth of knowledge as they work through multiple, interactive, information-gathering, application, and reinforcement activities that break the mold of lecture/textbook-based lessons.

chapter 18

How Relevant Is Relevance?[1]

James F. Valentine, Jr., and Lyn Margaret Repath-Martos

Curriculum designers, educators, and researchers have long searched for effective ways to facilitate and expedite language acquisition. With the shift toward methodologies focused on language use, such as the language for specific purposes movement (LSP), and away from those focused on language usage, such as grammar translation, the relationship between the content of second language instruction and learners' educational goals has come under careful scrutiny. One recent curricular innovation which claims to achieve this match is content-based instruction (CBI). Underlying both the LSP and CBI movements is the premise that providing language learners with subject matter relevant to their real-world needs will motivate them to acquire the language associated with those needs as well.

Proponents of LSP and its English language equivalent, English for specific purposes (ESP), however, have learned the hard way that relevance alone may not always motivate students:

> Teachers are realising that purpose-built ESP courses lacking some general components can be boring and demotivating to the very students they were especially designed for. It could well be that teachers, course book writers, and programme designers have been guilty of focusing too much on the desired *end-product*, without giving enough thought to the *process* of achieving it. (Kennedy & Bolitho, 1984, pp. 136–137)

This insight from the ESP literature (i.e., that designing curricula around the notion of relevance alone does not guarantee student satisfaction) is important

---

[1] This article originally appeared in *The CATESOL Journal, 1992, 5*(1) under the title, "How Relevant Is Relevance? An Examination of Student Needs, Interests, and Motivation in the Content-Based University Classroom." Reprinted with permission.

to keep in mind when investigating CBI and its underlying premises. The lingering suspicion when noting the purpose of such curricula and the claims made by CBI curriculum designers is that they may well be falling into the same trap. Thus, an investigation of the notion of relevance as it applies to CBI is in order.

The American university English as a second language (ESL) setting is a particularly interesting one in which to examine the dimensions of relevance and need satisfaction given the widely varying backgrounds of the current university student population, which consists of significant numbers of both immigrant and international students (Kayfetz, Cordaro, & Kelly, 1988; Zikopoulos, 1990).[2] In spite of such diversity in the university ESL context, instructional approaches such as CBI and LSP assume that meeting student needs (i.e., relevance) is both motivating and attainable. Indeed, proponents of CBI claim that "even though learner language needs and interests may not always coincide, the use of informational content which is perceived as relevant by the learner is assumed by many to increase motivation in the language course" (Brinton, Snow, & Wesche, 1989, p. 3). The broad purpose of this chapter is to examine this assumption by focusing on the relationship between motivation and instructional design with special attention to the role of relevance.

MOTIVATION AND SECOND LANGUAGE ACQUISITION

In the field of second language acquisition (SLA), the study of motivation has been largely limited to variations on the sociopsychological approach of Gardner and Lambert (1959, 1972), whose notions of instrumental and integrative motivation have dominated the literature for decades.[3] Instrumental motivation and motivation based on relevance share characteristics of perceived functionality and utility for students who are learning a second language. Nevertheless, Gardner and his followers have generally considered integrative motivation superior to instrumental motivation as a support for second language learning (Crookes & Schmidt, 1991). Crookes and Schmidt argue that in the field of SLA, past research emphases on naturalistic, subconscious second language learning

---

[2] Classified on the basis of length of stay in the United States and residency status, working definitions and refinements of these two groups as used in this chapter are as follows: *International* students have tourist or student visas and have been in the United States less than two years; *short-term immigrant* students have permanent resident visas or citizenship and have been in the United States from two to five years; *long-term immigrant* students also have permanent resident status or citizenship and have been in the United States longer than five years.

[3] Integrative motivation involves an orientation in which the second language learner's goals are derived from "positive attitudes towards the second language group and the potential for integrating into that group." Instrumental motivation, by contrast, "refers to more functional reasons for learning a language" such as getting a job or passing a required examination (Crookes & Schmidt, 1991, pp. 471-472).

and a concurrent lack of classroom-based research on motivation have made the adoption of more instructionally oriented definitions and theories of motivation both difficult and unlikely. They do emphasize, however, that the time is right for a more practical, interdisciplinary approach to motivation in SLA.

MOTIVATION AND INSTRUCTIONAL DESIGN

From educational psychology, Keller (1983) and Keller and Kopp's (1987) motivational theory of instructional design provides at least a theoretical basis for looking at motivation and relevance in the classroom. Motivation, according to Keller (1983), "is the neglected 'heart' of our understanding how to design instruction" (p. 390). His motivational-design model divides motivation into four conditions: interest, relevance, expectancy, and satisfaction. The most fundamental of these for the purpose of this study is relevance, which Keller claims "refers to the learner's perception of personal need satisfaction in relation to the instruction, or whether a highly desired goal is perceived to be related to the instructional activity" (p. 395). As is evident from this definition, relevance refers not only to the satisfaction of instrumental needs, that is, "when the content of a lesson or course matches what the students believe they need to learn" (Crookes & Schmidt, 1991, p. 482), but also to the satisfaction of personal-motive needs such as achievement and affiliation, or the need to interact with others (Keller, 1983, p. 408). In second language course design, instrumental needs are often ascertained through needs analyses, whereas needs for achievement and affiliation are often part of the rationale for such course activities as individual contracting and group work (Keller, 1983).

RELEVANCE OF CONTENT TO STUDENT NEEDS

As previously noted, it is not uncommon for curriculum developers to incorporate the needs of learners into the instructional design of language courses. Most often, this is achieved through formal and informal needs analyses. As we have seen, early practitioners of ESP may have placed too much emphasis on what Hutchinson and Waters (1987) call *target needs* (i.e., what learners need to do in the target situation) and not enough on their *learning needs* (i.e., what they need to do in order to learn). CBI, on the other hand, purports to balance both types of students' needs by combining subject-matter instruction with skills-based second language instruction. Indeed, proponents argue that content-based courses are

> based directly on the academic needs of the students and generally follow the sequence determined by a particular subject matter in dealing with the language problems which students encounter. The focus for the students is on acquiring information via the second language and,

in the process, developing their second language skills. (Brinton et al., 1989, p. 2)

In emphasizing both content instruction and second language skills, CBI attempts to meet both students' target and learning needs and to address students' relevance concerns based on instrumental and personal motives.

AN EXAMINATION OF THE RELEVANCE ASSUMPTION

From the background literature, it appears that several basic assumptions underlie CBI. First, the approach assumes that learners in a given academic setting will have similar linguistic needs. It also assumes that curriculum designers are able to identify those needs as well as create appropriate lessons from content materials to meet them. Finally, as has been indicated from the outset, an underlying assumption of CBI is that relevance is motivating, that is, that meeting the needs and goals of learners through subject-matter instruction will motivate students to learn. The two studies reported on in this chapter examine this last assumption in a content-based, university ESL classroom. Specifically, three research questions were addressed: What do university ESL students perceive their academic language needs to be? Given these perceived needs, to what degree is there a match between the CBI curriculum and students' stated needs? Do students indeed find the content-based curriculum relevant and motivating?

METHODOLOGY

Setting and Program Description

To investigate the role relevance plays in influencing student attitudes toward a given language curriculum, we chose to examine the advanced level of the UCLA ESL Service Courses, which purports to meet students' real-world academic needs through the use of content-based units. Participants in this program are concurrently enrolled students held by the university for an ESL requirement; thus, they are working toward their degree goals while improving their academic English language skills. Given this student profile, the program's multiskill curriculum incorporates language skills that are deemed to be most relevant to the students' academic goals, as determined by experience and expert opinion rather than by a formal needs analysis. Since the ESL course participants come from a wide range of disciplines, have varying degree goals, and have had widely different exposure to academic English, a true adjunct, in which all students are enrolled in the same linked ESL/content courses, is not feasible.

Instead the curriculum, henceforth referred to as the *simulated adjunct,* combines elements from a true adjunct with those of a theme-based model. It is considered a simulated adjunct in that the academic content–based units used in the ESL course consist of authentic video lectures taken from UCLA undergraduate general education courses, and the actual reading and writing assignments designated by the content professor. For example, a videotaped lecture on media and the First Amendment, from an introductory course in communication studies, combined with the corresponding readings, form an argumentation unit in the advanced-level ESL class. Following practice with listening comprehension, note taking, and reading strategies based on the videotaped lecture and readings, students write a persuasive essay on a topic relevant to the First Amendment. They also participate in a debate structured around an issue brought up in the lecture. In the advanced-level sections we studied, two academic modules were used: one based on an introductory lecture from a western civilization course, and the second from the communication studies unit just described. (See also Weigle and Jensen, Chapter 16 in this volume.)

Procedures

Two independent studies were conducted simultaneously. Study 1 employed questionnaires, observations, and interviews in four sections of an advanced-level ESL course. The goal was to get an overview of students' perceived needs and their views on the efficacy of the instructional sequence in meeting those needs. Through weekly observations and interviews, Study 2 focused in depth on one section of the same course. The studies are described in more detail below.

In Study 1, three questionnaires were administered to identify students' perceived needs and satisfaction with the curriculum. The first, an open-ended, precourse questionnaire administered in the first week of the course (n = 88), collected demographic information such as degree goal, major, and previous experience with ESL, EFL and CBI[4] and elicited areas of students' perceived needs. Students' responses to the final question, "What academic abilities and skills do you need to be successful in your courses at UCLA?" were tallied, and the most frequently mentioned skills were incorporated into a second, Likert-scale survey. Administered during the second week of classes (n = 76), this survey asked students to rate the importance of these skill areas for academic success. A postcourse questionnaire (n = 65), in which students were asked to rate the emphasis given in the instructional sequence to these same skill areas and the helpfulness of instruction in meeting their academic language needs, was given during the final week of the academic quarter.

Study 2 employed both weekly, participant observations and in-depth interviews to investigate the same issues as Study 1. However, whereas Study 1 broadly surveyed students without a previously stated theoretical frame, Study

---

[4] Additional demographic data were obtained from the departmental student information sheets, which are filled out at the beginning of each quarter. These forms include data on native country, languages spoken, length of time in the United States, and a self-rating of proficiency in ten English skill areas.

2 focused primarily on student needs and reactions ethnographically[5] in light of existing theories of motivation and relevance.

Both studies employed observations as a primary data source. Participant observation allowed the researchers to view the curriculum in use and get a sense for the motivational level of the students vis-à-vis instructional activities. Study 1 focused on how students interacted with course materials and each other. Each of the four class sections was randomly observed at least four times during the ten-week quarter. In Study 2, the second researcher routinely observed one section's class meetings on a weekly basis in order to monitor general motivational level and student reaction to the curriculum.

In both studies, observations yielded information on student personality type and were used to identify possible interview candidates. The researchers found that some students were consistently voluble and active during class time, whereas others participated very little. Taking volubility and activity as a sign of possible motivation and interest (cf. Maehr, 1982; Stipek, 1988), students from both high and low volubility groups were selected for in-depth interviews.

In addition, students were selected on the basis of length of stay in the United States to ascertain whether interest and motivation were related to previous exposure to academic English. In Study 1, the researcher interviewed thirty-six students both individually and in small groups using a loosely structured interview guide derived from observed student reactions to the instructional sequence. In Study 2, eight individual, in-depth interviews were conducted using a highly structured interview guide designed to elicit student needs, reactions to the curriculum, and motivations.[6]

Additional attitudinal information was obtained from students' midterm evaluations and informal journal entries in both studies. The midterm evaluations (n = 78), administered during the sixth week of the quarter, asked students to rate instructional activities and materials on a three-point usefulness scale. Students also rated the time spent on global skills (reading, writing, speaking, listening, grammar, and vocabulary) on a five-point scale, ranging from *not enough* (1) to *too much* (5). This midterm evaluation included three open-ended

---

[5] Watson-Gegeo (1988) notes the growing popularity of ethnography in educational and ESL research "because of its promise for investigating issues difficult to address through experimental research, such as . . . how to gain a more holistic perspective on teacher-student interactions to aid teacher training and improve practice" (p. 575). In order to obtain just such a holistic perspective of motivation in the university ESL classroom, ethnographic field observations were chosen for the current study. To satisfy another requirement of ethnographic research in ESL as outlined by Watson-Gegeo (1988), that of attempting to understand the situation "from the perspective of the participants" (p. 579), a decision to use in-depth interviews with students was also made.

[6] According to the ESP literature, the "structured interview has several advantages over the questionnaire" in identifying the nature of learners' needs, such identification of needs being one of the basic research foci of this study. From an ethnographic perspective, the greatest advantage of the interview comes from the fact that "the gatherer can follow up any avenue of interest which arises during the question and answer session but which had not been foreseen during the designing of the structured interview" (MacKay, 1978, p. 22).

queries on likes, dislikes, and suggestions for improving the course. Journal entries, in response to such instructor-generated prompts as "How module #1 helped me to be a success at UCLA" (n = 21) and "If you could design an English class for a group of students exactly like you, what would the class be like?" (n = 19), were a rich source of student commentary on needs and interests. Both provided valuable information regarding students' perceptions of the relevance of the curriculum to their needs.

RESULTS

Student Needs

Students expressed a wide range of achievement and affiliative needs on a variety of measures. In the academic domain, based on the questionnaire data from Study 1 (see Table 18.1), the most frequently expressed need was for writing instruction and practice, a finding which was later confirmed in the in-depth interviews. Reading comprehension was the second most highly rated skill area. In addition, reading speed was identified as a *somewhat important* skill, although one not as highly ranked as reading comprehension. A third area of perceived need was for listening comprehension, judged by 76 percent to be *very important*. It is interesting to note that while this finding is supported by the interview data, a strong endorsement of the need for listening comprehension was more often expressed by international students. Not surprisingly, many immigrant students, given their aural proficiency, felt that listening comprehension was of lesser importance. However, many of those same students felt that study skills, such as note taking, outlining, and test taking, were more important for their academic success. Another perceived need frequently expressed in student journals and interviews was for knowledge of grammar. The following excerpt from a Vietnamese

TABLE 18.1   Student-perceived needs (in percentages)

Skill Area	Very Important	Somewhat Important	Not Very Important	Not at All Important
Writing	89	11	0	0
Reading Comprehension	87	12	1	0
Reading Speed	47	46	7	0
Listening Comprehension	76	20	4	0
Note Taking	64	33	3	0
Grammar	62	34	4	0
Vocabulary	N/A	N/A	N/A	N/A
Speaking: Formal	50	38	12	0
Speaking: Informal	20	48	28	4

Note: n = 65

immigrant's journal is illustrative of the attitude many students hold regarding the curricular importance of both grammar and writing:

If I could design an English class for a group of students who are all equally leveled in all academic abilities as I am, I would specifically focus on grammars and writting abilities. Everyone knows that to be successful in the real world, you must earn your audience's respect by expressing your point of view in good sense and be able to persuade them with your words.

Similar findings were reflected in the questionnaire data (Table 18.1), with 62 percent feeling that grammar was *very important.* Another skill noted for its importance was that of speaking, although once again this skill appeared more important to the international than to the immigrant students. A final category to note is that of vocabulary. Although on the first open-ended survey, this skill category was not initially identified by students as being important for academic success, vocabulary later proved to be an area of great concern for many of the students, as indicated by observations, interviews, and the midterm evaluations.

Affiliative needs emerged as another important area of student needs, primarily through classroom ethnographic observations employed in the second study. Observed student behavior and interview data indicated that the students enjoyed interacting with each other and being part of groups both in the ESL class and out. Indicators of this need ranged from students' preference to be interviewed together, to anecdotes of the importance of groups in dealing with university academic life. One Taiwanese international student, for example, told of how classmates would intervene with professors who had difficulty understanding her. She added that this sense of group is particularly important in the ESL class: "We are in the same class and should know each other . . . make friends with each other." Although affiliative needs were vital for some individuals, for the majority of students they were not as highly stressed as the achievement needs.

Student Needs and the Curriculum

Now that the academic and affiliative needs of students have been described, it is important to examine the relevance of the curriculum to these needs—in other words, to look at the match between students' perceived needs and the instructional sequence—in order to assess the motivational potential of the curriculum and instruction. Both strong and weak matches were found in the academic domain between students' perceived needs and the instructional sequence, whereas in the area of affiliation, interesting data regarding the role of groups and the instructor emerged.

Strong curricular matches to student needs were found in the areas of academic writing and reading. Eighty-one percent of students felt that the instructional emphasis placed on these two important skill areas was *about right* (see Table 18.2). There was a similar match between perceived needs and curriculum in terms of note taking and listening skills. Seventy-one percent of the students surveyed at the end of the course rated note taking skills as highly emphasized. In the interviews, several students commented that this particular aspect of the course really "helped me with other courses." As for listening comprehension, 79 percent of the respondents expressed satisfaction with the present level of emphasis placed on listening in the instructional sequence.

However, weaker matches were found for other areas of perceived needs, namely those of grammar, vocabulary, and speaking. Forty-seven percent of the students claimed that there was *not enough* time spent on grammar instruction. The interview data showed a certain level of frustration with the lack of overt grammar instruction, especially among the long-term immigrant students. A second area of frustration was vocabulary: On the midterm evaluations, 60 percent of the students felt that *not enough* class time was spent on vocabulary activities. One student wrote: "I think an efficient way of building vocabulary would be very useful, i.e., more direct work on vocabulary." However, during the interviews, a Yugoslavian international student summed up his views of the content-based nature of the instructional sequence as follows: "Writing is most present [and] through that writing I improve vocabulary. . . . [There is] maybe less [emphasis on] grammar, but [I] have to pay attention [to grammar] in writing." For this student, who was somewhat exceptional in his understanding of the CBI model, the need for overt grammar and vocabulary instruction was

TABLE 18.2   Match of curriculum to student needs (in percentages)

	Emphasis/Time Spent On		
Skill Area	*Too Much*	*About Right*	*Not Enough*
Writing	3	81	16
Reading	5	81	14
Listening	4	79	17
Note Taking[a]	N/A	N/A	N/A
Speaking	1	52	47
Grammar	0	53	47
Vocabulary	0	40	60

Note: n = 78
[a] Although an evaluation of student perceptions of the emphasis placed on note taking was not included on the midterm evaluations, an emphasis scale on the third questionnaire in Study 1 (*n* = 65) did include this skill category. Seventy-one percent of the students indicated that note taking was *highly* emphasized in the curriculum; 25 percent felt the skill was *somewhat* emphasized; and 4 percent felt the study skill was *not very* emphasized.

unnecessary. As for the final academic area of speaking, 47 percent of the students responded that there were *not enough* activities in the instructional sequence to help them improve their oral skills.

Group interaction in the classroom did, however, allow students an opportunity to practice their informal speaking skills and to satisfy their affiliative needs. Classroom observations revealed that group work was an integral part of instruction, although not all students found it especially beneficial in terms of academic success. The classroom configuration of six square tables—each seating four students facing one another—marked a sharp contrast to the traditional university classroom with rows of seats facing a chalkboard and lectern. This configuration gave the impression that discussion and cooperative work were encouraged, an impression confirmed by both interviews and midterm evaluations. When asked to describe the class in the structured interviews, one student mentioned that "discussion is [the] most important part" of classroom activities and "it's always present." Another interviewee concurred, saying, "We sit in groups and sometimes . . . most of the time we talk . . .; we discuss a lot."

Students' affiliative needs were further met through the endeavors of the instructor. In many cases, students felt a tie to each other and the instructional sequence through the efforts of the teacher. In response to the midterm query of what they liked most about the class, five students commented about the classroom atmosphere, describing it as "comfortable" and "not boring." In addition, one noted the role of the instructor: "I think it's great the way it is. But in my opinion, it's also depends on the instructor too." This comment was reiterated by another student in her interview: "The teacher influences a lot. . . . The way I get interested is the teacher." This "teacher effect" is an important one to note, for it can greatly change students' perception of the relevance of instruction and their interest in it.

Relevance and Motivation

From the above discussion of student needs and the ESL curriculum, one begins to get a sense of the relationship between relevance and motivation. Students clearly expressed appreciation for their newfound ability to put study skills such as note taking to use in other settings. For example, one student commented in her interview that the goals of the ESL course were to "[give] us skills for our other courses—how to notetaking, how to read faster," a point expressed by several other students.

With regard to the other academic skills, students also perceived the writing component of the course to be both useful and relevant. Writing-related materials and activities, such as composition handouts, in-class essays, and brief or extended definitions, were rated by more than half the respondents to be *very useful* (see Table 18.3). Comments such as "[I have to do] daily work for class—including writting which is fantastic" and "[this class has] more writing [than the previous course], it's tough a little, but I think it is working," were made in response to being questioned about what students liked most. These kinds of

TABLE 18.3 Student ratings of usefulness of skill area activities (in percentages)

Skill Area	Very Useful	Somewhat Useful	Not Useful
Writing			
Writing in-class essays	63	37	0
Composition hand-outs	59	40	1
Writing brief/extended definitions	51	41	8
Journal writing	48	51	1
Reading			
Paced and timed readings	60	36	4
History textbook/reading activities	45	45	10
Study Skills and Academic Listening			
Paraphrasing/summarizing	67	26	7
Note Taking/Outlining	58	39	3
Video lecture	49	45	6
Group/Speaking Activities			
Class discussions	53	43	4
Group work	42	48	10
Group presentations[a]	34	36	14

Note: n = 78

[a] Sixteen percent of students (12), all from the classroom in which ethnographic observations were conducted, indicated that the category of group presentations was *not applicable,* perhaps reflecting the fact that no presentations had occurred up to that point in the quarter.

comments further indicate the value and usefulness of the writing component for these students.

Paced and timed reading practice, although not initially rated so highly by students, was strongly rated at the midpoint of the course with 60 percent of the students indicating that such activities were extremely helpful for them. Furthermore, one Iranian immigrant wrote in her journal:

> This class is more useful than I ever thought it would be. One of my worst problems in studying is my low speed which I never knew how to improve it. However, this method of speed reading has really helped me to know that I should set a time and try to read in a set amount of time.

This student, demonstrating what McCombs (1984) would call "continued motivation to learn," later reported near the end of the term that the timed reading activities were so beneficial to her studies that she was interested in taking another ESL course which focused specifically on reading skill development. The value of the timed reading activities was also strongly supported in the midterm evaluations, with ten students commenting that this reading activity was one of the things they liked most about the class.

The emphasis on study skills was also perceived to be quite motivating by students in the ESL service courses. One particularly salient activity was that of paraphrasing and summarizing, which 67 percent of the students found to be *very useful.* Note taking, as we have seen, was viewed by many students as relevant to their other academic course work, as was the skill of outlining, which a clear majority of the students rated as quite useful. The response to the video lecture component, the primary source for the listening and note-taking activities, however, was not strong at the time of the midterm evaluation. In fact, in addition to being less highly rated than the study skills, the video component was specifically mentioned by eight students in their open-ended comments as one of the elements they disliked most. As with the history reading activities, this less-than-enthusiastic response could in part reflect disinterest in the topic of the first content-based unit—early medieval European history—as an additional ten students commented negatively about that particular unit's subject matter.

With regard to group activities, students generally indicated a liking for group work, but not necessarily an appreciation for its usefulness in their academic work. Indeed, on the midterm evaluations only 42 percent ranked group work as *very useful*, but twelve students named group work as the aspect they liked most about the course. In addition, nine more proposed increased or more varied group work in their suggestions for improving the course.

Paralleling the mixed findings concerning the usefulness of group work, certain students seemed to make an implicit distinction in the academic domain between materials and activities that were helpful and relevant and those that were interesting and enjoyable. One student, when asked what she liked about the class, began to talk about how she found that skills like note taking and outlining "help" but are "boring" and later expressed her opinion that "this course is something you have to learn, you need to learn." A second student echoed this "no, but" refrain, responding that the aspect of the course he did not like was "writing so often, but I know it helps." Similarly, another international student said the aspect she disliked most was "writing papers" and then, laughing, responded immediately thereafter that the aspect she found most helpful was "writing papers." Lack of student interest certainly played a role in the relatively low rating of the history textbook and reading activities. Taken as a whole, such findings again emphasize that there is more to student motivation than mere relevance of instruction to student needs.

DISCUSSION

Face Validity: Meeting Students' Perceived Needs and Expectations

Grammar and vocabulary were the skills most often listed by students as not having been given enough curricular emphasis. From our observations, we found that virtually all the skills that students perceived as fundamental to academic success could be found in the curriculum as it stands; the problem may stem from students' confusion over the form, structure, and goals of a content-based approach to language teaching. Only one student seems to have fully grasped that through the writing process in this CBI model, grammar and vocabulary instruction take place indirectly. For many students, however, it was difficult to get beyond expectations of a traditional language skills curriculum with an overt grammar component and weekly vocabulary lists. In an effort to deal with these expectations, we feel that it is fundamental for the students to have a clear understanding of the CBI model, and that the instructor must overtly state the rationale for each classroom activity. It also may be necessary and useful to include more explicit grammar and vocabulary instruction, perhaps through incorporation of a grammar reference book within the content-based instructional context.

Relevance versus Interest in Instructional Design

Keller's (1983) instructional design theory of motivation distinguishes between *relevance* and *interest*. Instead of personal need or goal satisfaction, interest "refers to whether the learner's curiosity is aroused and whether this arousal is sustained appropriately over time" (p. 395). In this research, the distinction between perceived relevance and interest became apparent through findings that some instructional activities were perceived to be helpful, but not necessarily interesting or enjoyable. This was particularly the case for writing and study skills such as outlining and note taking. Furthermore, in light of students' negative reactions to the European history module, the notion of student interest appears to have particular bearing for CBI in that a poor choice of topic seems to greatly undermine student motivation based on interest and, to some extent, relevance. When selecting courses for a CBI model such as this simulated adjunct program, curriculum designers must consider the students' general interests, backgrounds, and educational goals. For this particular program, broad, introductory courses which captured student attention and fostered discussion, such as those in Communication Studies and Psychology, greatly enhanced student interest and general motivation.

Affiliative Issues: Group Interaction and Instructor Role

As we have seen, Keller's notion of relevance refers to the satisfaction of not only instrumental needs but also "personal needs," such as affiliation. The use of group work and the role of the instructor were found to be key variables in the affective and motivational reactions of these students to the instructional sequence. Although it was not always viewed as relevant to academic success, group interaction in the course was highly valued by significant numbers of students because it seemed to offer them an opportunity to speak and get to know one another in a protected, culturally tolerant environment. Not surprisingly, the instructor was often a key player in setting the tone for this classroom environment. Our research findings also indicated that students prefer occasional restructuring of groups in order to get to know all class members. A final variable to note is that of instructor conviction about the efficacy of CBI: Observations of different instructors using the same materials revealed that variations in approach led to differences in student perceptions of interest and motivation. This demonstrates the importance of instructors' beliefs in the validity of CBI as well as the significance of instructor interest in and experience with the topic areas.

Thus, although support was found for CBI's claim that the instrumentality and relevance of instructional design are motivating to students, other factors such as student interest, expectations for language learning, and need for affiliation also heavily influenced student motivation. In the ESP context, Hutchinson and Waters (1987) have already noted the complexity of motivation as well as the importance of motivational factors beyond the scope of traditional notions of instrumental relevance:

> Motivation, it appears, is a complex and highly individual matter. There can be no simple answers to the question: "What motivates my students?" Unfortunately, the ESP world, while recognising the need to ask this question, has apparently assumed that there is a simple answer: relevance to target needs. . . . But . . . there is more to motivation than simple relevance to perceived needs. . . . [If] your students are not fired with enthusiasm by the obvious relevance of their ESP materials, remember that they are people, not machines. The medicine of relevance may still need to be sweetened with the sugar of enjoyment, fun, creativity, and a sense of achievement. . . . In other words, they should get satisfaction from the actual experience of learning, not just from the prospect of eventually using what they have learnt. (p. 48)

As these ESP specialists have advocated, CBI must go beyond a mere reliance on relevance to motivate students. In addition to emphasizing skills that students find eminently helpful in their academic coursework, the model should address such additional motivational concerns as student interest and satisfaction through appropriate content choice, recognition of students' perceived language learning needs for grammar and vocabulary, careful instructor development and training, and the effective use of such instructional techniques as group work and cooperative learning.

CONCLUSION

Based on our findings, relevant instruction is important and motivating to students in the university ESL setting. Content-based instruction that simulates a university course while emphasizing authentic academic writing, reading, and study skills such as note taking and lecture comprehension can be both meaning-ful and quite powerful in motivating students. However, the lack of traditional and therefore expected ESL activities such as grammar and vocabulary instruc-tion, content topics which do not address the majority of students' background experiences and interests, and affiliative concerns such as group interaction and instructor role play additional, mitigating roles in student motivation and perceptions of relevance.

chapter 19

Enhancing Student Performance through Discipline-Based Summarization-Strategy Instruction

Lía D. Kamhi-Stein

College-level students enrolled in academic courses are required to complete a variety of academic literacy tasks, including such reading-to-write tasks as reading textbook chapters and writing book reports or reading content-area source articles and completing research paper assignments. Successful completion of these tasks demands mastery in subject-matter content and proficiency in the target language.

Common to all reading-to-write tasks is the need for students to summarize. This complex process requires the comprehension of written content and the subsequent condensation and transformation of important information at the expense of minor details (Brown, Day, & Jones, 1983; Solarz, 1994). While there is plentiful research on the summarization genre in the first language (L1) reading and cognitive psychology literature, interest in summary writing in content-based second language (L2) settings has only recently begun to grow.

L1 reading research has shown that good and poor readers differ in the strategies they utilize to summarize written information; good readers use global reading strategies which allow them to understand the gist of a source text (Hare & Borchardt, 1984; Hidi & Anderson, 1986; Winograd, 1984). In contrast, the local nature of the reading strategies used by poor readers prevents them from condensing information (Brown & Day, 1983; Brown, Day, & Jones, 1983; Johns, 1985; Solarz, 1994), creating topic sentences, and building summaries around them (Garner & McCaleb, 1985; Hare & Borchardt, 1984). When compared with inexperienced writers, expert writers study a source text more carefully, plan more, remain more objective, and take their audience into account (Taylor, 1984). Expert writers also produce topic-based and detached summaries that contain fully elaborated syntactic structures (Kaplan, Cantor, Hagstrom, Kamhi-Stein, Shiotani, & Zimmerman, 1994).

Although research on summary writing and L2 readers is still limited, low-proficiency L2 students have been found to function much like poor L1 summarizers; they frequently replicate (Campbell, 1990) or omit important information as well as fail to combine ideas across paragraphs (Johns & Mayes, 1990). Much of L2 research on summary writing has focused on either describing summarization strategies (cf. Endres-Niggemeyer, Waumans, & Yamashita, 1991; Sarig, 1993) or examining the effects of instruction on the summarization strategies of foreign language students (cf. Bensoussan & Kreindler, 1990; Cordero-Ponce, 1994) as opposed to immigrant students in ESL settings (cf. Johns & Mayes, 1990).

English for academic purposes courses often take one of two forms: skills-based language courses (Leki & Carson, 1994) or content-based courses (Brinton, Snow, & Wesche, 1989). Both promote the development of one or more language skills. Summarization instruction in skills-based language courses typically takes the following form: Appropriate source articles of perceived interest to the students are selected and procedures for summarizing are explained. Following this, students read and produce a summary of the source article. Model summaries of this article may be provided along with instructor or peer feedback of the student-produced summaries. It is important to note, however, that the subject matter of the source articles usually has no direct relation to subject matter that students are studying in their other academic courses. In content-based courses, on the other hand, the procedures followed to teach summarization are much the same but the source articles used are typically selected from the content materials students are studying across the disciplines. In the adjunct model of language instruction, for example, the source articles used in the language class are drawn from the linked content course readings. Thus, students already have some familiarity with the subject matter, and summarization practice reinforces their content learning.

Though the EFL reading literature is filled with examples pointing to the benefits arising from summarization instruction (e.g., Bensoussan & Kreindler, 1990; Holmes, 1996), still unclear is the extent to which the integration of summarization-strategy instruction in content-based language courses may affect the performance of L2 students in general, and the performance of immigrant students from non-English home backgrounds in particular. Given that the latter group of students is increasing in number (Waggoner, 1993) and is often at risk in an academic environment that requires a high level of literacy skills in English, there is a need for more research on pedagogical practices that may enhance these students' content and strategy learning.

The study described in this chapter was conducted under the premise that intensive exposure to subject-matter content combined with summarization-strategy instruction in adjunct courses would result in language benefits. The study set out to design a "discipline-based summarization-strategy instruction program" and to investigate the effectiveness of such a program. The study was guided by the following question:

To what extent, if any, do "at-risk" university-level freshmen from a Spanish-speaking background benefit from discipline-based instruction in summary writing, as measured by: (a) the students' holistic and main idea performance as well as by the students' summarization efficiency; (b) the students' use of appropriate reproduction strategies, including quoting and paraphrasing, and by the use of inappropriate reproduction strategies, including copying and nearly copying; and (c) the students' ability to combine information within and across paragraphs?

SUMMARY-WRITING: UNDERLYING COGNITIVE PROCESSES

Current models of summarization instruction draw on the work of Rumelhart (1977) and Kintsch and van Dijk (1978). For Rumelhart, summarizing text is much like trimming a tree; content at the lower level of importance in the structure of the text is discarded. The Kintsch and van Dijk model of text summarization relies on the mental operations required to produce the *gist* of a text, which can be generated by applying the following macrorules: (a) deleting propositions which are not needed for the interpretation of other propositions in the text, (b) generalizing or subsuming individual propositions into more general ideas, and (c) constructing a new proposition at the global level.

Drawing on the analyses of Kintsch and van Dijk's macrorules for text summarization, Brown and Day (1983) identify six basic rules for summarization: (a) deleting trivia, (b) deleting redundancies, (c) substituting a superordinate item for a list of items, (d) substituting a superordinate action for a list of actions, (e) selecting a topic sentence, if one is *not* present in the original text, and (f) inventing a topic sentence if none is available. Expanding on the work of Brown and Day (1983) and Winograd (1984), Hare and Borchardt (1984) add two summarization strategies: *combining paragraphs*—a strategy characteristic of mature summarizers, and *polishing a summary*—a strategy that helps differentiate between rough and finished summaries. The summarization-strategy instruction program involved in this study is based on the early work of Brown and Day (1983), Winograd (1984), and Hare and Borchardt (1984).

METHODOLOGY

Program Participants

The summarization program described in this chapter involved fifteen at-risk university level freshmen from a Spanish-speaking background. These students were enrolled in adjunct study group courses designed to enhance the academic literacy skills in English of underprepared L2 students at California State University,

Los Angeles (see Snow, Chapter 22 in this volume, for more discussion of the program model).

Of the 15 students in the study group courses, 7 were male and 8 were female, 13 were 20 years of age or below, and only 2 were between 21 and 25 years of age. Additionally, 11 of the 15 students in the program had lived in the United States for more than eight years and another 11 had been schooled in the United States since kindergarten or first grade. While in elementary school, these students had participated in a variety of language programs including ESL, bilingual, and English-only programs. The students' college placement scores revealed their lack of preparation for a general education curriculum requiring high levels of academic literacy skills in English. All the students had obtained scores of 150 or below on the Reading Skills section of the English Placement Test (EPT), 350 or below on the verbal section of the Scholastic Achievement Test (SAT), and 56 or below on the Gates-MacGinitie Reading Test.

Program Design and Rationale

The summarization-strategy instruction program developed for this study was embedded within an adjunct study group program in Health Science and Animal Biology. The study group courses met twice a week for a total of four hours per week for a period of ten weeks and were team-taught by a peer study group leader and a language specialist. Summarization instruction, as implemented in this study, relied on three complementary features: (a) discipline-based instruction, (b) training with awareness, and (c) assisted performance.

Discipline-Based Instruction.   The summarization instruction was discipline-based in that it was driven by the demands of the general education courses in which students were enrolled. First, the readings selected for summarization instruction in the adjunct study group courses were drawn from journals, magazines, and newspapers that the content professors required students to use in their classes. To ensure the appropriateness of the readings in terms of difficulty and content relevance, the content professors—working in cooperation with the language specialist and a reference librarian—identified and selected materials prior to the beginning of the term.

Second, instruction was discipline-based in that the readings selected for the purposes of summarization-strategy instruction were directly tied to one of the lecture topics presented by the content professors. It was expected that this narrow reading (Krashen, 1981a) or in-depth reading (Dubin, 1986) approach would provide students with opportunities to accumulate background knowledge and learn high-frequency vocabulary on a discipline-specific topic, ultimately leading them to more fully comprehend the discipline and to write more efficient summaries.

Third, because a goal of instruction was to promote the transfer of strategies learned in the study group to the linked general education courses, students worked toward the completion of a reading-to-write assignment (Flower, 1990), a content course requirement involving the use of textual sources to produce new texts which, in part, required students to summarize the written sources. The rationale behind this assignment was that the students would be highly motivated to immediately apply the summarization strategies learned in the study group to the requirements of the general education course in which they were enrolled. Additionally, it was expected that by reading and summarizing articles directly related to the topic of the content course assignments, students would develop expertise in the topics chosen.

Training with Awareness.   Training with awareness involved teaching students (a) what each summarization strategy was, (b) why the strategy had to be learned, (c) how and when to use the strategy, and (d) how to evaluate the use of the strategy (see Anthony & Raphael, 1989; Casazza, 1993; Garner, 1987; Weinstein & Mayer, 1986). It was expected that awareness training would promote the transfer of strategies learned in the study groups not only to the linked general education courses but also to future courses in which students would enroll (Anthony & Raphael, 1989; Shih, 1992). To emphasize the idea that summary writing is a skill that is needed across content areas, summarization-strategy instruction began with a class discussion about academic tasks requiring students to produce either oral or written summaries. After this, students were presented with the summarization strategies included in Figure 19.1. Each strategy was introduced and modeled through the think-aloud technique, which involved the instructor's articulation of her thought process (Nist & Kirby, 1986). The technique provided students with insights into the summarization process of efficient summarizers. In particular, it was useful to model strategies that poor summarizers lack, such as inventing a topic sentence, combining information from different paragraphs or sections of the source text, and paraphrasing ideas.

After introducing each of the summarization strategies, the instructor distributed copies of a discipline-specific article and an accompanying student-produced "model" summary. Working in dyads, the students read the article, and then read and evaluated the summary using the checklist provided in Figure 19.2.

The evaluation step had three main objectives: (a) to help the students determine which summarization strategies the writer had used and whether or not modifications were in order, (b) to provide students with exposure to a "model" summary which was within their range of reading/writing ability, and (c) to expose students to high-frequency vocabulary in the discipline to which the adjunct study group was linked.

After the students had discussed the appropriateness of the summarization strategies applied in the model summary and had (when necessary) engaged in a process of jointly correcting and revising the summary, they evaluated a "poorly" constructed summary using the checklist in Figure 19.2. This step (in retrospect, one of the most beneficial in the summarization-strategy instruction program) gave students a valuable opportunity to identify instances of plagiarism, discuss which summarization strategies had *not* been used, and determine how such strategies could be incorporated into the summary. It also promoted the

---

Strategies for Summary Writing

SUMMARIZING PROCESS

After reading the article to be summarized:

1. Put the article down and think:
   What is/are the main idea/s presented in the article?
   A. Make a mental picture of the article's main idea/s.
   B. Write down the main idea IN YOUR OWN WORDS.
   C. If you don't see the main idea, "invent" one.

2. Delete redundant and minor details.

3. Combine ideas from different paragraphs or sections of the article.
   Do NOT write one sentence for every paragraph.

4. Combine lists.
   A list of activities like "smoking" and "drinking" can be summarized into "high risk behavior."

5. Go over your summary when you have finished it.
   A. Read your summary, then read the article again.
   B. Is your summary complete? Does it emphasize the points that the author
      emphasized in his/her article?

6. Polish your summary.
   Is your summary easy to follow? The sentences and paragraphs in your summary should
   be connected with connecting words like "furthermore," "moreover," "in addition."

YOUR SUMMARY SHOULD

1. Show that it is based on other people's material. Mention the author of the article
   periodically.

2. Avoid plagiarism. To avoid plagiarism you should:
   A. Paraphrase (USE YOUR OWN WORDS) what the author has stated OR
   B. Use quotation marks if you use the author's words. Then, write the author's last
      name and year of publication in parentheses [e.g., (Smith, 1991)].

3. Present "the big picture." Do NOT worry about details.

FIGURE 19.1   Strategies for summary writing

SOURCE: Adapted from Brown & Day, 1983; Brown, Day, & Jones, 1983; Hare & Borchardt, 1984; Kirkland & Saunders, 1991.

critical evaluation and analysis of the summary from the point of view of content and structure and helped highlight the importance of paraphrasing information and of being concise and clear.

In class, the students then participated in a think-aloud session aimed at jointly constructing the summary of an article distributed by the instructor. When the summary was completed, the students used the checklist one more time to evaluate the summary and to justify their summarization decisions.

The next step in the summarization-strategy training process consisted of having students select and summarize one article related to the writing assignment in the linked content course. The students then were instructed to self- and peer-evaluate the summary using the checklist in Figure 19.2. Summarization instruction concluded with the students' selecting, summarizing, and connecting two

---

Summary Checklist

Instructions: Answer the following questions:

1. Has the author identified the main idea/s in the article?   YES   NO
   (Think: What was the author's message?)
   Suggestions for improvement?

2. Has the author deleted minor details?   YES   NO
   Suggestions for improvement?

3. Has the author reflected the emphasis of the article?   YES   NO
   (The title may help identify the emphasis.)
   Suggestions for improvement?

4. Has the author combined similar ideas?   YES   NO
   Suggestions for improvement?

5. Has the author paraphrased accurately?   YES   NO
   (Remember that quotation marks have to be used or the author's
   ideas have to be paraphrased.)
   Suggestions for improvement?

6. Has the author excluded personal opinion?   YES   NO
   Suggestions for improvement?

7. Has the author shown that the summary is based on other people's material?   YES   NO
   (Has the author used phrases such as "According to," "As stated by"?)
   Suggestions for improvement?

8. Has the author connected the sentences with words like "moreover,"   YES   NO
   "similarly," "in contrast," "first," "second"?
   Suggestions for improvement?

FIGURE 19.2   Eight steps to evaluating a summary

SOURCE: Adapted from Casazza, 1993; Kirkland & Saunders, 1991.

or three articles, which eventually were used in completing the research paper assignment or data collection project required in the general education courses.

Assisted Performance.   The third critical feature of the summarization-strategy training consisted of providing students with scaffolding (Wood, Bruner, & Ross, 1976) or assisted performance. Assisted performance, defined as what learners are able to do with the help of "more capable others" (Tharp & Gallimore, 1988, p. 35), involved providing students with support for learning until assisted performance was no longer needed.

Assisted performance procedures included adapting the complexity of the summarization tasks, modeling summarization strategy use as needed, and maintaining the students' level of interest (Rosenshine & Meister, 1994). Assisted performance also involved giving students opportunities for guided and independent practice. Guided practice began with the instructor's "expert" modeling and continued with the students supporting one another. As the students became competent strategy users, the role of the instructor diminished and the students were left to work independently.

Data Collection

In the Winter quarter, the Health Science and Animal Biology study group students completed a timed, in-class pre- and post-intervention summarization task on discipline-specific articles containing features characteristic of descriptive and comparative texts (Meyer, 1981). Word counts for the articles were similar, and ratios of sentence length to word length showed that both articles were aimed at the college level (Fry, 1977).

Before completing the pre-intervention summarization task, a measure of prior knowledge of the topics was obtained. The students were asked to write for five minutes on the topic about which they would be reading (Spivey, 1983). The students included in this study were those who obtained a score of 0, which indicated that they knew nothing about the topic (Alexander, Kulikowich, & Schulze, 1994).

Data Analysis

The summary protocols were analyzed in the following ways. First, following three 3-hour norming sessions, holistic scores were assigned to the essays by three trained ESL teachers using a 6-point holistic rating scale for summary protocols adapted from the TOEFL Test of Written English. Each summary protocol was assigned a composite score, consisting of the sum of the three independent scores. The scores obtained ranged from a low of 3 to a high of 18. Interrater reliability was .91 for the pre-intervention task and .90 for the post-intervention task.

Second, summarization efficiency was calculated by dividing the total number of main ideas present in the summaries by the total number of words included (Garner, 1982). It was expected that a high mean would be indicative of students who were able to express a great number of main ideas in a small number of words.

Third, in order to analyze the students' strategies in combining and reproducing main ideas from the source texts, the following steps were taken. Each main idea present in a summary protocol was identified by the three raters working jointly. Then, drawing on Kroll's (1977) and Carrell's (1985) categories of idea units, each main idea was deconstructed into its constituent units—including "an isolatable element of a discourse supporting the topic of a discourse" (Kaplan, personal communication; see also Kamhi-Stein, 1995, for categories of idea units). Idea units were further analyzed for *combination strategies* (Johns, 1985; Johns & Mayes, 1990; Winograd, 1984) and *reproduction strategies* (Campbell, 1990). The category *combination strategies* included *combinations within paragraphs* (i.e., combinations of two, three, or more idea units within and across sentences) and *combinations across paragraphs* (i.e., combinations of two, three, or more idea units from different paragraphs or from the same and from different paragraphs). The category *reproduction strategies* included instances of *copies*, *near copies*, *quotations*, and *paraphrases*. An idea unit was counted as a *copy* when all its content words were the same as those in the idea unit in the source text and as a *near copy* when all its content words but one or two were copied from the original unit or when syntax was rearranged (Campbell, 1990). An idea unit was counted as a *quotation* when quotation marks enclosed the unit and as a *paraphrase* when the syntax was substantially different from that of the original unit.

Finally, the summary protocols were examined to determine whether they exhibited three rhetorical features which characterize summaries produced by expert readers and writers. Specifically, the protocols were analyzed for whether they (a) revealed a detached tone (Kaplan et al., 1994), (b) included an explication of the pragmatic condition of the task (Connor & McCagg, 1987), and (c) presented a macroproposition giving the gist of the article (Garner & McCaleb, 1985; Hare & Borchardt, 1984; Johns & Mayes, 1990).

INSTRUCTIONAL OUTCOMES

The strong emphasis on training with awareness and assisted performance combined with content-based readings provided students with opportunities to master summarization strategies as well as the content of the general education courses. This section presents the outcomes arising from the discipline-based summarization-strategy instruction program. It focuses on the students' holistic performance, on the strategies they employed to reproduce and combine information from the source text, and on the rhetorical features revealed in the summaries.[1]

Holistic and Main Idea Performance

One of the benefits of instruction was a significant gain in the students' holistic performance. As shown by the holistic scores, prior to instruction the students demonstrated *some* developing competence in summary writing, but their summaries remained flawed at either the content, rhetorical, or syntactic level (mean score = 8). On completing the summarization instruction program, the students' holistic performance was indicative of summarizers who demonstrated *minimal* competence in summary writing at the content, rhetorical, and syntactic levels (mean score = 12). Two sets of pre- and post-intervention summary protocols are presented in Figure 19.3 to illustrate the typical performance of program students.

In addition, the students improved in their ability to identify a significantly higher number of main ideas (two in the pre-intervention task versus four in the post-intervention task) as well as in their ability to write more efficient summaries—that is, summaries that focused more on central ideas and that excluded irrelevant and redundant information (253 mean number of words in

---

[1] For a more detailed discussion of the study's results, see Kamhi-Stein, 1995.

the pre-intervention task versus 152 in the post-intervention task). This result, indicative of the higher quality of the content in the students' post-intervention summaries, can be attributed to two factors. First, in study group course discussions, the students challenged one another for greater specificity. Second, in their classes, the Health Science and Animal Biology professors gave mini-lectures emphasizing the idea that reader-based texts (i.e., those produced to be read by the content professors) had to be built around important information and had to avoid the inclusion of repetitious and irrelevant ideas.

Prior research has shown that "able" and "less able" readers differ in their sensitivity to the importance of textual ideas (Spivey, 1983; Winograd, 1984). The results of this study are consistent with these findings. Though the students exhibited improved ability to identify or reproduce important information, the mean number of main ideas recognized on instruction was still low. This deficiency in their sensitivity to important information did not result from their lack of awareness of the requirements of the summarization task. In fact, the study group students, much like the participants in other studies (cf. Garner,

FIGURE 19.3   Summary protocols of two participating project students

Subject 1: Pre-Intervention Summary (Composite score = 5)

The Safer Sex

The Safer Sex is an article that really have caught my attention. It happens because it gives a professional and kind of accurate in formation about heart disease affecting women in the United States and at the same compare it with heart disease affecting men. I am surprised about how statistic is given by the article in heart disease in women and men. It says, "during the first weeks after a heart attack women face twice the risk of death of men." Why I feel surprised is because according with the article heart disease is a man's problem but about what I read. It should be more a women's problem even this disease is the number one affecting both sexes. So, physicians have to work out very hard to try decreasing the heart disease that at the same time causes other diseases such as diabetes and high pressure which are also very risky in women's life. At last, I understood that even statistical are against women and a little bit in favor of men, both sexes may die by hearth disease even if they are using a coronary artery bypass in their body.

Subject 1: Post-Intervention Summary (Composite score = 12)

The Safer Sex

According to many researchers who have been trying to understand the differences between male and female in getting heart disease, men have preference in the way of treatment than women. Facklman states that most people think that heart disease affect more men. However, researchers have found that heart disease also affects women and is the number one killer of men and women in the U.S. Some researchers also found that the women tend to develop chronic heart failure after an attack more than twice the rate of men. Also, there is some bias in diagnosing cardiovascular problems in women. For example, Fiebach said "if a middle-aged woman is having chest pain one doesn't think of a heart attack. If a middle-aged man is having chest pain, one automatically thinks of heart attack." This shows why women tend to suffer severe complications after the heart attacks and are in more jeopardy to die faster than men. Furthermore, some studies point to the body-size as causes of technical difficulties during bypass operations. Finally, severe complications after hear attacks, some problems related to age, severity of heart attack, and illnesses like hypertension and diabetes are also seen as the causes of heart disease in women.

(continued on next page)

Subject 2: Pre-Intervention Summary (**Composite score = 8**)

Here Comes the Sun

The title of the article I read is *Here Comes the Sun.* It's a real interesting article. It deals with researches done to investigate more about the *Winter depression.* It talks about how different scientist have different cures for the cause of depression.

The winter depression takes place between late November to April. This depression affects men along with women. Studies have proven that premenopausal women are the vast majority of people affected by winter depression. Something that the article does not talk about is children. Whether or not they get this depression.

Researchers have done many researches to find a cure to this depression. They came up with 2 approaches to this treatments. The first one is to place a person in front of a screen emitting the light five time brighter than regular room light for 2 hrs. each day. The second one is using a screen which produces 20 brighter than regular room light for 30 minutes every day.

This treatment seems to cure patients. In some occasions it improves some patients health.

The article tries to explain as I told you before why this happens. Yet, nobody has an answer. Some believe that the light your eyes receives has something to do with this. But this hasn't been proven correct.

In conclusion I believe that the sun has something to do with the depression. Maybe because there is more sun brightness during this time. The answer is still in of found. Probably some of the treatments found could some day cure the Winter depression.

Subject 2: Post-Intervention Summary (**Composite score = 11**)

Here Comes the Sun

According to "Here Comes the Sun" people tend to have SAD (seasonal affective disorder) during the winter time in places farther from the equator. People with SAD have daytime drowsiness, extreme weight gain, difficulty awakening in the morning, and social withdrawal.

To treat SAD patients, researchers have placed patients in front of bright lights for one or two weeks. Scientists believe that this treatment "alters the circadian rhythms," but how it doe it is not clear. Although this treatment is good, researchers have not yet come out with the perfect cure.

FIGURE 19.3   Summary protocols (continued)

1985; Rinaudo, 1993; Winograd, 1984), were quite aware that summary writing involves the identification of main ideas and the subsequent reduction of information. Instead, this deficiency in performance, consistent with findings in prior studies (cf. Garner, 1985; Rinaudo, 1993), most likely resulted from the participants' inability to identify important content in partially descriptive source texts.

Reproduction and Combination Strategies

Additional benefits of instruction included an increase in the use of appropriate reproduction strategies, characteristic of better L1 and L2 readers (Brown & Day, 1983; Hare & Borchardt, 1984; Johns, 1985; Johns & Mayes, 1990; Winograd, 1984), and a reduction in the use of inappropriate reproduction strategies. The results of the post-intervention task show that the students found synonyms for content words and phrases, a skill that appears late and requires not only the understanding of written text but also the command of a large vocabulary (Campbell, 1990; Johns & Mayes, 1990). The increase in paraphrasing is believed to be the result both of extensive content-based paraphrasing practice and of exposure to discipline-based readings. Such exposure may have led project students to understand content-specific texts better and, ultimately, may have prompted them to rely less on inappropriate reproduction strategies such as copying and near copying.

Although Animal Biology students did not quote once prior to instruction, quoting was the second most common reproduction strategy exhibited by the Health Science students before strategy instruction. In general, these students simply embedded the quotations into their summaries without using introductory discourse markers such as "according to [author's name]" or "as stated by [author's name]." This is illustrated in the following student sample:

Most people know that heart disease represents the number-one killer of men in the U.S. but many don't realize that it's also the number one killer of women.

There are several possible explanations for this finding. Some students may have been aware of the inappropriateness of plagiarism: thus, once they identified important information, they decided to quote it instead of copying it directly. Other students may have thought that because their writing style did not match that of the published author, they should rely on the quotation strategy instead of attempting to paraphrase the idea.

The benefits of instruction did not extend to a significant improvement in the students' ability to abstract the global meaning of the text. Prior to instruction, students from both content courses directed their attention at individual sentences and paragraphs rather than at the global meaning of the text. On completing the summarization instruction program, the Health Science students still relied heavily on the use of local reading strategies, although they improved in their ability to combine information from different sentences within the same paragraph. In comparison, after instruction the Animal Biology students were relatively more successful than those in Health Science at combining information from different paragraphs, a characteristic of more competent summarizers.

Rhetorical Features

A further effect of instruction was an improvement in the tone revealed by the students in their summaries. Prior to instruction, nearly 45 percent of students in Health Science and 50 percent of students in Animal Biology maintained an involved tone; in fact, the students responded to the readings in a personal manner and very often wrote a personal reaction to the ideas presented in the source texts. The following example shows how, prior to instruction, a male writer in Health Science reacted to the source text by expressing his opinion about the topic:

> Why can't physicians just look at everyone else as human beings instead of discrimaniting, heart disease doesn't. Not to say the least about minority & females, they won't even think twice about helping us. The article doesn't specify what kind of males & females they use for their research. But I can positively assume that they were caucasians.

Prior to instruction, other students in Health Science and Animal Biology also responded explicitly to the source text:

> Why I feel surprised is because according with the article heart disease is a man's problem but . . .

> I understood from the article that there are people who actually get depressed during the Winter . . .

These findings are consistent in part with prior research regarding the "orientation toward topic" exhibited by Latino students (Basham, Ray, & Whalley, 1993). The tendency to include personal reactions in the summary may be attributed to the students' lack of acculturation to university culture. This explanation is based on the observation that lack of objectivity was noticed among project students who had had no more than two quarters of college experience and not among the Latino students enrolled in sophomore and junior courses.

Discipline-based summarization instruction can be considered effective in that 45 percent of the students in Health Science gained in their ability to begin their summaries with an explication of the pragmatic condition of the task, contributing to a detached, scientific tone. Following are three examples of summary openings in the Health Science corpus. The first two openings, from the pre-intervention task, were counted as inappropriate; the third one, drawn from the post-intervention task, was counted as good:

> Physicians in the 90's have largely ignored women who complain of chest pains which is a big potential sign of heart attack.

> Bruce Bower describes a women who is leing asleep, then a light bult being place near her bed.

In "The Safer Sex?" the author talks about . . .

As can be observed in the first two examples, Health Science students who failed to begin their summaries with an explication of the task's condition either did not attribute the ideas to sources or made false assumptions about the reader's shared knowledge of the topic. In contrast, nearly 85 percent of the students in Animal Biology began their pre-instruction summaries with an explication of the pragmatic condition of the task. An example from the pre-intervention summaries in the Animal Biology corpus illustrates this point:

In the article "Here Comes the Sun" the author reports research done on winter depression and . . .

The summarization-strategy training was reasonably successful in promoting an improvement in the students' ability to create macropropositions which give the gist of the article. Following is an example of a macroproposition around which the writer built her summary:

According to different studies reported in the "Safer Sex" it has been established that women have a greater chance of dying of cardiovascular disease than men do due to different factors.

The improvement in the students' ability to write macropropositions was unexpected, given the general finding in L1 and L2 reading research that summarization instruction does not result in the ability to create macropropositions (cf. Day, 1980; Hare & Borchardt, 1984). The Health Science and Animal Biology professors played an important role in this respect, emphasizing in their lectures the importance of opening any writing assignment with a generalization about the topic. Both instructors also provided students with sample openings.

CONCLUSION

The summarization-strategy instruction described in this chapter offered students valuable opportunities to practice summary writing, develop metacognitive control over their strategy-learning process, and at the same time manipulate content material. The strong emphasis on making students aware of *what* summarization strategy to use, *when* to use it, and *how* to use it helped them to become active summarizers as well as to gain control over their content-learning process. Additionally, the demands of the study group and the general education course in which the students were concurrently enrolled grounded strategy instruction in the reality of the content class. In the study group, the students learned how to use summarization strategies that they needed to apply to the content class; similarly, the study group students were exposed to material that they were required to read in the general education course. This programmatic feature not only increased the students' motivation to learn how to summarize content material but also provided them with multiple opportunities to acquire background knowledge on topics addressed in the general education course.

The approach to instruction described in this chapter prepared students to summarize content material, probably one of the most common—and critical—academic literacy demands of general education courses. However, an approach to instruction that combines training with awareness, assisted performance, and a discipline-specific curriculum should not be limited to summarization-strategy instruction. This approach could be applied to other academic literacy tasks, including synthesis tasks, and to other educational levels, including college preparatory programs and middle and high school ESL courses. In this way, at-risk L2 students can develop a repertoire of strategies that will ultimately contribute to their academic success.

chapter **20**

Linguistic Form, Pragmatic Function: Relevant Research from Content-Based Instruction

Jane Zuengler and Donna M. Brinton

The call for considering language function along with language form can be traced to Cazden, John, and Hymes's (1972) anthology *Functions of Language in the Classroom.* In his introduction to the volume, Hymes argues for a contextualized view of language:

> What is crucial is not so much a better understanding of how language is structured, but a better understanding of how language is used; not so much what language is, as what language is for. (p. xii)

This recognition of form/function relationships in language has spurred a large body of research in both first language (L1) and second language (L2) settings, and the examination of these relationships holds a major place in second language acquisition (SLA) research.[1] As Young (1995) states, the emphasis in language teaching on communication has made the social context of language use a significant area to study. One such context which is of increasing relevance to language researchers and teachers alike is the growing area of content-based instruction (CBI).

According to Wesche (1993), content-based approaches to language teaching are aimed at "the development of use-oriented second and foreign language skills" and are "distinguished . . . by the concurrent learning of a specific content and related language use skills." Within the content-driven curriculum that characterizes these approaches, emphasis is placed on "the incidental internalization of new

---

[1] In March 1995, for example, an academic session at TESOL in Long Beach, California was devoted to this topic. Entitled "Form and Function in Language Learning: Sociolinguistic Perspectives," the session was sponsored by the TESOL Research Interest Section.

knowledge by the learner from rich target language data" with a focus "on the meaning being communicated" (pp. 57–58). As such, content-based classrooms present a natural context for research into the relationship between grammatical form and pragmatic function—especially as this research relates to the *input* which learners receive in the classroom setting (either through interactions with their peers or teachers or through exposure to written text) and to the spoken or written *output* of learners who are using the target language to relay content-related concepts.

CBI as a movement is still in its infancy, and (as pointed out by Johns, Chapter 31 in this volume) its literature has tended until now to focus on curricular models, student affect, language proficiency gains, and instructional strategies.[2] Nonetheless, there is a burgeoning interest in CBI today in areas of research such as text analysis, pragmatics, and discourse communities—domains which have traditionally been examined by researchers in the field of English for specific purposes (ESP). Within this area of investigation is the existing CBI research into form/function relationships, which is the subject of this chapter.

A TYPOLOGY OF CLASSROOM INTERACTIONS

In their discussion of language use in the classroom, Richards and Lockhart (1994) note that the complex linguistic dimensions of classroom interactions generally fall into one of the four following areas:

1. Teachers' modifications of their language (e.g., speaking more slowly, using pauses, changing pronunciation, modifying vocabulary, modifying grammar, modifying discourse)
2. Teachers' questions (e.g., questions related to classroom procedures or routines, questions requiring a display of knowledge, questions eliciting an opinion or point of view)
3. Teachers' feedback methods (e.g., feedback on form, feedback on content)
4. Learners' language use in the classroom (e.g., communicative functions in classroom interaction, language used to complete classroom tasks)

Though the authors do not make specific reference to research in content-based classes, these four areas (with some minor modifications, as will be explained shortly) can be seen as the framework by which researchers have examined the CBI classroom. Thus, they provide useful means for capturing both the range and focus of existing research.

---

[2] We would add to this list the assessment of language proficiency gains in CBI programs.

By far the most productive area of research in CBI (and more specifically in sheltered classroom settings) concerns the language modifications or accommodations which occur in classroom discourse when teachers present content to L2 learners. This research encompasses both Areas 1 and 2 as outlined by Richards and Lockhart. Groundwork in this area was laid in the early experiments with sheltered classes offered through the bilingual University of Ottawa (Edwards, Wesche, Krashen, Clément, & Kruidenier, 1984; Hauptmann, Wesche, & Ready, 1988; Vanniarajan, 1987; Wesche & Ready, 1985). These studies documented important differences in the language addressed to L2 learners versus that addressed to L1 learners in the content classroom. Among these differences were the teachers' slower rate of speech, more careful pronunciation, use of stylistically more "neutral" vocabulary, and more frequent use of display questions.

The University of Ottawa findings are supported by additional studies of teacher discourse addressed to L2 learners in the content-area classroom at the university level (Mannon, 1986) and in the K–12 setting (Wong-Fillmore, 1985; Early, 1985; Pritzos, 1992; Kumpf, 1995). These studies are further augmented by the body of literature on the characteristics of academic language in general. Particularly pertinent are the data reported from a fifth-grade sheltered social studies class in which the teacher uses Socratic questioning and repeats student utterances with rising intonation to model the "critical discourse register" he wishes students to adopt as they discuss a filmstrip on the lifestyles of native peoples in northern Canada and the Arctic (Solomon & Rhodes, 1995).

While serving to further document modifications that occur in teachers' speech, the above studies raise additional questions, such as which types of accommodations make the content material most comprehensible to the learners, and whether such accommodations actually help students to develop the level of academic language proficiency needed to succeed in mainstream classes. Richard-Amato and Snow (1992b), Master (1992), Snow (1993; also Chapter 22 in this volume), and Peterson (Chapter 13 in this volume) provide useful insights into effective strategies which content-area faculty can employ to enhance the understanding of English language learners in the content-area classroom.

Another area of research is detailed in Richard and Lockhart's third category—feedback methods used by teachers. Included in this category is research examining teacher strategies for providing feedback on the content and form of learners' contributions. Such research may involve an analysis of informal feedback measures or more formal assessment tools. In CBI, when the content knowledge of English language learners is assessed, the measures are affected by students' language skills; conversely, when their language skills are assessed, any measurement is also affected by students' command of content (Mohan, 1986, 1990; Mohan, Low, & Wilson, 1995). Also of relevance to Richards and Lockhart's third area of research are the investigations into how teachers scaffold knowledge for learners (see, for example, Hawkins, 1988). This type of structured practice and feedback to learners is seen as essential to both the content and language development of English language learners. Finally, it is important to recognize that while the teacher may be the most likely assessor and feedback provider in CBI, learners can also take these important roles in helping each other develop both content and language. Duff's (1993, 1995) research on Hungarian EFL history classes effectively documents the change from traditional teacher-centered "recitation" activity as the norm toward other, more student-centered oral activities. The student-centered activities, Duff (1995) writes, involve more interactional negotiations among learners and a less teacher-controlled participation pattern that enables the learners to provide each other with feedback on content as well as language.

The final area mapped out by Richards and Lockhart consists of learners' interactions as they engage in and complete classroom tasks. This area of content-based research allows a close examination of the form/function relationships which exist in the learners' output at any stage in the developmental process; some of the research also examines changes that occur over time as learners expand their repertoire of forms and functions and approach a more target-like command of both.

There are some relevant studies of learners' language use in university content-based programs. Duffy (1995) examined the written production of learners in an adjunct model course at St. Michael's College and found evidence of growth in the learners' ability to use language to express concepts related to the subject-matter course material. Kamhi-Stein (1995, also Chapter 19 in this volume) documents growth in the summarization skills of language minority students enrolled in an adjunct model study course involving the academic disciplines of Animal Biology and Health Science. Finally, Koshik (1995) examined the activity of defining in a simulated adjunct model classroom, noting the effects of group work on the co-construction of definition sequences.

However, much broader-based research into form/function relationships has been carried out in the K–12 context, either in content-area or sheltered classes. It is important to note that outcomes of this research differ. Some have concluded that CBI is inadequate or problematic for developing L2 form/function relationships (see Eskey, Chapter 10 in this volume) and have recommended that instruction be more focused on language form. Other studies, however, provide pictures of content instruction which is rich in fostering form/function development. The divergent outcomes of these studies may be due in part to the heterogeneity of programs, levels, and settings in which the learners were studied. However, they may also be due to the differences among researchers in their conceptions of or assumptions about language and content learning. Recognizing that researchers' conceptions of language proficiency and language learning have a profound influence on their research questions and outcomes is certainly not a novel idea (e.g., see Harley, Allen, Cummins, & Swain, 1990; Firth & Wagner, 1996). Often, though, the researchers' assumptions are not elaborated on in the literature, and the outcomes are therefore limited in their generalizability. We will illustrate these considerations by discussing several studies which have differing outcomes.

Swain (1988) examined teacher-student discourse in third- and sixth-grade immersion classes in Canada. Studying interchanges in a history class, Swain concludes that while the content class setting can offer authentic form/function language use, the use may be too restricted or too *meaning-* (rather than *form*) oriented to be beneficial for language learning. Swain argues that some attention to form is necessary in order to develop correct form/function pairings; she did not, however, see much attention to form in the lessons as they were taught. Additionally, Swain looked for, but did not find, what she considered ample amounts of modified production by learners. The learners were engaged in a lot of listening, but relatively little speaking. Thus, the teacher-student inter-changes primarily consisted of students providing short answers to the teachers' questions. If students produced errors, the teachers tended to correct them only when there were problems conveying meaning, not form. The characterization of the discourse led Swain to suggest that content teaching was inadequate in providing learners with a good language learning experience. She concludes that content teaching should be made more conducive to language learning, recom-mending that content teachers modify their instruction to get learners to attend to and produce particular language forms.

In her recommendations, Swain has judged the content class discourse against a conception of generic, interactional discourse that much of the second language acquisition field considers potentially good for language learning (however, compare Firth & Wagner, 1996). It is discourse that involves inter-actional negotiations, comprehensible input, and modified output that occurs when learners are made aware of the need to revise what they produce (see Swain, 1985). Although unstated as such, Swain's conception of language allows at least some separation of it from content, enabling her to pose the question of whether content learning promotes language learning; it further leads her to suggest that manipulating one (i.e., content) might help the other (i.e., language).

A similar, generic conception of language and language learning appears to inform Musumeci's (1996) investigation of university-level CBI. Musumeci examined teacher-student interactions in three L2 Italian classes whose content was the social geography of Italy. Believing that modifications of both input and output are essential to any kind of language learning, Musumeci looked, in the data, for points at which comprehension failed; her purpose was to determine whether and how the interlocutors modified their speech toward mutual understanding. The common interactional pattern was similar to what Swain found, with teachers producing a lot of display questions and students responding to them, rather than initiating conversational turns themselves. In these interactional patterns, Musumeci found that teachers modified their output to learners when learners signaled that they had not understood them, but there were few cases of teachers requiring the learners to modify their own production. Musumeci's conclusion was that the interactions in these content-based classes were inadequate for language learning. Although there was evidence of modification of teacher input, there was little evidence of the modification of learner output that Swain and others argue is necessary for language acquisition to occur.

EXAMPLES OF FORM/FUNCTION DEVELOPMENT IN THE CONTENT-AREA CLASSROOM

Other studies draw more positive conclusions about the potential of CBI for developing L2 form/function relationships. As pointed out above, the researcher's conception of the language/content relationship influences the research questions asked and the interpretation of findings. While the studies we describe below do not directly state the researchers' conceptions, it is clear in the reporting process that these researchers believe that functional needs for communicating within any content area do arise. They further believe that any instruction in a content-based setting constitutes an environment where content-functional needs can lead directly to the development of L2 forms. In contrast to other conceptions of language and content, this view assumes no such dichotomization of content versus language, but considers the two inextricably linked. It is a view which corresponds more closely to the form/function opinions expressed in the introduction to this chapter. As Hymes (1972) has argued, it is important, in understanding language, to consider what it is used for within its context of use, rather than to examine and judge its form against a generic conception of proficiency.

When learners are engaged in a content area, they are acquiring knowledge of that content. Along with this acquisition of content knowledge come certain *functional needs* for communicating concepts. These lead directly to the development of *language forms* used to express the concepts. To illustrate this complex and reciprocal relationship between content and language form and function, we have selected two examples of research studies conducted in secondary-level science classes taught to L2 learners. Included in each example is an overview of the study along with "before and after" examples that illustrate ongoing language development.

The first example is drawn from Kessler and Quinn's (1984) year-long longitudinal study of one learner in a high school physical science class in San Antonio. The learner, a seventeen-year-old native speaker of Gujerati, had arrived at the high school with very little English and had spent his first year in the United States taking ESL and auditing classes such as mathematics. At the time of the study he was in his second year of high school. Although mainstreamed in his content courses, he was still enrolled in a "traditional" ESL course (i.e., one which had no integrated language/content focus).

Based on the premise that lab-based science experiences provide a rich potential for the development of second language/literacy skills, Kessler and Quinn decided to investigate written science lab reports to examine the learner's development of form/function relationships. (These totaled five reports written at four times throughout the academic year.) The reports entailed, among other functional needs, the ability to respond to written directions, to describe an experiment's procedures, to state hypotheses, and to draw conclusions. Figures 20.1 and 20.2 present reports written by the learner at the beginning (Stage 1) and end (Stage 4) of the school year.

Title:	The force of friction and the waight of a Body
Babelm:	what happned to the force book.
Materials =	spring scale; loop of thread; 4 testbook
Procedure -	Four textbook will be needed for this experiment, so should work in groups of four. Find the weight of book by means of a spiring scale, and record the weight

Number of book	weight of Book in newton	Force of (Friction) in Newten
1	9 N	$3 \frac{1}{2}$ N
2	18 N	$6 \frac{1}{4}$ N
3	27 N	10 N
4	36 N	1 N

Congusenel -   the book differce newten and twice time

FIGURE 20.1 Example of science laboratory report at the beginning of the school year (Stage 1)

FIGURE 20.2 Example of science laboratory report at the end of the school year (Stage 4)

Titals =	To Find the Solubility of Sodium Chloride by Evaporating a Saturated Solution	
Problem:	find solubility of socium chloride	
Materials =	100 m. graduate; evaporating dish; equal-arm balance stand; 4-inch ring, wire gauze; burner	
data:	1) mass of empty dish	44.2 g
	2) mass of dish plus solution	66
	3) mass of solution	21.8 g
	4) mass dish plus salt	51.4
	5) mass of salt	7.2
	6) mass of water	14.6
	7) volume of water (ml)	14.6
	8) solubility of NACl	49.3

$$\frac{\text{mass of salt} \ (g)}{\text{volume of water (ml)}}$$

Congulsen: Salt is very solubility in water.

These reports support the claim that content-area demands such as writing up lab reports contribute to second language development on the part of the learner. As may be evident from Figures 20.1 and 20.2, the science teacher in this study had given the students a format to follow in writing up their lab reports: (1) the title of the experiment, (2) the statement of the problem, (3) the materials needed, (4) a summary of the procedure, (5) a report of the experiment's findings, and (6) the conclusions. Although some portion of this format involved copying from the text (e.g., the title or procedure), other elements required the learner to condense and summarize the material from the text and to make original contributions in the form of the conclusions drawn from the available data.

According to the authors, the Stage 1 report presents evidence that the learner has a basic understanding of the concepts (i.e., he is able to list the weights, calculate the force of friction, and arrive at the correct conclusion). There remain clear difficulties, however, in his efforts to state the problem and conclusion. Over the course of the year, the lab reports become longer and more accurate in terms of the supporting data provided and the conclusions drawn. In Stage 4, Kessler and Quinn note that the learner is doing less copying[3] from the text and more paraphrasing and summarizing (see Figure 20.2 above). In producing his own language, he makes fewer errors in mechanics and in the forms required to express the appropriate linguistic functions. Overall, it is obvious that by the end of the year the learner is still producing errors, but many fewer ones. In the opinion of the authors, the language has become more targetlike in expressing scientific functions.

A similar case study was carried out by Spanos (1993), who investigated multiple learners' progress in integrated ESL math and ESL science classes. To better compare the findings with the Kessler and Quinn study, we focus here on the results from the ESL science class only. In this study, Spanos functioned as the ESL science teacher in a class of English language learners who were almost all L1 Spanish speakers. The learners were ninth or tenth graders who had recently exited from a bilingual program; they ranged from fifteen to eighteen years old and had been in the United States from one to three years. Spanos describes the learners as intermediate level, possessing basic conversational skills and reading abilities of between second- and fourth-grade levels. Some learners in the class needed assistance in transferring academic concepts from their L1 and therefore needed to develop the concepts in order to function in the L2. The goal of the science class was to teach basic physical and life science in order to prepare the learners to take a mainstream biology class. As a means of achieving this, Spanos (as the teacher) developed activities for practicing scientific language and reinforcing learning strategies. These activities followed the CALLA (Cognitive Academic Language Learning Approach) design

---

[3] In fact, when the learner does copy in Stage 4, he copies more accurately.

1. State the problem. (What are we trying to learn?)

2. Gather information about the problem. (What do we already know?)

3. Form a hypothesis. (What do you think will happen? Why?)

4. Perform an experiment to test the hypothesis. (How will we learn?)
   (a) materials used:
   (b) steps in the experiment:

5. Record and analyze data from the experiment. (What happened? Why?)

6. State a conclusion. (What have we learned?)

FIGURE 20.3 The scientific method procedure

(Chamot & O'Malley, 1987, 1994). To help the learners work with scientific knowledge and apply the scientific method, Spanos developed a protocol (see Figure 20.3) that closely resembles the lab report format used by Kessler and Quinn.

Spanos had the learners work with this protocol, the Scientific Method Procedure, four times early in the year and four times at the end of the year; students worked in pairs on experiments from their science lab book. For example, in fall and then again in spring, the learners performed investigations of how and why fire needs oxygen to burn. In fall, the student pairs were given matches, a votive candle, and a can of sterno. They were asked to light these and place a jar over each to determine which one extinguished first. In spring, they received two votive candles, matches, two dishes, and a small glass jar. They were to light both candles, wait until the flames grew, place the jar over one of the candles, and determine the result. Figure 20.4 presents fall-spring comparisons of how selected student pairs expressed Step 3 ("Form a hypothesis") in the Scientific Method Procedure—a process Spanos reports having heavily emphasized in class. In comparing the two sets, note that the fall responses use simple

FIGURE 20.4 Development of form/function relationships—forming a hypothesis (Step 3)

Example A

Fall:	Well, the fire of the candle is small and it take more time to use the oxigen. So the sterno Fire is bigger It take a few minute to eat the oxigen.
Spring	We think the candle is inside the jard won't stand for a long time.

Example B

Fall:	was because the oxigens was more longer that the other one.
Spring:	We think that the candle inside the jard won't stay lited as long as the other canle because the jar doesn't have a lot of oxygen.

Fall:	The candle has more oxygen that the sterno but the fire of the canle is more soft that the sterno because we know that the sterno has mor vapor.
Spring:	Whe we put the jar to cover the candles the candles turn off because the air was gone, because the vapor absorve the air that what happened.

FIGURE 20.5 Development of form/function relationships—recording and analyzing data (Step 5)

present or past tense to report facts and do not exhibit any of the linguistic or functional characteristics of a hypothesis. The spring responses continue to show formal errors in the writing; however, even though they are not clearly stated hypotheses, they express predictions and thus represent an improvement in the learners' ability to manage the functional scientific language.

Step 5 in the scientific method procedure involved having the learners record and analyze their data. In explaining what happened, they were to demonstrate an understanding of the relationship between fire and oxygen. Figure 20.5 presents fall and spring examples from the same pair of students. Spanos points out that the fall response not only fails to show what happened but also reveals a misunderstanding by the learners, who have not understood that the more intense burning of the sterno can used up oxygen more quickly than did the votive candle.[4] In contrast, the spring response shows a conceptually clearer understanding of the relationship between the burning candles and the oxygen. Concerning linguistic form, there is evidence of growing complexity in the use of the "when" clause used to introduce the sentence.

Spanos does not include comparative fall-spring data for Step 6 ("State a conclusion"). However, he notes signs of improvement in the learner responses in that more learners were able to respond to this step in spring than in fall; further, the spring responses (see Figure 20.6) often transcended the specific experiment to make general conclusions about the importance of oxygen.

FIGURE 20.6 Development of form/function relationships—stating a conclusion (Step 6)

Spring:	We learn that we need oxygen to make fire. The jar didn't have enough exygen that's why the fire couldn't stay on.
	We already have learned when we need more oxigen and is very important for us.
	We learn if in the place where we are not air we can't make fire because the air make fire thing that are natural.

---

[4] Instead, these learners appear to have thought that the sterno was stronger than the candle and so should have continued to burn longer.

CONCLUSION

The positive outcomes of the two studies we have just discussed, and the negative findings of the studies we summarized earlier, should be interpreted in light of the language/content conceptions which the researchers appear to hold. If we take the view that form and function are inextricably linked and that their relationship can only be understood within the context of use, we are less able to hold a generic view of language proficiency or language learning as a measurement by which to judge a given content-based class. Instead, we are more likely to view CBI as a potentially rich learning environment for second language learners—specifically as this relates to the acquisition of linguistic form and pragmatic function. In the conclusion of his study, for example, Spanos (1993) notes that his learners were able to process what they had learned in conducting the experiments and were able to convey their growing understanding of the Scientific Method Procedure in increasingly appropriate target language forms.

What do these successful outcomes indicate with respect to the potential for CBI to foster beneficial function/form relationships? In order to answer this question, we need to consider what facilitates the building of such a relationship. For this purpose, we return to the Richards and Lockhart framework. In Area 1, we believe it is critical to examine the pragmatic choices of forms used to "shelter" language to English language learners. Similarly, research in Area 2 (long an area of interest in classroom-centered SLA research) can inform us about the types of questions teachers in both the content-based language classroom and the content-area class use when addressing students; it can also help explicate the degree to which the choice of question type is influenced by the function the question performs in the larger discourse. Concerning feedback and assessment (Area 3), we need to examine both how teachers choose to frame their feedback to students and how the choice of certain syntactic forms may have bearing on the students' ability to display their knowledge of content. Finally, with reference to learner language use in the classroom (Area 4), we need to examine closely the symbiotic development of form and function in our learners' interlanguage as they gain control of academic language forms and functions in the discipline-specific language classroom. This promising area of research is still largely open to investigation.

chapter **21**

The English Language Fellows Program: Using Peer Tutors to Integrate Language and Content[1]

Richard Blakely

The English Language Fellows Program at the University of Rhode Island was conceived when a student, whom I will call Tran, who had taken two ESL courses with me in his first year, came back to take a literature course I was teaching four years later (in order to fulfill a general education requirement so that he could graduate) *and almost failed.* Most distressing to both of us was the obvious fact that in four years of taking courses toward his B.A. in Accounting, Tran's English not only had not improved but had actually deteriorated. As a first-year student Tran was one of the top students in his ESL classes, making discernible progress in all four skills, especially reading and writing. As a senior he could not write a complex sentence. A paragraph of Jack London or Ernest Hemingway was an impenetrable mystery, which he would spend agonizing hours trying to understand.

The following year I was given a copy of a letter written by another nonnative-speaking student who had also taken the two ESL courses offered by the University during his first year *and done well in them.* The letter has been transcribed exactly as it was written, with minor deletions; it is reproduced here with permission of the student, who said that if it can help people understand the plight of nonnative speakers at his own campus and beyond, it will at least have served a purpose.

---

[1] This is a slightly adapted version of an article which appeared in *College ESL*, 1995, Vol. 5(2), pp. 1–20. Reprinted with permission. The article was the winner of the 1997 Fred Malkemes Prize sponsored by the American Language Institute of New York University.

Cambodia is the Place origonaly bore. Then I alway wanted to be a constructor, civil Engineering and a Mathematician. I never have the opportunity to achieve all of these goals, because of the poverty of the country.

Now I am in the processing of getting the American's citizenship. . . . I am a senior in B.S. of Applies Mathematic and a sophomore in civil Engineering.

One day the [state agency that was sponsoring a special job training program] was introduced by one of the civil Engineering dean in my . . . (mechanical of solid) class. The movement I heard the program, I was so happy and affraid. The reason I affraid because I am not a 2.5 grade point average student and happy because I know that this is once of a life time opportunity that I alway dream off, and that the reason that I send this letter at the last minutes.

Again I am a senior in Applies Mathematic and sophomore in civil engineering. I had completed the requirements up to second year of civil engineering, I am interesting in constructing, built a building, road, bridge and house. I have no experience as I already prescribed but I had work experience at many place such as in the industrial, factory, Painting and fixing house.

Needless to say, the student did not get the job. Moreover, both he and his fiancée, also a native speaker of Khmer and a recent graduate of the University, have yet to find gainful employment in their chosen fields. Because of their limited (and limiting) English, one has to wonder if they ever will.

The stories of these students are not as uncommon as one would like to believe. In fact, they illustrate a problem that, if left unchecked, threatens to undermine the very foundation on which public higher education in this country is based: More and more immigrant, language minority students who graduate from U.S. colleges and universities are for all intents and purposes illiterate, unable to get jobs for which they have been trained, and incapable of becoming productive, integrated members of society. (See Stuart, 1990, for one assessment of this problem.)

The solution to this problem is not to give nonnative-speaking students one or two more courses in ESL (courses which often do not bear credit, and which the students themselves do not want to take), but to give them the opportunity, as well as the desire, to continue studying English throughout their years as undergraduates.

The English Language Fellows Program does just that. To encourage nonnative-speaking (NNS) students to persevere with the task of continuing to perfect their English while obtaining their degrees (and often working long hours to pay for their studies), continual and cumulative study of the language counts for *real* credit toward graduation. To make it relevant to other courses they are taking, and to their future plans for a career, this language study is content-based. (For more on content-based language instruction, see Benesch, 1988; Brinton, Snow, & Wesche, 1989; Cantoni-Harvey, 1987.)

The English Language Fellows (ELF) Program was originally supported by a grant from the Fund for the Improvement of Postsecondary Education, U.S. Department of Education. In fact, the program was modeled in part on the Brown Writing Fellows Program (Haring-Smith, 1994) and on Foreign Language Across the Curriculum programs that are now springing up all over the country (see Krueger & Ryan, 1993b), except that here the foreign language is the language of general instruction. The program pairs specially trained native-speaking undergraduates with NNS classmates to study the content of courses that both are taking together. Woven into that study of course content, for the benefit of the NNS students, is the study of language as it is used to communicate and understand the course material. This content-based English language study is generated by the specially trained Fellow who organizes and conducts the study sessions. For running those sessions, the Fellow is paid an hourly wage. For attending them regularly and doing the extra language study that they require, the ESL students receive an extra unit of credit in addition to the three units awarded for the content course.

SELECTION AND TRAINING OF FELLOWS

Every semester fifteen exceptional students with native or near-native proficiency in English, preferably in their first or second year, are selected as potential Fellows. Criteria for selection include strong faculty recommendations, good grades, high SAT scores, an interest and background in foreign languages and cultures, and a desire to make the university—and the world beyond it—a better place.

Once accepted, these fifteen students take a semester-long training seminar, now a regular three-credit university course. This course is divided into three parts: *who, what,* and *how.* The first part focuses on the people the program is designed to serve: specifically, growing numbers of NNS immigrants in this country—where they come from, why they are here, and some of the problems they face once they arrive. During this phase of the course students read texts, see films, and carry out activities that we hope will show them what it is like to be a nonnative speaker in this country. A good example of one of the shorter texts is "Mother Tongue" by Amy Tan (1990), in which the author describes how almost every aspect of her mother's life in the United States was adversely affected simply because she spoke with an accent. Because of her "impeccable broken English," her daughter says, "people in department stores, at banks, and at restaurants did not take her seriously, did not give her good service, pretended not to understand her, or even acted as if they did not hear her" (p. 5).

Part two of the training course, the *what,* explores the field of second language acquisition, with emphasis on particular difficulties a native speaker of another language is likely to encounter in learning English. In this phase we introduce the four traditional skills—listening, speaking, reading, and writing—and also spend some time discussing grammar and vocabulary acquisition.

In part three, students begin to think about *how* they will put this knowledge to use as Fellows in the program, working with ESL classmates in preparing for an exam, for example, or writing a paper, or rehearsing an oral presentation. During these last three to four weeks we try to impress on the future Fellows the newness of what they will be doing. Pairing high-achieving native speakers with at-risk language minority classmates in such an extensive, systematic fashion has never been done before. Nothing has yet been written which applies directly to what they will be called on to do in their one-unit study sections. So in order to define what Fellows are, we must first define what they are not. They will not be teachers, for example, nor tutors in the strictest sense, nor even peer tutors. In fact, *tutoring* and *helping* are words we caution them not to use, for both imply a power relationship between a giver and a receiver that runs counter to the cooperative spirit on which the program is based. Indeed, after three semesters of operation—forty-eight English language study sections offered in conjunction with other courses—Fellows are unanimous in saying they "received" as much in those sections as the NNS classmates with whom they worked. Thus, for lack of an appropriate term, we tell the Fellows-to-be to think of themselves as "privileged collaborators in learning," the privilege being their native understanding of the language of instruction.

One could also use Vygotsky's (1978) term *more capable peers* with the caveat that the greater capability of the native speaker is due only to her innate familiarity with the language, not to a higher "actual developmental level." Indeed, if her classmate were a native speaker of Vietnamese and they were studying at a university in Vietnam, it is the classmate who would be more capable. Bruffee (1993), although keeping the terms *peer tutors* and *tutees,* takes pains to stress their equality. "In peer tutoring this equality means, first of all, that the students involved—peer tutor and tutee alike—believe that they both bring an important measure of ability, expertise, and information to the encounter and, second, that they believe that they are institutional status-equals: both are students, clearly and unequivocally" (p. 83).

In comparison with other tutor training programs, most would agree that this is more broad-based and thorough. As a semester-long course, it involves 45 hours of class time and requires well over 100 hours of outside reading and preparation.[2] Moreover, it is for credit—an integral part of the university curriculum. But even in a fifteen-week course, no matter how demanding, we cannot do much more than introduce so many different areas, and this is why at the end of the semester we tell the students it is just the beginning. The real learning starts then.

---

[2] Most tutor-training programs, even those which are offered for credit, do not involve more than 30 hours—the number necessary to qualify for the "Master/Level 3" (highest) Certification of Tutor Programs by the national College Reading and Learning Association.

The course is called, simply, "Becoming an English Language Fellow," and the word *becoming* is important. Because it exposes traditional, native-speaking undergraduates to people and problems most of them were not aware of previously, it is, for many, an eye-opener. Students say that after taking the course they see things differently; they are not the same people they were before. An anecdote may serve as an example.

When this course was first offered in the spring of 1993, a student who was taking it came up after class to relate an experience he had had a few days earlier. For most people this experience would have seemed insignificant, but for Murray, in light of what he had been reading recently, it was earthshaking. Once or twice a week Murray would get together with friends to play volleyball. These were mostly people he knew, old friends from high school, but others who happened to be there would often join in. One day after they had finished playing, Murray was going around asking people if they wanted to go to a local campus hangout. The way he described it, he was going up to people one by one, asking if they wanted to come along, when suddenly he realized he had passed one person up—someone who turned out to be an immigrant from India. Realizing what he had done, Murray went back and asked him too, and the Indian gratefully accepted. What Murray found so amazing, and at the same time so difficult to admit, was that up until that moment this darker-skinned student, even though he'd played with them on several occasions, *had been to him invisible.* As Murray said after class, still visibly shaken, "How could I not have seen that guy before?"

And that is precisely the problem. At the University of Rhode Island—as, I suspect, at many other U.S. colleges and universities where language minorities have not yet become the majority—immigrant NNS students are marginalized not only by their own feelings of inadequacy and lack of confidence in English but by the fact that to large segments of the traditional campus population (students, faculty, and administrators), these students, and the problems they encounter, are virtually invisible (see Rose, 1989[3]).

So if this course causes blinders to be removed from the eyes of even a few of the students who take it, one could argue that the program has already succeeded. But as stated above, the end of the course is only the beginning.

THE STUDY SECTIONS

As to the "real learning" that goes on in the one-unit study sections, for both the Fellows and their NNS classmates, the best way to describe it here may be to present a typical example of one of those sections.

---

[3] "Class and culture erect boundaries that hinder our vision . . . and encourage the designation of otherness, differences, deficiency," says Rose (p. 205), whose book *Lives on the Boundary* was a source of inspiration for the ELF Program.

Rebecca took the Fellows training course during the second semester of her first year. The following semester, one of the courses she enrolled in was a "gen ed" anthropology course in which there were two NNS classmates: Y, a student in her third year from Japan, who plans to return to Japan after graduation; and D, a first-year student, who immigrated to this country from Cambodia in 1987. With the approval of the course instructor (and with his enthusiastic support), Rebecca arranged to meet with D and Y twice a week for the rest of the semester. Before their first meeting, Y and D both filled out a two-page questionnaire assessing their own strengths and weaknesses in English, and signed a brief "contract" enrolling them in a section of English Language Studies 201 (ELS 201). This is a one-unit tutorial course, offered under the auspices of the ELF Program, which qualifying nonnative speakers at the University can take "in conjunction with other courses" as many as twelve times.

After each meeting of these one-unit sections, Fellows are required to fill out "Daily Course Reports" which are intended to help the program staff keep track of what goes on in each of them. The following summary of this particular section of ELS 201 will consist of excerpts from these course reports, quoting directly from the Fellow who wrote them (with her permission, and with minor editorial changes), and interspersed with occasional explanatory notes as needed.

The complete report for meeting number 1, although that session lasted a full hour, is very brief:

We went through the chapters in the book that were going to be on the quiz. It was the first meeting so we talked about the program and got to know each other a little. I was very nervous.

Because of this last comment, the project director attended the beginning of the following session in an effort to help jump-start it, showing Rebecca, Y, and D how to go over notes from previous class lectures and how to use reading assignments as a tool for vocabulary enhancement, as well as pronunciation and grammar practice. Noteworthy here is the fact that even though Rebecca, in the training course, had read and talked extensively about these strategies and about working with students like Y and D, she still felt at a loss when it came to actually conducting a section of ELS 201 on her own. This is a very common occurrence among new Fellows, and understandably so, but it shows again that one can only learn by doing.

By the fourth meeting, Rebecca's course report gives ample indication that the section has now gotten off to a good start. The session lasted an hour and a half.

We talked about the quiz we took today. Then we went through all of the lectures and they asked me for things that they had not heard, spelled or written correctly in their notes. . . . They had a lot of questions and blank spaces where they had lost what the prof was saying.

Then we did vocabulary from the lectures—words in the course and everyday words that I had written down for them. Then I discovered Y's "l and r" problem. We did the mouth diagram and then one of those lap/rap [minimal pair] exercises. We spent about 15 minutes on the word "world." They both read a paragraph from the book and we talked about pronunciation w/D and flowing of the sentence w/Y. I felt good about this session. We accomplished a lot and did language stuff as well as studied. I think we're getting used to each other.

Meeting number 7 took place a week before the first exam. The course report for that session illustrates one of the major beneficial side effects of the program—the close personal relationships that often build among the participants:

1. We have an exam on Wed. so we rigorously went over the notes—they asked questions—we all discussed them. I had D explain the things he understood to Y and vice versa. All and all it was a great session. I got the feeling we all understood the material.
2. Of course, as usual, we did pronunciation (minimally). When they pronounced a word wrong I corrected them. I also discovered Y's hidden "v and b" problem. She wrote favor as "fabor."
3. I felt really good today because after the session we were talking and Y said they didn't have any programs like this at [another state university she had attended the year before]. She said it was a real help and that I was good at what I do. Before, she barely spoke, now she's doling out compliments. It's a good feeling. The 3 of us really get along. So far it's been a very positive experience.

Unfortunately, this enthusiasm was tempered by their grades on the exam. Although Rebecca got an A (97%), Y got a low C (70%) and D barely passed (61%). To Rebecca, these low grades were puzzling. From studying with Y and D, she knew they both had a good grasp of the course material. Why then did they do so poorly? During meeting number 9, while trying to prepare them better for an upcoming quiz, she comes upon a possible answer:

I had each of them give me a version of their main point of each chapter, which was successful. A few points they didn't understand, so we broke down each sentence in the paragraph and figured them out. I, in fact, learned a lot through that. Then we discussed what our prof had suggested we pay attention to for the quiz and I made sure they had those points down.

We talked a little about the exam, but I told them we'd go over it in more depth tomorrow.

I then had a light bulb flash over my head, slapped my forehead and said "Dah!" I realized they both knew the material and that on the previous quizzes (and the exam) it was the wording that threw them off. I had known this but had no solution. So I pulled out the last quiz with them and we talked about the wording of the questions and the answers. I told them to look at every word and how to eliminate answers more efficiently. Note the quiz attached. [Rebecca had attached a copy of the quiz to the course report. Here is Question 1, which she refers to below:

"Elizabeth Vrba's 'turnover-pulse' hypothesis states:

    a. that speciation and extinction follow major climatic (and thus environmental) fluctuations

    b. that cladistic analyses are based on false premises

    c. that evolutionary change is independent from climatic (environmental) change

    d. that dinosaurs evolved warm-bloodedness before mammals"]

D, on #1, had read "independent from" in letter C as "dependent on." So we talked about what prepositions go w/each (i.e., dependent on and independent from) thus stressing the importance of knowing the language and the grammar. We then went thru each question . . . then we eliminated each answer, either because it didn't make sense, didn't answer the question, wasn't even in the text, etc. I really think they felt better. . . . Tomorrow [while taking the quiz] I think they will take their time and look at every word (so will I, by the way).

Rebecca's discovery points to a major problem NNS students encounter in their studies and about which very little, in the ESL literature, has been written—namely, the deceptive simplicity of so-called "objective" exams. Faced with a choice between (a) a course graded primarily on the basis of written assignments, and (b) another section of the same course where the grade depends exclusively on multiple-choice or true/false exams, most NNS students will enroll in the second, assuming that it will be less challenging to their limited English and allow them to do better in the course. Rebecca's discovery here, and similar discoveries made by other Fellows in the program, indicate that the opposite may be true.

In their following meeting, Rebecca, Y, and D continued to explore this problem:

We talked a lot about the exam, once again we dissected some of the questions and analyzed each word's importance. They both realized why they got questions wrong. In doing this we realized that there were indeed an abundance of tricks. I.e., one question was about this guy that everyone associated with sufficient similarity. One of the answers had "insufficient" in it, which threw almost everyone off. D couldn't believe in [the prefix] made such a difference. . . .

Today I met w/ Prof. L [the course instructor]. I told him what we were doing in the sessions. We talked about the exam and he suggested the possibility of the 3 of us taking it separately from the class so that they could ask me questions about unclear wording.

One of the responsibilities of Fellows is to touch base periodically with the instructors of the content courses, to tell them what they are doing in their meetings with the NNS students and ask their advice about problems or difficulties those students might be having. Here, when Professor L learned of Rebecca's concern that Y's and D's low grades might have been due more to lack of proficiency in English than to lack of knowledge of course material, he proposed that the three of them take the next exam in his office so that Rebecca could answer any questions Y and D might have while taking the test—not about content, but about any wording or vocabulary that might not be clear to them because of their status as nonnative speakers.

Mindful now that she will be able to give them this sort of input, Rebecca focuses in their following meetings on the importance of looking at every word, something she discovers Y and D were not in the habit of doing.

On Friday we talked about reading a sentence and skipping over the words they don't know. I asked Y if she knew what the text meant by "get a feel for something." She said no, so I asked what she does when she comes to something she doesn't know. She said if she can't understand the sentence she'll look it up, but otherwise she just skips over it. D agreed, so I told them that that is precisely when they should put a question mark on it and ask me. I made a rather big deal about how important it is to better their English so I think they'll start doing it. [The end of this course report shows how much Fellows themselves stand to learn in these sessions—and not only about course material. Also in attendance at this session was C, another Cambodian student who is a member of the program staff.] . . .

In our class we had been talking about language so we continued the discussion in the session. I found out things like Y is only called Y by her parents. If anyone else called her that it would be an insult. All her friends call her Y-chan. I asked her if she wanted me to call her that so she'd feel more at home, but she said it didn't matter. I was really interested in C's and D's thoughts on assimilating. They both were saying they had to learn how to communicate with Americans entirely differently than [with] Cambodians, i.e., eye contact, closeness, touching. Fascinating stuff!

The course report for meetings 13 and 14 shows how much a Fellow's job has to do with trying to change habits, a process that for an immigrant student like D can be discouragingly slow and painful.

First I asked D [Y was absent for this session] if he had specific questions relating to the text. He had quite a few because the chapters are getting more and more complicated. We went over what he didn't understand and what was important to know. We then did vocabulary, which included "discordant", "novelty" or "novel" (he thought novelty was a book), "palate, manipulate, harem, promiscuous, ergo, enhanced." All these words, I told D, were important to the sentences they were in. I gave him an example of how one word can make or break your understanding. The more I stress this, hopefully, the more he'll write down what he doesn't know. I told him all he had to do was underline and ask me. He said he knows this, but just wasn't in the habit of it.

Anyway, we did pronunciation and the biggest problem we faced was, of course, "th." He has a BIG problem with it. We did diagrams and different words—we'll probably work on it every session from now on. Also a really big problem was that, when reading from the book, every word w/o an "s" on the end, he adds one, and every word w/an "s" on the end, he takes it off. It was the most frustrating thing for both of us. He couldn't stop doing it. "Differences" was "difference." "Trait" was "traits." We talked about why he does this. I couldn't really figure it out, but we just kept doing it and doing it until he said the sentence correctly. . . .

One thing that was difficult were the words "terrestrial" and "territorial." Both are used frequently in class and D can't distinguish between them. I told him to listen for the "s," then realized he throws "s" around all over the place so I just had him sound them out and say them over and over again. We also talked about how I can't remember a word in Italian, my 2nd language, unless I say it and learn the correct pronunciation. I don't think he knew exactly what I meant but he agreed. So any word that was important I had him sound it out.

In the next few meetings leading up to the second midterm, the pace picks up. Meeting number 18 was on a Sunday afternoon, the day before the exam, and lasted two hours. The course report shows the tension felt by all three. It also shows how richly Fellows deserve their hourly wage.

Y could only stay an hour so what I did w/ her was rushed. I gave her the practice exam of 25 questions that I had made up and she did really well. The ones she missed we talked about while D prepared questions to ask me about things he didn't understand. Then while Y finished the exam I explained some things that were unclear to D. I felt like I was really rushing both of them, but they seemed to get what I was saying. After Y finished the practice exam I quickly told her what points were important to study for the exam. I [had] spent almost an hour with L. [the professor] Friday asking him things I didn't understand and what was important to know for the exam. Luckily he was extremely helpful. So Y had a good idea of what to concentrate on when she left. I worry about her. She rushes around so much I don't think she does anything but study. . . . Basically today's session was devoted to recapping everything we've done since the last exam. I'm really nervous, actually, to take the exam, because I want to help them as much as I can w/o giving them the answers. We'll see how it goes. D is improving, I think, all the time. The more he talks the better I understand him. For the next meeting we'll start doing some more pronunciation, since we've slacked off a little in preparing for the exam.

As proposed by Professor L, Rebecca, Y, and D took the exam at the scheduled time, but in his office so that Rebecca could clear up any language problems Y and D might have as those problems arose. (To eliminate any doubts about what the three of them discussed during this time, a tape recorder was left on throughout the session.) Apparently the strategy worked, for on this second midterm, whereas Rebecca again earned an A (97%), this time Y and D scored very well also (95% and 92%, respectively).

Throughout the remaining third of the semester, the meetings between Rebecca, Y, and D continued to follow the pattern established before the second mid-term: reviewing readings and lecture notes in preparation for quizzes and the final, doing some pronunciation as time permitted, but paying particular attention to specific words and phrases Y and D had trouble understanding. While a lot of these words were specific to course content (and difficult even for native speakers to understand), many more were not, and the relative simplicity of that second category might seem surprising. Many educators at the college level tend to assume that their NNS students have already acquired a fairly extensive academic vocabulary, by virtue of having been admitted to the institution. The curious mix of content-specific, often very complex vocabulary, along with surprisingly simple words and phrases that Rebecca recorded in her course reports, reveals the urgent need of Y and D (and other students like them) to continue developing their vocabulary at a very basic level (see Bernier, Chapter 7 in this volume). Here is a good example of such a list, from an earlier session:

Vocabulary [that we discussed] included:

- retention—retain
- pentadactyly
- digits
- extensive
- simultaneous (D figured this out from T.V.; he knew the word "simulcast")
- elaboration
- de-emphasis
- repertoire
- modification
- ballpark figure
- more or less
- iffy—shaky
- self-aware
- relatively
- nocturnal
- hommoide, homminidae, hominoid, hommid
- tail between your legs

During these last four weeks Rebecca also kept in close touch with Professor L, who suggested they follow the same procedure for the final that they had followed for the second midterm. "I thanked him," Rebecca wrote, "for being so flexible and concerned. . . . He was really happy their grades had improved so dramatically" (from meeting number 22).

The course reports for this period, as the end of the semester draws nearer, have an increasingly frenetic, breathless quality about them. Reading them, one feels the mixture of apprehension and resignation that all students share at the end of the term, and that gives a college campus at that time of year the feeling of a storm about to break or a battle about to begin. Rebecca is by turns ecstatic and depressed, one day full of hope, the next day plunged into despair. Their session on December 12 was, she says, "by far the worst meeting ever." (Then she goes on to describe what sounds like one of the most interesting and beneficial sessions of the semester!) The following session, meeting number 24, she says "went great. We all had a couple of good laughs and got a lot done." Here is the report of meeting number 25, in its entirety:

Confusion was the trend of today. I was not prepared and very tired. Therefore, I spent a lot of time wondering if D and Y understood me. They weren't responsive at all. The more I thought they were confused, the more confused I became and then, of course, the more confused they became. Anyway we did get some things accomplished. We decided exactly what we need to study and how. Other than that, it was a loss.

The tone of the last course report, luckily, is more upbeat. "Today was a good meeting," Rebecca begins, then goes on to describe their elaborate preparations for the final exam.

OUTCOMES

Evident in these excerpts, and in fact in all of Rebecca's course reports throughout the semester, is an underlying element of doubt, a faint but constant questioning tone, as she is always wondering if she's doing the right thing, being as effective as she can be. "I'm not all that sure I'm doing everything I can," she says in one report, "but I'm trying." And in another, "I wish I could do more, but I don't know what."

This constant self-questioning is something Rebecca shares with all the Fellows, even the most experienced. Rather than being something to worry about, it can be seen as proof that the program is alive and well; for if the Fellows are constantly questioning and seeking, they are also finding answers and making discoveries. It is this constant process of discovery that makes being a Fellow so rewarding. Best of all, they are making these discoveries on their own, truly taking charge of their own education, learning that learning comes from within. In Rebecca's case, she has every reason to believe that the answers she found and the techniques she used were good ones; that if she wasn't necessarily doing "the right thing," she was certainly doing something right. On the final exam, Y scored very well (98%), giving her an overall course grade of A-, and D scored moderately well (75%), which earned him a C+. (Indicative that working as a Fellow has a positive impact on one's own performance, Rebecca scored 100% on the exam and got an A for the course.) Both Y and D agree that if they had not participated in the complementary section of ELS 201, they would not have done nearly so well in the course. In their final evaluative questionnaires, both said they did "much better" in the course because of these sessions, stressing in particular the value of going over lectures and focusing on content-specific vocabulary. As far as making progress in English, again both students gave the sessions the highest ranking, and in their written comments said the sessions were particularly beneficial in the areas Rebecca stressed throughout the semester: pronunciation and vocabulary acquisition.

This section of ELS 201 differs from most of the others only in the amount of time Rebecca devoted to writing her daily course reports and the extensive detail she put into them. In many other ways it is typical of all of them. Any other section in which there is more than one nonnative speaker, for example, poses the problem of finding a balance between each student's capabilities in English that Rebecca had to deal with here (and finally resolved by spending more time with D, whose lower level put him at greater risk in the course). The fact that Y was an international student and D an immigrant, with all the characteristic differences that distinguish those two groups, made Rebecca's balancing act even harder. But even those Fellows working with students who come from similar backgrounds, and who speak the same native language, soon discover that each student has widely divergent needs and learning styles. Hence our a priori assumption that every section of ELS 201 with more than one student in it will be a heterogeneous mix and will pose new and unexpected challenges to the Fellow.

Typical also is Professor L's readiness to make allowances in his testing procedures for the benefit of Y and D. One of the most gratifying reactions to this program has been the willingness—even eagerness—among faculty to accommodate it, and thereby accommodate the NNS students it serves. Examples of similar accommodations made by other instructors include giving special meetings for the students in the sections of ELS 201, along with their Fellows, to prepare for upcoming exams; giving NNS students additional lead time to prepare writing assignments; altering lectures to make them clearer to nonnative speakers by using more visuals, simplifying language, taking time to explain cultural references, and so on; and changing the wording of tests to make the questions easier for NNS students to understand.

Faced with drastically rising enrollments of NNS students on their campuses, some U.S. universities have undertaken extensive faculty development programs to sensitize professors to the problems these new students have, so that they will make appropriate changes in their courses (see Snow, Chapter 22 in this volume). The only drawback to this approach is the perception among some faculty that such changes will dilute their courses and start them slipping down the slope toward "remediation." Some professors see the administration's proddings as an unwelcome intrusion in their disciplines, even as a possible threat to academic freedom.

By comparison, the changes already brought about by the English Language Fellows Program at the University of Rhode Island have been remarkably easy and harmonious; and when one thinks about it, the reason for this difference in attitude is fairly obvious. When an outstanding native-speaking student like Rebecca makes an appointment with her professor to talk about difficulties her NNS classmates are having in reading a textbook or understanding lectures, that professor is likely to listen more carefully than if he were being addressed by a dean or an outside consultant. He is also likely to accept the changes he initiates, in consultation with the Fellow, not as a regrettable "dumbing down" of course material (which they are not) but as a natural response to changing student needs, of which he had been unaware. After three semesters of operation, with 20 Fellows conducting complementary sections in 41 courses taught by 38 different professors, not one participating faculty member has complained that the program was intrusive or had anything but a positive impact on the course. Instead, the majority have thanked the Fellows for bringing the problems of these nontraditional students to their attention, and so far eight report that they have changed the way they teach as a result. (See also Srole, Chapter 8 in this volume for a content faculty perspective.)

This potential of "peer tutors . . . to act as agents of institutional change" is the subject of an entire chapter in Bruffee (1993). As Bruffee describes it, this change seems almost subversive in nature, in that it "goes to the very root of the educational process. It is challenging traditional prerogatives and assumptions about the authority of teachers and the authority of knowledge. It is saying that peer tutors have the potential for helping to change the interests, goals, values, assumptions, and practices of teachers and students alike" (p. 82).

Another typical feature of Rebecca's section, and no doubt for some the most significant, was the effect it had on Y's and D's performance in the content course and the grades they both received. All NNS students who have completed complementary sections of ELS 201 say that those sections helped them do "better" or "much better" in the content courses. This subjective response appears to be corroborated by data. In spring semester 1994, the average grade of the NNS students in the fourteen content courses for which they were taking complementary sections of ELS 201 was 2.92. This compares to the overall average in those same courses, for native and nonnative speakers alike, of 2.34. Confirming again that conducting sections of ELS 201 has a beneficial effect on one's own grades, the average for Fellows in those courses was 3.62. The averages for both the Fellows and their NNS classmates in those courses were significantly higher than their overall grade point averages.

SUGGESTIONS FOR IMPLEMENTING PEER TUTOR PROGRAMS

People wanting to set up similar programs at their own institutions should bear in mind a few very important considerations:

1. Getting such a program up and running is a full-time job. In addition to a project director, staff for a similar-sized program should include some sort of research or teaching assistant, and secretarial support to help process the increasingly heavy load of paperwork.

2. The study sections conducted by the specially-trained native speakers *must be credit bearing,* and that credit must count toward graduation. There are many strong arguments to support this, and these arguments should be clearly understood by the administration before the groundwork is laid.[4]

3. Once the program is running, communication is the key to success— communication between the director and the Fellows; between the Fellows and the content faculty; and among the Fellows, the director, and all participating NNS students. For this reason, weekly or bimonthly meetings should be a built-in feature. Half or full-day workshops are also a good idea, and attendance at the meetings and workshops should be obligatory. Direct communication among all participants is now greatly enhanced by the use of electronic mail, a

---

[4] The issue of credit for ESL/FL is discussed at length in Blakely (in press).

communication venue that was undertaken recently in the Fellows program and that has been extremely successful.

4. In order for such a project to succeed and prosper it must have, a priori, the unqualified, enthusiastic support of the administration.

CONCLUSION

If the English Language Fellows Program continues to have such a positive impact on the grades of its participants and to produce other beneficial results, it seems safe to assume that pairing specially trained native speakers with at-risk language minority classmates is a good solution to the problems posed by ever-increasing numbers of immigrant students in our schools and colleges. Not only is it good for them, but it brings about changes in the parent institution that are good for us all.

chapter 22

Teaching Academic Literacy Skills: Discipline Faculty Take Responsibility

Marguerite Ann Snow

"My classes are filled with students who don't speak the language, can't read the textbook, and can't write a decent paper. These kids have graduated from American high schools, but they're not ready for college."

"I'm an Economics professor. You can't expect me to become an English teacher, and anyway, I don't have the time."

"I would really like to reach these students, but I don't have the background or training."

These three comments are just a sample of the reactions from faculty across the country who teach in today's multicultural university. They reflect a range of attitudes: from faculty who are having trouble accepting the reality that demographic changes have profoundly affected the profile of students entering our colleges and universities; to those so entrenched in their traditional roles that they refuse to change their instructional repertoire; to concerned faculty members who recognize that accommodations are in order but feel at a loss in terms of expertise and experience.

The dramatically changing face of American postsecondary education and its ensuing cultural, educational, and linguistic diversity present a significant challenge to faculty across the disciplines. Although many content-area faculty are skillful teachers, there is a growing mismatch between the teaching strategies they have honed over the years for mainstream students and approaches which will engage the linguistically and culturally diverse students presently enrolled in their classes. When old approaches no longer work and new approaches are unclear or untried, faculty in frustration often resort to one of two typically ineffective responses—they either lower their standards or fail more students.

Responsibility for meeting the needs of underprepared native English-speaking and nonnative English students has traditionally fallen to learning assistance and English as a Second Language (ESL) professionals. The literature in both fields is replete with examples of programs which seek to assist these students through supplemental instructional[1] or ESL programs *outside* their regular university courses. These approaches may indeed be effective in institutions with large, well-established supplemental instruction or ESL programs or, alternatively, where the commitment and resources exist to fund programs for small numbers of underprepared and second language students. However, as the spotlight focuses increasingly on student diversity, content-area faculty require assistance in dealing with the instructional demands of the burgeoning native-born and immigrant language minority population entering postsecondary education. This changing student profile, in which college-ready students are the exception rather than the norm, may require a reexamination of existing models in many institutions.

FACULTY DEVELOPMENT

In the past two decades, there has been a growing movement to involve content-area faculty in cross-disciplinary collaboration aimed at promoting meaningful educational equity for linguistically and culturally diverse students. Faculty development programs have increasingly begun to offer assistance to faculty across the disciplines. Perhaps the best documented cross-curricular intervention is Writing Across the Curriculum (WAC) programs, which emerged in the 1970s as an effort "to improve student learning and writing by encouraging faculty in all disciplines to use writing more often and more thoughtfully in their class-rooms" (Young & Fulwiler, 1986, p. 1). More recently, priorities have been expanded to sensitize faculty to an increasingly multicultural student population. A workshop series and peer visit program at the University of Maryland's University College, for example, aims to help faculty face the challenge of teaching minorities and the disadvantaged (Mills, n.d.). At Pace University in New York, a series of fictitious case studies was developed for use in faculty development workshops. For instance, workshop participants consider the case of Grant Eldridge, a professor at Metropolitan University, who, when blowing off steam to a close colleague, characterizes his Introduction to Sociology course as "a goddamn United Nations in there" (Silverman & Welty, 1992, p. 1). Participants discuss the causes of his (and their) frustration and work to develop solutions to some of the challenges raised in the case study.

Other recent perspectives have focused on assisting faculty to expand their instructional repertoires. Weimer (1987) and colleagues offer strategies for teaching large classes more effectively, and Angelo and Cross's (1993) work on

---

[1] For further background on supplemental instruction, see Blanc, DeBuhr, & Martin, 1983; Elifson, Pounds, & Stone, 1995; Stahl, Simpson, & Hayes, 1992.

classroom assessment techniques has led to an influential handbook aimed at the college and university teacher. The handbook was designed "to give teachers some practical tools (which they could freely adapt) for standing back and looking at different aspects of their teaching" and for designing "measures to see how well what they were doing was working with students" (National Center for Research to Improve Postsecondary Teaching and Learning, 1992, p. 1).

A collaborative faculty development project at Georgia State University sought to address retention issues for high-risk students through a focus on academic literacy requirements in various disciplines (Carson, Chase, & Gibson, 1993). Academic literacy was defined, for the purpose of the project, as the "language skills (reading, writing, speaking, and listening) that are developed in, and required by, the academy" (p. 6). It is, the authors note, a specific kind of school-related literacy, one that is both the goal of education and a tool by which other educational goals are achieved. In the first phase of the project, the academic requirements of selected classes from four disciplines—biology, English, history, and political science—in an urban high school and urban university were examined. Faculty of the targeted courses from both settings then participated in a series of "dialogues" to learn about academic literacy from the perspectives of high school preparation, university expectations, and students' experiences and to collaborate on ways by which they could promote the development of academic literacy.

This chapter reports on another approach to the development of academic literacy through faculty development. Project LEAP: Learning English for Academic Purposes,[2] based at California State University, Los Angeles (CSULA), assists faculty in integrating language and content instruction within their courses and, thereby, assisting students to develop complex academic literacy skills through guided learning tasks and practice with peer and faculty feedback opportunities. The goal of the project is to integrate the teaching of language and critical analysis skills along with course content to make instruction more accessible to language minority students while maintaining or increasing the courses' academic rigor.

Given the demographics of CSULA, where approximately 75 percent of entering freshmen are underrepresented students (most of whom are first-generation college students, with some 70 percent coming from non-English home backgrounds), we have taken the view that responsibility must be extended to all faculty for improving the academic literacy skills of our language minority students. From the outset of the project, we have fought against the pervasive myth that expectations and course requirements should differ from one population of students to another. In other words, we endeavor to avoid the perception that we are advocating "dumbing down" the curriculum for language minority students. Yet it is well documented that the skills brought to the university classroom by underprepared students are deficient. How, then, can this seeming conflict be reconciled?

---

[2] The faculty development project described in this chapter has been funded by two grants from the Fund for the Improvement of Postsecondary Education (FIPSE), U.S. Department of Education.

One answer lies in Meyer's admonition: "Teachers should have two goals: to teach the content, and to teach the necessary conditions for learning it" (1993, p. 106). We believe that student access and academic rigor need not be contradictory. In this project, content-area faculty have learned to "scaffold" their teaching—to guide students through the analytical processes underlying complex academic tasks. They have modified their syllabi and teaching strategies with the expressed purpose of teaching the academic literacy skills which enable students to meet the heavy conceptual and linguistic demands of their courses.

MODIFIED GENERAL EDUCATION COURSES

Participating faculty have successfully modified the syllabi and teaching methods of courses in the Departments of Anthropology, Biology, Health Sciences, History, Political Science, Psychology, Sociology, and Speech Communication. General education courses in these eight departments were targeted because of their reputation for being particularly conceptually or linguistically difficult. Teams consisting of the course professor, a language specialist,[3] and a peer study group leader are assigned to each targeted course and work together over the course of an academic year.

During the Fall term, team members attend a four-hour weekly training seminar led by the project director. The seminar has two main objectives. The first objective is to familiarize the participants with principles and issues in second language acquisition and English for Academic Purposes (EAP), and with instructional strategies for integrating language and content. Participants are assigned readings each week which provide both the theoretical underpinnings and the practical applications of the various topics. The sessions are run seminar-style, with many opportunities to react to and discuss the readings and course materials from the various perspectives represented on the teams—the content issues concerning the professor, the language demands addressed by the language specialists, and the student perspective provided by the peer study group leaders.

The second objective of the Fall seminar is to rethink the existing course structure and assignments of the targeted courses, and by the middle of the term to design "language-enhanced" versions of the courses which are compatible with the project philosophy, the state of the art in EAP, and the requirements of the participating departments. Critical to meeting this objective is creating an environment in which the teams can build good working relationships and positive rapport and respect, despite the varied perspectives and the differential power hierarchy created by asking team members from vastly different experiences and educational backgrounds to work effectively together.

---

[3] We have purposely chosen to refer to the ESL teachers in the project as "language specialists" out of a sensitivity to the many U.S.-born language minority students participating in the project who do not view themselves as ESL students.

During the Winter term, the modified or language-enhanced general education courses are offered. In conjunction with each of these courses, a two-unit
study group which meets four hours a week is team-taught by the peer study
group leaders and language specialists. The teams continue to meet on a weekly
basis to coordinate all activities. The teams and the project directors meet as a
group in the middle of the Winter term to discuss issues that arise; they meet
again at the end of the term for a final debriefing about the enhanced courses.
All participants write up their course innovations during the Spring quarter. The
activities and exercises implemented in the language enhanced courses are then
edited and formatted into training manuals developed for each targeted course.[4]

INSTRUCTIONAL ENHANCEMENTS

The following sections present examples of the instructional enhancements
implemented in the targeted courses. Although numerous exercises and activities
to teach academic literacy skills were also implemented in the adjunct study
group, the strategies presented here are those used by the content professors
in the lecture portion of the targeted courses.[5] The various strategies can be
grouped into six categories: improving lectures; making the textbook accessible;
assembling academic information; writing essays, exams, and research papers;
preparing students for exams; and involving students actively in learning.

Improving Lectures

Project faculty worked to improve the quality and accessibility of their lectures
by incorporating a variety of instructional strategies they had not previously
employed. One strategy involves writing an agenda on the chalkboard for each
class session to provide students with a "roadmap" for both the scope of the
day's lecture and the new concepts to be covered. Another involves provision
for interactive review of the key concepts from the previous lecture. In Health
Science, for example, the professor begins each lecture with a review routine

---

[4] Three training manuals for nine general education courses are available: *Training Manual I*
(History, Human Biology, Psychology), *Training Manual II* (Political Science, Sociology, Speech),
and *Training Manual III* (Animal Biology, Anthropology, Health Science). These manuals document
innovations for the specific courses. In addition, a manual entitled *Teaching Academic Literacy
Skills: Strategies for Content Faculty* presents a variety of exercises and activities applicable to
any course. A training video is also available in which course instructors and language specialists
describe many of the course enhancements implemented in the project. Requests for the manuals
and video should be directed to: Project LEAP; King Hall A2036; School of Education; California
State University, Los Angeles; Los Angeles, California 90032.

[5] It should be noted that the inspiration for certain activities or the actual activity used in the
lectures may have come from the other team members as well.

in which students are divided into groups and assigned different questions based on the previous lecture. Each group is required to briefly provide its collective answers to the class and to answer questions posed by members of other groups. The instructor fills in any important information not adequately covered. This routine accomplishes several goals besides the opportunity to review key material. Because students expect the review each class period and know that they will be held accountable in their groups, they come to class better prepared, having completed the assigned reading and having reviewed their lecture notes from the previous class. The routine also gives students an opportunity to talk about the material—an often neglected component of a typical lecture course. Not only do they practice speaking skills, but they also have an opportunity to "translate" course material into their own words.

Perhaps the most fundamental change in the way the participating professors approach lectures is a heightened awareness of their *own* use of language. Faculty were impressed by the findings of two studies conducted at CSULA which had direct implications for instruction. In a comparison of the language demands of science and social science courses, McCurry (1991) found dramatic differences in the degree to which professors defined terms. Of the four courses McCurry observed, the science professors defined 79 percent of the terms used in the Chemistry lecture and 65 percent of the terms in Engineering. In contrast, the Sociology professor defined 32 percent of the terms in lecture, followed by the Political Science professor at 28 percent. In the second study, Bernier (Chapter 7 in this volume) examined the challenge faced by second language and working-class students in dealing with the language used in the lectures, textbooks, and examinations in the CSULA general education History course and developed a taxonomy of vocabulary difficulty. It includes three categories: content terms; language terms; and language masking content (defined as terminology appropriated by historians and other scholars with shared understanding, but which also has colloquial, literal, or alternative meanings).

In the training seminar, faculty came to realize they had sometimes mistakenly assumed that the students understood their lectures. In the classroom, their newly heightened sensitivity to potential misunderstanding leads to conscious monitoring of language choices. For instance, project faculty pay increased attention to their use of (a) technical and sub-technical, discipline-related terms (e.g., "V.J. Day," "scalawags"); (b) general academic vocabulary (e.g., "hypothesis," "watershed"); and (c) collocations, idioms, and slang with cultural, generational, or social class connotations which may not be part of students' background experiences (e.g., "Alice in Wonderland," "Gary Cooper," "mortgage payment").

Greater sensitivity to language use was also manifested in a variety of pedagogical strategies, such as (a) routine perusal of lecture notes before class to anticipate and/or minimize potential problem terms; (b) explicit attempts to embed both discipline-specific and general academic terms by providing extended definitions and elaborated explication; and (c) conscious efforts to recycle vocabulary in different and increasingly more sophisticated contexts.[6] Faculty also make increased use of the chalkboard or overhead projector to provide visual cues as well as verbal cues. (In this way, "survival of the fittest," which appeared as "survival of the fetus" in a student's Political Science notes during a previous term, could have been avoided.) Employing another strategy, the Sociology instructor sets up a box at the back of the lecture hall in which students leave questions or ask for clarification of language or content terms at the end of each class. The Animal Biology professor deals with the huge volume of new terms and concepts by preparing skeletal outlines for each lecture. The outlines are available in the library in advance of the lectures. Armed with the outlines, students do not have to struggle through the "noise" of highly technical, difficult, unfamiliar terms and waste critical lecture time worrying about correct spelling; their attention instead is freed up to concentrate on the lecture itself and the important connections the instructor makes among the plethora of terms. The outlines provide the added benefit of modeling good lecture notes. All in all, participating faculty became extremely adept at providing multiple cues to meaning through a rich combination of verbal, visual, and experiential associations— techniques often advocated for sheltered subject-matter instruction (see Rosen and Sasser, Chapter 3 in this volume).

Making the Textbook Accessible

Participating faculty implemented a variety of strategies to assist their students in dealing with course readings, the sheer amount of which is perceived by most students as overwhelming. Course enhancements include orienting students to college-level textbooks through a textbook overview activity, modeling techniques for taking reading notes and outlining in the margins, preparing model chapter study guides, and building periodic quizzes into the syllabus as a way to keep students accountable for course readings. One of the most effective strategies was "Reading from the Outside In"—an approach to textbook reading which breaks students of the habit of reading in an exclusively linear or chronological manner and which incorporates features of SQ4R (Robinson, 1962), Directed Reading Thinking Activity (DR-TA) (Stauffer, 1969), and the more recent work of reading educators such as Schumm and Hinchman (1994). Content faculty walk students through the first chapter of the course text, disabusing them of the notion that they should read page by page. During this orientation, faculty demonstrate how to analyze the structure of the chapter, how to read the introduction and conclusion, how to make use of the headings and subheadings, and most important, how to ascertain the thesis of each section and the overall thesis of the chapter.

---

[6] For further discussion of strategies for vocabulary development in history courses, see Srole, Chapter 8 in this volume.

Assembling Academic Information

Assessments of academic literacy have revealed the importance of integrating information from multiple sources and weaving it into a coherent whole on essays, exams, and papers (Campbell, 1990). Project faculty came to understand that considerable attention must be paid to assisting students to make sense of lecture, text, and other source material (e.g., interviews, data, primary sources) before they can be expected to complete paper assignments. Again, project faculty realized they had taken for granted that students received this kind of exposure in high school or even in other introductory college courses. Faculty became adept at "dissecting" complex academic tasks and guiding students through the component steps.

Teaching students to assemble academic information involves a variety of interesting techniques, depending on the discipline. In the History course, the professor requires every student to turn in a "thesis card" after every lecture. In a sentence or two, students must state the thesis of each lecture, a requirement which continues up to the point in the term at which 85 percent of the students can correctly identify the thesis (typically accomplished after four or five weeks). Activities have also been devised to teach students that compiling and organizing relevant information are prerequisite steps to answering most exam questions or paper assignments. Students in the History course, consequently, practice list-making. During the week before the take-home mid-term exam, for instance, students work in groups to make lists containing evidence of both "change" and "continuity" in preparation for answering the essay question: "Was the Civil War and Reconstruction Era a watershed event in the South? Why or why not?" In Anthropology, students are given a list of statements taken from a novel (which is required reading) and are asked to group them into common anthropological categories that have been discussed in lecture and the textbook (e.g., kinship systems, rituals, sex roles, witchcraft). To teach students how to collect and analyze data, the Anthropology instructor stages a mock interview and provides handouts with interviewing tips to prepare students to obtain informants' views on cultural values. In Animal Biology, students receive practice in interpreting tables and figures in preparation for analyzing a class data set for their scientific paper. (See Kamhi-Stein & Snow, 1997.)

Writing Essays, Exams, and Research Papers

Project faculty in the general education courses have seen significant improvement in the quality of student writing *and* content understanding after redesigning their previous "one-shot" term paper assignments into multi-step exercises whereby students submit parts of the paper in stages. Faculty became much more skillful in crafting writing assignments which make explicit the critical thinking or analytical requirements of the tasks.[7] The multi-step assignments guide students

---

[7] See Reid & Kroll, 1995, for a useful discussion of issues in the design and assessment of writing tasks.

through the writing process, teaching them the skills underlying the assignment (e.g., accessing sources in the library, learning to summarize information for the literature review, collecting and analyzing data, discussing what is significant, and drawing conclusions). Moreover, students benefit from peer feedback as the content faculty make extensive use of check-lists and peer editing groups in an effort to help students develop metacognitive awareness about their writing strategies (for these and future assignments in other courses). From the faculty perspective, the checklists and peer editing groups also help control the avalanche of paper grading which can occur when assignments are due in stages.

The Political Science instructor readily admits that prior to project partici-pation her syllabus contained only a few lines describing the required research paper, and that she rarely answered questions regarding the assignment during the term. She generally felt disappointed in the final products but did not know how to go about changing her approach. After the Fall training, she recast the research paper into a multi-step assignment, scaffolding the underlying tasks in a series of smaller assignments due throughout the term. The syllabus provided detailed guidelines as well as grading criteria. At the beginning of the term, the students participated in a library orientation and completed a graded homework assignment geared toward fulfilling the research requirements of the term paper. In this activity, students learned to use on-line data retrieval systems such as LEXIS/NEXIS, OCLC, and CARL to access sources. After reviewing model student papers, they turned in the introduction and literature review sections of their research papers at the midterm point; two weeks later they added a discussion and conclusion, incorporating peer and instructor feedback in the production of the final draft.[8]

Preparing Students for Exams

Project faculty have also experimented with different ways to prepare students for exams. In the Humans and Their Biological Environment course, for instance, the professor encourages students to submit multiple-choice questions to be used on examinations. By the third midterm exam, 42 percent of the questions which appeared on the exam were student-generated. In the Anthropology course, the professor has seen an increase in the number of "A" and "B" grades awarded after asking students to formulate mock essay questions as homework and giving them time during class to brainstorm possible answers in groups.

Involving Students Actively in Learning

Project faculty have sought to accommodate diverse learning styles through increasing wait time when calling on students, avoiding "spotlighting" students, and using group work to encourage active class participation, especially in large

---

[8] For other examples from Animal Biology, Anthropology, and History, see Koch, Krilowicz, Srole, Galanti, Kamhi-Stein, and Snow, 1997.

lecture courses. Project faculty use the first class meeting not only to introduce the course and discuss its requirements but also to emphasize assignment deadlines and to assist students in making a calendar with a class work schedule and assignment due dates.

One of the most successful course innovations aimed at getting students actively involved is the added requirement that students visit the faculty member during office hours. Some faculty require two visits, but they encourage students to come in pairs. Another faculty member requires students to come with two prepared questions, a "content" question and "language" question. The requirement has created more interaction between faculty and students and is particularly effective with students who are unwilling to ask questions in class and were previously too intimidated to visit faculty in their offices. In some cases, faculty good-naturedly complain that the office hour requirement has opened the floodgates and that they have had to add additional office hours, but most are gratified by the increased contact with students and the breaking down of hierarchical barriers (see Kamhi-Stein, Koch, & Snow, 1997).

SHORT-TERM FACULTY TRAINING

We have also had success with a less extensive training model which does not include the adjunct study group. In this model, faculty participate in a four- or five-session (12–20 hour) training seminar and choose to enhance an aspect of any course (general education, upper division, or graduate) which they feel needs improvement. The faculty participants are required to design "mini-projects" dealing with a selected academic literacy skill and submit critiques of their mini-projects at the conclusion of the training and implementation phases. The write-ups have been all very informative; they reveal the ability of the participants to critique their efforts constructively, illuminating both what works and what does not work during the course of innovating. The write-ups also reveal participants' abilities to focus on student outcomes—and most important, on how their own teaching innovations influence student learning. Two examples of course enhancements, one from a lower-division course and one from an upper-division course, are described below.

A challenge faced by the instructor of an upper-division Chicano Studies course is that no standard textbook is available. Instead, students read a variety of leading works on the history of Mexicans in Los Angeles, many of which are in the form of oral histories and firsthand accounts. Students typically have trouble with this kind of reading because there is no distillation of the information in the form of prereading questions, chapter summaries, end-of-chapter discussion questions—or any of the other features which tend to be found in the typical survey text for a first course in a field. As a result of participation in project training, the professor realized that he must provide some kind of structure within the organization of his class to assist students with the difficult reading demands of the course. Consequently, he now creates cooperative learning discussion groups which meet during each class period, under his guidance, to practice the analytical skills needed to identify the thesis and supporting evidence of each reading. In discussing his expectations for the groups, he notes that "students [become] aware that discussion is more demanding than copying down lecture notes. The purpose of a discussion is to organize, integrate, analyze, interpret, and question the lectures, readings, videos, and other course materials."

In the first meeting of the training workshops, the instructor of a lower-division Introduction to Philosophy course had expressed considerable frustration at the students' difficulty with the conceptually dense course material, a problem exacerbated by the large lecture format. For her mini-project, she embraced the notion of scaffolding discussed in the training sessions and recast her writing assignment into a series of three smaller, discrete projects, each following a specific sequence. Each assignment starts with "rather simple questions and concepts and progresses through steps of increasing complexity." Each project ends with a question requiring students to draw from concepts and theories they have learned and answer a question requiring them to think critically on a subject which they find interesting and immediate. The keys to the success of this course enhancement are twofold: (a) Students are guided through the analytical process, going from simpler to more complex applications of the course material; and (b) perhaps more important, they have an opportunity to practice this analytical thought process *three* times over the course of the ten-week term. The instructor concluded that the quality of student products was "clearly superior" to those of her previous assignment. She expressed concern, however, that the new approach brought a tremendous increase in her work load, and she vowed to find a way to teach the desired skills while easing the grading demands of the three-project format. Perhaps, she suggests, guiding the students through the analytical process twice rather than three times might balance her instructional aspirations with the realities of grading in a large class.

PROJECT RESULTS

The effort expended by project faculty to improve instruction for language minority students has resulted in documentable improvements in student performance. Project students, despite being identified as at risk because of low scores on the Scholastic Achievement Test and on measures of entering reading and writing skills, have performed as well as or better than control students (not enrolled in the study group courses) in terms of grade point average, persistence in completing the courses, fewer "D"s and "F"s received, and a higher percentage of "B"s attained (Tricamo & Snow, 1994). In addition, post-course evaluations indicate that students consistently rate project courses very highly and point to the emphases on reading, writing, and study skills as the most valuable aspects of the courses. Perhaps the most revealing signs of the students' endorsement is that many enroll in sections of other project courses, and that they are virtually unanimous in saying they would recommend the program to their friends.

FACULTY "BUY-IN"

It is clear from our experience at CSULA that faculty do not have to and should not have to lower expectations or decrease course rigor for underprepared students. On the contrary, they can and should require that *all* students perform at the highest levels of academic potential. However, given the gaps in academic and linguistic preparation that many language minority students bring to the postsecondary classroom, faculty must assume increased responsibility for teaching academic literacy skills and for scaffolding instructional routes to success. Even though we have seen dramatic changes in the attitudes of faculty who have experienced positive results from being attentive to students' language needs and altering their instructional strategies accordingly to teach academic literacy skills, getting faculty to "buy in" to cross-curricular collaboration is indeed a formidable challenge.

We have learned much about motivating change by interacting intensively with hand-selected faculty and less intensively with faculty at large in general campus workshops. We have worked with a diverse mix of faculty, similar to that found on any typical college campus. Our audiences have included (a) highly motivated instructors who consciously work to improve their teaching; (b) competent but pedagogically unaware, discipline-focused faculty who do not introspect much about their teaching and probably teach much as they were taught as undergraduates; and (c) rigid, unimaginative faculty who, in frustration over their students' lack of preparation, blame the students and take no responsibility for changing their teaching methods in light of changing student needs.

As ESL professionals we have to think realistically about what will motivate content-area faculty to assume an expanded instructional role. Several strategies have proven effective in our experience. First, content-area faculty must be convinced that they will see improvement in their students' mastery of course content by assisting them with academic language skills. Successful "marketing" of cross-curricular collaboration must therefore cast as its ultimate objective the raising of standards and course rigor, rather than expecting less of students. We have discovered that framing discussion about language as a vehicle for improving *content mastery* strikes a deeper chord with content-area faculty than discussion about improving students' reading and writing skills. The bottom line for content-area faculty is (and should be) mastery of course material. Framed in this way, language instruction which accomplishes content goals is easier to promote. Second, the requisite instructional skills must be similarly scaffolded for our colleagues in the disciplines as we assist them in expanding their instructional repertoires. This requires several steps. Discipline faculty must receive some theoretical underpinning in second language acquisition, such as familiarizing themselves with the distinction between academic and social language. They must also be exposed to extensive presentation of practical applications in a variety of content areas. The critical final step is to provide time for faculty to reflect on their *own* courses and an opportunity within the training session to begin some substantive course modifications (e.g., redesigning their syllabus, rethinking writing assignments).

In teaching underprepared language minority students, faculty are challenged to bridge their expectations as instructors and their students' level of skill development. In our project, we have adopted the transformative model of faculty development (Angelo, 1994), which is not predicated on remediating poor teachers but rather on assisting them with the skills needed to respond effectively to the increasingly diverse population in their classes. Although it is indeed easier to influence faculty who are motivated to change, the readiness of the more entrenched faculty to complain about the poor preparation of their students provides an excellent "back door" opening to begin discussion about successful strategies developed by their faculty colleagues to address similar "lamentable" instructional problems. Training sessions, thus, typically begin with a round of introductions in which participants report their reasons for attending the workshops. Invariably, the complaints which mark the beginning of the session change into enthusiastic sharing about possible solutions by the end of the workshop. This is possible because there are, in fact, many practical strategies which faculty can integrate into their courses to make instruction more accessible to language minority students—ranging from such simple, nontaxing teaching enhancements as writing unfamiliar words on the chalkboard to more complex solutions such as the multi-step paper assignments described earlier in this chapter.

In recruiting project faculty, we have found that even though many faculty members are very committed to improving their instructional skills, they are also wary of being perceived in their departments as "too" involved in teaching concerns when it comes time for promotion. Or, when they have innovated and produced positive results (i.e., students performed better in their classes), they are criticized for giving too many high grades or grading too leniently. We must accept that these biases and misperceptions exist and be prepared to help content-area faculty demonstrate to their colleagues that they have, in fact, raised course standards by giving more complex assignments and that they are indeed holding students accountable for high levels of content knowledge and language skill.

We have also found that junior-level faculty who themselves were educated in a multicultural milieu may be more likely to embrace the notions of diversity and equity in education. Of course, nontenured faculty generally do not hold leadership positions within their departments; thus, the multiplier effect may be harder to achieve than aiming at the outset to convert senior faculty to cross-curricular collaboration. Moreover, many senior faculty came to the profession when teaching was a top priority (over research and publications) and continue to maintain a deep commitment to excellent teaching. In our experience, however, the two most critical characteristics in selecting faculty for project participation are a commitment to student success and willingness to change—attributes which know no age or status limits.

A strong institutional commitment to the ideals of language and content integration is obviously a huge boost to project success. Our campus is increasingly committed to improving instruction for language minority students, and faculty are becoming more aware that institutional support exists from the highest administrative levels downward. More convincing to the resistant faculty member, however, is positive word of mouth. On our campus, faculty members from more than seventeen departments have participated in project training; thus, more and more "disciples" are espousing project ideals. We have publicized the classroom accomplishments of project faculty in various campus newsletters and have encouraged faculty themselves to participate in workshops dealing with issues of pedagogy and multiculturalism. Moreover, department-based initiatives have spun off. Faculty in the History department, for instance, now meet quarterly to discuss pedagogy and share strategies they have found to influence student learning outcomes; hiring criteria have been revised to give priority to applicants with interest and/or experience in teaching linguistically and culturally diverse students.

CONCLUSION

We encourage others to undertake cross-disciplinary collaboration. The following advice may help spur faculty and curricular reform:

1. Give faculty and staff adequate time, resources, and freedom to innovate.
2. Start small. A tightly managed project can accomplish in-depth work without compromising the comprehensiveness or transferability of the outcomes.
3. Work from the bottom up. Enhance specific courses taught by carefully selected faculty, then generalize to other courses and departments.
4. Maintain and, preferably, increase the academic rigor of the courses you enhance. Students will learn meaningful skills that they can transfer to other courses, and faculty and students will participate in more stimulating teaching/learning experiences.
5. Involve both ESL and content-area faculty from the beginning in the design of an approach that is appropriate to the needs of the particular institution; empower them to define the problem and develop a plan to address it within their own context.

Our experience at CSULA has demonstrated that content-area faculty can and will accept responsibility for meeting the needs of second language students by making significant changes in their instructional repertoires. The two principles of faculty development discussed—teaching academic literacy as the vehicle for content mastery, and motivating concerned faculty with practical solutions—have influenced a large number of faculty to rethink their pedagogy in an effort to improve instruction, not only for language minority students but for all students.

A core of highly effective faculty mentors has emerged to assist other faculty in improving instruction. After working across a variety of campus departments, with course formats ranging from seminars to large lecture classes, and with both undergraduate and graduate courses, we have assembled a rich toolbox of activities and strategies that offers something for all faculty. Although there are many challenges inherent in cross-curricular endeavors, our experience shows that ESL and content-area faculty can successfully join forces to ensure that language minority students are exposed to the academic literacy skills needed for success at the university level.

PART I

Questions for Follow-Up Thought and Application

Focus on Theoretical Underpinnings

1. Grabe and Stoller in Chapter 1 note several sources of theoretical support for content-based instruction: second language acquisition theories, training studies, research in educational and cognitive psychology, and CBI program outcomes. In your opinion, which of these sources presents the most compelling rationale for CBI? Why?

2. For each context (K–12 ESL, K–12 foreign language, postsecondary ESL, postsecondary foreign language, or language across the curriculum), characterize the various applications of CBI that are reported in the literature. What models are typically implemented in the various settings?

3. Although program outcomes are generally used as an argument for the success of CBI, Grabe and Stoller note that there are, in fact, few empirical studies documenting student gains in content knowledge or language proficiency. Does this dearth of empirical evidence argue against the continued implementation of CBI? Why or why not?

Focus on K–12 Instruction

1. In Chapter 2, Sheppard, in summing up the results of the survey conducted by the Center for Applied Linguistics (CAL), is struck by the "diversity" that characterizes content-ESL programs as they are currently being implemented. Applying what you know about K–12 education, what do you think are some of the factors that account for this diversity?

2. The results of the CAL survey found that 79 percent of the programs reported no language proficiency requirement for participation in the content-ESL program. How can this finding be reconciled with the conventional wisdom in CBI that students need to be at the high beginning or intermediate level to benefit from this approach? What are the instructional implications of this finding?

3. Rosen and Sasser state in Chapter 3 that "the zone of overlap between content and language development activities is constantly shifting." How does the vignette from the sheltered World History classroom illustrate this overlap?

4. Kinsella offers a rather critical appraisal of sheltered instruction in Chapter 4. What is her main concern? What focus does she propose? Do you think there is a place for "teacher-driven"/"curriculum-centered" *and* "learning to learn" methods? What strategies discussed by Rosen and Sasser, and by Kinsella, might be most appropriate for English language learners at different proficiency levels? Cite specific examples to support your answer.

5. In Chapter 5, Tang presents the case for explicit teaching of knowledge structures and graphic representations. What are the advantages of such an approach? Can you think of any weaknesses of this methodology?

6. Drawing from the four chapters in this section, outline the key features of an ideal instructional program for K–12 English language learners.

Focus on Postsecondary Instruction

1. Theme-based courses are often criticized for their lack of coherence across units. How does the Six T's approach presented by Stoller and Grabe in Chapter 6 address this criticism? Are you persuaded?

2. From your experience as either a student or teacher, do any other examples of academic vocabulary come to mind after reading Bernier's account in Chapter 7? Can you think of any additional categories of vocabulary to add to Bernier's classification?

3. What insights as an ESL/EFL teacher did you gain from the perspective on content and language teaching provided by the content specialist (History professor Carole Srole) in Chapter 8?

4. Speculate on the reactions of Srole's colleagues to her approach to teaching history.

5. The instructional techniques outlined by Bernier and Srole in Chapters 7 and 8 are aimed at undergraduates who lack experience with and exposure to common academic literacy tasks. What might be done earlier in these students' academic lives—for example, in high school—to better prepare them for college-level study?

6. In Chapter 9, Murphey describes some of the unique issues associated with implementing a content-based approach in the EFL setting. If you have had experience abroad teaching EFL in countries other than Japan, what would you add to his list?

7. Research in second language acquisition suggests that student attention to the teacher's use of the target language is critical. How can you rationalize the implementation of CBI in the foreign language setting where few native speaking instructors are available?

8. Three diverse postsecondary settings served as the backdrops for CBI in these chapters—a U.S. language institute primarily serving international students, the general education curriculum of a four-year institution, and a foreign university with a homogeneous EFL student population. Do you see any common issues across these diverse settings?

9. What strategies can you suggest for assisting students in any of these post-secondary settings to build the kind of general academic background knowledge required of content-based instruction?

Focus on Syllabus, Materials, and Course Design

1. According to Eskey in Chapter 10, what are the three dimensions of syllabus design? Explain how these three dimensions apply to CBI.

2. Eskey notes that content-based instruction, like many communicative language teaching approaches, tends to "come down hard on the side of fluency" and that therefore "attending to grammar in any systematic way is difficult." He suggests that CBI practitioners must realize that what they are teaching is not the *content* but the *discourse* of this content. Elaborate on the distinction, and discuss what such an approach might look like in practice.

3. In Chapter 11, Gianelli describes a six-step procedure for creating thematic units. Select a theme and map out the possible subtopics and activities that would constitute an integrated unit for language arts, science, art, social studies, and music; outline the six steps for thematic unit development.

4. Examine a commercial theme-based textbook for the ESL or EFL market. Based on Gianelli's suggestions for preparing thematic units, critique the text.

5. In Chapter 12, Iancu notes that in the initial stages of implementing the adjunct model at George Fox University, "students focused on mastering content and neglected their language skills, while the ESL instructor struggled to balance the roles of language and content specialist." How might Eskey respond to this situation?

6. Iancu differentiates between an adjunct *course* and an adjunct *program*. Elaborate on these concepts, using concrete examples to illustrate each.

Focus on Teacher Preparation

1. Do you think it is possible to separate the competencies required of effective ESL/EFL teachers from those required for effective teaching of content-based instruction?

2. How do you see the Freeman (1989) model (discussed by Peterson in Chapter 13) with its constituent teacher competencies of "knowledge," "skills," and "attitudes" reflected in the TESOL, science, and social studies teacher candidates' reflections discussed by Kaufman in Chapter 14?

3. Do you know of any other training programs that prepare teachers for content-based instruction? If you were to design such a program, what would your training/staff development model include?

Focus on Assessment

1. Many language teachers might argue that Turner's eight stages of test development presented in Chapter 15 require too much time and effort. What counter-arguments could you provide to persuade these teachers of the importance of following such guidelines?

2. How does the focus of assessment differ in theme-based, sheltered, and adjunct courses according to Weigle and Jensen in Chapter 16?

3. Applying Bachman and Palmer's (1996) categorization of language texts as high or low in terms of authenticity and interactiveness, how would you characterize the assessment tasks in the sample content-based language test described by Turner in Chapter 15?

4. Does content-based assessment pose particular threats to the three principles of test usefulness discussed by Weigle and Jensen in Chapter 16? If so, what? And how might these be overcome?

5. According to Mohan (1986), "Greater awareness is needed of the content factor in language tests and of the language factor in content tests." Do the chapters in this section present any solutions to this problem?

Focus on Research

1. How can the data in integrated language and content classrooms described by Short in Chapter 17 assist classroom teachers in improving their instructional practice?

2. Which instructional strategies reported by Short did you find most appealing? Are there any that you would be hesitant to use? Why?

3. One claim typically made by advocates of CBI is that students will be highly motivated because the content is relevant to their academic needs and interests. How would Valentine and Repath-Martos (Chapter 18) respond to this claim? What is your own personal opinion?

4. According to results of Valentine and Repath-Martos's study, the students felt that vocabulary and grammar teaching were not emphasized enough. Discuss ways to give them more prominence within the existing simulated adjunct program.

5. Many researchers today suggest that the idea of "student needs" requires closer examination. How can we further differentiate this concept?

6. Look at the Strategies for Summary Writing presented by Kamhi-Stein in Chapter 19 (Figure 19.1). Are there any strategies that you disagree with? Any that you would add?

7. Select one of the sample student pre- and post- summaries in Chapter 19. What feedback would you give the student on his/her improvement in performance?

8. Zuengler and Brinton in Chapter 20 note that relatively few empirical research studies have been carried out to document language gains by learners in content-based classrooms. Think of a context that you are familiar with where learners are engaged in integrated language and content learning. What aspect of this learning would you want to investigate? How would you design your study?

9. Swain (1988) argues that not all content teaching is necessarily good language teaching. Brainstorm research questions that might illuminate fruitful contexts for CBI.

Focus on Alternative Models

1. Briefly describe the rationale for the projects at the University of Rhode Island (Chapter 21) and California State University, Los Angeles (Chapter 22), respectively, and give examples of positive outcomes for (a) peer tutors, (b) ESL students, and (c) faculty.

2. Although both projects described in this section by Blakely and by Snow involved peer tutors, their approach to faculty involvement was very different. How were they different? What kinds of conditions or variables might affect the choice of approaches? Apply your answer to a postsecondary setting with which you are familiar.

3. Two very different attitudes are often expressed in discussing underprepared students: (a) We must adjust our expectations because these students lack the skills to compete academically; or (b) we must guard at all costs against "dumbing down" the curriculum. What evidence from these two programs can you provide to counter both points of view?

4. The peer tutors in the English Language Fellows Program and the general education faculty in Project LEAP gained many insights as a result of their participation. From reading about their insights, what did you learn that you can apply to content-based instruction?

5. What interested you most about these two projects?

Practical Issues at a Glance

Part II explores a range of issues that impact the implementation and delivery of content-based instruction. The chapter authors raise questions, note challenges, and offer solutions for designing content-based programs, working with content-area faculty, and administering programs.

In Chapter 23, "Collaborating with Content-Area Teachers: What We Need to Share," Annela Teemant, Elizabeth Bernhardt, and Marisol Rodríguez-Muñoz offer readers ten principles that underlie effective collaboration with content-area teachers. In Chapter 24, "Content-Based Instruction: Is It Possible in High School?" Eva Wegrzecka-Kowalewski describes an interdisciplinary program in which language and content-area teachers restructured their courses, shared their teaching aims and objectives, and successfully integrated the teaching of language and content. On the community college level, Young Gee (Chapter 25, "ESL and Content Teachers: Working Effectively in Adjunct Courses") explains how ongoing communication and respect for each other's disciplines enabled a language and a content instructor to collaborate in an adjunct program. Basing their discussion on implementation issues reported in the growing literature on content-based programs, Lynn Goldstein, Cherry Campbell, and Martha Clark Cummings (Chapter 26, "Smiling through the Turbulence: The Flight Attendant Syndrome and Writing Instructor Status in the Adjunct Model") highlight the differential status of content and language faculty as one factor that presents special challenges in adjunct model courses.

The final chapter in Part II takes a different perspective. In Chapter 27, "The Challenges of Administering Content-Based Programs," Donna Brinton draws on her experience to identify ways in which administrators can foresee and address issues that arise when a content-based curriculum is in place.

chapter 23

Collaborating with Content-Area Teachers: What We Need to Share[1]

Annela Teemant, Elizabeth Bernhardt, and Marisol Rodríguez-Muñoz

The twenty-first century promises that ever-increasing numbers of students from diverse language backgrounds will enter the public school system (Lange, 1990). In an ideal twenty-first century, ESL students would learn science, math, and other important academic content in their native languages. Most often, however, ESL students must learn English and academic content simultaneously, through their second language—English.

Given these less than ideal circumstances, ESL teachers understand that they alone cannot meet all the language and content needs of their students through limited contact programs, whether daily or weekly (Barker & Bohlman, 1991). Fortunately, the broader school community can become a valuable resource. For example, science, math, literature, and history teachers who have daily contact with ESL students can help support their content learning and acquisition of English.

This chapter identifies ten principles that ESL educators need to address in collaboration with content-area teachers. The principles represent real-world concerns that emerged during several interdisciplinary classroom-based research projects (e.g., Bernhardt, Destino, Kamil, & Rodríguez-Muñoz, 1995; Bernhardt, Dickerson, Destino, & McNichols, 1994; Destino, Bernhardt, & Rodríguez-Muñoz, 1994) and extensive focus-group discussions with public school science teachers in Florida and Ohio. For each principle we describe a concern, outline a response, and present a relevant example. As a result, these principles summarize what content-area teachers need to know about the ESL students in their classes, and what strategies ESL professionals can offer to help them.

---

[1] From "Collaborating with Content-Area Teachers: What We Need to Share" by A. Teemant, E. Bernhardt, & M. Rodríguez-Muñoz, 1996, *TESOL Journal*, 5(4), pp. 16–20. Reprinted with permission.

PRINCIPLE 1: LANGUAGE AND CONTENT
GO HAND IN HAND

Students cannot wait until they speak English fluently to be deemed "ready" for content instruction. There tends to be a wide gap between what ESL students can understand, write, and conceptualize in English, and what they can say, write, and conceptualize in their native languages. This gap poses problems for students and sometimes leaves parents, teachers, counselors, or administrators saying, "Send them when they know English." Although content-area educators understand that waiting for content can mean academic disaster for ESL students who may never catch up to their peers, the rationale for sending non-English speakers to their math or science classes eludes them.

Several concepts familiar to ESL professionals can make this easier to understand. First, content-area teachers benefit from learning that it takes six to eight years for ESL students to become fluent enough in English to compete with native-speaker peers in an academic setting (Collier, 1987). Second, content teachers need to learn that students typically understand much more of English than they can say or write. For example, a student may grasp why hot air rises but not be able to express that concept in English. Therefore, waiting until ESL students are fluent or precluding them from academic work is a detriment rather than an act of support in preparing them for academic competition.

PRINCIPLE 2: CONCEPT AND LANGUAGE
GAPS REQUIRE DIFFERENT APPROACHES

Determining whether a problem is conceptual or linguistic is a challenge for content teachers when they cannot probe for clarification in their students' first language (L1). Content-area teachers must learn that teaching students who share a common native language differs from teaching students who have heterogeneous language backgrounds. In the monolingual setting, teachers can check students' knowledge of the relationship between words and their associated concepts. In the heterogeneous language setting, however, teachers must do this and more. They must also determine whether ESL students can communicate their knowledge—for example, whether they know the science but not the language, or the language but not the science.

When they themselves are limited to English for probing students' understanding, content-area teachers benefit from learning that a wrong word does not always indicate an incorrect understanding of the concept. It is misleading to equate linguistic accuracy with conceptual accuracy. Working with ESL students, teachers may inadvertently be filling in not only the students' conceptual blanks but the linguistic ones as well.

Words like *force* exemplify another issue familiar to ESL professionals. *Force* has both a common and a scientific meaning. Content-area teachers found it useful to be reminded that whereas the native speaker probably knows the common meaning of the word, the ESL student may need to learn both its common and its scientific meaning. In this case, the word *force* is more complicated for ESL students than a less common word, such as *photosynthesis*.

Content-area teachers have also noted that information about the ESL student's cultural background, academic background (e.g., in science), and language proficiency would be useful in helping them determine whether problems are linguistic or conceptual in nature. Content-area teachers need to see ESL educators as an important resource for this type of information.

PRINCIPLE 3: SECOND LANGUAGE LEARNING IS DEVELOPMENTAL

Although all teachers must deal with errors in students' work, content-area teachers may not understand that for ESL students these errors frequently reflect signs of learning. Understanding that there are stages of development in language learning can be useful to content-area teachers in helping them make sense of the oral and written language their students produce.

As an example, second language acquisition (SLA) research has shown that learners progress through clear stages in their use of verbs (Larsen-Freeman & Long, 1991). The content-area teachers we spoke with responded favorably to finding out that ESL students tend to learn irregular verbs first, then regular verbs, then past tense, and finally more complex tenses. Although ESL students may say *I had previously thinked* or write *I did poured* as they make sense of what they are learning, these errors in advanced forms are good indicators of language development. When content teachers recognize these stages in language learning, they can become better facilitators in the language learning process.

PRINCIPLE 4: CONTENT SHOULD NOT BE COMPROMISED OR DILUTED

Helping second language students does not mean compromising content. In an effort to accommodate the needs of ESL students, some content-area teachers may falsely believe they must water down course content by simplifying grammar or vocabulary, selecting simplified readers, or doing away with textbooks altogether. Content-area teachers are interested in knowing what modifications to materials actually help ESL students; however, they also fear that making such modifications means compromising content for their native English-speaking students (see Srole, Chapter 8, and Snow, Chapter 22, in this volume).

Content-area teachers benefit from understanding two principles. First, they do not need to invest in special or different materials designed especially for ESL students. It is more important to exploit the materials they use every day, with all their students, to the benefit of the ESL students they teach. Second, in exploiting materials, the modifications that count are elaborative adjustments rather than simplifications (Parker & Chaudron, 1987; Widdowson, 1978). Simplifying materials denies ESL students access to the very language they need and limits their opportunities for learning. Giving ESL students more than one word, more than one reading, or more than one avenue for understanding a concept can be more useful than watering down the content. Content-area teachers need to know that instead of compromising content, these more appropriate elaborative techniques benefit both ESL and native English-speaking students.

PRINCIPLE 5: LINGUISTIC ADJUSTMENTS MAKE CONTENT ACCESSIBLE TO STUDENTS

Some states require content-area teachers to participate in ESL endorsement programs. Content-area teachers have expressed resentment toward such programs, noting that the techniques presented are nothing more than good teaching strategies. The science teachers we interviewed, for example, were well versed in the benefits of using concept maps, hands-on activities, cooperative learning activities, and written instructions to complement oral instruction. Moving beyond good teaching strategies, content teachers responded favorably to learning that various linguistic adjustments in linguistic/speaking interaction, made in the process of teaching, work to support learning and make content more accessible to ESL students.

ESL professionals know from classroom-based research (Chaudron, 1988; Long & Porter, 1983) and SLA research (Larsen-Freeman & Long, 1991) that comprehension is related to the negotiation of meaning, and that many types of adjustments help ESL learners make sense of the language they hear from teachers and peers. Content-area teachers benefit from learning that adjustments, such as asking yes/no questions or either/or questions, lighten students' linguistic load in their attempts to participate in classroom interaction. Techniques such as breaking difficult ideas into manageable units (conceptual and linguistic), pausing during speech to allow students to catch up, stressing the main word of a sentence, demonstrating, or elaborating are all adjustments that make content more accessible to ESL students (see Rosen & Sasser, Chapter 3 in this volume).

PRINCIPLE 6: STRATEGIC USE OF READING AND WRITING ACTIVITIES IS IMPORTANT

ESL students rely on different language skills in various content courses. For example, a history class may focus on listening to lectures or reading books. A science class, on the other hand, may put greater focus on students' ability to listen and speak, with reading and writing playing a secondary role in the classroom.

Content-area teachers do not always understand the elusiveness of information transmitted to ESL students in a listening/speaking mode. Words are difficult to retain when not supported in writing on handouts, the chalkboard, or transparencies. Allowing students to approach content from several angles, by reading and writing or by reading and doing, gives them the chance to show comprehension without having to master the control needed in speech (Bernhardt et al., 1994). Content-area teachers can make strategic use of reading and writing activities to support what is delivered in a listening/speaking mode. These activities help ESL students gain and demonstrate their understanding.

PRINCIPLE 7: GRADING SHOULD BE FAIR TO ESL STUDENTS

Grades based on multiple assessments are more fair for second language students. Because ESL students' test performances do not always reflect their understanding, it is important that content-area teachers not be unduly influenced by any one assessment. ESL students may perceive standardized, essay, or performance-based tests as intimidating, depending on their particular language abilities. For example, if students are nervous about their oral skills, a performance assessment in biology may reflect more their anxiety than their knowledge. The students may actually be very knowledgeable in biology but demonstrate that competence more accurately in writing than in speaking.

Bernhardt et al. (1995) observe that second language students are in "double jeopardy" each time they are asked to demonstrate "knowledge in a language over which they have only partial control" (p. 6). Multiple assessments—reading, writing, performance, and standardized scores—give content-area teachers a more accurate picture of all the content an ESL student has mastered (see Turner, Chapter 15, and Weigle and Jensen, Chapter 16, in this volume).

PRINCIPLE 8: AFFECTIVE FACTORS INFLUENCE LEARNING

Language learning is a psychological and affective phenomenon as well as a linguistic one. Content-area teachers are generally aware of the difficulties ESL students face in learning to adjust to a new culture, language, and school system. However, they may not be aware of how these adjustments manifest themselves in language learning. For example, an ESL student's silence may be misinterpreted. Content-area teachers benefit by knowing that a silent period often precedes production in language learning; that fear of correction can keep students quiet; and that to feel safe, students may withdraw psychologically, if not literally, to the back of the class. A teacher's efforts to get to know ESL students on an individual basis—for instance, showing interest in a student's culture and language—create connections that help ease the psychological adjustment to the classroom.

Affective factors that influence language learning extend beyond the classroom to the community as well. Content-area teachers often lack information about their ESL students' home environment and need strategies for getting parents involved in their children's learning. By providing important cultural information and expectations to content-area teachers, the ESL teacher demystifies not only the language learning process but the cultural, ethnic, racial, or language differences that hinder integration and encourage psychological or physical segregation in the classroom and community.

PRINCIPLE 9: ACADEMIC LANGUAGE SHOULD BE DEVELOPED AS A SEPARATE SKILL

Conversational fluency does not guarantee fluency in the language needed for academic success. Content-area teachers are often baffled by the disparity between ESL students' social and academic language abilities. Some students may struggle with school talk while others struggle with face-to-face interaction. Skill in one area does not guarantee skill in the other.

Content-area teachers play an important role in preparing students to succeed academically. ESL students often need to be introduced to the U.S. education system, instructed in academics, and guided in their academic use of language (Adamson, 1993; Bernhardt, 1994; Cummins, 1992). Generally, ESL professionals recognize the academic demands on students in terms of reading, writing, listening, and speaking skills for all disciplines. However, content-area teachers can help ESL students succeed by making explicit the academic requirements specific to their fields. For example, content-area teachers can show ESL students what is expected in their course by giving them prototypes of written work, guidelines for completing assignments, or lists of common mistakes. These types of resource materials provide clarity to students in both content-area and ESL courses.

PRINCIPLE 10: CROSS-DISCIPLINARY COLLABORATION IS ESSENTIAL

Collaboration between content-area and language teachers can have high returns for second language students if ESL teachers approach the collaboration with several strategies in mind. There is much to be gained in sharing the responsibility for ESL students' academic success with the broader community of teachers who also interact daily with ESL students. But collaboration across content areas takes foresight and sensitivity. Obstacles are plentiful: School systems are not always set up to encourage collaboration, community biases may need to be addressed, and resentment may arise when content-area teachers are asked to take on additional responsibilities. If, however, we as ESL professionals are both selective and strategic in our efforts to collaborate, we will be able to advocate more effectively for our students (see Snow, Chapter 22 in this volume).

STRATEGIES FOR COMMUNICATING WITH CONTENT-AREA TEACHERS

From our focus group discussions with public school science teachers, it became evident that several strategies must guide our dialogue with content-area teachers. Because people respond differently, any approach must be on an individual basis. Nevertheless, ESL teachers can avoid misunderstandings if they keep in mind the following four strategies.

Clarify Teaching Roles

Be clear about teaching roles, specifically acknowledging the content-area teacher as the content expert. An ESL teacher who teaches science *vocabulary* cannot necessarily teach science *content* any more than a person who speaks English can teach English grammar or literature. One science teacher said about his experience with ESL teachers, "They are not the science teacher. They're there for support in the language area, not to take over the class." By recognizing and delineating the limits of our own expertise, we will underscore emphatically the responsibility all content-area teachers have to support ESL student learning.

Focus on Reasons for Activities

Conscientious teachers are aware of good teaching strategies; however, they may not realize why strategies such as using reading and writing activities to reinforce learning are of particular importance to the ESL student. The ESL professional's role in communicating this kind of information to content-area teachers cannot be overemphasized.

Create Bridges between Language and Content Objectives

Emphasize the establishment of both language and content objectives in lesson planning (Destino et al., 1994). Content-area teachers routinely make thoughtful decisions about how best to approach content (e.g., through a reading activity or speaking activity). It is important to emphasize in addition that content-area teachers should make content more accessible to ESL students when they make the language requirements—vocabulary, grammar, or rhetorical structure—more explicit, for example, by highlighting vocabulary or language structure on the chalkboard.

Be Diplomatic

Collaboration with content-area teachers requires a proper balance between tenacity and diplomacy. How directly you approach collaboration depends on your school's readiness to recognize the needs of ESL students. Content-area teachers stressed to us that collaboration is most effective within small groups, where a need is recognized and participation is voluntary. The information shared must be succinct, easy to assimilate, well packaged, and conveyed in terms everyone understands.

The ESL teacher who reinforces content-area teachers' domains can avoid marginalization by being tactfully persistent even if that means staying on the periphery in attempts to raise awareness among faculty. Collaboration efforts may begin, for example, by encouraging a content-area teacher who is sensitive to the needs of ESL students to organize a departmental workshop to discuss issues related to ESL student learning. Follow-up activities can be devised to focus on individual, class, or school initiatives. How involved you are as an ESL professional may depend on your colleagues' preferences. Clearly, negotiating a protocol for effective collaboration among ESL and content-area faculty is an issue worthy of discussion.

CONCLUSION

As ESL professionals, we have much to offer and can best help our ESL students by enlisting the cooperation of content-area teachers. We can enlist that aid by responding to what content-area faculty want to know about helping ESL students, by providing them with principles to guide their practice, and by strategically impressing on all school faculty the responsibility each teacher has to support the academic success of ESL students. Any one principle or combination of these ten principles will help encourage conversation. They represent a starting point for focused and strategic collaboration with content-area teachers, who share with us the opportunity and challenge of educating ESL student populations.

chapter 24

Content-Based Instruction: Is It Possible in High School?[1]

Eva Wegrzecka-Kowalewski

Researchers and language teachers have pointed out that there is a strong need for integrated language and content programs for ESL learners at the elementary and secondary level (Cantoni-Harvey, 1987; Mohan, 1986). The chief goal of such programs is to focus on academic competence in addition to language communication skills. Educators such as Gianelli (Chapter 11 in this volume) who have implemented thematic units in their ESL curriculum report positive results. The question to be answered is no longer whether it is effective to implement content-based instruction, but how the integration of language and content can take place in traditional school settings.

THE ESL HUMANITAS PROGRAM

To investigate this question I have chosen to describe a content-based ESL program at Thomas Jefferson High School in Los Angeles, where I taught until recently. The official name of the program is ESL Humanitas. The program originated at Cleveland Humanities Magnet High School a decade ago, envisioned and created by teacher Neil Anstead. In 1986, the Los Angeles Educational Partnership received a grant from the Rockefeller Foundation to fund mainstream English interdisciplinary programs in non-magnet settings. Jefferson High School was one of the first eight sites to launch Humanitas. The project has now expanded to more than thirty schools in the Los Angeles Unified School District, and new teams of teachers are trained each year. In 1990, the ESL section of

---

[1] This article originally appeared in *The CATESOL Journal, 1992,* 5(1) under the title "How Can Content-Based Instruction Be Implemented at the High School Level?" Reprinted with permission.

Humanitas was established as an experimental program in four Los Angeles high schools. It was designed to utilize content for language acquisition and develop students' awareness of the interconnection among all areas of knowledge. Some of the philosophical premises of the Humanitas program are to break down artificial boundaries between disciplines and to develop written, oral, and critical thinking skills through a writing-based curriculum.

The design of the Jefferson ESL program resembles the adjunct model of content-based instruction, which is more typically found in postsecondary settings. Participating students are concurrently enrolled in coordinated classes of ESL, biology, and U.S. history. The curriculum of each semester is divided into three thematic units, and all language assignments are related to these pre-determined themes. The classes are linked through a sharing of the themes, and they complement each other through mutually coordinated assignments. The content of biology and U.S. history is reinforced in the language class; thus, the students use English in the language class to read and write about the topics covered in the two content classes.

All ESL students in the program at Jefferson High come from Latin America and have low-intermediate to intermediate levels of English proficiency when they enter the program. They are classified as ESL 3 during the first semester and ESL 4 during the second semester. Classes meet in a four-hour block of instruction every day; there are two periods of ESL instruction, one period of biology, and one period of U.S. history.

The umbrella theme for the two-semester program is Human Relations. The subthemes, three for each semester, are related to each other and are recycled throughout the school year. The subthemes are introduced in the following order:

Fall Semester
1. Culture and Human Behavior
2. Identity and Self-Awareness
3. The Protestant Ethic and the Spirit of Capitalism

Spring Semester
4. Immigration and Racial Prejudice
5. Individual and Group Power
6. The Atomic Age—Conflicts and Resolutions

Key concepts link the subthemes and are addressed in all three classes. For example, the first unit on Culture and Human Behavior includes the following concepts:

1. Culture is the collection of values, beliefs, customs, and language that people share in common and that can be taught to the next generation.
2. Culture is necessary for survival and the existence of human beings as human beings.
3. Human beings are the product of culture and biology.

4. Learning a language involves learning a culture; it is a process of forming one's identity. (The concept of identity introduced here becomes a natural bridge for the next unit on Identity and Self-Awareness.)

The ESL class for the first unit on Culture and Human Behavior covers different components of culture, introduces key vocabulary, and analyzes the process of acquiring a language and entering the cultural domain of human life as exemplified by the life of Helen Keller. In the biology class, students study the difference between human and nonhuman behavior and focus on how human behavior is culturally determined. The U.S. history class focuses on the cultural roots (Indian and European) of Hispanic populations and explores the historical causes of cultural differences between the United States and Latin America.

Integrating Content

One of the major challenges of interdisciplinary instruction is integrating the content across participating classes. The students, accustomed to the traditional high school program, have to adjust to this connection between the English and content classes, which they perceive as unrelated. Theme integration is achieved through a variety of assignments. One such assignment involves the students in presenting a visual-oral self-awareness project in the ESL class in which they explore their Indian-Hispanic cultural roots. In another assignment, the students create a new civilization on an unknown planet with a focus on the biological adaptation of a group of humans to a new environment. In still another integrated activity, students produce a movie based on the short story "On the Sidewalk Bleeding" by Evan Hunter, which they have read and analyzed in the ESL class. This video project is the culminating activity of the unit. It follows discussions and written assignments pertaining to life choices and consequences and reflects the students' explorations of their awareness of these choices. The project exemplifies how art can be brought into the classroom to provide opportunities for creative self-expression; it also provides a transition to the second subtheme of identity and self-awareness.

Written assignments are another method of integrating the curriculum. The team structure of Humanitas allows all three instructors to work with the students on particular assignments from the very beginning of the program. Moreover, the students are able to work throughout the day on one topic, developing their ideas and written products as they move from one class to another.

Being the ESL teacher in this program, I observed incredible development in the Humanitas students' language skills compared to those of the students in the traditional ESL classes, which I also taught. One of the main areas of growth is in essay organization. As a teaching strategy, I provide students with authentic models of essay writing from primary sources such as Bertrand Russell's autobiography. During the first semester, the Humanitas students are able to produce coherent multiparagraph essays which evidence higher-order thinking skills, whereas their peers in non-Humanitas classes are still working on paragraphs retelling their personal experiences. The Humanitas students' essays, for example, discuss such concepts as the loss of the Indians' identity under the Spanish occupation of the Americas. The success of such conceptual writing in the content-based program supports the view that content teaching facilitates language learning and that academic progress need not be delayed by deferring content-area instruction until students are proficient in the second language (Curtain, 1986).

The fact that the Humanitas students are taught by a team of teachers who simultaneously discuss the same concepts and often disagree about them provides an atmosphere which stimulates intellectual curiosity. It also encourages students to take risks in defining their own point of view. Initially students are often confused when they find out that teachers do not want them to repeat their opinions but prefer instead that they search for their own. Gradually they sharpen their critical judgment skills and start asking questions. Such questioning of concepts, in my experience, occurs less frequently in traditional ESL classes.

Program Outcomes

Evaluation of the general Humanitas program revealed a significant improvement in students' writing over the course of a year. Furthermore, the study found that "The impact [of the program] was particularly noticeable on students' conceptual understanding, where Humanitas students made their largest gains and comparison students made virtually no improvement during the year" (Aschbacher, 1991, p. 18).

At the end of the first year of the ESL Humanitas program at Jefferson High, we also had a very strong impression that the Humanitas ESL students were ahead of other ESL students in English skills and cognitive abilities. The progress of our ESL students was congruent with the overall progress of the mainstream Humanitas students, who surpassed their peers and improved their school performance in such areas as writing skills and grades earned (Merl, 1991).

I attempted to capture this growth empirically in a study which compared the ESL Humanitas and non-Humanitas ESL groups. To this end, I collected data from the ESL 2 and ESL 4 exit exams (mandatory district tests) and the Gates-MacGinitie Reading Test. The results revealed that students in the content-based ESL Humanitas group made greater gains in reading skills than the regular ESL students and scored higher on two of the three district-mandated exit exams; surprisingly, however, their writing scores were lower than those of the regular ESL students. Overall, I was gratified to find that the ESL Humanitas students had higher grade point averages than the regular ESL students and that more of the ESL Humanitas students took the Scholastic Aptitude Test than did regular ESL students, offering insight into their increased motivation to pursue a college education (Wegrzecka-Monkiewicz, 1992).

Expansion of the current ESL Humanitas program at Jefferson High is presently being considered. Possible directions being discussed are post-ESL (students continuing on after they exit ESL classes) and ESL 2 (low-intermediate) entry options. Although students who leave the current program can function very successfully in regular mainstream classes, the mainstream Humanitas program is still too challenging for them linguistically. The post-ESL section would create an opportunity for them to continue their conceptual development at an appropriate language level. Moreover, it is hoped that a three-year program commencing at the ESL 2 level would prepare these students for the academic rigors of college work.

CONCLUSION

Our year-and-a-half experience with the Humanitas program at Jefferson High has revealed several important issues which can serve others as guidelines for setting up a content-based program in a traditional school setting. Since the instructional teams are creating an original curriculum, they need various kinds of support. Funding for many of the above support services has come from the Los Angeles Educational Partnership, the Rockefeller Foundation, and other private institutions. Similarly, the teams need access to good photocopying facilities since they teach primarily from teacher-produced materials adapted from a number of resources. Teachers and program coordinators also need support of a different kind—namely, release time to develop these teaching materials, to attend training workshops, and to plan and coordinate field trips and cultural events. There are presently three training centers for the districtwide Humanitas program where the instructional teams are able to receive in-service training. Additional funds are also made available for a two-week Summer Academy, which provides an invaluable opportunity for all teachers who wish to share experiences and refine their programs.

Finally, our experience with content-based instruction at the secondary school level has revealed that setting up a team that can work effectively together is a key ingredient to success. It is important, in my opinion, that instructors be allowed to create their own teams voluntarily. Developing a new curriculum, adapting materials to the students' developing language levels, and meeting with team members to coordinate instruction requires a great deal of effort. Being a Humanitas ESL teacher means learning other subjects to integrate the concepts and assignments, taking risks and experimenting with new ideas, and being alert to shortcomings and ready to make changes constantly. If a team of teachers is willing to face these challenges, a content-based program can provide a long-awaited opportunity for tremendous linguistic and conceptual growth, for both students and their teachers.

chapter 25

ESL and Content Teachers: Working Effectively in Adjunct Courses[1]

Young Gee

The ESL teacher must develop an effective working relationship with the content-area instructor if an ESL adjunct course is to be successful. ESL instructors face many challenges in doing this for any number of reasons: the content instructor's unfamiliarity with second language learning; disregard for ESL as a discipline; or hidden agendas to have the ESL class serve in a tutoring function rather than as a language acquisition class. There will be more opportunities for collaboration if colleagues are flexible, caring, and concerned; it is especially critical that they be sensitive to language issues. How can ESL teachers develop a good working relationship with content instructors? Allow me to describe the modified adjunct course I teach at Glendale Community College and explain how I fostered this critical relationship.

ADJUNCT COURSE DESCRIPTION

In 1990 the College Access Program at Glendale Community College proposed the creation of a number of *special paired classes* or *connected courses,* which were meant to improve the performance of students in content classes. This led to the creation of a content-based ESL course in which the ESL students were separated from the general student population in the classroom. In the sheltered adjunct class, we decided to pair the advanced reading and composition class with a course in social science—Asians in America. We limited enrollment to twenty-five students and arranged our class schedules so that the students would

---

[1] This article originally appeared in *The CATESOL Journal, 1992, 5*(1) under the title "How Can ESL and Content Teachers Work Together Effectively in Adjunct Courses?" Reprinted with permission.

go to their ESL class on Mondays and Wednesdays from 9:00 to 11:00 A.M. and then immediately to their social science class from 11:00 A.M. to noon on Mondays, Wednesdays, and Fridays. Since this was the first attempt at Glendale to implement an adjunct class in this area, I felt that an analysis of student needs in the social science class had to be done before the ESL class materials development could begin.

Needs Analysis

Hutchinson and Waters (1987) state that a needs analysis must determine the "necessities, lacks, and wants" of learners as well as the course objectives. Such an analysis brings the learners into the design of the syllabus and materials development. The *necessities* of our course were the required instructional objectives which had been predetermined by the course outlines used at Glendale Community College. The *lacks* could be defined as skills, knowledge, or abilities that the students lacked as determined by someone other than the learners. To determine lacks, I created a questionnaire for the social science content instructor, Mako Tsuyuki, to complete (see Appendix at the end of this chapter for a copy of the questionnaire). His answers helped me determine what skills and areas to emphasize in my syllabus and materials. Additionally, I attended three of his class lectures to determine lacks. The *wants* were determined by questionnaires given to all students (native English-speakers as well as nonnative speakers) in Dr. Tsuyuki's regular sections of the social science class.

The needs analysis got my relationship with the content instructor off to a good start. Our meeting to discuss the results of the questionnaire presented an excellent opportunity to get his comments and correct any of my misunderstandings or omissions in regard to his responses. The responses to the questionnaire revealed the instructor's concerns in a number of areas. The first lay in the area of speaking skills. He felt that students needed to ask questions about the readings and respond to questions in class. Listening skills were important because of his rapid speaking style in lectures. Reading skills were needed for understanding vocabulary and main ideas. Writing was also very important. After meeting with the content instructor, I realized that new information presented in his lectures was very important, and I responded to his needs by incorporating exercises to develop skills he felt were necessary to get good grades in his class. I believe that being responsive to the content instructor's needs from the very beginning was an important first step in building mutual respect. It showed him I was on his side.

The meeting also gave me the opportunity to inform the content instructor of the instructional goals of my own class and how I proposed to integrate the language skills of writing, reading, listening comprehension, and speaking with a focus on content. I asked him to let me review essay topics from past exams so I could use them for practice essays in my class. I assured him that I would alter these questions and that I wanted them so that students could practice writing in the same discourse modes. For example, comparison and contrast were frequently used, as in this prompt: "Describe the similarities and differences between early Chinese and Japanese immigrants." Descriptive questions were common, as in this question: "What were some 'push and pull' factors affecting the early immigrants?"

Ongoing Communication between Instructors

Because we jointly built the foundation of the ESL class, the content-area instructor and I developed a team spirit and reached mutual goals. In our subsequent meetings he asked me questions about student progress, ESL methodology, and language acquisition. I, of course, asked him to clarify content information and had opportunities to further sensitize him to specific language issues in his classroom. These meetings also helped to build trust in each other and respect for our two very different disciplines. When he asked, I explained ESL techniques used to foster language acquisition, such as discussion groups or peer correction, and offered suggestions about how to use these techniques in his class. However, I felt it was important to offer only when asked because my suggestions could be taken as a pedagogical criticism rather than a sharing of teaching techniques.

Additionally, we both realized the need to maintain frequent communication by having weekly or biweekly meetings. In my modified adjunct, I used the content text from the social science class as the reading text. This required me to keep pace with the content instructor's lectures so that I wouldn't go too slowly or too rapidly in our content-related class discussion and writing activities. While we tried to have regular weekly meetings in the beginning, we found that these weren't always necessary, so we met informally as needed. Sometimes the meetings would last much longer than we had expected (two hours); sometimes they would be no more than ten minutes. During the meetings we caught up on what we were doing in our respective classes and discussed the progress of the class in general and of particular students in need of help. We also used these opportunities to share information about our respective disciplines.

At about the middle of the semester, we met to discuss student progress and restate our goals for the remainder of the term. This was important because it allowed us to negotiate a balance between the remaining course objectives of our respective classes and what the students could realistically complete. The midsemester and subsequent meetings helped strengthen ties. Developing ties can take many forms, from strictly business—that is, discussing students—to more personal ones, such as inviting the content instructor out to lunch or to have a cup of coffee. Informal meetings give both instructors the opportunity to meet in a neutral setting without pressure to be strictly professional. This was another important means to build a working relationship.

Language Mastery versus Content Mastery

At our meetings, I tried to guide the content-area instructor into seeing educational issues in terms of language rather than content mastery alone. When we could agree on some issue being language-based rather than content-based, I could affect his class. Meetings which were held after his tests provided excellent opportunities for this. After his first test, we met to discuss the problems the students experienced. I was quite frank with him about comments from the students. Most said that vocabulary on the test was difficult or unfamiliar and that they simply hadn't had enough time to finish the test. They had spent more time trying to understand the questions than answering them. I suggested using simpler vocabulary and sentence structures in the explanations and test items, giving more examples, grouping similar test-question types together, and, especially, allowing enough time for ESL students to finish what would take native English speakers less time. For example, a later test included a multiple-choice section and an essay section. I let him know that most students did poorly on the essay because of time limitations. I suggested administering such a test over two days because ESL students need more time to write. He agreed to do this with later tests. (See also Blakely, Chapter 21 in this volume.) Of course, constructive criticism is a two-way street, so it was important to always ask the content instructor what I could do better in my class. How could I have helped the students better prepare for that test? What weaknesses did the content instructor see that might be language related?

When teaching in an adjunct framework, the language teacher should expect that ESL students will ask questions about the content. I handled this by stating from the beginning that I was the ESL instructor, not the content instructor. Although I became familiar with enough content material to correct the students' factual errors, I made it a point to stress that the students were the content masters. If the students disagreed about information, I asked them to speak to the content instructor. It was important to follow up on these questions, and I always asked him what they had asked. This process served to keep a professional separation between content and ESL. The content instructor knew I was not treading in his area of expertise, and I believe this helped strengthen our relationship.

CONCLUSION

Content-based instruction is, in my opinion, ideal for ESL instruction at the community college level. Students at this level are above survival ESL needs. But the academic demands placed on them in regular content classes, which are usually taken in addition to ESL classes, are taxing. While traditional ESL classes serve to bridge the linguistic gaps between the students' first and second languages, they typically focus on language, not content. Content-based ESL classes, where language is the vehicle to content mastery, provide an effective way to assist students with the transition to regular content courses. This necessitates, however, many practical considerations—one of the most critical being the need to build a strong working relationship with content-area instructors.

Appendix

Instructor's Needs Analysis*

Instructions: Please respond to the following items by checking the appropriate column. Only think about your students who are NOT native speakers of English in the social science course.

There are *weaknesses* in these *speaking skills*:	Often	Sometimes	Never	N/A
1. Participating in class discussions	☐	☐	☐	☐
2. Participating in small in-class groups	☐	☐	☐	☐
3. Formulating questions clearly	☐	☐	☐	☐
4. Responding to questions	☐	☐	☐	☐
5. Interacting with the instructor via comments/questions	☐	☐	☐	☐
6. Giving oral presentations	☐	☐	☐	☐
7. Pronunciation	☐	☐	☐	☐
8. Other (specify) _____	☐	☐	☐	☐

There are *weaknesses* in these *listening skills*:	Often	Sometimes	Never	N/A
9. Following oral dictation	☐	☐	☐	☐
10. Understanding lectures in class	☐	☐	☐	☐
11. Understanding comments/questions of classmates	☐	☐	☐	☐
12. Understanding films/videos shown in class	☐	☐	☐	☐
13. Other (specify) _____	☐	☐	☐	☐

There are *weaknesses* in these *reading skills*:	Often	Sometimes	Never	N/A
14. Vocabulary	☐	☐	☐	☐
15. Reading speed	☐	☐	☐	☐
16. Making connections between important ideas from reading assignments to lectures	☐	☐	☐	☐
17. Distinguishing facts from opinions	☐	☐	☐	☐
18. Interpreting charts, graphs, statistics	☐	☐	☐	☐
19. Making logical inferences	☐	☐	☐	☐
20. Understanding the writer's biases/positions on issues	☐	☐	☐	☐
21. Other (specify) _____	☐	☐	☐	☐

---

* Adapted by permission from Kate Kinsella, *Assessing and Meeting ESL Learner Needs across the Disciplines,* an unpublished handout.

There are *weaknesses* in these *writing skills*:	Often	Sometimes	Never	N/A
22. Grammar (e.g., subject-verb agreement)	☐	☐	☐	☐
23. Mechanics (e.g., punctuation)	☐	☐	☐	☐
24. Proper essay form (e.g., indentation)	☐	☐	☐	☐
25. Organization of ideas (i.e., orderly presentation of ideas)	☐	☐	☐	☐
26. Essay development (i.e., enough supporting details)	☐	☐	☐	☐
27. Clearly stating main ideas	☐	☐	☐	☐
28. Being specific enough (i.e., not overgeneralizing)	☐	☐	☐	☐
29. Summarizing and synthesizing	☐	☐	☐	☐
30. Explaining/defining ideas	☐	☐	☐	☐
31. Comparing and contrasting	☐	☐	☐	☐
32. Arguing/defending a point	☐	☐	☐	☐
33. Describing events in order or a process	☐	☐	☐	☐
34. Showing causes and effects	☐	☐	☐	☐
35. Classifying/grouping together related ideas	☐	☐	☐	☐
36. Other (specify) _____	☐	☐	☐	☐

There are *weaknesses* in these general *academic skills:*	Often	Sometimes	Never	N/A
37. Coming to see the instructor for help	☐	☐	☐	☐
38. Using available resources (e.g., library, tutoring)	☐	☐	☐	☐
39. Taking efficient lecture notes	☐	☐	☐	☐
40. Completing reading assignments on time	☐	☐	☐	☐
41. Completing writing assignments on time	☐	☐	☐	☐
42. Coming to class late	☐	☐	☐	☐
43. Plagiarism	☐	☐	☐	☐
44. Reading interactively (i.e., marking in text, outlining)	☐	☐	☐	☐
45. Time management	☐	☐	☐	☐
46. Other (specify) _____	☐	☐	☐	☐

Instructions: In this section, DON'T think about language problems. Only think about course requirements. Please rate the importance of the following for ANY STUDENT in the social science course to get a good grade. Circle only one number per item.

	Degree of Importance Low ———————— High				
47. How important is writing essays?	1	2	3	4	5
48. How important is asking questions?	1	2	3	4	5
49. How important is making comments about lecture/reading?	1	2	3	4	5
50. Writing argumentation/persuasion	1	2	3	4	5

	Degree of Importance				
	Low				High
51. Writing comparison/contrast	1	2	3	4	5
52. Describing	1	2	3	4	5
53. Explaining events/processes in logical order	1	2	3	4	5
54. Showing causes and effects	1	2	3	4	5
55. Classifying/grouping together related ideas	1	2	3	4	5
56. Analyzing and summarizing ideas	1	2	3	4	5
57. Synthesizing ideas drawn from many sources	1	2	3	4	5
58. Drawing main ideas from readings	1	2	3	4	5
59. Drawing main ideas and details from readings	1	2	3	4	5
60. Reading critically and arguing with author's ideas	1	2	3	4	5
61. Thinking critically and arguing with instructor's ideas	1	2	3	4	5
62. Giving oral presentations	1	2	3	4	5
63. Participating in whole-class discussions	1	2	3	4	5
64. Participating in small-group discussions	1	2	3	4	5
65. Other (specify) _____	1	2	3	4	5
66. Other (specify) _____	1	2	3	4	5

chapter **26**

Smiling through the Turbulence: The Flight Attendant Syndrome and Writing Instructor Status in the Adjunct Model[1]

Lynn Goldstein, Cherry Campbell,
and Martha Clark Cummings

In examining any pedagogical approach, it is important to consider the settings in which the approach is implemented as well as the constraints inherent in those settings. For example, many practitioners advocate the use of adjunct-model writing courses as a means of helping students learn content at the same time that they learn to write academic papers for these content courses. In the adjunct model the students who attend, for example, a writing course offered by the ESL department also attend a content course such as political science or second language acquisition offered by another academic department. The writing course focuses on the genres students need to use in the content course and, among other writing activities, uses the actual papers assigned in the content course as a means of helping students master these genres. On the whole, however, the literature on adjunct-based writing courses does not emphasize factors that impinge on the success of such courses. Our collective experience in teaching adjunct writing courses in a variety of settings has shown that certain factors can have serious consequences.

What follows are observations of difficulties that teachers may encounter in implementing adjunct writing courses in higher education. We do not describe a particular adjunct-model course but generalize from our experiences teaching a number of such courses, particularly from those in which we encountered problems. We refer to teacher and student journals and particular examples of courses to illustrate issues where appropriate. We begin from the point of view of the university student, for clarity's sake, but we recognize that student and teacher issues are inherently intertwined.

---

[1] This article originally appeared in *The CATESOL Journal, 1994, 7*(1) under the title, "Smiling Through the Turbulence: The Flight Attendant Syndrome and Other Issues of Writing Instructor Status in the Adjunct Model." Reprinted with permission.

STUDENT ISSUES

The literature expounding content-based language courses tells us that content-based language courses are intrinsically motivating for students (Brinton, Snow, & Wesche, 1989; Leaver & Stryker, 1989). The adjunct model predicts that students will be writing about content that is meaningful to them, at the very least because they need to understand content in order to be successful in the companion content course (Goldstein, 1993). Consider, however, situations where the content course seems either irrelevant or uninteresting to students. It is our experience that when students take a writing course adjuncted to a content course which they consider irrelevant or uninteresting, their resistance to the content course can lead to considerable resistance in the writing course. As one teacher noted in her journal, "Every time I've ever taught an adjunct or content-based course, there have been complaints about the content." A student remarked in a journal entry, "It's really frustrating. I am push into a class and the instructor teach to me something I do not want any help with. I need grammar, spelling, organization not more of political science course."

Students also bring expectations from their previous academic experience about what their writing courses should cover. We have found that some students expect a "standard" writing class which covers a range of genres applicable to a variety of disciplines rather than a subset of genres applicable to only one discipline or course. In addition, some students expect the course to focus heavily on grammar and vocabulary. They may balk at being limited to in-depth study of specific types of writing related to their content course and may also feel that they are, therefore, not receiving appropriate generalized instruction (see, for example, Valentine & Repath-Martos, Chapter 18 in this volume).

For example, in a writing class for native and nonnative speakers enrolled in a required political science research course, we met a lot of resistance to working on the particular writing assignments of the course. Students viewed these papers as unique to the policy course and wanted instead to work on genres that they perceived as applicable to a wider range of courses. Some students came away feeling that the instruction they received was inappropriate or not helpful beyond the confines of this particular combination of writing and content courses. One student in an adjunct writing class stated this concern in an evaluation, "I do not know if you realize it or you are doing it specifically, but it seems we are being taught the principles of political science rather than conventional English writing."

Another issue of concern is students' trust in the adjunct writing course. This trust can be undermined when students believe they are not receiving adequate writing instruction. Of equal concern is the students' sense of who has authority over the content being taught in the content course. Traditionally the academy has vested that authority in the content teacher, and writing teachers have taken pains not to tread on it. However, the adjunct model makes the issue of authority central because students are writing papers in the adjunct writing course which focus on the content of the companion course. Moreover, following current pedagogical practices, we teach and respond in ways that demonstrate that the writing is not separable from the content (see Shih, 1986, for example). Adjunct writing teachers therefore find themselves having to both know the content themselves and respond to the content in students' papers. Although the writing teacher may feel confident that she does know the content and can respond to its use in the students' papers, the students are not always so willing to vest this authority in their writing teachers.

I do believe the class is helping an awful lot in sharpening my political science writing skills. There is no doubt about that. The doubt is how well, you, an English instructor, can disseminate and give feedback on my political science writing. . . . I realize that the main purpose of this course, is to hone my skills at political science writing. But let's make a distinction here—it is simply improving writing skills and definitely not imparting knowledge about the principles of political science, for that is the forte of political science faculty members.

(excerpt from a student evaluation)

This lack of trust on the part of the students can be further exacerbated when the writing teacher is learning the content along with the students by attending the content course. Students may wonder if their teacher knows the content as well as they do, or they may feel that their writing teacher is just "one step ahead." A teacher wrote in her journal, "[A student] wondered if and why the institution was going to keep making its English teachers teach things they don't know anything about."

The issue of authority leads to another concern expressed by students in adjunct writing courses: serving two masters. In some instances, students are confused by what they perceive as differing expectations on the part of the writing teacher and the content teacher. Unless the writing teacher and the content teacher share knowledge and perceptions about writing processes, products, responses, evaluation, and assessment, students may feel they are receiving conflicting messages about what is important in their writing and how it will be evaluated. In a number of instances, students have been thoroughly dismayed by the disparity between the responses of the writing teacher (who focuses on process as well as product and responds to and evaluates rhetoric, content, and language) and the responses of the content teacher (who focuses on product and evaluates solely on content and/or language).

She [the student] told me after class that she was really angry at JA [content teacher] because she had given him a draft of her critique and he had said it was all right, he had even marked it "good" in places (I have a copy) and then when he gave it back to her he had given her an A– (a low grade for her) and told her the policy evaluation was all wrong. Step 10 she got all wrong. So what is she supposed to do/think? Why didn't he tell her it was all wrong when he read the draft? He wasn't reading carefully, that's why.

(excerpt from an adjunct writing instructor's journal)

In sum, from the students' point of view, adjunct courses are not always as effective as we might believe or hope. Students perceive them as working well when these courses fit their expectations about what a writing course should be and do, when they are invested in the content of the content course, and when they trust the writing teacher's control of the content and feel that their writing teacher and content teacher are in sync. Too often, however, some combination of these factors is not present, and students are left feeling that they are not receiving the kind of instruction that will help them become better writers.

TEACHER ISSUES

One of the things that really upsets me about adjunct writing courses in general and this one in particular is that it makes me feel like a flight attendant. I keep picturing us in our little uniforms going up and down the aisles, taking care of the student-passengers, while the big boys fly the plane. We rattle down the aisle of a 747 handing out plastic wrapped chicken sandwiches, smiling through the turbulence, while the big professors sit up in the cockpit. The question is: Aren't we giving up our authority over our own "content" by doing this? Pretty soon we'll be bringing them coffee, too. Won't we?

(excerpt from an adjunct writing instructor's journal)

As this journal entry illustrates, adjunct writing teachers may have difficulty with authority, status, and rank. But this is not only a problem for adjunct courses. More often than not, writing courses are considered "skill" courses by most members of the academy; and although learning to write is considered important, it is still regarded as only a skill. Rose (1985) comments, "It is absolutely necessary but remains second-class" (p. 347). In addition, language learning in general and ESL in particular are often categorized as skill courses and not as important in the university hierarchy as content courses. Auerbach (1991) has argued that, "A fact of life for ESL educators is that we are marginalized. The official rationalization for our marginal status is that ESL is a skill, not a discipline."

(p. 1). A writing course for ESL students, then, is doubly marginalized in the eyes of the rest of the university faculty and administration.

In the case of adjunct-model courses, the writing course is often taught by a part-time instructor and the content course by an associate or full professor. In one case we know of, two deans were teaching the content course. This situation has been variously dealt with. Johns (1989) suggests accepting the asymmetry between the content course and the adjunct writing course. Benesch (1992), on the other hand, states that

> Paired arrangements can easily turn the ESL class into a tutoring service which sustains large classes, one-way lectures, incomprehensible text-books, and coverage of massive amounts of material. Rather than acting as support for this type of instruction, we should be fighting for smaller classes, a more interactive teaching approach, and better readings. We can model a more appropriate style of teaching in ESL classes, including small group discussion, journals, student-generated questions, and we can work with our colleagues in other disciplines to implement these methods. (p. 8)

Johns and Benesch represent two ends on the continuum of teacher attitudes regarding the place of ESL adjunct writing courses vis-à-vis the content course. Before embarking on this kind of teaching, a prospective instructor of an ESL adjunct writing course should seriously consider how much status and authority she needs to have to function adequately in the classroom.

We have found that the belief still persists among content instructors that writing instruction is a skill that can be learned through memorizing rules and applying them. That is, these content professors expect

> that writing courses will address sentence-level concerns whereas [writing] instructors emphasize a process approach to writing wherein audience, purpose, organization, and development of ideas are primary concerns. Grammatical or sentence-level issues are addressed only after audience, purpose, organization, and development are clearly addressed. (Choi, Cramp, Goldsborough, Nashiro, & Tuman, 1993, p. 5)

We have heard the following comments from content instructors on what is important in writing instruction:

1. Student writers use too many *ing* words.
2. I tell students to look at every *the* and see if they can strike it.
3. Only quote quotes.
4. Not to spellcheck is rude.

Further, some content instructors feel that writing instructors should limit their remarks to sentence-level grammatical and mechanical issues. In this view, writing instructors have no business making suggestions about students' ideas because they are not experts on the course content. On the other hand, most writing teachers, educated by Halliday and Hasan (1976), think of a text as a semantic unit—a unit of meaning, not form. It is therefore virtually impossible for them to disregard content in their writing instruction, because disregarding content would mean disregarding the text.

Finally, if and when writing instructors attempt to share their expertise, it may not be appreciated by content instructors. In fact, more often than not, content instructors behave as if there is no content in writing classes, as if writing were something any well-educated person could teach. They seem to hold the attitude that writing, like riding a bicycle or driving a car, is a means to an end we all use but a tedious skill to teach and one in which they have no interest in participating. It does not even seem to occur to them that they could participate in their students' development as writers.

Even though adjunct writing instructors feel that content cannot be disregarded, they will never understand the content to the same degree as the content instructors (with the exception of those writing instructors who are degreed in another field besides applied linguistics, TESOL, language education, etc.). Nor should they. The task of content-based instruction is to make explicit "the assumptions, conventions, and procedures of [the particular] discourse communities" (Eskey, Chapter 10 in this volume, p. 140). Indeed, adjunct writing instructors should take on the role of discourse analysts, working with the content instructors and course material to determine the written discourse parameters of that discipline. Some previous research in this area may be helpful, primarily that carried out by ESP specialists (e.g., Bazerman, 1984; Dudley-Evans & Henderson, 1990; Johns, 1991b; Swales, 1990). But for the most part, adjunct writing instructors need to investigate the discourse of the disciplines of their content assignments as part of their own course development.

This is no easy task. They face at least two obstacles. First, regardless of their attempts to inform themselves, adjunct writing instructors face the students' mistrust of their authority vis-à-vis content instructors. Such mistrust can become contagious, infecting the writing instructors' own self-confidence. This is illustrated in the following diary excerpt by a writing instructor whose course was linked to a political science research methods course:

Today in class I was totally stumped by a student question: Do we just have to take concepts, operationalize them, and thereby turn them into variables? Before this question came, I thought I understood concepts and variables completely. The student jolted me into realizing I didn't know how operationalization related the two together. And that after preparing a writing lesson on operationalization! I've got to go back to the political science material after all—wonder what else I don't yet understand completely!?!

[The next day] Yikes! Have I got concept-phobia now that I found out from my student that I didn't realize how operationalization affects concepts & variables? Here on page 23 of the political science textbook there's a discussion of whether concepts have to be observable or not. I had to read and reread over and over. I guess concepts have to at least be indirectly observable—a concept's empirical referents allow us to observe it at least indirectly. I guess even if it's not directly observable, it should still be precise and theoretically important. Okay, that should be good enough understanding of that—calm down, and try not to panic like that.

(excerpt from an adjunct writing instructor's journal)

A second obstacle arises when writing instructors try to elicit content information from their content colleagues. The writing instructors may find that content instructors, not being discourse analysts themselves, are unable to articulate readily the discourse expectations of their fields. Their language awareness of the discourse patterns of their fields is lacking, even though their general understanding of the content of their fields may be excellent. Their responses to questions about what the writing is like in their fields tend to reflect their views of academic writing per se: for example, expectations of organization and grammatical or orthographical correctness. Thus, adjunct writing instructors should acquire enough knowledge of the content to be able to discuss specific issues of discourse expectations with the content instructors.

We have found it futile to ask content instructors in the field of policy studies, for example, the extent to which they define terms in their writing and the extent to which they expect their students to do so. However, when we have asked about the need to define specific terms like *civil strife* or *agenda-setting* within the field of political science, we have found ourselves in the midst of a fruitful discussion on the discourse of defining terms. Content instructors need to be prepared to work with the adjunct writing instructors introspectively and analytically to help build an understanding of the discourse of their discipline. The discussion and analysis carried out between adjunct writing and content instructors may need to cover discourse parameters of professional writing in the field as well as university student writing, in order for the writing instructor to determine appropriate discourse parameters for a particular adjunct course. Not that they should, but even if adjunct writing instructors immersed themselves in course lectures, discipline-specific reading material, and sample student papers, they might still be unable to develop an insider's perspective without consulting the content instructors as members of that discourse community.

Just as adjunct writing instructors need to learn the discourse of the content area, content instructors need to learn aspects of the field of writing pedagogy in order to provide complementary instruction to our common students. Of primary concern is that content instructors respond to student writing during the writing process in a manner that corresponds pedagogically to our own manner of response to writing. We also hope that content instructors will assess final drafts of papers in ways that correspond to our assessment procedures. We need to develop with the content instructors a common understanding of the expectations of the discourse community that we are teaching, sharing views on guiding students during their writing processes, responding to student work in progress, and assessing final papers.

As anyone who has been involved in writing-across-the-curriculum knows, writing instructors can encounter content instructors who consider it their responsibility merely to present writing assignments, answer questions if students seek help during office hours, and put letter grades along with a few justifying remarks on final papers. What must occur in the adjunct model is serious communication between adjunct writing instructors and content instructors regarding many issues, for example (a) the types of written discourse the students should be working on, (b) the most appropriate ways to clarify writing assignments, (c) the types of difficulties students are experiencing in writing various assignments, (d) characteristics of both excellent and inadequate papers from the content instructor's perspective and ways to clarify this for the students well before final drafts are due, (e) given specific assignments, the areas in which adjunct writing instructors should help students and the areas in which content instructors should help them, and (f) those aspects of the assignment that the adjunct writing teacher should assess and those that the content teacher should assess.

Clearly, what we are suggesting here—developing an understanding of the discourse community at hand as well as sharing a common view of writing pedagogy—requires work from both the content instructor and the writing instructor. There must be reciprocal communication regarding entire fields of academic thought. Such communication cannot be accomplished during a handful of meetings before the term begins; it requires consistent communication throughout the course. According to the literature, a most important factor ensuring the success of an adjunct language program is regularly scheduled meeting time with content and language instructors—meeting time which is paid and scheduled at a time of the working day when all instructors have plenty of energy (Brinton, Snow, & Wesche, 1989; Mundahl, 1993). Without paid, rested time, meaningful communication cannot occur among content and adjunct language instructors; neither can communication take place successfully if the status of the adjunct writing instructor remains marginal. Boundaries must be crossed by both the adjunct writing instructors and the content instructors such that the pedagogical responsibility and authority for writing and content are shared.

CONCLUSION

Teachers need to approach adjunct courses with caution. Institutional parameters find many of us working under conditions that do not easily lend themselves to sound adjunct courses. We are suggesting that ESL writing teachers be wary of situations in which they have lower status, in which the content teachers do not value the writing teacher's content nor attempt to learn it, in which the institution does not support the adjunct model by providing paid time for collaboration, in which there is not common ground for teaching and responding to writing between the content and writing teachers, or in which the students themselves are not vested in the content or the adjunct model. We are not suggesting that teachers avoid these situations; but we do believe that for the adjunct model to work, these conditions must be overcome. In the end, working under such conditions is not only demoralizing to students and teachers alike, but it ends up separating what is inherently inseparable—content and writing.

In the right circumstances, or where there is the flexibility or willingness to experiment with different programmatic components (see Iancu, Chapter 12 in this volume, for example), adjunct courses are a powerful means by which to integrate content and writing instruction. They allow us to open doors to the academic world for our students, helping them to understand the content and discourse of the communities within which they are learning and to become more effective writers within that community.

chapter 27

The Challenges of Administering Content-Based Programs[1]

Donna M. Brinton

Some years ago my colleagues Ann Snow, Mari Wesche, and I addressed practical considerations of content-based program implementation in our book *Content-Based Second Language Instruction* (1989, pp. 70–88). The treatment of the topic was not meant to be exhaustive, but rather intended to highlight the particular issues and challenges germane to administering content-based programs. None of us had had a great deal of experience administering such programs, and content-based instruction (CBI) was still more or less in its infancy. My experience in the past few years has been more intensively in this realm—that is, I have been involved in administering a year-long content-based ESL program for concurrently enrolled university students at UCLA[2] as well as a summer adjunct program for visiting international students. Being in the administrative "hot seat" for these programs has enabled me to see the issues more clearly than I did before, and it is with this in mind that I share my experience here.[3]

Program administrators wear many hats, regardless of the type of program involved. Most frequently, they spearhead innovation and oversee the implementation of curricular philosophy as reflected in course objectives, syllabus specifications, and course activities and materials. They also assume responsibility for budgeting, hiring instructors and support staff, selecting and ordering

---

[1] This article originally appeared in *The CATESOL Journal, 1992, 5*(1) under the title "What Challenges Do Content-Based Administrators Face?" Reprinted with permission.

[2] See Valentine and Repath-Martos, Chapter 18 in this volume, for a more complete description of the curriculum in this program.

[3] In both programs I was fortunate to share administrative duties with my colleagues Brian Lynch (academic director, UCLA ESL Service Courses) and Jean Turner (co-director, UCLA Summer Sessions Advanced English Program). Though the opinions stated here are my own, I owe a large debt to both Brian and Jean for facilitating the administration of these ventures.

textbooks, scheduling class times and rooms, and providing for duplication facilities and audiovisual needs. On the student end, they produce and distribute promotional materials, contact program sponsors, and recruit and advise students. Finally, they direct ongoing evaluation efforts—student placement and achievement testing, instructor observation, program evaluation, and the like (see Matthies, 1991, and Pennington & Xiao, 1990, for a more detailed discussion of these activities). Carrying out these duties requires a combination of pedagogical savvy, market insight, managerial talent, and crisis intervention skills.

The above picture is a generic portrait of the ESL program administrator and does not take into account any of the special challenges of content-based program administration. I maintain that Murphy's Law, which prevails in all of program administration, is all the more prevalent in CBI, since in CBI we are mapping new boundaries in general. This redefinition of boundaries entails an accompanying redefinition of the program administrator's responsibilities.

The following insights from my administrative experience with the ESL summer adjunct program for international students may serve to alert others to salient aspects which need special attention if content-based programs are to be effectively administered.[4] I share these experiences with the UCLA Advanced English Program (AEP) at the risk of being recognized as a novice program administrator. Nonetheless, I believe that the hurdles which I encountered during the course of this program are not uncommon ones, and that anyone involved in the administration of content-based programs can benefit from being forewarned as to what may lie ahead.

Our job was facilitated by a supportive sponsor, UCLA Summer Sessions, whose staff understood the issues involved and were committed to the long-range goal of implementing CBI, even if it meant operating at a loss for the first year or two. My co-administrator and I were fully prepared to deal with the types of problems discussed in the 1989 work cited above—for example, inadequate funding for the program, insufficient compensation for teaching faculty, lack of collaborative spirit among teachers, incomplete faculty understanding of CBI principles, unsuitable facilities, scheduling problems, and excessive teacher work load.

In fact, none of these occurred. Because of the favored status our program enjoyed with the administration, we received priority room scheduling; further, we were able to budget adequately for our material needs (e.g., photocopying, audiovisual supplies) and even received support which exceeded our expectations (e.g., access to the university's computer lab facilities and tutorial services

---

[4] This program, like the UCLA Freshman Summer Program (FSP), follows the adjunct model of program design (see Brinton, Snow, & Wesche, 1989). However, it differs in terms of audience (international students studying in the United States during the summer, not immigrant freshman students who are regularly admitted to a U.S. university) and in certain of its design elements. For example, students attend two linked courses (ESL and a content-area course) plus a general (nonadjuncted) speech course, unlike FSP in which students attend only two linked classes.

and a modest entertainment budget which covered an end-of-term student barbecue). We requested (and received) 150 percent summer pay for the teachers in our program, arguing that since they were working from a reactive curriculum in which they had to respond on a day-to-day basis to what was being presented in the content course, they would be developing most of their own teaching materials. Finally, through a brief but fruitful pre-sessional workshop with the teachers involved, we were able to build on an already existing collaborative spirit and further orient teachers to the most critical underlying principles of CBI.[5]

CHALLENGES

The following challenges, however, caught us unprepared.

Student Recruitment

We were scheduled to offer two back-to-back six-week sessions, for which UCLA Summer Sessions had promised us 150 students each. The reality of offering a content-based program for the designated proficiency level,[6] however, soon became clear, as rosters for the first session showed only 12 students enrolled in the program. Eventually we were able to secure 18 students who both fit our desired profile (i.e., academically oriented with the required TOEFL level) and were interested in participating in the program. The second summer session fared slightly better, with a Japanese client providing the majority of the 88 students who participated. However, this brought a problem of a different nature, namely that the Japanese/non-Japanese (i.e., European and South American) mix in this session was extremely uneven, leading to certain cross-cultural problems which impacted negatively on the effectiveness of the program. This was particularly evident in the speech component, in which the oral proficiency differences of the Japanese and non-Japanese students were most evident, and in which student needs diverged most radically.

Marketing the Program

We had attempted to communicate the nature of the program through specially designed promotional materials. Where possible (both in Japan and later when students arrived on campus), we also held a student orientation to present program specifics and answer questions. However, we found that explaining a complex venture like CBI in language which is accessible to students (and especially within the confines of brochure copy) is a nearly impossible task. The

---

[5] See Peterson, Chapter 13 in this volume, for more information on preservicing and in-servicing teachers in the CBI context.

[6] This program was designed for students at the higher end of the proficiency spectrum (TOEFL 500+).

student orientation session at UCLA was slightly more successful; however, the students' complete unfamiliarity with this model of instruction made it difficult for them to imagine the integrated language and content teaching they would be experiencing. Many were puzzled by the information presented and opted instead to enroll in the more traditional intensive language program that was also available on campus.

Red Tape

Working within a bureaucratic hierarchy has its rewards (e.g., staff available to assist in various aspects of the program) and its punishments. Because our program was part of the regular summer offerings, our students enrolled through the central office, which also handles drop/add requests and the like. Staff in the Summer Sessions office did not understand that in our model of linked courses, section changes entailed a change in not one course but in the entire suite of courses which constituted the program (ESL, speech, and the content course). This was but the beginning of numerous red tape snags, which included confusion regarding the credit status of the three linked classes, lack of compliance with our request for a certificate of program completion, and the like.

Selection of Content Classes

We wanted to offer a wide variety of content courses. However, in order to facilitate curriculum and materials development efforts, we had to team ESL teachers and attach multiple sections of ESL to a given content area. This limited the number of content courses we could offer. The eventual AEP content course offerings (Economics; Psychology; Western Civilization; American History, 1900–present; and Communication Studies) were selected with a view toward allowing students to choose from introductory courses across a broad spectrum of disciplines. In selecting these courses, we also considered factors such as the instructional effectiveness of the professors involved and their willingness to include international students in their classes. Unfortunately, we did not always have access to the instructors' syllabuses or reading lists, nor did we know in advance the academic backgrounds and interests of our student population. What in fact occurred was that the majority of students preferred the Communication Studies course, with far fewer selecting the remainder of the classes.

One of the issues we did not adequately anticipate in content course selection was the degree to which students' prior background knowledge would figure in their content course performance. This proved to be the case in Western Civilization, Economics, and American History. Especially in the American History class, the American students had a distinct cultural advantage over the international students—most of whom had never heard of Malcolm X, the WPA, the New Deal, and so forth (see also Bernier, Chapter 7 in this volume). Finally, the six-book course reading load for the American History course (which included a novel and several autobiographies as well as several academic textbooks) overwhelmed the international students and caused several to abandon their attempt to keep up with the content course material.

Cultural Misunderstandings

Cultural misunderstandings are bound to occur in any program, especially those involving recently arrived international students who may be experiencing culture shock. In a content-based program, students not only experience the predictable kinds of cultural alienation but suffer as well from lack of prior exposure to the university system. Perhaps the most interesting of our summer experiences in this regard involved a student from France who, misunderstanding the scantron instructions on his midterm psychology exam, designated the *no post grade* column, assuming that this meant the grade would be reported to him personally rather than mailed to him. When he did not find his grade listed on the midterm grade roster, he interpreted this as meaning he had failed the exam. Disappointed, he stopped attending the psychology class. Only through intervention by his ESL instructor, who sensed that something was wrong, was the situation corrected. These kinds of misunderstanding may seem trivial or even amusing when first encountered; however, they clearly undermine students' efforts to achieve their academic goals and thus impact seriously on the program administrator's attempts to maintain the integrity of the program.

Attrition

No doubt all programs suffer from problems of attrition. However, in an adjunct model program, the attrition factor is compounded by the fact that a student who is failing one class is in all likelihood at risk in the linked course as well; thus, once the failure factor sets in, it is multiplied over the number of courses involved, and students do not have the usual recourse of redoubling their efforts in their "other" courses. This was the case in AEP, especially in those courses (e.g., Economics, American History) where background knowledge played a larger role. Since these courses had lower student enrollments to begin with, the backwash effect was particularly disruptive to the effective implementation of the adjunct model, and teachers in both the linked courses experienced a high degree of frustration as a result.

CONCLUSION

Having detailed the setbacks which impeded the smooth administration of the program, I'd like to end with several recommendations. First, adjunct programs at the postsecondary level require a high level of student proficiency. Student recruitment at this end of the proficiency scale is difficult, since there may not be sufficient numbers of students who meet the designated cutoff requirements. Without focused, long-term efforts on the part of the sponsor, such programs will not be realizable. Second, recruitment efforts need to be backed up by well-planned and professional program packaging. In other words, the program must be described in such a way that students understand its purpose and intent. Planning ahead for the future of AEP, for example, we assembled video footage in which participants candidly gave their own assessment of the program. Once available in enrollment centers, this video marketing tool should pique students' curiosity and present a more valid picture of what this type of language study entails. Finally, these programs need to be adequately funded—either through institutional funding or external grant sources.

Next, although being a part of a centralized bureaucracy can provide a program with important support services, content-based programs have special requirements which fall outside the realm of the procedures normally followed in the centralized administration. Such programs definitely benefit from having a decentralized structure (or at least a clearly detailed set of special procedures) to handle admissions, enrollment, and scheduling. This would prevent situations in which students are misdirected or falsely informed and would simplify program administration. In terms of content class selection and cultural misunderstandings, a more sensitive administration (i.e., one aware of the types of pitfalls encountered in AEP) would be able to more effectively orient students to the U.S. university system and select courses which require less cultural background knowledge on the part of the students.

Even in the administratively difficult arena of CBI, the ends do justify the means. Satisfied students and teachers and documented program success are the administrator's ultimate reward; and it is my belief that an effectively administered content-based program, by virtue of the meaningful language exposure and practice it provides, produces these desired end results.

Students in AEP made measured gains in their writing and speaking skills, and (as measured via a self-assessment instrument) increased in their perceived ability to perform a variety of academic tasks (e.g., take notes from a lecture, read an academic textbook, or ask a professor a question during office hours). They also showed gains in academic writing skills on a pre/post composition measure. When asked to rate the program's effectiveness, they gave it high ratings for improving their academic writing and listening skills as well as their English conversation and textbook reading skills. The teachers, too, expressed satisfaction in their end-of-term reviews of curriculum, as summarized by the following comment:

My overall experience with the Summer Adjunct Program this year was quite positive—certainly the best of my four summers teaching summer-institute-type programs. Where the content class was concerned, students received clearly presented, comprehensible input. . . . As for [the ESL class], the class worked much of the time in an almost magical way. If an ordinary [ESL class] were half as involved with the material and the discussions as this class was, it would still be a good class.

Given these kinds of rewards, I heartily encourage others to embark on the venture of content-based program administration. I further urge them to document their administrative efforts, thus building on the groundwork which I lay in this chapter.

PART II

Questions for Follow-Up Thought and Application

1. Teemant et al. (Chapter 23), Wegrzecka-Kowalewski (Chapter 24), and Gee (Chapter 25) discuss factors that contribute to the successful implementation of content-based instruction. In your opinion, which suggestions provided by the authors are the most useful?

2. According to the above authors, what conditions present the most serious threat to the implementation of content-based instruction?

3. Goldstein, Campbell, and Cummings (Chapter 26) discuss the delicate power relationship that exists between the content and language instructors in an adjunct model program. Would Gee agree with their characterization of the "pilot" and the "flight attendant"? Why or why not?

4. Brinton (Chapter 27) lists numerous challenges that she faced in administering a content-based program. Map out a strategy for how she might avoid these challenges the second time around.

5. Many of the content-based programs described in this volume benefited from outside funding. Why do these programs require significant resources? Brainstorm possible funding sources (e.g., local, state/provincial, national, or private). Are there contexts in which content-based instruction can be implemented without special funding? If so, what conditions would need to be met for the program to succeed?

Connections between Content-Based Instruction and Other Teaching Approaches

Part III considers the relationship between content-based instruction and other instructional approaches being used extensively in language teaching settings across a variety of educational levels. All the authors in this section were asked to consider specifically the connections among current approaches to second and foreign language teaching.

David Freeman and Yvonne Freeman (Chapter 28, "Whole Language Teaching and Content-Based Instruction: Are They Compatible?") assess the compatibility of content-based teaching and a popular approach in elementary and secondary school instruction—whole language teaching. At the adult level, Rosemary Henze and Anne Katz (Chapter 29, "The Role of Content-Based Instruction in Workplace Literacy") examine the application of content-based instruction to workplace literacy programs. In Chapter 30, "VESL and Content-Based Instruction: What Do They Have in Common?" Kathleen Wong explores the commonalities between content-based instruction and vocational ESL. Ann Johns (Chapter 31, "English for Specific Purposes and Content-Based Instruction: What Is the Relationship?") highlights the similarities and differences between English for Specific Purposes and content-based instruction. In Chapter 32, "The Role of Content in Task-Based EAP Instruction," Joan Carson, Josephine Taylor, and Laureen Fredella take a critical look at the role of content in task-based language teaching programs.

The last two chapters in Part III reprise two traditional components of language teaching curricula, namely, culture and literature. Sharon Hilles and Dennis Lynch (Chapter 33, "Culture as Content") and Christine Holten (Chapter 34, "Literature: A Quintessential Content") argue that culture and literature, respectively, serve as ideal content for content-based teaching.

chapter 28

Whole Language Teaching and Content-Based Instruction: Are They Compatible?[1]

David Freeman and Yvonne Freeman

The answer to this question is, "Yes, absolutely!" A whole language approach is appropriate for teaching second language through content-based instruction for learners of all ages and in all subject areas. However, in order to understand how whole language supports content-based instruction, it is necessary to recognize two things: (a) Whole language is not limited to the teaching of reading and writing in lower elementary school grades, and (b) whole language is an approach to teaching and learning rather than a method or a series of materials. Teachers who use a whole language approach with second language learners realize the importance of teaching language through subject-area content.

ROOTS OF WHOLE LANGUAGE

Whole language has its roots in the eighteenth-century writings of Rousseau and Pestalozzi, both of whom encouraged a holistic approach to all education. They believed that learning moves "from concrete, sensory experience" and should not be "drilled through rote memorization and corporal punishment" (Miller, 1988, p. 7). Shannon (1991) points out that the current whole language movement is based on two historical traditions: student-centered education and social reconstruction. In whole language classes, teachers teach "to and from the experiences of their students" (Olsen & Mullen, 1990), and they involve students in critical assessment of their social reality (Freeman & Freeman, 1991). These

---

[1] This article originally appeared in *The CATESOL Journal, 1992, 5*(1) under the title "Is Whole Language Teaching Compatible with Content-Based Instruction?" Reprinted with permission.

goals can best be accomplished in whole language classes that offer solid subject-matter teaching.

Current whole language practices in the United States are the result of a grassroots movement of elementary teachers who were dissatisfied with being forced to teach reading from carefully structured materials such as basal readers and writing from grammar rules and language workbooks. The research in first language (L1) reading and writing by K. Goodman (1986), Y. Goodman (1985), Harste, Woodward, and Burke (1984), Smith (1971), and Graves (1983) and in second language (L2) literacy by Edelsky (1986) and Hudelson (1984) supports an approach that uses authentic reading materials, process writing, and organization around theme cycles (Edelsky, Altwerger, & Flores, 1991).

However, whole language is not limited to the teaching of literacy or the use of theme cycles in the lower grades. Whole language has also been successfully implemented in upper-grade content classes, including classes with second language students (Freeman & Freeman, 1989a, 1989b, 1992). Content-area teachers realize that their current students are socially, economically, and ethnically diverse and that any one set of educational programs, textbooks, and workbooks cannot meet their needs. ESL students need more than language drills or exercises designed to develop communicative competence. They do not have years to practice English before they acquire academic knowledge. They need to be offered an education that allows them to learn English through meaningful content so they can achieve academic and social success, and that is the goal of whole language teachers for their second language students.

THE QUESTIONING LESSON PLAN: WHOLE LANGUAGE CONTENT PLANNING

Content-based instruction for second language students involves students in reading and writing in all subject areas. Content-area teachers using whole language often organize their instruction around themes that come out of the students' own questions. These themes engage students in meaningful activities that move from whole to part, build on students' interests and backgrounds, serve their needs, provide opportunities for social interaction, and develop their skills in oral and written language as they use their first and second languages.

Clark (1988) has pointed out that curricula should involve students "in some of the significant issues in life." He therefore encourages teachers to design their curricula around "questions worth arguing about" (p. 29), suggesting questions for different age groups, such as: "How am I a member of many families?" (grades K–1); "What are the patterns that make communities work?" (grades 2–3); "How do humans and culture evolve and change?" (grades 4–5); "How does one live responsibly as a member of the global village?" (grades 6–8).

Sizer (1990) draws on the same idea by suggesting that organizing around *essential questions* leads to "engaging and effective curricula." In social studies, teachers responsible for teaching U.S. history might begin with broad questions that are especially appropriate in our diverse society, such as "Who is American? Who should stay? Who should stay out? Whose country is it anyway?" (p. 49). Sizer suggests larger questions for long-term planning and smaller, engaging questions to fit within the broader ones. For example, an essential question in botany might be, "What is life, growth, 'natural' development, and what factors most influence healthy development?" (p. 50). A smaller engaging question might be, "Do stems of germinating seedlings always grow upwards and the roots downwards?" (p. 50).

In all the above examples, the goal is to make the curriculum student centered rather than teacher centered by involving students in answering relevant, real-world questions that they help to raise. Whole language teachers often organize curriculum by using questions for day-by-day lesson planning. It is important to point out that in learner-centered classes, the questions come primarily from the students; however, as a member of the learning community, the teacher can also raise questions.

A method for planning that is consistent with whole language and suitable for content classes is the following Questioning Lesson Plan (see Figure 28.1).

FIGURE 28.1   Questioning lesson plan

1. **What is the question worth talking about?**
   Can the topic for this lesson be formulated in a question? What is the engaging smaller question that fits into your broader question for your overall theme?

2. **How does the question fit into your overall plan?**
   What is the broad question/theme that you and your students are exploring over time? How does the smaller, engaging question support the concepts you are working on with this broad question?

3. **How will you find out what the students already know about the question?**
   What are different ways your students might show what they already know about answering the question? You might brainstorm, do an experiment, interview someone, and so forth.

4. **What strategies will you use together to explore the question?**
   What are ways the question might be answered? You and your students might read, do an experiment, brainstorm, ask an expert, work out a problem together, and so forth. Ask the students if they have ideas about how to answer the question.

5. **What materials will you use together to explore the question?**
   List the resources, including people, that students might use to answer the question. Again, ask the students if they have ideas about this.

6. **What steps will you and the students take to explore the question?**
   In order to be sure that you are keeping in mind principles about learning, consult the *Whole Language Checklist*.

7. **How will you observe the students' learning?**
   What are some different ways to evaluate the process of your students' learning? Be sure to consider alternatives to traditional tests, including group presentations, a group-produced book or newspaper, the results of an experiment, a drawing or schemata, and so forth.

8. **What specific techniques will you use to ensure that the input is comprehensible for your second language students?**
   Have you planned to use sheltering techniques, including visuals, gestures, group work, and first language support?

- Does the lesson move from the general to the specific? Are details presented within a general conceptual framework?

- Is there an attempt to draw on student background knowledge and interests? Are students given choices?

- Is the content meaningful? Does it serve a purpose for the learners?

- Do students work together cooperatively? Do students interact with one another, or do they only react to the teacher?

- Do students have an opportunity to read and write as well as speak and listen during the lesson?

- Is there support for the students' first language and culture?

- Does the teacher demonstrate a belief that students will succeed?

FIGURE 28.2   Whole language checklist

This lesson plan format is designed to help teachers reconceptualize a curriculum as a series of questions generated by the students and the teacher as they explore topics together. The format also encourages teachers to keep in focus the broad concepts they are studying. It asks them to consider how each lesson might connect to broader themes. It also asks them to consider specific ways they can make the input comprehensible for their second language students. Planning lessons with this format is one way teachers can put whole language theory into practice with second language students. In addition, teachers have found that the whole language checklist (see Figure 28.2), drawn from whole language principles (Freeman & Freeman, 1988), is useful in evaluating their content lessons.

CONCLUSION

The popular view that whole language means literacy instruction for elementary students is too narrow. Whole language extends to math, science, social studies, and all the content areas and to secondary as well as elementary education. Whole language means instruction that centers on students' needs and interests. Teachers applying whole language with second language students teach language through content because they recognize the importance of their students' developing not only language but also academic competence. Whole language without content instruction is not whole language.

chapter 29

The Role of Content-Based Instruction in Workplace Literacy[1]

Rosemary Henze and Anne Katz

Workplace literacy has been defined as

> more than just knowing how to read. It's also more than having the narrow skills for a specific job. When we use the term "literacy" we include the full array of basic skills that enable an individual to "use printed and written information to function in society, to achieve one's goals, and to develop one's knowledge and potential." (National Assessment of Educational Progress, 1985, cited in Sarmiento & Kay, 1990, p. 3)

In this general definition, the authors conceive of workplace literacy as a benefit to both native speakers and nonnative speakers of English. In this chapter we focus on workplace literacy as it applies to the ESL population. The vignettes that follow give the flavor of two such situations.

> The room contains long tables placed end to end. Large tinted windows look down over Market Street, where pedestrians and cars speed on their way. At 10 minutes before the hour a few students have already arrived for class, dressed for the work day that will begin at the end of their two-hour block of English for the Workplace. The students come from a myriad of language backgrounds and represent a variety of departments and employment positions within this large bank; the one thing they share is a common need to improve their English language skills. By doing so, employees believe they will improve their current job performance and increase their opportunities for advancement. During the class, they will focus on increasing their proficiency using content drawn from the workplace environment—the

---

[1] This article originally appeared in *The CATESOL Journal, 1992, 5*(1) under the title "What Is the Relationship Between Workplace Literacy and Content-Based Instruction?" Reprinted with permission.

company newspaper, interactions among employees and between employees and managers, telephone protocols, computer mail. Lessons are based on these real-life uses of language. The two instructors are independent contractors hired by the bank to provide ten-week-long blocks of instruction.

In another part of the city, a small but growing bakery known for its rich desserts made with fresh ingredients employs a production work force that is Hispanic, Vietnamese, Indonesian, and Chinese. While most of the time employees are involved in actions—weighing, mixing, baking, decorating—they also need to be able to use English language skills. They need, among other things, to understand instructions, acquire the ability to read a work order, and follow safety instructions and maintenance work procedures. In worksite-based classes designed on the basis of a "literacy audit," workers develop English language proficiency in areas directly related to the needs of their jobs. Classes are offered in six-week segments provided by Project EXCEL, a workplace literacy program funded by the U.S. Department of Education as a training program offered by the Career Resources Development Center.

Though a great deal of variation exists among workplace literacy programs, these two vignettes illustrate some aspects of the relationship between workplace literacy and content-based approaches. To clarify this relationship, we compare the two approaches in terms of several key dimensions: audience, location, purpose, content, and teachers.

DIMENSIONS

Who is it for? Workplace literacy programs such as Project EXCEL are designed for adults who are working. Participants may be native speakers of English or may be in various stages of acquiring English as a second language. Content-based ESL instruction, on the other hand, can be designed for any age group all the way from elementary school children through college students. The participants are by definition acquiring English as a second language.

However, the differences in the two audiences go beyond age and native language. Though rarely articulated, there is an essential class difference in that workplace literacy programs are most often geared for workers such as those in the bakery example, whereas content-based instruction is typically geared for students pursuing an academic program. When and if these students eventually join the work force, they will probably not be working at the lowest levels of the production force. In this sense, the distinction between the two types of programs reflects the vocational/academic split which runs through so much of our educational system. (This is not limited to the United States. Many, if not most, other countries make a similar or stronger separation.)

Where does it take place? Workplace literacy programs may take place at a worksite or at a site near the workplace. Content-based ESL programs generally take place in a school or university setting.

What are the purpose and content? Both types of programs make the same basic assumption—that it is better to teach language-related skills in context than in isolation (Mohan, 1986). The purpose of both is to integrate language development with content so that language and/or literacy will be learned in a more meaningful context. In the case of content-based approaches, the content is usually math, science, history, or other academic disciplines. In the case of workplace literacy, the content is the knowledge and skills needed for particular jobs. For example, some of the employees in the bank example needed to learn how to write more effective memoranda. Others needed to improve their skills at decoding and sending computer mail. Still others, customer service representatives, needed to work on telephone protocols for handling customer complaints. All these employees were working on language set within specific workplace contexts.

How is the content determined? In content-based ESL, academic needs and state frameworks determine the content to be taught, although individual teachers do usually have some flexibility in adapting the frameworks to the proficiency levels and needs of individual classes. In workplace literacy programs, on the other hand, the determination of content depends on two major variables. One is the linguistic demands of the particular workplace. To determine these linguistic demands, an instructor or curriculum specialist studies the particular job to find out what kinds of language the employees need in order to function effectively in that environment. For example, in the second job situation described above, Project EXCEL curriculum developers conducted a literacy audit to determine what reading, computation, and communicative skills were required for workers to perform job tasks effectively. EXCEL staff collected all printed materials and observed the working environment on several occasions. They also videotaped and audiotaped the working environment, including workers' performance and communication. These data provided an exhaustive inventory of language functions in the workplace. The second major variable is the level of participants' communicative skills, usually determined through some form of needs assessment at the beginning of the program. The literacy audit provides a specific description of the communicative demands of the workplace, whereas the needs assessment considers students' skills in relation to those workplace demands.

Who teaches it? Both content-based ESL and workplace literacy programs use similar teaching configurations. In some cases, a language teacher teams with a content or skills instructor in either the same classroom or separate ones. In other cases, a content or skills instructor who has been trained in language and literacy development assumes responsibility for both content and language. In a third configuration, a language teacher who has a background in a skill or content area assumes full responsibility. No matter what configuration is used, both types of programs require some cross-fertilization of teachers who are skilled in language development and teachers who are skilled in the particular work or content area.

CONCLUSION

ESL professionals need to consider the relationship between content-based ESL and workplace literacy because the ESL workplace itself is changing. Older students are coming into programs, the numbers of immigrants and refugees are increasing, and some employers are beginning to take over the responsibility of training their workers in language skills. We need to be aware that opportunities exist to work with employers as ESL professionals and to consider the role we want to play in workplace literacy. Is there a place for us outside of schools and colleges? This brief foray into the world of workplace literacy suggests that there is.

chapter 30

VESL and Content-Based Instruction: What Do They Have in Common?[1]

Kathleen Wong

Vocational English as a second language (VESL) has, in general, been defined as English language instruction that concentrates on the linguistic and cultural competencies required for employment. If we assume the definition of content-based instruction to be "the integration of particular content with language-teaching aims" (Brinton, Snow, & Wesche, 1989, p. 2), then the connection between the two should be obvious. In fact, VESL serves as an excellent example of content-based instruction.

MODELS OF VESL INSTRUCTION

Basically, there are three types of VESL instruction: (a) general VESL, (b) occupational-cluster VESL, and (c) occupation-specific VESL.

General VESL refers to language instruction related to finding a job, maintaining a job, and advancing on the career ladder. Known also as prevocational ESL, it is content-based language instruction insofar as it focuses on teaching English in the context of employment. General VESL courses normally introduce language—communicative skills, grammatical structures, vocabulary—and cultural information, all relating to the world of work. For the most part, students enrolling in general VESL have an array of occupational interests. The unifying element is that all the students seek general work-related language and content. A typical class covers such topics as reading and interpreting want ads, filling out job applications, answering questions for job interviews, and reading

---

[1] This article originally appeared in *The CATESOL Journal, 1992, 5*(1) under the title "What Do VESL and Content-Based Instruction Have in Common?" Reprinted with permission.

and interpreting transportation and schedule information. Other topics might include understanding and giving directions, clarifying information, making excuses, and apologizing.

Developing cultural competency in a general VESL course is as important as developing linguistic competency. Instructors must provide students with pertinent information regarding the workplace culture as an integral component of instruction. The areas covered in teaching cultural competency may include understanding work schedules, time sheets, paychecks and deductions, benefits, employee forms, safety rules, and unions. This cultural information is taught through discussions or readings in English and is followed up with other language activities for reinforcement. It may also be communicated in the students' native language when concepts are too complicated to be explained in English at the particular ESL level being taught. For students who are literate in their first language, these types of cultural notes may also be presented in written form, as in the VESL textbook *English That Works* (Savage, How, & Yeung, 1982).

The second model of VESL instruction, *occupational-cluster VESL,* provides instruction for a group of occupations that are bound together by common language needs, technical skills, and work culture. VESL for health workers, VESL for restaurant workers, and VESL for service workers all fit into this category of occupational-cluster VESL. As an example, VESL for service workers may cover linguistic competencies and cultural competencies relevant to work in stores, restaurants, hotels, gas stations, and repair shops (see, for instance, Wrigley, 1987). Such a course aims for students to gain mastery in communicative language skills, reading and writing skills, grammatical structures, and terminology that are basic to survival in all service work. In addressing cultural competence, the instructor would also teach content, including job interviewing, job performance, on-the-job expectations, customer relations, employee evaluations, and critical thinking for the workplace—all specific to service work.

The primary objective of the third type of VESL instruction, *occupation-specific VESL,* is to develop linguistic and cultural competence in a specific occupation. Occupation-specific VESL enables students to enter or continue in a vocational training program, find employment, and function on a job. The linguistic and cultural competencies parallel what is taught in occupational-cluster VESL. However, the focus is much narrower, such as VESL for janitorial workers or VESL for electronics workers.

VESL bridge classes, such as those offered at City College of San Francisco, are a variation of the occupation-specific model. These bridge classes were instituted primarily because ESL students were not succeeding in mainstream vocational courses and programs, even though they had reached the recommended ESL level for entry into such courses. Bridge classes involve the application of various ESL instructional techniques to teach a specific vocational skill. Although communicative language skills, certain grammatical structures, and vocabulary are taught, the instruction emphasizes gaining proficiency in the content (i.e., vocational skill). VESL bridge instruction employs many of the techniques typically used in sheltered content instruction (see Rosen & Sasser,

Chapter 3 in this volume). In order for students to gain competency, the instructor incorporates oral, aural, and visual ESL teaching strategies. Students are asked to repeat information and answer as in a choral language activity, and the instructor solicits constant verbal feedback from students to check their comprehension of the content. Because of the teaching techniques involved, VESL bridges have historically been taught by ESL instructors who are also competent in the vocational skill, such as use of the computer and computer applications or typing. Ideally, vocational instructors should receive training in ESL teaching methodology, especially when teaching sheltered content sections in which ESL students are taught in a homogenous grouping.

VESL instruction arose out of the need for ESL adults to become employed. This targeted population has found it difficult to succeed in traditional vocational training programs and, moreover, to find actual employment because of limited language skills and cultural knowledge critical for job success. General VESL, occupational-cluster VESL, and occupation-specific VESL have all evolved as instructional models to answer the content-specific language needs of this population.

DELIVERY SYSTEMS FOR VESL

In order to understand VESL as it relates to content-based language instruction, it is important to examine the delivery systems (or settings) through which VESL instruction is currently being offered. The four types of delivery systems include (a) the ESL program approach, (b) the vocational program approach, (c) the work experience approach, and (d) the workplace approach.

In the *ESL program approach,* courses are offered in general VESL, occupational-cluster VESL, and occupation-specific VESL. These courses may or may not have direct links to vocational training programs in the sense that they directly relate to the content covered in existing vocational courses. Their development is often a precursor to the implementation of the other approaches that will be discussed below and comes from the sheer numbers of requests by students to institute such courses because they cannot enter existing vocational programs or because they cannot find employment due to their limited language proficiency. General ESL classes may also include VESL units on employment, emphasizing work-related language and cultural competencies.

The *vocational program approach* usually prepares ESL students for entry-level positions in a particular field of work, such as office occupations. It is essential that along with vocational training the students receive VESL instruction of the general, occupational-cluster, or occupation-specific type. For the most part, VESL in this setting focuses on language and cultural competencies specific to the occupation or occupational cluster. Instructional materials used in the VESL component are based on content in the designated occupation(s). The vocational instructor and VESL instructor work closely together so that there is continuity between their respective courses. Drawing from the materials and language used in the content class, the VESL instructor is thus able to develop language activities that facilitate the students' assimilation of the content as well as further develop their language skills. In addition, it is important for the vocational instructor to obtain feedback from the VESL instructor as to what adjustments must be made in teaching content and skills to ESL students, especially if the vocational course is taught as a sheltered class of all ESL students as opposed to a class combining both ESL and native English speakers.

In the *work experience approach* a student is placed at a worksite for on-the-job experience, in addition to receiving VESL and vocational instruction in the classroom. As with the vocational program approach, general VESL, occupational-cluster, or occupation-specific are the types of VESL instruction implemented. However, what makes this approach unique is that VESL and vocational instruction can be directly applied to a real work situation and vice versa. Hence, VESL instructors can draw on actual experiences on the job to structure classroom activities. Moreover, students are introduced to experiential language learning via their direct immersion in the working world. This kind of exposure allows them to build communicative language skills in a natural setting with native speakers as well as gain pertinent occupational and cultural knowledge.

The *workplace approach* provides VESL instruction (occupational-cluster or occupation-specific) to ESL employees already on the job. The purpose of VESL instruction in this setting is to facilitate the adjustment that ESL employees must make in an English-speaking work environment. The intended outcome is that they, in turn, will become more productive workers. (See Henze & Katz, Chapter 29 in this volume, for further discussion of issues in workplace literacy.)

CONCLUSION

VESL shares many of the same concerns as other content-based language instructional models. Staff development training is necessary for vocational instructors in how to better accommodate ESL students and for VESL instructors in strategies for working with vocational instructors on content course development. Content information and materials need to be gathered from both vocational instructors and industry to develop appropriate VESL curriculum and materials. VESL instructors, like other content-based language instructors, must ensure that language instruction relates to language in the content course (i.e., vocational training or the workplace). Also, administrators and industry must support VESL. Without such support, this type of instruction will never have the opportunity to develop. Finally, in this age of budget cuts and fiscal restraint, those of us in the field need to seek out creative opportunities for collaborative efforts between not only education and private industry, but also between ESL and vocational programs within our own institutions.

chapter 31

English for Specific Purposes and Content-Based Instruction: What Is the Relationship?[1]

Ann M. Johns

$\mathbf{W}$hen I was initially asked to answer this question, I felt I could sum up the relationship in one sentence: *English for specific purposes (ESP)* is a super-ordinate term for all good ESL/EFL teaching, and content-based instruction (CBI) is a central force in this movement. However, after some reflection and a review of a few standard references on CBI and ESP (see, for example, Johns, 1991a; Johns & Dudley-Evans, 1991; Robinson, 1991; Snow, 1991b; and Swales, 1985a, 1985b, 1985c), I have concluded that there is more to this relationship than a single sentence can express.

My purpose here is to discuss the ESP and CBI movements in a more complete manner than my original one-sentence response would have allowed. First, I will discuss in what ways the two movements appear to be similar. Then, I will examine some of the features of the two movements that appear to make them different, that separate them in the minds of researchers, curriculum designers, and practitioners. This discussion is constructed by my own experience and reading; no doubt, others would—and perhaps will—take issue with my claims.

SIMILARITIES

I begin with the similarities between ESP and CBI, for they are the most obvious to me. Both movements stem from practitioners' unease about the separation of language instruction from the contexts and demands of real language use. We

---

[1] This article originally appeared in *The CATESOL Journal, 1992, 5*(1) under the title "What Is the Relationship Between Content-Based Instruction and English for Specific Purposes?" Reprinted with permission.

worry that general purpose language instruction, or TENOR (Teaching English for No Obvious Reason), cannot prepare students for the demanding linguistic, rhetorical, and contextual challenges of the real world (e.g., the workplace or the academic classroom). There is considerable evidence for our concerns, as Mohan (1986) notes:

> A language is a system that relates to what is being talked about (content) and the means to talk about it (expression). Linguistic content is inseparable from linguistic expression. *But in research and in classroom practice, this relationship is frequently ignored* [italics added]. . . . In language learning we overlook the fact that content is being communicated. (p. 1)

In both movements there is an effort to discover and use genuine discourse from the real world in the language classroom to ensure that classroom content reflects the target situation. There is also an effort to engage students in meaningful use of language, rather than in activities that focus on the language itself. Thus, as Johns and Davies (1983) put it, language becomes a "vehicle for communication," not merely a "linguistic object" studied in isolation for its grammatical and lexical features. Practitioners in both movements recognize that language classroom activities should be designed to assist students in interacting with content and discourse in cognitively demanding ways, or at the very least in ways that are similar in use to those in the target language situation.

How do we determine what is authentic language and what are authentic activities? We work closely with experts in the target situation, people who know what students must do and who understand the purposes of content and discourse in their particular contexts. In CBI there are models for working with content experts (e.g., adjunct and sheltered classes—see Brinton, Snow, & Wesche, 1989); in ESP there are related models (e.g., team teaching—see Johns & Dudley-Evans, 1991). Thus, both ESP and CBI encourage the transfer of language skills and content to real life by bringing genuine language and authentic classroom activities to students.

DISSIMILARITIES

If these are the similarities, what are the differences between the two movements? One difference relates to the scope of each movement's influence. CBI is generally limited to the English as a second language (ESL) setting, in places like the United States, the United Kingdom, Canada, Australia, and New Zealand. ESP, on the other hand, prides itself in being an international movement; in fact, much of the interesting ESP work takes place in countries in which English is a foreign language.

This difference in instructional setting has resulted in the use of a variety of labels to describe courses in which language and content are integrated. Thus,

ESP is the conventional term used to designate specific purposes language programs in the English as a foreign language (EFL) setting. In the ESL setting, however, terms such as *workplace ESL* and *English for academic purposes* prevail.[2] In Australia, for example, there is "a degree of resistance to using the term *ESP*" (Judy Coleman, personal communication). Instead, Australians employ phrases such as *technical and further education for immigrant students (TAFE)* and *English in the workplace (EWP)*.

We don't find the same resistance to using ESP in the EFL setting, as evidenced by the publications and conferences with ESP in the titles coming out of Latin America, Europe, the Middle East, and Asia. *English for Specific Purposes: An International Journal,* provides ample evidence for the scope of this movement: Nearly half of the journal's contributors and more than half of its subscribers work in EFL contexts.

ESP can be distinguished from CBI in other ways as well: Courses are often designed for adult students whose needs are more immediate, identifiable, and specific than those of children. These courses tend to be short, needs-based, and focused.[3] One such student population enrolls in Workplace ESL classes; teachers from this ESP area represent a large proportion of the ESP Interest Group in TESOL. For the most part, CBI is identified with sheltered English and the education of children in primary and secondary grades. In some parts of the United States, such as the Southwest, CBI has been mandated for curricula at these levels.

There are other contrasts, at least in the minds of EFL curriculum designers and teachers. Whereas CBI is generally a multiskill approach, integrating the four skills in order to make the language learning experience authentic and to reflect the learning styles and strategies of the variety of students enrolled (Chamot & O'Malley, 1987), ESP has often been limited to one skill—reading—because this is what students in foreign countries badly need in order to access texts in science and technology. In fact, there are so many ESP reading courses in EFL settings that Mohan (1986) likens the movement to "reading in the content areas" (p. 15). For those interested in this phenomenon, Hudson (1991) provides a useful discussion of a well-developed overseas ESP reading program.

Finally, there are theoretical and research-related differences in scope and focus. ESP has a long research tradition, dating from the early 1960s (Swales, 1985a)—a tradition that has drawn from linguistic analyses, from discourse studies, from pragmatics, and recently from studies of genres and discourse communities (Swales, 1990). The journal *English for Specific Purposes* has published many articles that could just as well have appeared in journals such as *Discourse Processes* or *International Review of Applied Linguistics.* In most conferences held in EFL contexts, there are many more presentations on

---

[2] It should be noted that Peter Master continues in his attempt to bring the English for Specific Purposes terms to all settings. See the columns he edits in *TESOL Matters* and *CATESOL News.*

[3] Holden (1996/1997) argues quite convincingly that we should base all course design on student needs, whatever the context.

text-based research than on pedagogy. This is because ESP researchers, particularly those concerned with reading subject texts, are convinced that a thorough and systematic analysis of written discourse is essential to creating a successful curriculum. Over time, ESP research has expanded from item counts (e.g., the percentage of passives in a scientific text) to form/function analyses (see Robinson, 1991, and Swales, 1985a, for overviews) and, more recently, into genre analysis (see Berkenkotter & Huckin, 1995; Bhatia, 1993; and Swales, 1990). Though much of the more recent research and resultant pedagogical practice is related to academic English (see Freedman & Medway, 1994; Johns, 1997; and Swales & Feak, 1994), the fastest-growing area of ESP practice and pedagogy in all parts of the world continues to be in business and the professions (St. John, 1996).

CONCLUSION

In sum, ESP practitioners are, for the most part, researchers—completing text and genre analyses, needs assessments, and other studies before designing their curricula. On the other hand, CBI practitioners seem to focus almost exclusively on pedagogy: discussing student affect, instructional strategies, and classroom models. At this point, there is a dearth of rigorous CBI research to support its claims.

I teach in an ESP program[4] at my own university, and I find the pedagogical contributions of CBI valuable to my practice. However, I still consider myself primarily an ESP person, for I find that this movement illuminates my research and, not incidentally, enables me to travel and exchange ideas with colleagues throughout the world.

---

[4] I call it "ESP" because that's my background; however, Brinton, Snow, and Wesche (1989) would identify the adjunct (linked) model as CBI.

chapter 32

The Role of Content in Task-Based EAP Instruction

Joan G. Carson, Josephine A. Taylor, and Laureen Fredella

> *"Task-based learning, discipline referred, rather than discipline determined."*
> *(Widdowson, 1993, p. 35)*

Content-Based Instruction (CBI) and Task-Based Language Teaching (TBLT) are both based on the idea that "real language learning is most likely to occur when the context of that learning is not only typical, but real, when the learners are not merely acting out roles, but trying to use their new language to fulfill genuine communicative purposes" (Eskey, Chapter 10 in this volume, p. 136). However, the difference between these two approaches lies in the selection of a curriculum organizing principle. For CBI, the curriculum is organized around *content*, the dual purpose of CBI models being "the learning of a second language and the mastery of content knowledge" (Brinton, Snow, & Wesche, 1989, p. 182). For TBLT, the curriculum is organized around *tasks*, the rationale being that language acquisition occurs when the learner is focused on the completion of a task rather than on the language used in the process (Prabhu, 1987).

Nevertheless, content plays a significant role in TBLT in general, and in task-based English for Academic Purposes (EAP) programs in particular. Rather than tasks *emerging from the content* to be learned as happens in the CBI approach, the tasks to be learned *determine the content* in a task-based approach. In fact, as Long and Crookes (1993) point out, one of the main strengths of task-based language teaching is "its principled approach to content selection" (p. 41)—that is, content is selected to *support the acquisition of specific tasks.* In this way, task-based EAP instruction expands on the CBI focus on language as a vehicle for learning content by then using content as a vehicle for task mastery. Task-based EAP instruction also requires mastery of content, but it is the task that focuses the way that language learners will read/write/listen/speak about content.

Crookes (1986) defines a task as something that is done, not said, "a piece of work or an activity, usually of a specified objective, undertaken as part of an educational course, or at work" (p. 1). Language learners' tasks are both *real-world tasks*, which are based on an analysis of learner's needs, and *pedagogic tasks*, which are based on second language acquisition theory and research. A real-world task would be, for example, to comprehend the prompt specifications for a constructed response exam question (e.g., short answer question, essay exam question). A pedagogical task related to the real-world task would be teaching/learning the pragmatic interpretation of vocabulary used in this type of exam question (e.g., "Describe . . ." or "Explain . . ." or "Give reasons for . . ."). A needs analysis provides an inventory of the target tasks that learners are preparing to undertake. These real-world tasks can then be classified into task types from which pedagogic tasks are derived. Ideally, tasks would be both real world and pedagogic, but these two kinds of tasks are necessarily interrelated. Nunan writes:

> The dilemma for the syllabus designer is on selecting and sequencing tasks which are not only psycholinguistically motivated [the pedagogic tasks], but which are also related in some principled fashion to the things which the learner might actually or potentially wish to do outside the classroom [the real-world tasks]. (1993, p. 55)

In TBLT, content and task are graded and sequenced relative to the priority of learners' needs and with respect to their difficulty, and the selection of both content and task depends on the learners' target goals.

For task-based EAP instruction, the tasks to be taught are identified through a needs analysis to determine what students will be expected to do in post-secondary academic settings. The tasks are academic in nature—for example, writing essay exams, reading textbooks, doing lab reports, taking lecture notes, reading multiple-choice questions, participating in class discussions, and preparing study summaries. Content is then selected to maximize the opportunities to master these specific academic tasks. For example, an essay exam is a task that usually requires synthesis of material from several chapters of a course text. In order to teach this task, certain content requirements would have to be met. The content would include multiple chapters of a single text and/or multiple texts in which content is interrelated. Furthermore, the content for this task (as well as for all tasks in an EAP curriculum) would have to be academic in nature and in style, because a significant aspect of academic tasks involves comprehending material at a certain level of cognitive difficulty and of a certain discourse tone and form. In other words, the task would constrain the content to be presented and learned in ways that are specific to academic settings.

TASK AS AN ORGANIZING PRINCIPLE

If CBI and TBLT share so many overlapping features, why is TBLT more appropriate for academic preparation programs? More specifically, for EAP programs why is task a more appropriate curriculum organizing principle than content?

According to Johns (Chapter 31 in this volume), EAP and CBI models both recognize the need for students to interact with content in cognitively demanding ways and/or in ways similar to those in which content is used in target language situations. However, using content as the *basis* for curriculum design in EAP instruction is problematic for several reasons.

First, evaluation criteria for content selection are a problem for EAP programs. Content is relatively easy to specify for K–12 instruction, being whatever is taught in the mainstream curriculum. Content is also determined in adjunct classes by whatever is specified for the content class. However, for theme-based EAP programs, the criteria for content selection are less straightforward (see, however, Stoller & Grabe, Chapter 6 in this volume).

According to Snow, Met, and Genesee (1989), "content must be chosen that is important and interesting to the learner" (p. 202). While the idea that content must be "important" and "interesting" is intuitively appealing and seemingly reasonable, the constructs of "importance" and "interest" are difficult to operationalize (see Valentine and Repath-Martos, Chapter 18 in this volume). Furthermore, it is not altogether clear that "importance" can be used as a criterion for selecting content in EAP classes, because content needs, as well as students' perceptions of content needs, are likely to vary significantly. Language learners preparing for postsecondary academic work will face a wide range of content subjects, only a few of which will be shared by all students in an EAP classroom. Thus, what content will be "important" to EAP students is difficult to specify.

Because of the difficulty of identifying important content, EAP teachers who have attempted to utilize CBI—most commonly through theme-based instruction—have had to rely on the criterion of "interest" in making content selections. If students do not recognize the importance of the content (i.e., if there is no evidence that the content *is* important to EAP students' goals and needs), then the claim is often made that students will learn language in order to provide access to content that is of interest to them. In other words, interest will motivate students to engage with subject matter that has been designated as the context for language learning. Although the notion that interesting content motivates students is unarguable, the question remains: How will teachers be able to determine what content will be interesting to their students? It is inevitable that not all students' interests will be accommodated by content selections; and even when multiple content themes are used, some students will undoubtedly be uninterested in one or more of the particular topics. The argument here is not that interest is an unimportant criterion. Rather, it is that interest is difficult to gauge and, thus, is an unreliable guide to content selection.

Because content cannot be specified for general EAP populations in the same way that it can for K–12 and adjunct class populations, designating content mastery as a primary course objective poses a problem of face validity for theme-based EAP classes. It would be difficult to convince students that learning about the environment or the civil rights movement in the United States, to name two popular topics in theme-based classes, will be essential to their success in postsecondary academic settings. As Brindley (1984) argues, goals that reflect the communicative needs of learners have greater face validity. Thus, the dual purpose of all CBI models—learning a second language and gaining mastery of content knowledge—poses problems for EAP programs. The goal of content mastery in a theme-based EAP program is not likely to relate to the future academic needs of the language learners, so the knowledge that is gained will not be seen as beneficial to the students if it is not perceived as transferable to the postsecondary academic context.

Finally, without the *need* for content mastery inherent in K–12 and adjunct classes, CBI lacks a focus for EAP programs. What underlies CBI is the notion that language learning will emerge from a focus on learning content from which are extracted the language structures, skills, or functions that are characteristic of various content areas. However, a general sense of "learning content" leaves a great deal of information unspecified. If content mastery is not one of the primary goals of the course, then the language teacher will need to create a focus for the content, and this focus will vary with the instructor and/or the instructor's sense of students' needs. In other words, CBI does not provide a principled basis for deciding on course focus in cases where content mastery is either unnecessary or inappropriate.

CONCLUSION

For EAP curricula, the main problem with content-based instruction resides in "content as the curriculum organizing principle" (Wesche, 1993, p. 61). In CBI, content bears a heavy burden which it cannot sustain in EAP programs wherein content selection may fail to reflect students' interests and needs, and wherein a focus on content mastery lacks face validity. However, in a *task-based* EAP program, content plays a justifiable role because task is the focus/organizing principle and content is needed to support the acquisition of tasks.

The issue of focus is important because it involves the questions of both real-world context and real-world communicative purposes. In CBI K–12 classes and in adjunct classes where content mastery *is* an actual student need, then content-based instruction is strongly justified. But when there is no need for content mastery and the CBI language teacher must decide the purposes and tasks for the course, then the connection with real-world context and communication is more tenuous. Because task-based curricula are grounded in learners' needs, EAP instruction that focuses on task mastery does maintain a clear connection with genuine language in genuine communicative interactions. Content is indispensable, but not for the primary purpose of acquiring information. Rather, the focus is on the cognitive, academic, and linguistic abilities needed for various academic tasks—tasks that are available for transfer to actual learning situations and that can be used to access and integrate subject matter in content courses.

chapter 33

Culture as Content[1]

Sharon Hilles and Dennis Lynch

Culture lessons in most ESL classrooms, from preschool through college or adult level, are in principle pretty much the same. We share and celebrate the holidays, food, and music of our students' various native cultures. We also give brief lessons on American holidays as they come up: a unit on the pilgrims in November, some Christmas carols (and possibly a chorus of "Dreydl, Dreydl, Dreydl") in December, and valentines in February. All this is done because most of us are committed to the notion that "language cannot be taught apart from culture" and that "to learn a language is to learn a culture." However, most of us would be hard-pressed to actually explain, let alone defend, either statement.

The notion of *culture* which is often reflected in classroom lessons is undoubtedly interesting and helpful to newcomers. Through it we orient students with procedural information and make them feel more comfortable in an alien culture because we acknowledge their own. However, this aspect of culture is not particularly problematic. Holidays and music may be the focus of curiosity and interest, but they seldom become the source of misunderstanding—at least of the sort that can distort the dynamics of a classroom. However, another aspect of culture is very problematic and potentially quite disruptive to the multicultural classroom. This aspect of culture is less visible and, as a result, less intelligible to teacher and student alike. Following the work of early twentieth-century phenomenologists and of more recent sociologists and sociolinguists such as Goffman (1963), Garfinkel (1967), and Ochs (1988), we invite ESL teachers to rethink their definitions of culture in light of the evidence that culture is a far more powerful and potentially disruptive force than most of us imagine. Moreover,

---

[1] This article originally appeared in *The CATESOL Journal, 1992, 5*(1) under the title "What Is the Role of Teaching Culture in Content-Based Instruction?" Reprinted with permission.

we argue that culture, in this sense, deserves consideration as content in any discussion of content-based instruction.

CULTURE AS SHARED UNDERSTANDING

The aspect of culture which interests us most is not the obvious differences in food, music, and dress but rather the mundane, the ordinary, the everyday stuff of which reality—especially social reality—is made. It is that which "everyone knows" or which is common sense. It is never (or rarely) up for question, but it differs—sometimes dramatically—from one cultural group to another. It is part of the background of our lives, the setting, the given. This aspect of culture is very much like a pair of contact lenses. We look through it, we experience reality in terms of it, but we do not see it except under the most unusual conditions. Yet this transparent aspect of culture is vitally important because it is the shared understanding inherent in our daily practices that determines how we organize, experience, and (perhaps) constitute reality. It determines what we experience in life. As a result, people from various cultures may experience the same situation in markedly different ways depending on how, when, and by whom they have been enculturated.

The fact that people experience or constitute reality in different ways and that they cannot see the lenses through which they look is not particularly alarming or problematic for the multicultural classroom. However, according to Garfinkel (1967) there is more to this aspect of culture than its near invisibility, and we think this is very important: There is evidence that this aspect or level of culture also has a moral status. That is, cultural breaches are treated as if they were moral breaches. Our reactions to such cultural breaches are the same as they might be to someone who lies to us—but when someone lies, we know what is wrong. However, when someone breaches a cultural expectation of the sort we are talking about, we do not see what is being breached (because it is transparent to our daily activity) yet we may feel outraged—often in staggering disproportion to the gravity of the transgression.

A good example of this might be the student who "cheats" on an exam. In some cultures cheating is viewed positively, as a sign that one is willing to share and is not so arrogant as to refuse help from others. Students who grow up in societies with such an interpretation represent generations of cheating in which their teachers—and their teachers' teachers before them—assisted each other on exams, often in clever and ingenious ways. Now imagine these same students at an American university. When they put these deeply ingrained strategies to work in a new environment, their professors react quite differently. Even when teachers know that such behavior is acceptable in the students' native country, they still react emotionally. Often the response involves moral justification: "People just shouldn't do that! It isn't right!"

Plagiarism is another example of a potential cultural misunderstanding. In some countries, using the words of others is considered good scholarship, a way to demonstrate that one knows the words of authorities (Gadda, 1994). In American schools, though, such an act flies in the face of our own deeply embedded understanding of what constitutes acceptable scholarly behavior. When students plagiarize, teachers feel personally insulted and betrayed.

These two examples involve acts that, from a Western point of view, are unambiguously immoral. For this reason they can be misleading, because the level of culture to which we hope to draw attention is really much broader than issues such as plagiarism and cheating. It involves acts which may be unconsciously construed as immoral, even though the standards by which the interpretations are made are not visible to the interpreters. These cultural differences might include how close or far to stand from those with whom one is speaking, what is considered bad breath or offensive body odor, what constitutes the proper way to look at the person with whom one is talking (such as a student staring blankly at the teacher even though he or she understands), or what counts as an interruption or rude behavior during class (such as sharpening a pencil during a teacher-directed portion of the lesson, or asking fellow students for confirmation of teacher instructions which have just been given orally and written on the chalkboard). Not only do these cultural differences disrupt the teacher-student relationship per se (for affective factors are unarguably important), but they also distort the discursive dynamics of a classroom, that is, all the factors that go with language and how it is used. Teachers and students, from elementary school through university level, can find themselves exasperated, frustrated, and offended but unable to say exactly why, and therefore unable to remedy the situation.

Let us now return to the focus of this volume: content-based instruction. The basic premise of content-based instruction for second language learners is that students will learn the target language better and more efficiently if they are taught not the language directly but other subjects in the language. We argue that culture, particularly its moral status and its invisibility, is a critical topic which should be addressed in content-based teaching.

Dividing the lesson into its "into," "through," and "beyond" phases (see, for example, Brinton, Goodwin, & Ranks, 1994), a content-based unit on culture for any level might begin with the obvious differences in food, dress, language, and custom and then move to the aspect of culture that isn't so obvious but is much more problematic.

ELEMENTARY SCHOOL STUDENTS

For elementary school children, a good "into" activity might involve bringing in pictures from *National Geographic, The Smithsonian*, or any other source that has attractive color photos of people from other cultures. As a prereading activity, students could discuss different cultural customs that they see in the pictures and their reactions to them. Follow-up questions could include what language the people in the pictures might speak and whether the students have had any experience with languages other than the ones represented in the classroom.[2] The "through" phase of the cultural lesson could center around any number of children's multicultural texts such as *I Hate English!* by Ellen Levine (1989) or student-generated and -illustrated language experience texts about customs, holidays, food, and language from students' native countries.

Finally, the "beyond" activity could exploit a natural ability of young children. Elementary students can (and spontaneously do) imagine "other places" where "up is down and people think differently, and there are no doors on houses and where every home has seventeen television sets because the sets usually break, but there are no repairmen."[3] This kind of play helps students think about the possibility and acceptability of other points of view. Students can imagine other worlds, write descriptions of them, and draw pictures of them. They can share their creations with the class. They can assume the role of someone from the imaginary place, make costumes, and answer questions in character from the teacher and class about their "home." Other students can play the parts of reporters and interview the aliens. The teacher can set the tone and pace of the interviews if necessary, move from descriptive questions to more subjective questions about feelings, ask about classroom rules, procedures, and tasks: "Do children go to school in your world? If not, how do they learn? If they do go to school, what is it like? Is it very different from here? Does this classroom seem strange to you? Why? Do you have brothers and sisters? How old are they? Do you miss your friends? What are their names? What do they like to do? Do you think they would like it here? Do you like it here? Why or why not?" The final task might include a written summary of the interview and possibly even a class newspaper with interviews and news from other worlds. The idea is that young thinkers get used to the idea that there are deep cultural differences and that these differences seem perfectly normal and commonplace (invisible) for someone who is a part of that group.

HIGH SCHOOL STUDENTS

A very evocative and exciting series of cultural lessons for older students could be organized around an adaptation of *Ways with Words* (Heath, 1983) or the article "What No Bedtime Story Means" (Heath, 1986b). In these studies, Stanford anthropologist Shirley Brice Heath describes three cultures within the United States with respect to language socialization and literacy practices and the extent to which this socialization matches the expectations held by schools. An excellent high school "into" activity for Heath's work can be based on an excerpt from Clyde Kluckhohn's (1949) "Mirror for Man," in which the author defines what

---

[2] We are grateful to Donna Brinton and the members of the 1989 UCLA Teaching Analytical Reading and Writing Program for sharing this and several other teaching ideas mentioned in this chapter.

[3] This is part of an actual story recently told to us by a seven-year-old.

anthropologists mean by culture and explains culture's influence on how people think, feel, and behave.

The activity starts out with pictures from *National Geographic* (as described above) and then moves to group clustering activities. The first task is to brainstorm the function of culture and to cluster the ideas elicited on the chalkboard. The ensuing discussion is eventually led to the significance of items mentioned by more than one group. The class is divided into groups again to repeat the clustering activity, this time using information about a culture which is assigned to them. Following the clustering activity, groups present their cluster to the class, which decides on the accuracy of information, the existence of stereotypes, and the overlaps between cultures. Class discussion also explores which characteristics are important or superficial. The final step in this stage is to lead the class to a consensus regarding the benefits of understanding another culture and what potential problems might exist between cultures. Teachers should encourage students to explore how culture can be used to define an individual and if there are any dangers in allowing a culture to speak for an individual.

To help students work through the Kluckhohn reading, they can be divided into jigsaw groups, each of which is assigned a portion of the reading. Group members become experts on their portion of the text. The groups are then reconfigured, with one expert in each group. In the reconfigured groups students construct a complete definition of culture, drawing on the specialized knowledge of each of the experts in their group. This activity can be followed up with other "through" activities, including T-graph exercises in which examples are taken from the text (e.g., "Chinese dislike milk and milk products") and written in the left-hand portion of the diagram; the generalizations which these examples illustrate (e.g., "Likes and dislikes for food are learned cultural behavior") are written in the right-hand portion of the diagram.

A "beyond" activity in this unit might be an adaptation of one of UCLA sociologist Harold Garfinkel's exercises. Students can assume the role of a stranger—or even of an alien. In this role they observe and record the everyday academic and social behaviors of their multicultural peers (including native English-speakers) and the reactions of others. Finally, they compare what they see with their own background behaviors. They keep journals, produce a group report or paper, or put on a television show in which their subjects are interviewed or observed in their natural settings.

UNIVERSITY STUDENTS

Older students might benefit from a more direct approach. The sociologist Erving Goffman (1963) explored certain invisible aspects of culture by studying settings in which cultural norms did not apply, such as mental institutions. Garfinkel sent out students to purposely breach cultural agreements to illustrate various aspects of culture, including its invisibility and moral status. Lessons organized around portions of these readings and sources cited therein could be a rich source of cultural insight for older students. Like their younger counter-parts, they could become investigators themselves in a "beyond" activity, observing and describing the multicultural environment of their own classrooms, schools, and neighborhoods.

At this level, students could even participate in adaptations of some of Garfinkel's breaching exercises as a way of making visible that which is normally invisible. Students could make a point of standing closer (or further away) than feels acceptable while talking with other students, teachers, parents, and so forth. Afterwards they should explain the experiment to their subjects and note their own responses to the experiment and the reactions of their interlocutors to both the experiment and its explanation. Such observations can be very revealing to those who have not previously thought about the hidden influences of social and linguistic practices. Variations include having students speak too loudly or too softly, interrupt or avoid responding appropriately, digress or give only short, direct responses, begin each statement with a brief narrative that winds slowly into the main point, and so forth. Writing up these exercises and follow-up discussions regarding how students felt during the experiments as well as open discussion about cheating, interrupting instructors, or people who stand too close (and what *too close* means) would contribute to the students' developing understanding of how cultural differences can distort speech situations, especially between teacher and student. Needless to say, these activities also provide an engaging occasion for the practice of language. (See also Devenney, 1991, for an *observe-and-record approach* used in conjunction with a language class.)

CONCLUSION

All the sample lessons, regardless of educational level, demonstrate that many aspects of culture are invisible to its practitioners and that breaches of this aspect of culture pack a wallop. Learning these two simple points would empower both students and teachers. Breaches of the sort we have described were relatively unusual in American schools some years ago because they simply didn't arise. Most teachers and students were from the same background: mainstream, middle class.[4] This is no longer the case. We feel that a knowledge of culture, what it is, and how it is reflected in our own group and in the various groups of our students is essential if we are to truly *promote* rather than merely *tolerate* diversity. Culture, as a topic, offers many possibilities as content in the content-based class.

---

[4] As Heath (1986b) points out, "Terms such as *mainstream* and *middle-class* are frequently used in both popular and scholarly writings without careful definition. In general, the literature characterizes this group as school-oriented, aspiring toward upward mobility through formal institutions, and providing enculturation that positively values routines of promptness, linearity (in habits ranging from furniture arrangement to entrance into a movie theater), and evaluative and judgmental responses to behaviors that deviate from their norms" (p. 123).

chapter 34

Literature: A Quintessential Content

Christine Holten

LITERATURE IN CONTENT-BASED INSTRUCTION

To say that literature has been banned from curricula and methodologies designed to teach ESL for academic purposes would be an overstatement, but to say that its role has been greatly reduced and its place more narrowly circumscribed would be accurate. Whereas at one time literature was *the* quintessential content in language classrooms and the end goal of all foreign language instruction, it now has an incidental place in most curricula and methodologies or has been relegated to its own "elective" course.

A personal anecdote will call to mind why such an exile may have occurred. As a student pursuing foreign language study fifteen years ago in U.S. public schools, I spent one year in junior high school, four years in high school, and one semester in college memorizing vocabulary, repeating dialogues, and practicing pronunciation before I finally "arrived." After this drill-based study of French, I was ready for the "real thing"—reading poetry by Verlaine, short stories by de Maupassant, novels by Flaubert, and plays by Molière. Along the way, reading St.-Exupéry's *Le Petit Prince* in high school, we got glimpses of the end goal. These glimpses had a dual purpose: to give us a foretaste, but also to tell us how far our language still needed to come before we could read more than children's literature.

In my second semester of college, I was finally ready to enroll in my first real French literature course. I can't remember the reading list largely because I didn't understand much of what I read. The previous five years of training proved woefully inadequate, and the leap from controlled vocabulary and grammatical structures to the rich, varied, nuanced language of literature was quantum. When I finally went to study in France, exactly two years and some dozens of pieces of French literature later, I felt comfortable with the language of literature, explicating texts, tracing themes and images, even writing an occasional literary analysis in French.

But my supposed competence was challenged when I spent my junior year studying in Paris. My language skills were up to the readings and lectures in literature and art courses, but we were required to take a political science course on the Fourth French Republic. The linguistic demands of the readings and lectures taxed my "literary" French. I had never had to comprehend and take notes in lectures designed for French students, and these were delivered in rapid-fire, culturally bound language. My training in explicating literature had not prepared me to pass a five-minute oral examination based on any area of French political history covered in a course that lasted for nine months. And I lacked the vocabulary to read the complex economic and political texts assigned.

My experience with French seems to adequately reflect the deficits in students' linguistic competence left by curricula and methodologies that projected toward and culminated in the study of great literary texts in the target language. In fact, such gaps in language instruction were the impetus for the development of many current second language teaching methodologies, of which content-based language instruction is one. Its goal is to increase communicative competence in specified academic content areas by teaching the language prevalent in the content area's texts, both written and oral. Advocates of content-based instruction argue that most academic disciplines have as their central content nonliterary texts whose linguistic structures and lexicon are very different from those found in most works of literature. Literature as the only content has also been criticized, because the types of language and analytical tasks called for in studying literature are of limited use in other academic content areas. Literary analysis, for instance, doesn't require the application of theory or critique and formal argumentation based on warrants and claims—all types of critical thinking required in various disciplines throughout the university.

LITERATURE AS REMEDY TO GAPS IN CONTENT-BASED INSTRUCTION

Given these convincing reasons for leaving literature out of content-based instruction and the deficits in my own foreign language abilities left by such an approach, why am I about to submit that literature be reinstated as a viable, even essential, element in content-based second language instruction? Again, personal experience sheds light on my change of heart. After a decade as a composition and EAP instructor and materials developer, I was assigned to teach a literature class—not a content-based literature class, but an elective course in American literature. As part of the course requirements I assigned two small written analyses of the literature we were reading. Since the focus was on literature and not on composition skills, I made conferences on student drafts optional. Accordingly, I did not have high expectations for the students' analytical pieces. To my great surprise, however, I received some of the best papers in my teaching career from students whose overall language proficiency was lower than that of the students who normally took my content-based EAP composition courses. What could explain the difference in these pieces and in the students' attitudes? The only appreciable difference, I concluded, was that we were NOT focusing on the skills involved in writing; instead, we were conducting more small group discussions and activities to help students arrive at their own interpretations of the literature. Although I had read Mangelsdorf (1989), who claims that discussions can enhance the quality of ESL students' written products, this could not completely explain what had occurred because many of my students had analyzed stories and poetry that we had not read or discussed together as a class. It had to be the literature.

The effect that studying literature had on my students' writing and analytical thinking impelled me to rethink the role that literature could play in improving ESL students' *academic* language skills. If literature worked so well in a course of its own, where the literary texts and their language were the central focus, what benefits could derive from including literature in content-based EAP courses? Even more interesting, the process of rethinking literature's place shed light on the problems posed by content-based instruction itself. It provided some fairly straightforward answers to some of those anecdotal struggles ESL instructors have in implementing content-based instruction, and it filled some of the gaps documented through empirical studies.

To outline the advantages that literature might offer content-based instruction, I want to "turn the tables" for a moment, pointing up the problems its successful implementation has posed for practitioners and suggesting how a return to the use of literature might provide a remedy.

Basing ESL materials on content that students are actually studying is sound, but not easily realized. Not all content-based programs have the luxury of linking their ESL courses directly to other university courses in science or social sciences being offered during the same quarter or semester. Curriculum coordinators in such programs are instead often put in the position of developing materials and units based on content they choose from a given academic field. For example, a ten-week course might contain two "content" units: one focusing on theories of immigration and assimilation from American history, and one focusing on animal behavior from biology. This approach, some argue, denies students the opportunity to select content areas of inherent interest to them. Students who are interested in the sciences may have to spend six weeks in the required ESL course studying sociology or history, whereas those majoring in economics may have to master information from biology (see Valentine & Repath-Martos, Chapter 18 and Carson, Taylor, & Fredella, Chapter 32 in this volume for a discussion of the "interest" issue). Such programmatic considerations have inescapable effects on student motivation, causing certain students to struggle against the very "idea" of the selected content. End-of-quarter comments from students in a content-based ESL curriculum reflect this:

> I really dislike the format of this course because the subject [i.e., readings about schizophrenia] is beyond the course of study. . . . It seems like a psychology class rather than an English class.

> I think that whoever's choosing the topic should concern that it is just a English class not a "biology" class. I could not see a point which we spent $\frac{1}{3}$ of the quarter discuss about [heredity] and environment. I strong recommend the cancelling of this unit!

LITERATURE IS MOTIVATING CONTENT

Literature, on the other hand, appears to be a more universally appealing content, one that students are motivated to tackle. What makes literature more motivating, say, than the sociology of deviance or the history of immigration patterns in the United States? The subject matter of literature is instrinsically accessible because literature is about us. No special expertise or knowledge is required. This alone can make it fascinating and, in a classroom, can motivate students.

This is not to say that students are not put off by the language, subjects, and types of analysis required to study works of literature. At first they distance themselves as much from literature as they do from other content areas that are not directly within their major fields. Just as in adopting other types of content materials, there is "no free lunch" for the teacher. She must do the same work to raise students' interest and schema about the particular problem being discussed in the literature and the author's treatment of it. But once students are shown that literature centers to a greater or lesser degree around the same conflicts, emotions, and enduring questions that they deal with in their everyday lives, they usually want to learn more, discuss more, read more, and eventually analyze more. Ultimately, the motivational work entailed in getting students to read and enjoy literature seems to take less time than it does with materials from other content areas. With content-area materials, teachers must often spend the entire instructional period "rallying" the students, building their confidence, bringing in collateral readings or anecdotes from the news or personal experience to prove the topic's relevance to the students' intellectual and personal lives.

I am not suggesting that we replace the content drawn from core disciplines of the university with literature; I am, however, suggesting that we supplement the readings and lectures drawn from content areas with literature that is compatible with the unit's focus and with the wider themes suggested by the content. For example, in one of the most successful content units in our ESL program at UCLA, students study several theories from American history about how new immigrants affiliate with the host country and culture. The unit begins with two literary pieces—one a short story, "The Juk-Sing Opera" by Genny Lim (1988), a second-generation Chinese immigrant; and the other an excerpt from the novel *Breath, Eyes, Memory* by Edgwidge Danticat (1994), a first-generation Haitian immigrant. The two pieces broadly raise some of the unit's themes: the difficulty of leaving one's homeland for another country, the cultural divide that separates first- and second-generation immigrants, and the barriers that the host culture raises to the full acceptance of immigrants. Before students listen to the history lectures or read the history texts about assimilation or the melting pot, they read these literary pieces and, in a journal and class discussion, relate the two authors' stories to their own experience as immigrants in this country. Literature is used similarly with a much less "user friendly" content unit from atmospheric sciences: the formation of *foehn* winds (e.g., the Santa Ana winds in California, the *mistral* in France, the *harmattan* in West Africa). In this unit, students read Joan Didion's (1968) piece about the negative effects of the Santa Ana winds on people's behavior. They are then asked to call to mind a *foehn*-type wind in their own region or some other meteorological phenomenon that is purported to negatively affect people's behavior, health, or moods. Discussion of Didion's piece reminds students of what they already know about such winds and stimulates their curiosity about how these winds are created.

Beginning each unit with literary excerpts can get the unit started in the right way, raising interest in the content while simultaneously motivating students to learn more. This good beginning can and often does spill over into the unit's other texts and activities, lessening the teacher's role as cheerleader and advocate for the more academic and theoretical texts.

REDUCING THE COGNITIVE DEMANDS OF CONTENT-BASED INSTRUCTION

Students in content-based ESL courses may not be motivated to study unfamiliar content because it puts new intellectual and cognitive demands on them. They may feel intimidated by these demands and "write off" the content. Rather than admit their own fear that their language, their intellect—in short, they themselves—might prove inadequate to the challenge, they dismiss the content as boring, inapplicable, and unsuited to their academic needs. Indeed, if we are to believe research and our own experience as teachers, the challenge of content-based courses and curricula is great.

Content-based instruction is predicated on the fact that academic literacy can only be promoted as students engage in the same tasks and encounter the same language as they will find in their university courses. Content-based materials replicate as faithfully as possible the texts and tasks of specific academic fields while adding activities that will scaffold the students' learning process and thus help them transfer the skills and language learned in the content-based ESL course to other college courses. The whole enterprise is designed as a sort of "cognitive apprenticeship" (Belcher, 1994, p. 24) that places heavy demands on the student—much heavier than conventional academic ESL courses. Unless students read widely or have already taken courses in a given area, they approach the content materials in each unit of the ESL course as novices. Being novices, they need to acquire several levels of knowledge: the vocabulary of the content area; the issues being discussed and the theoretical perspectives within which the content area studies them; and the analytical and argumentative tools required to discuss and write critically about the topic. All this must usually be accomplished within a semester or even half a semester.

Students and teachers alike often complain that the quality of their work suffers because of these demands. Students grumble that their ESL teachers are asking them to perform at a higher level than their content professors (because we expect them to write essays which are linguistically accurate and draw on the content and theories of a given unit). Students in an ESL class also don't see the rationale for learning, for example, about the symptoms and treatment of schizophrenia. Teachers find that lesson planning becomes something akin to juggling; they must teach the content of the unit, as well as reading, writing, and listening skills. At the same time, they must make sure not to neglect grammar and vocabulary.

Here again, incorporating literature into content-based materials may help in one of two ways. The first alternative would be to incorporate one work of literature into the unit's academic readings. As suggested earlier, this could be read at the beginning of the unit in order not only to motivate students and orient them to the unit but also to give them a lens through which they can understand, assess, and eventually write about concepts presented in the more academic sources. In one of our own content-based curricula, a unit from sociology, students learn about group theory—more particularly the definitions of *in groups* and *out groups* and the ways in which people affiliate with them. As part of the unit, students read excerpts from Golding's *Lord of the Flies* (1954), relating the groups they find in the story to the theories and facts they have been studying in the sociology unit. In their final writing assignment, a multiple draft essay, they apply what they have learned about in groups and out groups to a scene from the novel or to a group that they are familiar with.

A second alternative would be to replace one of several content units completed during a given semester with a unit composed entirely of related literary texts. Similar to traditional theme-based units, this could be a combination of poetry, short stories, and some films, unified around a common theme or issue. One such unit I have developed centers around two broadly drawn themes: a journey to self-identity, and the place of women in society. Students read *As We Are Now*, a novel by May Sarton (1973); "Sweat," a short story by Zora Neale Hurston (1993); and *'night, Mother*, a play by Marsha Norman (1991), which also has a film adaptation. The works can be read in their entirety or selected excerpts can be accompanied by a short introduction to the characters and synopsis of the plot up to the beginning of the excerpt. In their final paper, students either trace one of the unit's themes through one of the works or compare the realization of the theme in two or more works.

Neither use of literature in content-based units represents a return to literature as the only content worthy of study in a language classroom. By interweaving literature with concepts and theories from nonliterary disciplines, students are still provided with the skills to deal with academic discourse in a very wide sense and in a way that is authentic to the types and breadth of college courses they will take. In addition, complementing source texts with literature or focusing solely on literary texts for one unit decreases the multiple demands placed on students to master content concepts while learning language and academic skills. In the first use of literature (literature integrated into the academic sources), the literature makes the abstract concrete. That is, the short story or excerpt from a novel, film, or play helps students apply the theory to situations from everyday life, thereby contextualizing the theory and making it easier to learn. (This is often not done adequately in the actual content courses themselves). This process, in turn, makes the subsequent analysis and application required in the analytical writing assignment much easier.

The second use of literature (a theme-based literature unit as one of several content-based units) also scaffolds both the cognitive and content demands of content-based materials in one of two ways: by reducing some of the levels of knowledge that students must confront, or by adding content and background knowledge which will help students engage these levels eventually. While short stories and novels may contain unfamiliar words, the plot and action are often so compelling that they carry readers along, enabling them to understand the basic elements of the story without having to know each word or master new terms before understanding an explanation of a concept. In poetry, understanding individual lexical items is more crucial; but since there are fewer items to process, the reader has both the time and the motivation to attend to every word and see the patterns created. There are no theoretical perspectives to be mastered, at least not at the level of literary analysis expected in an ESL composition or multi-skills course. (No understanding of Derrida or Foucault is required, for instance.) Thus, the content to be mastered is limited to that of understanding a short story's basic plot and conflict, and the characters' development. This leaves room for students to become familiar and comfortable with the barebone tools of literary analysis (plot structure or poetic form, theme, symbol and image, point of view, and the language of literature including simile and metaphor). All these can be defined in a paragraph or two, and students can be helped to learn these tools by incorporating them in overt and subtle ways into class discussion or analysis activities. In such an approach, students think carefully about a certain aspect of a text and its meaning (i.e., plot, theme, symbols) and then compose a cogent analysis of the work they have read. In retrospect, I attribute the surprising quality of my students' papers to the fact that the analysis of literature, by its nature, laid a systematic and more accessible foundation for the written analysis that they had to undertake.

LITERATURE: A CRUCIBLE FOR TEACHING THE GRAMMAR OF ACADEMIC TEXTS

The final gap in content-based curricula and methodologies that I would like to address may be more of a personal failing than an actual problem with the content-based approach to ESL instruction. It is this: Either I fail to spend enough time on grammar and vocabulary, or, when I do focus on language, basing what I teach on the discourse the students are comprehending or on the tasks they will have to complete, they often fail to perceive it as grammar instruction because it doesn't bear enough resemblance to the kind of instruction they are used to. (See Eskey, Chapter 10 in this volume, for a critique of content-based instruction vis-à-vis its ability to integrate the teaching of linguistic form.) The problem of failing to emphasize grammar and vocabulary adequately, at least as I experience it, grows out of the second problem in content-based instruction treated above: that is, content-based materials, by definition, model the rich, authentic texts and demands of academic content areas. This not only places difficult cognitive demands on students but also increases the number of areas in which the teacher must provide instruction and assistance. I tend to pay attention to whatever or whoever is crying the loudest. In content-based courses, the problems that seem to loom the largest for students usually involve recognizing the content area's theoretical perspectives, mastering the skills involved in comprehending the texts, and composing responses or analyses of the material. As a consequence, I often deemphasize grammar in favor of what seem to be more pressing issues.

Putting literature back into the content-based curriculum may provide a solution for the dilemma of what to focus on—if we rethink the way that we use literature. It is tempting, for instance, to add a work of literature to a content-based unit because it is linguistically and cognitively less demanding than the other academic sources the students are reading. The work of literature viewed in this light provides a "breather" in the midst of difficult tasks and challenging content. It often provides a break for the teacher as well, since it might be discussed without preparing extra vocabulary, grammar, or schema-building activities.

But, by taking this attitude, we may be missing a very important opportunity. Precisely because short stories or excerpts from novels are easier for students to comprehend, they may provide an excellent crucible for language work. Once students have felt the success of understanding the gist of the plot and are familiar with characters and themes of a short story, they may be more willing to look more closely at the grammatical structures and vocabulary that make up the text itself. They may not be willing to do the same with academic texts which they have struggled to understand and whose content they find less compelling than that of a good short story. Their willingness to do concentrated language work on a piece of literature that they like may well carry over into the grammar of academic readings and lectures.

The activities that follow illustrate the part that I believe literature can play in language instruction. All the activities have been adapted to specific works of literature taken from Lazar (1993), a useful teacher's reference. One activity that students have found useful is adapted for use with Kate Chopin's (1993) "The Story of an Hour" (see Figure 34.1). The students are given a worksheet with five groups of words taken from the short story. Each group of students is assigned a group of words and must discover the words' basic meaning (denotation), closest synonyms, meaning in the story, and context of use. Finally, they

---

VOCABULARY WORKSHEET

EXERCISE: You will work in groups to complete this activity. Each group will be assigned one of the lists of words.

1. Discuss the most common meaning that the word has (i.e., the meaning most commonly associated with this word or the meaning this word has in everyday usage).
2. Discuss the meaning of the word in the context of the story. Check the paragraph and sentence in the text to find the word's specific meaning. You may use a dictionary to help you, but you should note that the particular vocabulary word may take on a slightly or greatly different meaning in the context of the short story.
3. Why did the author choose this word? Were there other words she could have chosen? What are they? Why didn't she use these?

Word List I	Word List II	Word List III	Word List IV	Word List V
a heart trouble (pg. 252, ¶ 1)	veiled (pg. 252, ¶ 2)	spent itself (pg. 252, ¶ 3)	paralyzed (pg. 252, ¶ 3)	pressed down (pg. 252, ¶ 4)
haunted (pg. 252, ¶ 4)	tumultuously (pg. 252, ¶ 10)	possess (pg. 252, ¶ 10)	abandoned (pg. 252, ¶ 11)	vacant (pg. 252, ¶ 11)
procession (pg. 253, ¶ 1)	illumination (pg. 253, ¶ 2)	impulse (pg. 253, ¶ 3)	elixir (pg. 253, ¶ 6)	riot (pg. 253, ¶ 7)

FIGURE 34.1 Vocabulary in context activity accompanying Kate Chopin's short story "The Story of an Hour"

must decide why the author chose to use these words and not their synonyms. This is usually their favorite part of the activity because they get to play "author." They discover that many of the words are related to the story's central theme or to the character's motivation or personality, both of which have usually been treated in class discussion before this activity is done. The activity can lay the groundwork for doing the same type of analysis in the academic texts the students are reading. After all, they are really being asked to explore a text's lexical cohesion. They can examine their academic texts for chains of synonyms or repeated words and discuss how each chain contributes to the main idea or argument of the text.

Another short story, "I Stand Here Ironing" by Tillie Olsen (1993), has wonderful adjective and adjective-adverb strings, all of which add a rich texture to the language Olsen uses. After reading and discussing the story, students are given three excerpts describing the central character during three different periods of her life. The excerpts have blanks in front of key nouns and verbs. Students are asked, without looking at the original text itself, to fill in the appropriate single or multiple adjectives that precede each noun or to determine the adverbs that precede or follow each verb. Students then compare their choices with those made by Olsen, discussing why she chose a particular word or words. This leads to a review of the position and ordering of attributive adjectives in English, but also to a discussion of the "writerly" reasons why adjectives may appear in strings in the first place. Expanding this technique to the more academic realm, students can explore the use of adjectives and adverbs alone or in strings in their assigned academic texts and perhaps even explore how texture is created in academic discourse.

While poetry is the type of literature that students resist the most and enjoy the least, poems often convey important syntactic lessons. Poets play with the language, repeating certain key syntactic patterns for effect and breaking others to convey their themes. Having students recognize these repetitions or reconstruct the normal word or clause order from the original lines of a poem teaches them much about English syntax. In several stanzas of "The Road Not Taken," Robert Frost (1995) plays with English syntax to achieve rhyme. The second and third lines of this familiar poem's first stanza demonstrate an interesting syntactic construction and the poet's license to play with standard English word order. "Sorry I could not travel both/and be one traveler, long I stood" demonstrates a construction that is stylistically sophisticated and useful in academic writing: an adjective clause preceding the main clause. Students can also examine the main clause itself, "long I stood," and construct the more usual word order and wording. This can lead to an interesting lesson on the elements of a sentence that can be fronted and when, in discourse, such fronting might occur. Students can then identify syntactic structures that resemble those found in the poetry in their academic texts. They can also do style imitations of certain syntactically interesting lines of a given poem, adding their own words and meaning to the text. While style imitations are most often done with literature, there is no reason that students can't identify interesting sentences or phrases from their academic texts and do the same type of imitation (accompanied by the necessary caveats about plagiarism, of course).

Another criticism that might be lodged against the language work incorporated into content-based materials and instruction relates to the broader question of what constitutes true language proficiency. This criticism is the opposite of that previously made against foreign language instruction centered solely around the study of literature. Such literature-based instruction was accused of teaching students archaic, little-used lexicon and structures and of not preparing students for the practical uses of language that were much more useful and widespread than literary study. This approach thus narrows the range of language, focusing almost exclusively on academic discourse. But content-based instruction may err on the side of narrowing and restricting language too much. In glancing through I.S.P. Nation's text, *Teaching and Learning Vocabulary* (1990), I noticed that, at the back of this text, there is what is called a university word list, a list of those lexical items most commonly used in academic writing. The list was surprisingly short and made me think just how restricted the register is that we may be exposing our students to. A second experience brought home the same point. Recently, several colleagues and I have been taping some of the most dynamic and skilled lecturers from disciplines across our campus giving lectures on topics that would later be used in materials development for content-based ESL units. Although the lectures come from disciplines as different as atmospheric science and sociology, these lecturers all had one thing in common: They succeeded in making their lectures accessible by setting the issue or theory within the range of students' real-life concerns and experiences, using the latest slang expressions or the most current references from popular culture. These segments of the lecture were delivered in surprisingly non-academic language. One professor, an astronomer, even read aloud from a popular science fiction novel and had students read and relate a piece of science fiction to ideas presented in class. This is in sharp contrast to ESL teachers who, in an attempt to faithfully replicate content classes, expose students exclusively to "real" academic register in the form of dry textbook readings and journal articles.

CONCLUSION

At first glance, it may seem that incorporating literature into existing materials will tax EAP teachers' and materials developers' time and creativity even further. In my experience, incorporating one piece of literature into an existing content-based unit can be done quite easily and have very beneficial effects. Choices of literature should be driven by the content itself, a precondition which significantly limits the type and subject matter of literature that would be suitable. An appropriate piece of literature can even serve to focus a very broad topic in a certain way and to unify loosely related academic lectures and reading texts in a unit. This may, in turn, force the teacher's or materials developer's hand to discard or edit down parts of academic readings and lectures.

By exploring the language of literature, students are being exposed to a broader and deeper range of language. Literature can enhance existing content-based curricula and solve some of the practical problems that are presented by a very rich, contextualized approach to language teaching. This does not imply a return to bygone days, the days of second language study for the sake of literature. Rather, it implies a new approach to using literature which has, at its core, the purpose of promoting ESL students' academic literacy and critical thinking skills. Literature does not need to be *the* quintessential content, but it can be *a* quintessential part of content-based curricula and methodology.

PART **III**

Questions for Follow-Up Thought and Application

1. List several reasons why it is important to seek connections across various teaching approaches and CBI.

2. Make the case for using whole language techniques in the content-based classroom.

3. The majority of chapters in this volume focus on the application of content-based instruction to academic settings. The chapters by Henze and Katz (Chapter 29) and Wong (Chapter 30), on the other hand, deal with workplace and vocational settings. Do you think the rationale for CBI applies with the same force? Why or why not?

4. In Chapter 31, Johns makes numerous distinctions between ESP and CBI. Do you agree? Why or why not?

5. Johns states that ESP has a long research tradition; Grabe and Stoller in Chapter 1 state that "there is typically little empirical evidence of program success because ESP programs seldom evaluate program results through controlled research methods." How can these authors hold such different points of view? Discuss.

6. How is the content determined for use within tasks in the approach advocated in Chapter 32 by Carson, Taylor, and Fredella? How do they differ in their view of the role of task from that of Stoller and Grabe in Chapter 6?

7. Stoller and Grabe make the claim that "all content-based instruction is fundamentally theme-based." How do you think Carson, Taylor, and Fredella would react to this statement? What is your position?

8. The teaching of culture and literature are mainstays of the foreign language teaching tradition. Critique the arguments made by Hilles and Lynch (Chapter 33) and Holten (Chapter 34) that culture and literature can serve as appropriate content in CBI. Do the arguments apply equally as well to ESL as EFL?

9. Holten (Chapter 34) disagrees with Eskey's claim that content-based instruction does not adequately provide for a focus on language form. Review Holten's classroom activities. Do you find her point of view persuasive?

10. Having read some or all of the chapters in *The Content-Based Classroom*, what do you see as the key issues in content-based approaches to second/foreign language teaching?

References

Ackerman, D. B. (1990). Intellectual and practical criteria for successful curriculum integration. In H. H. Jacobs (Ed.), *Interdisciplinary curriculum: Design and implementation* (pp. 25-37). Alexandria, VA: Association for Supervision and Curriculum Development.

Ackerman, J. (1993). The promise of writing to learn. *Written Communication, 10,* 334-370.

Adamson, H. D. (1993). *Academic competence: Theory and classroom practice—Preparing ESL students for content courses.* New York: Longman.

Alexander, P. A., Kulikowich, J. M., & Jetton, T. L. (1994). The role of subject-matter knowledge and interest in the processing of linear and nonlinear texts. *Review of Educational Research, 64*(2), 201-252.

Alexander, P. A., Kulikowich, J. M., & Schulze, S. K. (1994). How subject-matter knowledge affects recall and interest. *American Educational Research Journal, 31*(2), 313-337.

Aljaafreh, A., & Lantolf, J. (1994). Negative feedback as regulation and second language acquisition in the Zone of Proximal Development. *Modern Language Journal, 78,* 465-483. [Special issue on sociocultural theory and L2 learning, J. Lantolf, Ed.]

Anderson, J. R. (1983). *The architecture of cognition.* Cambridge, MA: Harvard University Press.

Anderson, J. R. (1990a). *Cognitive psychology and its implications* (3rd ed.). New York: W. H. Freeman.

Anderson, J. R. (1990b). *The adaptive character of thought.* Hillsdale, NJ: Erlbaum.

Anderson, J. R. (1993). Problem solving and learning. *American Psychologist, 48,* 35-44.

Anderson, R. C., Wilson, P., & Fielding, L. (1988). Growth in reading and how children spend their time outside of school. *Reading Research Quarterly, 23,* 285-303.

Angelo, T. A. (1994, June). From faculty development to academic development. *American Association of Higher Education Bulletin,* 3-7.

Angelo, T. A., & Cross, K. P. (1993). *Classroom assessment techniques: A handbook for college teachers* (2nd ed.). San Francisco: Jossey-Bass.

Anthony, H. M., & Raphael, T. E. (1989). Using questioning strategies to promote students' active comprehension of content area material. In D. Lapp, J. Flood, & N. Farman (Eds.), *Content area reading and learning: Instructional strategies* (pp. 244-257). Englewood Cliffs, NJ: Prentice-Hall.

Artigal, J. (1991). *The Catalan immersion program: A European point of view.* Norwood, NJ: Ablex.

Aschbacher, P. R. (1991). Humanitas: A thematic curriculum. *Educational Leadership, 49*(2), 17-19.

Asher, J. (1969). The total physical response approach to second language learning. *Modern Language Journal, 53,* 3-17.

Asher, J. (1982). *Learning another language through actions: The complete teachers' guidebook.* Los Gatos, CA: Sky Oaks.

Auerbach, E. (1991). Politics, pedagogy, and professionalism: Challenging marginalization in ESL. *College ESL, 1*(1) 1-9.

Auerbach, E. (1993). Reexamining English only in the ESL classroom. *TESOL Quarterly, 27*(1), 9-32.

Bachman, L. F. (1990). *Fundamental considerations in language testing.* Oxford: Oxford University Press.

Bachman, L. F., & Palmer, A. S. (1996). *Language testing in practice: Designing and developing useful language tests.* Oxford: Oxford University Press.

Baetens-Beardsmore, H. (Ed.). (1993). *European models of bilingual education.* Clevedon, Avon: Multilingual Matters.

Baetens-Beardsmore, H. (1994). Language policy and planning in Western European countries. In W. Grabe, C. Ferguson, R. B. Kaplan, G. R. Tucker, & H. G. Widdowson (Eds.), *Annual review of applied linguistics, 14. Language policy and planning* (pp. 93-110). New York: Cambridge University Press.

Barker, D. J., & Bohlman, C. (1991). ESOL in U.S. secondary schools. *TESOL Journal, 1,* 12.

Barnitz, J. (1986). Toward understanding the effects of cross-cultural schemata and discourse structure in second language reading comprehension. *Journal of Reading Behavior, 18*(2), 95-116.

Barsalou, L. (1992). *Cognitive psychology: An overview for cognitive scientists.* Hillsdale, NJ: Erlbaum.

Basham, C., Ray, R., & Whalley, E. (1993). Cross-cultural perspectives on task representation in reading to write. In J. Carson & I. Leki (Eds.), *Reading in the composition classroom: Second language perspectives* (pp. 299-314). Boston: Heinle & Heinle.

Bazerman, C. (1984). Modern evolution of the experimental report in physics: Spectroscopic articles in *Physical Review,* 1893-1980. *Social Studies in Science, 14,* 163-196.

Beck, I. L., & McKeown, M. G. (1991). Social studies texts are hard to understand: Mediating some of the difficulties. *Language Arts, 68,* 482-490.

Beck, I. L., McKeown, M. G., & Gromoll, E. W. (1989). Learning from social studies texts. *Cognition and Instruction, 6*(2), 99-158.

Belcher, D. (1994). The apprenticeship approach to advanced academic literacy: Graduate students and their mentors. *English for Specific Purposes, 13,* 23-34.

Bell, I. (1985) *This book is not required.* Fort Bragg, CA: The Small Press.

Benesch, S. (Ed.). (1988). *Ending remediation: Linking ESL and content in higher education.* Alexandria, VA: Teachers of English to Speakers of Other Languages.

Benesch, S. (1992). Sharing responsibilities: An alternative to the adjunct model. *College ESL, 2*(1), 1-10.

Benjamin, J. R. (1991). *A student's guide to history* (5th ed.). New York: St. Martin's Press.

Bensoussan, M., & Kreindler, I. (1990). Improving advanced reading comprehension in a foreign language: Summaries vs. short-answer questions. *Journal of Research in Reading, 13*(1), 55–68.

Bereiter, C., & Scardamalia, M. (1993). *Surpassing ourselves: An inquiry into the nature and implications of expertise.* Chicago: Open Court Press.

Berkenkotter, C., & Huckin, T. (1995). *Genre knowledge in disciplinary communities.* Hillsdale, NJ: Erlbaum.

Bernhardt, E. B. (1994). A content analysis of reading methods texts: What are we told about the nonnative speaker of English? *Journal of Reading Behavior, 26,* 159–189.

Bernhardt, E. B., Destino, T., Kamil, M., & Rodríguez-Muñoz, M. (1995). Assessing science knowledge in an English/Spanish bilingual elementary school. *COGNOSOS, 4,* 4–6.

Bernhardt, E. B., Dickerson, T., Destino, T., & McNichols, M. (1994). Writing science and writing in science: Perspectives from minority children. *COGNOSOS, 3,* 7–10.

Bhatia, V. K. (1993). *Analyzing genre: Language use in professional settings.* London: Longman.

Blackey, R. (1981). A guide to the skill of essay construction in history. *Social History, 45,* 178–182.

Blakely, R. (in press). Creating and funding an instructional resource center for language minority students. In T. Smoke (Ed.), *Adult ESL: Politics, pedagogy, and participation in classroom and community programs.* Mahwah, NJ: Erlbaum.

Blanc, R. A., DeBuhr, L. E., & Martin, D. C. (1983). Breaking the attrition cycle: The effects of supplemental instruction on performance and attrition. *Journal of Higher Education, 54*(1), 80–90.

Brindley, G. (1984). *Needs analysis and objective-setting in the adult migrant education program.* Sydney: Adult Migrant Education Service.

Brinton, D. M., Goodwin, J., & Ranks, L. (1994). Helping language minority students to read and write analytically: The journey into, through and beyond. In F. Peitzman & G. Gadda (Eds.), *With different eyes: Insights into teaching language minority students across the disciplines* (pp. 57–88). New York: Longman.

Brinton, D. M., & Holten, C. (1989). What novice teachers focus on: The practicum in TESL. *TESOL Quarterly, 23*(2), 343–350.

Brinton, D. M., Holten, C. A., & Goodwin, J. M. (1993). Responding to dialogue journals in teacher preparation: What's effective? *TESOL Journal, 2*(4), 15–19.

Brinton, D. M., Snow, M. A., & Wesche, M. B. (1989). *Content-based second language instruction.* Boston: Heinle & Heinle.

Britten, D. (1985). Teacher training in ELT: Part 1. *Language Teaching, 18,* 112–128.

Brophy, J. E., & Alleman, J. (1991). *Social studies instruction should be driven by major social education goals.* East Lansing: Michigan State University, Institute for Research on Teaching.

Brown, A. L., & Day, J. D. (1983). Macrorules for summarizing texts: The development of expertise. *Journal of Verbal Learning and Verbal Behavior, 22*(1), 1–14.

Brown, A. L., Day, J. D., & Jones, R. S. (1983). The development of plans for summarizing texts. *Child Development, 54,* 968–979.

Brown, R., Pressley, M., Van Meter, P., & Schuder, T. (1996). A quasi-experimental validation of transactional strategies instruction with low-achieving second-grade readers. *Journal of Educational Psychology, 88,* 18–37.

Bruffee, K. A. (1993). *Collaborative learning: Higher education, interdependence, and the authority of knowledge.* Baltimore: Johns Hopkins University Press.

Brumfit, C. J., Paulston, C. B., & Wilkins, D. A. (1981). Notional syllabuses revisited. *Applied Linguistics, 2*(1), 20–32.

Bruner, J. (1978). The role of dialogue in language acquisition. In A. Sinclair, R. J. Jarvella, & W. J. M. Levelt (Eds.), *The child's conception of language* (pp. 44–62). New York: Springer.

Bruner, J. (1986). *Actual minds, possible worlds.* Cambridge, MA: Harvard University Press.

Bullock, T., Laine, C., & Slinger, E. (1990). Reading instruction in secondary English and social studies classrooms. *Reading Research and Instruction, 29,* 27–34.

Burkart, G. S., & Sheppard, K. (1994). *Content-ESL across the USA: A training packet* (Vol. 3). Washington, DC: Center for Applied Linguistics.

Byram, M., & Leman, J. (Eds.). (1989). *Bicultural and trilingual education: The Foyer model in Brussels.* Clevedon, Avon: Multilingual Matters.

Caine, R. N., & Caine, G. (1990). Understanding a brain-based approach to learning and teaching. *Educational Leadership, 48,* 66–70.

Campbell, C. (1990). Writing with others' words: Using background reading text in academic compositions. In B. Kroll (Ed.), *Second language writing: Research insights for the classroom* (pp. 211–230). Cambridge: Cambridge University Press.

Campbell, P. (1996). Using content-based courses and activities for student success at the university. *The Language Teacher, 20*(2), 25–28.

Cantoni-Harvey, G. (1987). *Content-area language instruction: Approaches and strategies.* Reading, MA: Addison-Wesley.

Carrell, P. L. (1985). Facilitating ESL reading by teaching text structure. *TESOL Quarterly, 19*(4), 727–752.

Carrell, P. L. (1987). Content and formal schemata in ESL reading. *TESOL Quarterly, 21*(3), 461–481.

Carrell, P. L. (1989). Metacognitive awareness and second language reading. *Modern Language Journal, 73,* 121–134.

Carson, J. G., Chase, N. D., & Gibson, S. U. (1993). *A model for faculty collaboration: Focus on academic literacy.* Atlanta: Georgia State University, Center for the Study of Adult Literacy.

Carson, J. G., Chase, N. D., Gibson, S. U., & Hargrove, M. F. (1992). Literacy demands of the undergraduate curriculum. *Reading Research and Instruction, 31*(4), 25–50.

Carter, M. (1990). The idea of expertise: An exploration of cognitive and social dimensions of writing. *College Composition and Communication, 41,* 265–286.

Casazza, M. E. (1993). Using a model of direct instruction to teach summary writing in a college reading class. *Journal of Reading, 37*(3), 202–208.

Casey, J. L. (1991). *A survey of ESL teaching methodologies being used in American intensive English programs.* Unpublished doctoral dissertation, University of Southern California, Los Angeles.

Castaneda, L. V. (1993). Alternative visions of practice: An exploratory study of peer coaching, sheltered content, cooperative instruction and mainstream subject matter teachers. In *Proceedings of the third national research symposium on limited English proficient student issues: Focus on middle and high school issues* (Vol. 1, pp. 431–467). Washington, DC: Office of Bilingual Education and Minority Languages Affairs, U.S. Department of Education.

Cazden, C. B., John, V. P., & Hymes, D. (Eds.). (1972). *Functions of language in the classroom.* New York: Teachers College Press.

Celce-Murcia, M. (1983). Problem-solving: A bridge-builder between theory and practice. In J. E. Alatis, H. H. Stern, & P. Strevens (Eds.), *Applied linguistics and the preparation of second language teachers: Toward a rationale* (pp. 97–105). Washington, DC: Georgetown University Press.

Chamot, A. U., & O'Malley, J. M. (1987). The cognitive academic language learning approach: A bridge to the mainstream. *TESOL Quarterly, 21*(2), 227-249.

Chamot, A. U., & O'Malley, J. M. (1994). *The CALLA handbook: Implementing the cognitive academic language learning approach.* Reading, MA: Addison-Wesley.

Chaudron, C. (1988). *Second language classrooms: Research on teaching and learning.* New York: Cambridge University Press.

Choi, E., Cramp, M., Goldsborough, J., Nashiro, R., & Tuman, J. (1993). *BA writes needs analysis.* Unpublished manuscript, Monterey Institute of International Studies.

Chomsky, N. (1957). *Syntactic structures.* The Hague: Mouton.

Chomsky, N. (1965). *Aspects of the theory of syntax.* Cambridge, MA: MIT Press.

Chopin, K. (1993). The story of an hour. In E. MacMahan, S. Day, & R. Funk (Eds.) *Literature and the writing process* (3rd ed. pp. 252-253). New York: Macmillan.

Christian, D. (Ed.). (1995). *Directory of two-way bilingual programs in the United States.* Washington, DC: Center for Applied Linguistics.

Christie, F. (Ed.). (1991). *Literacy for a changing world.* Victoria: Australian Council for Educational Research.

Christie, F. (1992). Literacy in Australia. In W. Grabe, C. Ferguson, R. B. Kaplan, G. R. Tucker, & H. G. Widdowson (Eds.), *Annual Review of Applied Linguistics, 12. Literacy* (pp. 142-155). New York: Cambridge University Press.

Clair, N. (1994). ESL teacher certification: A call for conversation. *TESOL Matters, 4*(2), 1, 3.

Clark, E. (1988). The search for a new educational paradigm: Implications of new assumptions about thinking and learning. *Holistic Education Review, 1*(1), 18-30.

Cochran, J. A. (1993). *Reading in the content areas for junior high and high school.* Boston: Allyn and Bacon.

Coelho, E. (1982). Language across the curriculum. *TESL Talk, 13*(3), 56-70.

Coley, J. D., & Hoffman, D. M. (1990). Overcoming learned helplessness in at-risk readers. *Journal of Reading, 33*(7), 497-502.

Collerson, J. (Ed.). (1988). *Writing for life.* Rozelle, New South Wales: Primary English Teaching Association (distributed through Heinemann).

Collier, V. P. (1987). Age and rate of acquisition of second language for academic purposes. *TESOL Quarterly, 21*(4), 617-641.

Collier, V. P. (1989). How long? A synthesis of research on academic achievement in a second language. *TESOL Quarterly, 23*(3), 509-531.

Collier, V. P. (1992). A synthesis of studies examining long-term language-minority student data on academic achievement. *Bilingual Research Journal, 16,* 187-212.

Collier, V. P. (1994, March). Promising practices in public schools. Plenary address presented at annual meeting of Teachers of English to Speakers of Other Languages, Baltimore, MD.

Commission on Teacher Credentialing. (1992). *Standards of program quality and effectiveness for professional teacher preparation programs for multiple and single subject teaching credentials with a (bilingual) crosscultural, language and academic development (CLAD/BCLAD) emphasis.* Sacramento: California State Department of Education.

Connor, U. M., & McCagg, P. (1987). A contrastive study of English expository prose paraphrases. In U. Connor & R. B. Kaplan (Eds.), *Writing across languages: Analysis of L2 text* (pp. 73-86). Reading, MA: Addison-Wesley.

Cordero-Ponce, W. L. (1994, March). *Facilitating L2 reading comprehension through summarization instruction.* Paper presented at the annual conference of the American Association of Applied Linguistics, Baltimore, MD.

Crabtree, C., Nash, G., Gagnon, P., & Waugh, S. (Eds.). (1992). *Lessons from history: Essential understandings and historical perspectives students should acquire.* Los Angeles: University of California, Los Angeles, National Center for History in the Schools.

Crandall, J. A. (Ed.). (1987). *ESL through content-area instruction.* Englewood Cliffs, NJ: Prentice Hall Regents.

Crandall, J. A. (1993). Content-centered learning in the United States. In W. Grabe, C. Ferguson, R. B. Kaplan, G. R. Tucker, & H. G. Widdowson (Eds.), *Annual Review of Applied Linguistics, 13. Issues in second language teaching and learning* (pp. 111–126). New York: Cambridge University Press.

Crookes, G. (1986). *Task-classification: A cross-disciplinary review* (Tech. Rep. No. 4). Honolulu: University of Hawaii at Manoa, Social Science Research Institute, Center for Second Language Classroom Research.

Crookes, G., & Schmidt, R. W. (1991). Motivation: Reopening the research agenda. *Language Learning, 41*(4), 469–512.

Csikszentmihalyi, M. (1990). *Flow: The psychology of optimal experience.* New York: Harper and Row.

Csikszentmihalyi, M. (1993). *The evolving source: A psychology for the third millennium.* New York: HarperCollins.

Csikszentmihalyi, M., & Csikszentmihalyi, I. S. (1988). *Optimal experience: Psychological studies of flow in consciousness.* New York: Cambridge University Press.

Csikszentmihalyi, M. K., Rathunde, K., & Whalen, S. (1993). *Talented teenagers: The roots of success and failure.* New York: Cambridge University Press.

Cummins, J. (1981). The role of primary language development in promoting educational success for language minority students. In California State Department of Education, *Schooling and language minority students: A theoretical framework* (pp. 3–49). Los Angeles: California State University; Evaluation, Dissemination and Assessment Center.

Cummins, J. (1984). *Bilingualism and special education: Issues in assessment and pedagogy.* Clevedon, Avon: Multilingual Matters.

Cummins, J. (1989). *Empowering minority students.* Sacramento: California Association for Bilingual Education.

Cummins, J. (1992). Language proficiency, bilingualism, and academic achievement. In P. Richard-Amato & M. A. Snow (Eds.), *The multicultural classroom: Readings for content-area teachers* (pp. 16–26). New York: Longman.

Cummins, J. (1994). Primary language instruction and the education of language minority students. In California State Department of Education, *Schooling and language minority students: A theoretical framework* (2nd ed., pp 3–46). Los Angeles: California State University, Evaluation, Dissemination and Assessment Center.

Curtain, H. A. (1986). Integrating language and content instruction. *ERIC/CLL News Bulletin, 9*(2), 10–11.

Curtain, H. A., & Pesola, C. A. (1994). *Languages and children: Making the match* (2nd ed.). New York: Longman.

Danticat, E. (1994). *Breath, eyes, memory.* New York: Soho.

Day, J. D. (1980). *Teaching summarization skills: A comparison of training methods.* Unpublished doctoral dissertation, University of Illinois, Urbana.

Destino, T., Bernhardt, E., & Rodríguez-Muñoz, M. (1994). Meeting science objectives in a bilingual setting. *COGNOSOS, 3,* 1–5.

Devenney, R. (1991). Teaching culture in language classes: One approach. *The CATESOL Journal, 4,* 83–90.

DeVries, R., & Kohlberg, L. (1987). *Programs of early education: The constructivist view.* New York: Longman.

Didion, J. (1968). Los Angeles notebook. In *Slouching toward Bethlehem* (pp. 217–221). New York: Dell.

Donato, R. (1994). Collective scaffolding in second language learning. In J. P. Lantolf & G. Appel (Eds.), *Vygotskian approaches to second language research* (pp. 33–56). Norwood, NJ: Ablex.

Driver, R. (1983). *The pupil scientist?* Philadelphia: Open University Press.

Drum, P. A. (1984). Children's understanding of passages. In J. Flood (Ed.), *Promoting reading comprehension* (pp. 61–78). Newark, DE: International Reading Association.

Dubin, F. (1986). Dealing with texts. In F. Dubin, D. Eskey, & W. Grabe (Eds.), *Teaching second language reading for academic purposes* (pp. 127–160). Reading, MA: Addison-Wesley.

Dubin, F., & Olshtain, E. (1986). *Course design.* New York: Cambridge University Press.

Duckworth, E. (1987). *"The having of wonderful ideas" and other essays on teaching and learning.* New York: Teachers College Press.

Dudley-Evans, A., & Henderson, W. (Eds.). (1990). *The language of economics: The analysis of economics discourse* (ELT Documents No. 134). London: Modern English Publications, in association with the British Council.

Duff, P. A. (1993). *Changing times, changing minds: Language socialization in Hungarian-English schools.* Unpublished doctoral dissertation, University of California, Los Angeles.

Duff, P. A. (1995). An ethnography of communication in immersion classrooms in Hungary. *TESOL Quarterly, 29*(3), 505–536.

Duffy, C. B. (1991, March). *Content-based instruction: The evolution of an adjunct model.* Paper presented at the annual conference of Teachers of English to Speakers of Other Languages, New York.

Duffy, C. B. (1995, March). *Adjunct model content-based language instruction: Effects on language and concept development.* Paper presented at the annual conference of the American Association of Applied Linguistics, Long Beach, CA.

Duffy, G. G. (1993a). Rethinking strategy instruction: Four teachers' development and their low achievers' understandings. *The Elementary School Journal, 93*(3), 231–247.

Duffy, G. G. (1993b). Teachers' progress toward becoming expert strategy teachers. *The Elementary School Journal, 92*(2), 109–120.

Dweck, C. S. (1989). Motivation. In A. Lesgold & R. Glaser (Eds.), *Foundations for a psychology of education* (pp. 87–136). Hillsdale, NJ: Erlbaum.

Early, M. (1985). *Input and interaction in the content classroom: Foreigner-talk and teacher talk in classroom discourse.* Unpublished doctoral dissertation, University of California, Los Angeles.

Early, M. (1990). ESL beginning literacy: A content-based approach. *Canada Journal, 7*(1), 82–94.

Early, M., Mohan, B. A., & Hooper, H. R. (1989). The Vancouver School Board language and content project. In J. H. Esling (Ed.), *Multicultural education and policy: ESL in the 1990s* (pp. 107–122). Toronto: The Ontario Institute for Studies in Education.

Early, M., & Tang, G. M. (1991). Helping ESL students cope with content-based texts. *TESL Canada Journal, 8*(2), 34–45.

Edelsky, C. (1986). *Writing in a bilingual program: Habia una vez.* Norwood, NJ: Ablex.

Edelsky, C., Altwerger, B., & Flores, B. (1991). *Whole language: What's the difference?* Portsmouth, NH: Heinemann.

Edwards, H. P., Wesche, M., Krashen, S., Clément, R., & Kruidenier, B. (1984). Second language acquisition through subject matter learning: A study of sheltered psychology classes at the University of Ottawa. *Canadian Modern Language Review, 41*(2), 268-282.

Eggins, S. (1994). *An introduction to systemic functional linguistics.* London: Pinter Publishers.

Elifson, J. M., Pounds, M. L., & Stone, K. R. (1995). Planning for and assessment of developmental programs. *Journal of Developmental Education, 19*, 2-11.

Eliot, T. S. (1962). The four quartets. In *The complete poems and plays: 1909-1950* (pp. 117-145). New York: Harcourt, Brace and World.

Elley, W. (1991). Acquiring literacy in a second language: The effect of book-based programs. *Language Learning, 41*, 375-411.

Endres-Niggemeyer, B., Waumans, W., & Yamashita, H. (1991). Modeling summary writing by introspection: A small-scale demonstrative study. *TEXT, 11*(4), 523-552.

Enright, D. S. (1986). "Use everything you have to teach English": Providing useful input to young language learners. In P. Rigg & D. S. Enright (Eds.), *Children and ESL: Integrating perspectives* (pp. 115-162). Washington, DC: Teachers of English to Speakers of Other Languages.

Enright, D. S., & McCloskey, M. (1988). *Integrating English.* Reading, MA: Addison-Wesley.

Erikson, F., & Shultz, J. (1982). *The counselor as gatekeeper.* New York: Academic Press.

Eskey, D. E. (1983). Meanwhile, back in the real world . . . *TESOL Quarterly, 27*(2), 315-323.

Eskey, D. E. (1984). Content: The missing third dimension in syllabus design. In J. A. S. Reid (Ed.), *Case studies in syllabus and course design. RELC Occasional Papers, 31*, 66-77.

Esposito, M., Marshall, K., & Stoller, F. L. (1997). Poster sessions by experts. In D. Brinton & P. Master (Eds.), *New ways in content-based instruction* (pp. 115-118). Alexandria, VA: Teachers of English to Speakers of Other Languages.

Estes, W. K. (1989). Learning theory. In A. Lesgold & R. Glaser (Eds.), *Foundations for a psychology of education* (pp. 1-49). Hillsdale, NJ: Erlbaum.

Faltis, C. J. (1993). *Joinfostering: Adapting teaching strategies for the multilingual classroom.* New York: Merrill.

Fathman, A., & Kessler, C. (1993). Cooperative language learning in school contexts. In W. Grabe, C. Ferguson, R. B. Kaplan, G. R. Tucker, & H. G. Widdowson (Eds.), *Annual Review of Applied Linguistics, 13. Issues in second language teaching and learning* (pp. 127-140). New York: Cambridge University Press.

Filene, P. G. (1993). Narrating progressivism: Unitarians v. pluralists v. students. *Journal of American History, 79*, 1546-1561.

Firth, A., & Wagner, J. (1996, August). *On discourse, communication, and (some) fundamental concepts in second language acquisition.* Paper presented at the International Association of Applied Linguistics (AILA) Congress, Jyväskylä, Finland.

Flower, L. (1990). Introduction: Studying cognition in context. In L. Flower, V. Stein, J. Ackerman, M. J. Kantz, K. McCormick, & W. C. Peck (Eds.), *Reading-to-write: Exploring cognitive and social process* (pp. 3-32). New York: Oxford University Press.

Forman, G., & Kuschner, D. (1977). *The child's construction of knowledge.* Belmont, CA: Wadsworth.

Fosnot, C. (1993). Rethinking science education: A defense of Piagetian constructivism. *Journal of Research in Science Education, 30*, 1189-1201.

Freedman, A., & Medway, P. (Eds.). (1994). *Learning and teaching genre.* Portsmouth, NH: Heinemann Boynton/Cook.

Freeman, D. (1989). Teacher training, development, and decision making: A model of teaching and related strategies for language teacher education. *TESOL Quarterly, 23*(1), 27-45.

Freeman, D. (1995). *Teacher education and structures of knowing.* Paper presented at the Third International Conference on Teacher Education in Second Language Teaching, City University of Hong Kong.

Freeman, D. E., & Freeman, Y. S. (1988, Summer). Whole language content lessons. *ESOL Newsletter,* 1-2.

Freeman, D. E., & Freeman, Y. S. (1989a). A road to success for language minority high school students. In P. Rigg & V. Allen (Eds.), *When they don't all speak English: Integrating the ESL student into the regular classroom* (pp. 126-139). Urbana, IL: National Council of Teachers of English.

Freeman, Y. S., & Freeman, D. E. (1989b). Changing contexts in secondary classes by altering teacher assumptions. *The CATESOL Journal, 2*(1), 27-43.

Freeman, Y. S., & Freeman, D. E. (1991). Doing social studies: Whole language lessons to promote social action. *Social Education, 55*(1), 29-32, 66.

Freeman, Y. S., & Freeman, D. E. (1992). *Whole language for second language learners.* Portsmouth, NH: Heinemann.

Frost, R. (1995). The road not taken. In E. V. Roberts & H. E. Jacobs (Eds.), *Literature: An introduction to reading and writing* (p. 898). Englewood Cliffs, N.J.: Prentice Hall.

Fry, E. (1977). Fry's readability graph: Clarifications, validity, and extension to level 17. *Journal of Reading, 21*(3), 242-253.

Gadda, G. (1994). Writing and language socialization across cultures: Some implications for the classroom. In F. Peitzman & G. Gadda (Eds.), *With different eyes: Insights into teaching language minority students across the disciplines* (pp. 43-56). White Plains, NY: Longman.

Ganeles, D., & Darcy, C. M. (1977). A practical and moral approach to the assessment of attitudinal development in competence-based education. In J. F. Fanselow & R. L. Light (Eds.), *Bilingual, ESOL, and foreign language teacher preparation: Models, practices, issues* (pp. 210-218). Washington, DC: Teachers of English to Speakers of Other Languages.

Gardner, H. (1993). *Multiple intelligences.* New York: Basic Books.

Gardner, R. C., & Lambert, W. E. (1959). Motivational variables in second language acquisition. *Canadian Journal of Psychology, 13,* 266-272.

Gardner, R. C., & Lambert, W. E. (1972). *Attitudes and motivation in second language learning.* New York: Newbury House.

Garfinkel, H. (1967). *Studies in ethnomethodology.* Englewood Cliffs, NJ: Prentice-Hall.

Garner, R. (1982). Efficient text summarization: Costs and benefits. *Journal of Educational Research, 75*(5), 275-279.

Garner, R. (1985). Text summarization deficiencies among older students: Awareness or production ability? *American Educational Research Journal, 22*(4), 549-560.

Garner, R. (1987). *Metacognition and reading comprehension.* Norwood, NJ: Ablex.

Garner, R., & McCaleb, J. L. (1985). Effects of text manipulations on the quality of written summaries. *Contemporary Educational Psychology, 10*(2), 139-149.

Garrett, N. (1991). Theoretical and pedagogical problems of separating "grammar" from "communication." In B. F. Freed (Ed.), *Foreign language acquisition research and the classroom* (pp. 74-87). Lexington, MA: D. C. Heath

Gaskins, I. (1994). Classroom applications of cognitive science: Teaching poor readers how to learn, think, and problem solve. In K. McGilly (Ed.), *Classroom lessons: Integrating cognitive theory* (pp. 129-154). Cambridge, MA: MIT Press.

Gee, J. P. (1990). *Social linguistics and literacies.* New York: The Falmer Press.

Genesee, F. (1994a). ESL and classroom teacher collaborations: Building futures together. *TESOL Matters, 4*(6), 3.

Genesee, F. (1994b). *Language and content: Lessons from immersion* (Educational Practice Report No. 11). Washington, DC: Center for Applied Linguistics, and National Center for Research on Cultural Diversity and Second Language Learning.

Goffman, E. (1963). *The presentation of self in everyday life.* Garden City, NY: Doubleday Anchor Books.

Golding, W. (1954). *Lord of the flies: A novel.* New York: Perigree.

Goldstein, L. (1993). Becoming a member of the "teaching foreign language" community: Integrating reading and writing through an adjunct/content course. In J. Carson & I. Leki (Eds.), *Reading in the composition classroom: Second language perspectives* (pp. 290–299). Boston: Heinle & Heinle.

Goldstein, L., & Liu, N. F. (1994). An integrated approach to the design of an immersion program. *TESOL Quarterly, 28*(4), 705–725.

Goodman, K. (1986). *What's whole in whole language?* Portsmouth, NH: Heinemann.

Goodman, Y. (1985). Kidwatching: Observing children in the classroom. In A. Jaggar & M. T. Smith-Burke (Eds.), *Observing the language learner* (pp. 9–18). Newark, DE, and Urbana, IL: International Reading Association, and the National Council of Teachers of English.

Grabe, W. (1986). The transition from theory to practice in teaching reading. In F. Dubin, D. E. Eskey, & W. Grabe (Eds.), *Teaching second language reading for academic purposes* (pp. 25–48). Reading, MA: Addison-Wesley.

Grabe, W. (1995). Discourse analysis and reading instruction. In T. Miller (Ed.), *Functional approaches to written text: Classroom applications.* Paris: TESOL France.

Grandin, J. (1993). The University of Rhode Island's international engineering program. In M. Krueger & F. Ryan (Eds.), *Language and content: Discipline- and content-based approaches to language study* (pp. 130–137). Lexington, MA: D. C. Heath.

Graves, D. (1983). *Writing: Teachers and children at work.* Portsmouth, NH: Heinemann.

Grennon Brooks, J. (1990). Teachers and students: Constructivists forging new connections. *Educational Leadership, 47,* 68–71.

Grennon Brooks, J., & Brooks, M. (1993). *The case for constructivist classrooms.* Alexandria, VA: Association for Supervision and Curriculum Development.

Halliday, M. A. K. (1993). Towards a language-based theory of learning. *Linguistics and Education, 5,* 93–116.

Halliday, M. A. K., & Hasan, R. (1976). *Cohesion in English.* London: Group Ltd.

Hamayan, E. V., & Perlaman, R. (1990). *Helping language minority students after they exit from bilingual/ESL programs: A handbook for teachers.* Washington, DC: National Clearinghouse for Bilingual Education.

Handscombe, J. (1989). Mainstreaming: Who needs it? In J. H. Esling (Ed.), *Multicultural education and policy: ESL in the 1990s* (pp. 18–35). Toronto: Ontario Institute for Studies in Education Press.

Hare, V. C., & Borchardt, K. M. (1984). Direct instruction of summarization skills. *Reading Research Quarterly, 20*(1), 62–78.

Haring-Smith, T. (1994). *Writing together.* New York: HarperCollins.

Harklau, L. (1994). ESL vs. mainstream classes: Contrasting L2 learning environments. *TESOL Quarterly, 28*(2), 241–272.

Harley, B., Allen, P., Cummins, J., & Swain, M. (1990). The nature of language proficiency. In B. Harley, P. Allen, J Cummins, & M. Swain (Eds.), *The development of second language proficiency* (pp. 7–25). Cambridge: Cambridge University Press.

Harste, J., Woodward, V., & Burke, C. (1984). *Language stories and literacy lessons.* Portsmouth, NH: Heinemann.

Hauptman, P. C., Wesche, M. B., & Ready, D. (1988). Second language acquisition through subject-matter learning: A follow-up study at the University of Ottawa. *Language Learning, 38*(3), 439–482.

Hawkins, B. (1988). *Scaffolded classroom interaction in a language minority setting.* Unpublished doctoral dissertation, University of California, Los Angeles.

Heath, S. B. (1983). *Ways with words.* Cambridge: Cambridge University Press.

Heath, S. B. (1986a). Sociocultural contexts of language development. In California State Department of Education, *Beyond language* (pp. 143–182). Los Angeles: California State University; Evaluation, Dissemination and Assessment Center.

Heath, S. B. (1986b). What no bedtime story means: Narrative skills at home and school. In B. Schieffelin & E. Ochs (Eds.), *Language socialization across cultures* (pp. 97–124). Cambridge: Cambridge University Press.

Hidi, S., & Anderson, V. (1986). Producing written summaries: Task demands, cognitive operations, and implications for instruction. *Review of Educational Research, 56*(4), 473–493.

Holdaway, D. (1979). *The foundations of literacy.* Sydney: Ashton, Scholastic.

Holden, W. (1996/1997, December/January). Proceeding from learner needs. *ESP News,* 11.

Holiday, A. (1994). *Appropriate methodology and social context.* Cambridge: Cambridge University Press.

Hollingsworth, S. (1989). Prior beliefs and cognitive change in learning to teach. *American Educational Research Journal, 26,* 160–189.

Holmes, J. (1996, March). *Becoming critical: From submissive reading to writing back.* Paper presented at the annual conference of the Teachers of English to Speakers of Other Languages, Chicago, IL.

Holten, C. A., & Brinton, D. M. (1995). "You shoulda been there": Charting novice teacher growth using dialogue journals. *TESOL Journal 4*(4), 23–36.

Hudelson, S. (1984). Kan yu ret an rayt en ingles: Children become literate in English as a second language. *TESOL Quarterly, 18*(2), 221–237.

Hudson, T. (1991). A content comprehension approach to reading in English for science and technology. *TESOL Quarterly, 25,* 77–104.

Hurston, Z. N. (1993). Sweat. In E. MacMahan, S. Day, & R. Funk (Eds.), *Lieterature and the writing process* (3rd ed., pp. 321–328). New York: Macmillan.

Hutchinson, T., & Waters, A. (1987). *English for specific purposes: A learning-centered approach.* New York: Cambridge University Press.

Hymes, D. (1972). Introduction. In C. B. Cazden, V. P. Hymes, & D. Hymes (Eds.), *Functions of language in the classroom* (pp. xi–lvii). New York: Teachers College Press.

Jacobs, H. H. (1990). The growing need for interdisciplinary curriculum content. In H. H. Jacobs (Ed.), *Interdisciplinary curriculum: Design and implementation* (pp. 1–11). Alexandria, VA: Association for Supervision and Curriculum Development.

Jarolimek, J. (1989). In search of a scope and sequence for social studies. *Social Education, 53*(6), 376–385.

Johannsen, E. (1993). Portraits of middle and high school instructional, programmatic, and teaching/learning processes in multiple-language contexts. In *Proceedings of the third national research symposium on limited English proficient student issues: Focus on middle and high school issues* (Vol. 1, pp. 883–887). Washington, DC: Office of Bilingual Education and Minority Languages Affairs, U.S. Department of Education.

Johns, A. M. (1985). Summary protocols of "under-prepared" and "adept" university students: Replications and distortions of the original. *Language Learning, 35*(4), 495–517.

Johns, A. M. (1986). Coherence and academic writing. *TESOL Quarterly, 20*(2), 247–264.

Johns, A. M. (1989, March). *English for academic purposes course design: The issue of transferable skills.* Paper presented at the meeting of Teachers of English to Speakers of Other Languages, San Antonio, TX.

Johns, A. M. (1991a). English for specific purposes (ESP): Its history and contributions. In M. Celce-Murcia (Ed.), *Teaching English as a second/foreign language* (pp. 67–78). New York: Newbury House.

Johns, A. M. (1991b). Interpreting an English competency examination: The frustrations of an ESL science student. *Written Communication, 8*(3), 379–401.

Johns, A. M. (1997). *Text, role and context: Developing academic literacies.* Cambridge: Cambridge University Press.

Johns, A. M., & Dudley-Evans, T. (1991). English for specific purposes: International in scope, specific in purpose. *TESOL Quarterly, 25*(2), 297–314.

Johns, A. M., & Mayes, P. (1990) An analysis of summary protocols of university ESL students. *Applied Linguistics, 11,* 253–271.

Johns, T. F., & Davies, F. (1983). Text as vehicle of communication: The classroom use of written texts in teaching reading in a foreign language. *Reading in a Foreign Language, 1,* 1–19.

Johns, T. F., & Dudley-Evans, T. (1980). An experiment in team-teaching of overseas post-graduate students of transportation and plant biology. *ELT documents 106: Team teaching in ESP.* London: The British Council (ETIC).

Johnson, D. W., Johnson, R. T., Holubec, E. J., & Roy, R. (1984). *Circles of learning.* Alexandria, VA: Association of Supervision and Curriculum Development.

Jurasek, R. (1993). Foreign languages across the curriculum: A case history from Earlham College and a generic rationale. In M. Krueger & F. Ryan (Eds.), *Language and content: Discipline- and content-based approaches to language study* (pp. 85–102). Lexington, MA: D. C. Heath.

Kagan, S. (1986). Cooperative learning and sociocultural factors in schooling. In California State Department of Education, *Beyond language: Social and cultural factors in schooling language minority students* (pp. 231–298). Los Angeles: California State University; Evaluation, Dissemination and Assessment Center.

Kagan, S. (1988*). Cooperative learning resources for teachers.* Laguna Niguel, CA: Resources for Teachers.

Kamhi-Stein, L. D. (1995). *The effect of explicit instruction on the summarization strategies of "underprepared" native Spanish-speaking freshmen in university-level adjunct courses.* Unpublished doctoral dissertation, University of Southern California.

Kamhi-Stein, L. D., Koch, N., & Snow, M. A. (1997). Making the most of office hours. In D. M. Brinton & P. Master (Eds.), *New ways in content-based instruction* (pp. 240–242). Alexandria, VA: Teachers of English to Speakers of Other Languages.

Kamhi-Stein, L. D., & Snow, M. A. (1997). Interpreting tables and figures. In D. Brinton & P. Master (Eds.), *New ways in content-based instruction* (pp. 36–43). Alexandria, VA: Teachers of English to Speakers of Other Languages.

Kamii, C. (1981). The application of Piaget's theory to education: The preoperational level. In I. E. Sigel, D. M. Brozinsky, & R. M. Golinkoff (Eds.), *New directions in Piagetian theory and practice* (pp. 231–265). Hillsdale, NJ: Erlbaum.

Kamii, C. (1985). *Young children re-invent arithmetic.* New York: Teachers College Press.

Kaplan, R. B., Cantor, S., Hagstrom, C., Kamhi-Stein, L. D., Shiotani, Y., & Zimmerman, C. B. (1994). On abstract writing. *TEXT, 14*(3), 401–426.

Kauffman, D., with Burkart, G. S., Crandall, J., Johnson, D. E., Peyton, J. K., Sheppard, K., & Short, D. J. (1994). *Content-ESL across the USA: A Practical Guide* (Vol. 2). Washington, DC: Center for Applied Linguistics.

Kaufman, D., & Grennon Brooks, J. (1996). Interdisciplinary collaboration in teacher education: A constructivist approach. *TESOL Quarterly, 30,* 231-251.

Kayfetz, J., Cordaro, M., & Kelly, M. (1988). *Improving ESL instruction for college bound students.* Final report of the project conducted July 1, 1987, through June 30, 1988, for the California Community College Fund for Instructional Improvement. Fountain Valley, CA: Coastline Community College. (ERIC Document Reproduction Service No. ED 307 946)

Keller, J. M. (1983). Motivational design of instruction. In C. M. Reigeluth (Ed.), *Instructional design theories and models: An overview of their current status* (pp. 283-434). Hillsdale, NJ: Erlbaum.

Keller, J. M., & Kopp, T. W. (1987). An application of the ARCS model of motivational design. In C. M. Reigeluth (Ed.), *Instructional theories in action: Lessons illustrating selected theories and models* (pp. 289-320). Hillsdale, NJ: Erlbaum.

Kennedy, C., & Bolitho, R. (1984). *English for specific purposes.* London: Macmillan.

Kessler, C. (1992). *Cooperative language learning: A teacher's resource book.* Englewood Cliffs, NJ: Prentice Hall Regents.

Kessler, C., & Quinn, M. E. (1984). *Second language acquisition in the context of science experiences.* (ERIC Document Reproduction Service No. ED 248 713)

Kintsch, W., & van Dijk, T. A. (1978). Toward a model of text comprehension and production. *Psychological Review, 85*(5), 363-394.

Kirkland, M. R., & Saunders, M. A. P. (1991). Maximizing student performance in summary writing: Managing cognitive load. *TESOL Quarterly, 25*(1), 105-121.

Kluckhohn, C. (1949). Mirror for man. Reprinted in J. R. McCuen & Anthony C. Winkler (Eds.), *Readings for Writers* (4th ed., pp. 226-233). New York: Harcourt Brace Jovanovich.

Koch, N., Krilowicz, B., Srole, C., Galanti, G. A., Kamhi-Stein, L. D., & Snow, M. A. (1997). The multistep writing assignment. In D. M. Brinton & P. Master (Eds.), *New ways in content-based instruction* (pp. 243-257). Alexandria, VA: Teachers of English to Speakers of Other Languages.

Kolb, D. (1984). *Experiential learning: Experience as the source of learning and development.* Englewood Cliffs, NJ: Prentice-Hall.

Kornblum, H., with Garschick, E. (1992). *Directory of professional preparation programs in TESOL in the United States.* Alexandria, VA: Teachers of English to Speakers of Other Languages.

Koshik, I. (1995, March). *The activity of defining in ESL classroom discourse.* Paper presented at the meeting of the American Association for Applied Linguistics, Long Beach, CA.

Krahnke, K. (1987). *Approaches to syllabus design for foreign language teaching.* Englewood Cliffs, NJ: Prentice-Hall.

Krapp, A., Hidi, S., & Renninger, K. A. (1992). Interest, learning, and development. In K. A. Renninger, S. Hidi, & A. Krapp (Eds.), *The role of interest in learning and development* (pp. 3-25). Hillsdale, NJ: Erlbaum.

Krashen, S. D. (1981a, December). The case for narrow reading. *TESOL Newsletter,* 21.

Krashen, S. D. (1981b). Bilingual education and second language acquisition theory. In California State Department of Education, *Schooling and language minority students:*

A theoretical framework (pp. 51-79). Los Angeles: California State University; Evaluation, Dissemination and Assessment Center.

Krashen, S. D. (1982). *Principles and practices in second language acquisition.* New York: Pergamon Press.

Krashen, S. D. (1985). *The input hypothesis: Issues and implications.* New York: Longman.

Krashen, S. D. (1989). We acquire vocabulary and spelling by reading: Additional evidence for the Input Hypothesis. *Modern Language Journal, 73,* 440-464.

Krashen, S. D. (1993). *The power of reading.* Englewood, CO: Libraries Unlimited.

Krashen, S. D., & Terrell, T. D. (1983). *The natural approach.* New York: Pergamon.

Kroll, B. (1977). Combining ideas in written and spoken English: A look at subordination and coordination. In E. O. Keenan & T. L. Bennett (Eds.), *Discourse across time and space* (pp. 69-108). Southern California Occasional Papers in Linguistics, Vol. 5. Los Angeles: University of Southern California.

Krueger, M., & Ryan, F. (1993a). Resituating foreign languages in the curriculum. In M. Krueger & F. Ryan (Eds.), *Language and content: Discipline- and content-based approaches to language study* (pp. 3-24). Lexington, MA: D. C. Heath.

Krueger, M., & Ryan, F. (Eds.). (1993b). *Language and content: Discipline- and content-based approaches to language study.* Lexington, MA: D. C. Heath.

Kumpf, L. (1995, March). *Teachers' talk in high school science classes.* Paper presented at the annual meeting of the American Association of Applied Linguistics, Long Beach, CA.

Lange, D. L. (1990). A blueprint for a teacher development program. In J. C. Richards & D. Nunan (Eds.), *Second language teacher education* (pp. 245-268). Cambridge: Cambridge University Press.

Lantolf, J. (Ed.). (1994). *Sociocultural theory and second language learning.* [Special issue of *The Modern Language Journal, 78*(4).]

Lantolf, J., & Appel, G. (Eds.). (1994). *Vygotskian approaches to second language research.* Norwood, NJ: Ablex.

Lantolf, J., with Pavlenko, A. (1995). Sociocultural approaches to second language acquisition. In W. Grabe, C. Ferguson, R. B. Kaplan, G. R. Tucker, H. G. Widdowson (Eds.), *Annual Review of Applied Linguistics, 15* (pp. 125-150). New York: Cambridge University Press.

Larsen-Freeman, D. (1983). Training teachers or educating a teacher. In J. E. Alatis, H. H. Stern, & P. Strevens (Eds.), *Applied linguistics and the preparation of second language teachers: Toward a rationale* (pp. 264-274). Washington, DC: Georgetown University Press.

Larsen-Freeman, D., & Long, M. H. (1991). *An introduction to second language acquisition research.* New York: Longman.

Lazar, G. (1993). *Literature and language teaching: A guide for teachers and trainers.* Cambridge: Cambridge University Press.

Leaver, B. L., & Stryker, S. B. (1989). Content-based instruction for foreign language classrooms. *Foreign Language Annals, 22,* 269-275.

Leki, I., & Carson, J. G. (1994). Students' perceptions of EAP writing instruction and writing needs across the disciplines. *TESOL Quarterly, 28*(1), 81-101.

Levine, E. (1989). *I hate English!* New York: Scholastic.

Lewitt, P. J. (1995). The means of meaning: A why and a how of teaching content. *The Language Teacher, 19*(11), 33-36.

Lightbown, P., & Spada, N. (1994). An innovative program for primary ESL students in Quebec. *TESOL Quarterly, 28,* 563-579.

Lim, G. (1988). A juk-sing opera. In G. Soto (Ed.), *A California childhood* (pp. 33-40). Berkeley, CA: Creative Arts.

Long, M. H., & Crookes, G. (1992). Three approaches to task-based syllabus design. *TESOL Quarterly, 26*, 27–56.

Long, M. H., & Crookes, G. (1993). Units of analysis in syllabus design: The case for task. In G. Crookes & S. M. Gass (Eds.), *Tasks in a pedagogical context: Integrating theory and practice* (pp. 9–54). Clevedon, Avon: Multilingual Matters.

Long, M. H., & Porter, P. A. (1983). Group work, interlanguage talk, and second language acquisition. *TESOL Quarterly, 19*, 207–228.

Lorenz, E. B., & Met, M. (1988). *What it means to be an immersion teacher.* Rockville, MD: Office of Instruction and Program Development, Montgomery County Public Schools.

Lucas, T. (1993). What have we learned from research on successful secondary programs for LEP students? A synthesis of findings from three studies. In *Proceedings of the third national research symposium on limited English proficient student issues: Focus on middle and high school issues* (Vol. 1, pp. 81–111). Washington, DC: Office of Bilingual Minority Languages Affairs, U.S. Department of Education.

Lucas, T., & Katz, A. (1994). Reframing the debate: The roles of native languages in English-only programs for language minority students. *TESOL Quarterly, 28*(3), 537–562.

Lynch, B. K., & Davidson, F. (1994). Criterion-referenced language test development: Linking curricula, teachers, and tests. *TESOL Quarterly, 28*(4), 727–744.

Lynch, B. K., & Hudson, T. (1991). EST Reading. In M. Celce-Murcia (Ed.), *Teaching English as a second or foreign language* (2nd ed., pp. 216–232). New York: Newbury House.

Macdonald, E. (1991). *High school science testing project.* Unpublished manuscript, Language Testing, Monterey Institute of International Studies, Monterey, CA.

MacKay, R. (1978). Identifying the nature of the learner's needs. In R. MacKay & A. J. Mountford (Eds.), *English for specific purposes: A case study approach.* London: Longman.

Macrorie, K. (1988). *Searching writing* (2nd ed.). Portsmouth, NH: Boynton/Cook.

Maehr, M. L. (1982). *Motivational factors in school achievement.* (Contract No. 400-81-0004.) Washington, DC: Department of Education, National Commission on Excellence in Education. (ERIC Document Reproduction Service No. ED 227 095)

Mangelsdorf, K. (1989). Parallels between speaking and writing in second language acquisition. In D. M. Johnson & D. H. Roen (Eds.), *Richness in writing: Empowering ESL students* (pp. 134–145). New York: Longman.

Manning, M., Manning, G., & Long, R. (1994). *Theme immersion: Inquiry-based curriculum in elementary and middle schools.* Portsmouth, NH: Heinemann.

Mannon, T. M. (1986). *Teacher talk: A comparison of a teacher's speech to native and non-native speakers.* Unpublished master's thesis, University of California, Los Angeles.

Martin, J. (1993). Genre and literacy: Modeling context in educational linguistics. In W. Grabe, C. Ferguson, R. B. Kaplan, G. R. Tucker, & H. G. Widdowson (Eds.), *Annual Review of Applied Linguistics, 13. Issues in second language teaching and learning* (pp. 141–172). New York: Cambridge University Press.

Master, P. (1992). What are some considerations for teacher training in content-based instruction? *The CATESOL Journal, 5*(1), 77–84.

Matthies, B. F. (1991). Administrative evaluation in ESL programs: "How'm I doin'?" In M. C. Pennington (Ed.), *Building better English language programs: Perspectives on evaluation in ESL* (pp. 241–256). Washington, DC: National Association for Foreign Student Affairs.

McCafferty, S. G. (1994). The use of private speech by adult ESL learners at different levels of proficiency. In J. P. Lantolf & G. Appel (Eds.), *Vygotskian approaches to second language research* (pp. 117–134). Norwood, NJ: Ablex.

McCombs, B. L. (1984). Processes and skills underlying continued motivation to learn. *Educational Psychologist, 19*(4), 199–218.

McCurry, J. (1991). *Comparing the sciences and social sciences: An assessment of the English language needs of second language undergraduates.* Unpublished master's thesis, California State University, Los Angeles.

McKeon, D. (1994). When meeting "common" standards is uncommonly difficult. *Educational Leadership, 51,* 45–49.

McLaughlin, B. (1992). *Myths and misconceptions about second language learning: What every teacher needs to unlearn.* (Educational Practice Report No. 5.) Santa Cruz, CA: National Center for Research on Language and Cultural Diversity.

Meinbach, A. M., Rothlein, L., & Fredericks, A. D. (1995). *The complete guide to thematic units: Creating the integrated curriculum.* Norwood, MA: Christopher-Gordon.

Menke, D. J., & Pressley, M. (1994). Elaborative interrogation: Using "why" questions to enhance the learning from text. *Journal of Reading, 37*(8), 642–645.

Merl, J. (1991, February 21). A bore no more: Humanities classes designed for "community" of teachers, students draw rave reviews. *The Los Angeles Times,* pp. B1, B4.

Met, M. (1988). *Second language acquisition in children.* Rockville, MD: Office of Instruction and Program Development, Montgomery County Public Schools.

Met, M. (1993). Second language learning in magnet school contexts. In W. Grabe, C. Ferguson, R. B. Kaplan, G. R. Tucker, & H. G. Widdowson (Eds.), *Annual Review of Applied Linguistics, 13. Issues in second language teaching and learning* (pp. 71–85). New York: Cambridge University Press.

Meyer, B. J. F. (1981). *Prose analysis: Procedures, purposes, and problems.* (Prose Learning Series, Research Report No 11.) Tempe: Arizona State University. (ERIC Document Reproduction Service No. ED 201 972)

Meyer, D. (1993). Recognizing and changing students' misperceptions: An instructional perspective. *College Teaching, 41*(3), 104–108.

Milk, R. D. (1985). The changing role of ESL in bilingual education. *TESOL Quarterly, 19*(4), 657–672.

Miller, R. D. (1988). Two hundred years of holistic education. *Holistic Education Review, 1*(1), 5–12.

Mills, B. J. (n.d.). *Using a workshop series to help faculty capitalize on student diversity.* Unpublished manuscript, University of Maryland, University of Maryland University College, College Park.

Mohan, B. A. (1986). *Language and content.* Reading, MA: Addison-Wesley.

Mohan, B. A. (1989). Language socialization. *Word, 4,* 100–114.

Mohan, B. A. (1990). LEP students and the integration of language and content: Knowledge structures and tasks. In C. Simich-Dudgeon (Ed.), *Proceedings of the first research symposium on limited English proficient students' issues* (pp. 113–160). Washington, DC: Office of Bilingual Education and Minority Languages Affairs, U.S. Department of Education.

Mohan, B. A., Low, M., & Wilson, K. (1995, March). *The assessment of language and the assessment of content: Compatible discourses?* Paper presented at the meeting of the American Association for Applied Linguistics, Long Beach, CA.

Moll, L. (Ed.). (1990). *Vygotsky and education: Instructional implications and applications of socio-historical psychology.* Cambridge: Cambridge University Press.

Munby, J. (1978). *Communicative syllabus design.* New York: Cambridge University Press.

Mundahl, J. (1993, April). *Educating teachers for content-based language instruction.* Panel presentation at the meeting of Teachers of English to Speakers of Other Languages, Atlanta, GA.

Murphey, T. (1992). Action logging: Letting the students in on the teacher training processes. *The Teacher Trainer, 6*(2), 20-21.

Murphey, T. (1993, January). Why don't teachers learn what learners learn? Taking the guesswork out with action logging. *English Teaching Forum,* 6-10.

Murphey, T. (1995). Identity and beliefs in language learning. *The Language Teacher, 19*(4), 34-36.

Murphey, T. (Ed.). (1996). *The medium is the message: Japanese teachers of English using English in the classroom.* Nagoya, Japan: South Mountain Press.

Murphey, T., Deacon, B., & Murakami, K. (1996). An analysis of JTE's classroom English and students' impressions. In T. Murphey (Ed.), *The medium is the message: Japanese teachers of English using English in the classroom* (pp. 43-46). Nagoya, Japan: South Mountain Press.

Murphey, T., & Purcell, W. (1996). Survey results of JTE's use of English in class. In T. Murphey (Ed.), *The medium is the message: Japanese teachers of English using English in the classroom* (pp. 47-52). Nagoya, Japan: South Mountain Press.

Musumeci, D. (1993). Content language learning: Symbiosis in the academe. In J. E. Alatis (Ed.), *Language, communication, and social meaning* (pp. 147-157). Washington, DC: Georgetown University Press.

Musumeci, D. (1996). Teacher-learner negotiation in content-based instruction: Communication at cross-purposes? *Applied Linguistics, 17*(3), 286-325.

Nation, I. S. P. (1990). *Teaching and learning vocabulary.* New York: Newbury House.

National Center for Research to Improve Postsecondary Teaching and Learning. (1992). Classroom assessment/classroom research: Four years into a hands-on movement. *The National Teaching and Learning Forum, 1*(6), 1-4.

National Clearinghouse for Bilingual Education (NCBE). (1991, March). Integrating language and content. *Forum, 14,* 1-3.

National Council for the Social Studies. (1992). Curriculum guidelines for multicultural education. *Social Education, 56*(5), 274-294.

National Council of Teachers of Mathematics. (1989). *Curriculum and evaluation standards for school mathematics.* Reston, VA: Author.

National Science Teachers Association. (1991). *Scope, sequence, and coordination content core: A guide for curriculum designers.* Washington, DC: Author.

Neering, R., & Grant, P. (1986). *Other places, other times.* Toronto: Gage Educational.

Nell, V. (1988). *Lost in a book: The psychology of reading for pleasure.* New Haven, CT: Yale University Press.

Nelson, K. (1977). Cognitive development and the acquisition of concepts. In R. C. Anderson, R. J. Spiro, & W. E. Montague (Eds.), *Schooling and the acquisition of knowledge* (pp. 215-239). Hillsdale, NJ: Erlbaum.

Nelson, K. (1986). *Event knowledge.* Hillsdale, NJ: Erlbaum.

Newman, D., Griffin, P., & Cole, M. (1989). *The construction zone: Working for cognitive change in school.* New York: Cambridge University Press.

Nist, S. L., & Kirby, K. (1986). Teaching comprehension and study strategies through modeling and thinking aloud. *Reading Research and Instruction, 25*(4), 254-264.

Norman, M. (1991) 'Night, mother. In R. Scholes, N. R. Comley, C. H. Klaus, & M. Silverman (Eds.), *Elements of literature* (4th ed., pp. 1405-1441). New York: Oxford University Press.

Nunan D. (1990). Action research in the language classroom. In J. C. Richards & D. Nunan (Eds.), *Second language teacher education* (pp. 62-81). Cambridge: Cambridge University Press.

Nunan, D. (1993). Task-based syllabus design: Selecting, grading and sequencing tasks. In G. Crookes & S. M. Gass (Eds.), *Tasks in a pedagogical context: Integrating theory and practice* (pp. 55–68). Clevedon, Avon: Multilingual Matters.

O'Brien, D., Stewart, R., & Moje, E. (1995). Why content literacy is difficult to infuse into the secondary school: Complexities of curriculum, pedagogy, and school culture. *Reading Research Quarterly, 30,* 442–463.

Ochs, E. (1988). *Culture and language development.* Cambridge: Cambridge University Press.

Office of Bilingual Education and Minority Language Affairs. (1993). *Proceedings of the third national research symposium on limited English proficient student issues: Focus on middle and high school issues* (Volumes 1, 2). Washington, DC: Author, U.S. Department of Education.

Olsen, L., & Mullen, N. (1990). *Embracing diversity: Teachers' voices from California classrooms.* San Francisco: California Tomorrow.

Olsen, T. (1993). I Stand Here Ironing. In E. MacMahan, S. Day, & R. Funk (Eds.), *Literature and the writing process* (3rd ed. pp. 363–368). New York: Macmillan.

O'Malley, J. M. (1990). The cognitive basis for second language instruction. In J. E. Alatis (Ed.), *Linguistics, language teaching, and language acquisition: The interdependence of theory, practice, and research* (pp. 478–496). Washington, DC: Georgetown University Press.

O'Malley, J. M., & Chamot, A. U. (1990). *Learning strategies in second language acquisition.* New York: Cambridge University Press.

O'Malley, J. M., & Waggoner, D. (1984, June). Results of a U.S. survey: Public school teacher preparation in the teaching of ESL. *TESOL Newsletter, 3.*

Oxford, R. (1990). *Language learning strategies: What every teacher should know.* New York: Newbury House.

Paivio, A. (1986). *Mental representations: A dual coding approach.* New York: Oxford University Press.

Pajares, F. M. (1992). Teachers' beliefs and educational research: Cleaning up a messy construct. *Review of Educational Research, 62,* 307–332.

Palinscar, A. S., & Brown, A. L. (1986). Interactive teaching to promote independent learning from text. *The Reading Teacher, 39*(8), 771–777.

Palmer, B. (1993). Eastern Michigan University's programs in language and international business: Disciplines with content. In M. Krueger & F. Ryan (Eds.), *Language and content: Discipline- and content-based approaches to language study* (pp. 138–147). Lexington, MA: D. C. Heath.

Parker, K., & Chaudron, C. (1987). The effects of linguistic simplifications and elaborative modifications on L2 comprehension. *University of Hawaii Working Papers in ESL, 6,* 107–133.

Peitzman, F., & Gadda, G. (Eds.). (1994). *With different eyes: Insights into teaching language minority students across the disciplines.* White Plains, NY: Longman.

Penfield, J. (1987). ESL: The regular classroom teacher's perspective. *TESOL Quarterly, 21*(1), 21–39.

Pennington, M. C. (1990). A professional development focus for the language teaching practicum. In J. C. Richards & D. Nunan (Eds.), *Second language teacher education* (pp. 132–151). New York: Cambridge University Press.

Pennington, M. C. (1995). The teacher change cycle. *TESOL Quarterly, 29,* 705–732.

Pennington, M. C., & Xiao, Y. (1990). Defining the job of the ESL program director: Results of a national survey. *University of Hawaii Working Papers in English as a Second Language, 9*(2), 1–30.

Peregoy, S. F., & Boyle, O. F. (1993). *Reading, writing, and learning in ESL: A resource book for K-8 teachers.* New York: Longman.

Piaget, J. (1954). *The construction of reality in the child.* New York: Basic Books.

Piaget, J. (1967). *The child's conception of the world.* Totowa, NJ: Littlefield, Adams.

Piaget, J. (1970). *The science of education and the psychology of the child.* New York: Basic Books.

Popham, W. J. (1978). *Criterion-referenced measurement.* Englewood Cliffs, NJ: Prentice-Hall.

Popham, W. J. (1981). *Modern educational measurement.* Englewood Cliffs, NJ: Prentice-Hall.

Porter, P., Goldstein, L., Leatherman, J., & Conrad, S. (1990). An ongoing dialogue: Learning logs for teacher training. In J. C. Richards & D. Nunan (Eds.), *Second language teacher education* (pp. 227-242). Cambridge: Cambridge University Press.

Prabhu, N. S. (1987). *Second language pedagogy.* Oxford: Oxford University Press.

Pressley, M., Almasi, J., Schuder, T., Bergman, J., Hite, S., El-Dinary, P., & Brown, R. (1994). Transactional instruction of comprehension strategies: The Montgomery County, Maryland, SAIL program. *Reading & Writing Quarterly, 10,* 5-20.

Pressley, M., El-Dinary, P. B., Gaskins, I., Schuder, T., Bergman, J. L., Almasi, J., & Brown, R. (1992). Beyond direct explanation: Transactional instruction of reading comprehension strategies. *Elementary School Journal, 92*(5), 513-555.

Pressley, M., & Woloshyn, V. (Eds.). (1995). *Cognitive strategy instruction that really improves children's academic performance* (2nd ed.). Cambridge, MA: Brookline.

Pritzos, S. C. (1992). *Teacher communication in regular and sheltered science classes.* Unpublished master's thesis, California State University, Long Beach.

Ratekin, N., Simpson, M., Alvermann, D., & Dishner, E. (1985). Why teachers resist content reading instruction. *Journal of Reading, 28*(5), 432-437.

Reid, J., & Kroll, B. (1995). Designing and assessing effective classroom writing assignments for NES and ESL students. *Journal of Second Language Writing, 4*(1), 17-39.

Renninger, K. A., Hidi, S., & Krapp, A. (Eds.). (1992). *The role of interest in learning and development.* Hillsdale, NJ: Erlbaum.

Resnick, L. B. (1987). Constructing knowledge in school. In L. S. Liben (Ed.), *Development and learning: Conflict or congruence?* (pp. 19-50). Hillsdale, NJ: Erlbaum.

Reyner, J., & Davison, D. M. (1993). Improving mathematics and science instruction for LEP middle and high school students through language activities. In *Proceedings of the third national research symposium on limited English proficient student issues: Focus on middle and high school issues* (Vol. 1, pp. 549-578). Washington, DC: OBEMLA, U.S. Department of Education.

Rhodes, N. (1995). *Total and partial immersion language programs in U.S. elementary schools, 1995.* Washington, DC: Center for Applied Linguistics.

Richard-Amato, P., & Snow, M. A. (Eds.). (1992a). *The multicultural classroom: Readings for content-area teachers.* White Plains, NY: Longman.

Richard-Amato, P., & Snow, M. A. (1992b). Strategies for content-area teachers. In P. Richard-Amato & M. A. Snow (Eds.), *The multicultural classroom: Readings for content-area teachers* (pp. 145-163). White Plains, NY: Longman.

Richards, J. C. (1987). The dilemma of teacher education in TESOL. *TESOL Quarterly, 21*(2), 209-226.

Richards, J., & Lockhart, C. (1994). *Reflective teaching in second language classrooms.* Cambridge: Cambridge University Press.

Richardson, V. (1990). Significant and worthwhile change in teaching practice. *Educational Researcher, 19,* 10–18.

Rinaudo, M. C. (1993). Metacognición y estrategias de aprendizaje [Metacognition and learning strategies]. *Lectura y Vida, 14*(3), 5–12.

Roberts, P. L. (1993). *A green dinosaur day: A guide for developing thematic units in literature-based instruction, K-6.* Boston: Allyn and Bacon.

Robinson, F. P. (1962). *Effective teaching.* New York: Harper & Row.

Robinson, P. (1991). *ESP today: A practitioner's guide.* Englewood Cliffs, NJ: Prentice-Hall.

Roe, R. B., & Warren, G. C. (1988). *Instructor's manual with test items.* (For Norton, M. B., Katzman, D. M., Escott, P. D., Chudacoff, H. P., Paterson, T. G., Tuttle, W. M., & Brophy, W. J. *A people and a nation: A history of the United States.* Brief ed., 2nd ed.). Boston: Houghton Mifflin.

Rogoff, B. (1990). *Apprenticeship and thinking.* New York: Oxford University Press.

Rose, M. (1985). The language of exclusion: Writing instruction at the university. *College English, 47*(4), 341–359.

Rose, M. (1989). *Lives on the boundary.* New York: Penguin.

Rosenshine, B., & Meister, C. (1994). Reciprocal teaching: A review of the research. *Review of Educational Research, 64*(4), 479–530.

Ruddell, M. R. (1993). *Teaching content reading and writing.* Boston: Allyn and Bacon.

Rumelhart, D. E. (1977). Understanding and summarizing brief stories. In D. Laberge & S. J. Samuels (Eds.), *Basic processes in reading: Perception and comprehension* (pp. 265–303). Hillsdale, NJ: Erlbaum.

Rumelhart, D. E. (1980). Schemata: The building blocks of cognition. In R. J. Spiro, B. C. Bruce, & W. F. Brewer (Eds.), *Theoretical issues in reading comprehension* (pp. 33–58). Hillsdale, NJ: Erlbaum.

Russel, T. (1993). Learning to teach science: Constructivism, reflection, and learning from experience. In K. Tobin (Ed.), *The practice of constructivism in science education.* (pp. 247–258). Hillsdale, NJ: Erlbaum.

Sadoski, M., Paivio, A., & Goetz, E. (1991). Commentary: A critique of schema theory in reading and a dual coding alternative. *Reading Research Quarterly, 26*(4), 463–484.

Sarig, G. (1993). Composing a study-summary: A reading/writing encounter. In J. Carson & I. Leki (Eds.), *Reading in the composition classroom: Second language perspectives* (pp. 161–182). Boston: Heinle & Heinle.

Sarmiento, A. R., & Kay, A. (1990). *Worker-centered learning: A union guide to workplace literacy.* Washington, DC: AFL-CIO Human Resources Development Institute.

Sarton, M. (1973). *As we are now.* New York: Norton.

Sasser, L., & Winningham, B. (1994). Sheltered instruction across the disciplines: Successful teachers at work. In F. Peitzman & G. Gadda (Eds.), *With different eyes: Insights into teaching language minority students across the disciplines* (pp. 22–42). New York: Longman.

Savage, K. L., How, M., & Yeung, E. (1982). *English that works.* Glenview, IL: Scott, Foresman.

Saville-Troike, M. (1984). What *really* matters in second language learning for academic achievement? *TESOL Quarterly, 18*(2), 199–219.

Schinke-Llano, L. (1993). On the value of a Vygotskian framework for SLA theory and research. *Language Learning, 43,* 121–129.

Schumm, J. S., & Hinchman, K. A. (1994). Helping learners complete assigned work. In B. A. Herrmann (Ed.), *The volunteer tutor's toolbox* (pp. 47–76). Portsmouth, NH: International Reading Association.

Shannon, P. (1991). *The struggle to continue: Progressive reading instruction in the United States.* Portsmouth, NH: Heinemann.

Shavelson, R. J., & Stern, P. (1981). Research on teachers' pedagogical thoughts, judgments, decisions, and behavior. *Review of Educational Research, 51,* 455-498.

Sheppard, K. (1994). *Content-ESL across the USA: A technical report* (Vol. 1). Washington, DC: Center for Applied Linguistics.

Shih, M. (1986). Content-based approaches to teaching academic writing. *TESOL Quarterly, 20,* 617-648.

Shih, M. (1992). Beyond comprehension exercises in the ESL academic reading class. *TESOL Quarterly, 26*(2), 289-318.

Shor, I. (1992). *Empowering education.* Chicago: University of Illinois Press.

Short, D. J. (1991). *How to integrate language and content instruction: A training manual* (2nd ed.). Washington, DC: Center for Applied Linguistics.

Short, D. J. (1993a). Assessing integrated language and content instruction. *TESOL Quarterly, 27*(4), 627-656.

Short, D. J. (1993b). Integrating language and culture in middle school American history classes. (Educational Practice Rep. No. 8.) Santa Cruz, CA: National Center for Research on Cultural Diversity and Second Language Learning.

Short, D. J. (1994). Expanding middle school horizons: Integrating language, culture, and social studies. *TESOL Quarterly, 28*(3), 581-608.

Short, D. J. (1996). *Integrating language and culture in the social studies.* (Final report submitted to the Office of Educational Research and Improvement, U. S. Department of Education.) Washington, DC: Center for Applied Linguistics.

Short, D. J., Mahrer, C., Elfin, A., Liten-Tejada, R., & Montone, C. (1994). *Protest and the American revolution.* Washington, DC: Center for Applied Linguistics, and the National Center for Research on Cultural Diversity and Second Language Learning.

Short, D. J., Montone, C., Frekot, S., & Elfin, A. (1996). *Conflicts in world cultures.* Washington, DC: Center for Applied Linguistics, and National Center for Research on Cultural Diversity and Second Language Learning.

Sigel, I. E., Brozinsky, D. M., & Golinkoff, R. M. (1981). *New directions in Piagetian theory and practice.* Hillsdale, NJ: Erlbaum.

Silverman, R., & Welty, W. M. (1992). *Case studies for faculty development: Grant Eldridge.* New York: Pace University, Center for Case Studies in Education.

Simon, S. B., Howe, L. W., & Kirschenbaum, H. (1972). *Values clarification: A handbook of practical strategies for teachers and students.* New York: Hart.

Singer, M. (1990). *Psychology of language: An introduction to sentence and discourse processing.* Hillsdale, NJ: Erlbaum.

Sizer, T. (1990, January). *Student as worker, teacher as coach.* Morristown, NJ: Simon and Schuster.

Slavin, R. E. (1995). *Cooperative learning* (2nd ed.). Boston: Allyn and Bacon.

Smith, F. (1971). *Understanding reading.* New York: Holt, Rinehart and Winston.

Smith, F. (1975). *Comprehension and learning.* New York: Holt, Rinehart and Winston.

Snow, M. A. (1989). *Negotiation of meaning in the immersion classroom.* Rockville, MD: Office of Instruction and Program Development, Montgomery County Public Schools.

Snow, M. A. (1991a). Content-based instruction: A method with many faces. In J. E. Alatis (Ed.), *Linguistics and language pedagogy: The state of the art* (pp. 461-470). Washington, DC: Georgetown University Press.

Snow, M. A. (1991b). Teaching language through content. In M. Celce-Murcia (Ed.), *Teaching English as a second/foreign language* (pp. 315-327). New York: Newbury House.

Snow, M. A. (1993). Discipline-based foreign language teaching: Implications from ESL/EFL. In M. Krueger & F. Ryan (Eds.), *Language and content: Discipline- and content-based approaches to language study* (pp. 37–56). Lexington, MA: D. C. Heath.

Snow, M. A., & Brinton, D. (1988). Content-based language instruction: Investigating the effectiveness of the adjunct model. *TESOL Quarterly, 22,* 553–574.

Snow, M. A., Met, M., & Genesee, F. (1989). A conceptual framework for the integration of language and content in second/foreign language instruction. *TESOL Quarterly, 23*(2), 201–217.

Solarz, F. Perelman de. (1994). La construcción del resumen [Summary writing]. *Lectura y Vida, 15*(1), 5–20.

Solomon, J., & Rhodes, N. (1995). *Conceptualizing academic language.* (Research Rep. No. 15.) Santa Cruz, CA: University of California, National Center for Research on Cultural Diversity and Second Language Learning.

Spanos, G. (1990). On the integration of language and content instruction. In R. B. Kaplan *et al.,* (Eds.), *Annual Review of Applied Linguistics, 10* (pp. 227–240). New York: Cambridge University Press.

Spanos, G. (1993). ESL math and science for high school students: Two case studies. In *Proceedings of the third national research symposium on limited English proficient student issues: Focus on middle and high school issues* (Vol. 1, pp. 383–420). Washington, DC: Office of Bilingual Education and Minority Languages Affairs, U.S. Department of Education.

Spiro, R., Vispoel, W., Schmitz, J., Samarapungavan, A., & Boerger, A. (1987). Knowledge acquisition for application: Cognitive flexibility and transfer in complex cognitive domains. In B. Britton & S. Glynn (Eds.), *Executive control processes in reading* (pp. 177–199). Hillsdale, NJ: Erlbaum.

Spivey, N. N. (1983). *Discourse synthesis: Constructing texts in reading and writing.* Unpublished doctoral dissertation, University of Texas at Austin.

Srole, C. (1993). *Teaching analytical skills and history.* Unpublished manuscript, California State University, Los Angeles.

St. John, M. J. (1996, August). *The rise of business English.* Paper presented at the 11th World Congress of Applied Linguistics, Jyväskylä, Finland.

Stack, L. (1993). Assessing an innovative practice: The writing portfolios of high school second language learners in an interdisciplinary thematic core grouping. In *Proceedings of the third national research symposium on limited English proficient student issues: Focus on middle and high school issues* (Vol. 1, pp. 873–882). Washington, DC: OBEMLA, U.S. Department of Education.

Stahl, N. A., Simpson, M. L., & Hayes, C. G. (1992). Ten recommendations from research for teaching high-risk college students. *Journal of Developmental Education, 16,* 2–10.

Stahl, R. J. (Ed.). (1994). *Cooperative learning in social studies: A handbook for teachers.* Reading, MA: Addison-Wesley.

Stauffer, R. G. (1969). *Directed reading maturity as a cognitive process.* New York: Harper & Row.

Stern, H. H. (1981). Communicative language teaching and learning: Toward a synthesis. In J. E. Alatis, H. B. Altman, & P. M. Alatis (Eds.), *The second language classroom* (pp. 133–148). New York: Oxford University Press.

Stevick, E. W. (1976). *Memory, meaning and method.* Rowley, MA: Newbury House.

Stewart, D. (1993). *Immigration and education: The crisis and opportunities.* New York: Lexington Books.

Stillings, N. A., Feinstein, M. G., Garfield, J. L., Rissland, E. L., Rosenbaum, D. A., Weisler, S. E., & Baker-Ward, L. (1987). *Cognitive science: An introduction.* Cambridge, MA: MIT Press.

Stipek, D. J. (1988). *Motivation to learn: From theory to practice.* Englewood Cliffs, NJ: Prentice-Hall.

Straight, H. S. (Ed.). (1994). *Languages across the curriculum: Translation perspectives VII.* Binghamton: State University of New York, Center for Research in Translation.

Strickland, D. S., & Morrow, M. L. (1990). Integrating the emergent literacy curriculum with themes. *The Reading Teacher, 43,* 604-605.

Stuart, D. K. (1990, January/February). ESL in secondary education and articulation with post-secondary programs. *TESOL Higher Education Interest Section Newsletter,* 6-7.

Sudermann, D., & Cisar, M. (1992). Foreign languages across the curriculum: A critical appraisal. *Modern Language Journal, 76,* 295-308.

Swain, M. (1985). Communicative competence: Some roles of comprehensible input and comprehensible output in its development. In S. Gass & C. Madden (Eds.), *Input in second language acquisition* (pp. 235-253). Rowley, MA: Newbury House.

Swain, M. (1988). Manipulating and complementing content teaching to maximize second language learning. *TESL Canada Journal, 6*(1), 68-83.

Swain, M. (1991). French immersion and its offshoots: Getting two for one. In B. F. Freed (Ed.), *Foreign language acquisition research and the classroom* (pp. 91-103). Lexington, MA: D. C. Heath.

Swain, M. (1993). The output hypothesis: Just speaking and writing aren't enough. *The Canadian Modern Language Review, 50,* 158-164.

Swain, M. (1995a, March). *Collaborative dialogue: Its contribution to second language learning.* Plenary address presented at the meeting of the American Association of Applied Linguistics, Long Beach, CA.

Swain, M. (1995b). Three functions of output in second language learning. In G. Cook & B. Seidlhoffer (Eds.), *Principle and practice in applied linguistics: Studies in honour of H. G. Widdowson* (pp. 125-144). Oxford: Oxford University Press.

Swain, M., & Lapkin, S. (1989). Canadian immersion and adult second language teaching: What's the connection? *The Modern Language Journal, 73,* 150-159.

Swales, J. M. (1985a). *Episodes in ESP.* Englewood Cliffs, NJ: Prentice-Hall.

Swales, J. M. (1985b). ESP—The heart of the matter or the end of the affair? In R. Quirk & H. G. Widdowson (Eds.), *English in the world* (pp. 212-223). Cambridge: Cambridge University Press.

Swales, J. M. (1985c). ESP comes of age? 21 years after "Some measurable characteristics of modern scientific prose." In M. Perrin (Ed.), *Today's provisions for tomorrow's needs* (pp. 1-20). New York: UNESCO.

Swales, J. M. (1990). *Genre analysis: English in academic and research settings.* Cambridge: Cambridge University Press.

Swales, J. M., & Feak, C. B. (1994). *Academic writing for graduate students: Essential tasks and skills.* Ann Arbor: University of Michigan Press.

Swales, J. M., & Feak, C. B. (1995). From information transfer to data commentary. In T. Miller (Ed.), *Functional approaches to written text: Classroom applications.* Paris: TESOL France.

Tan, A. (1990). Mother tongue. *Threepenny Review 43,* 7.

Tang, G. M. (1992). The effects of graphic representation of knowledge structures on ESL reading comprehension. *Studies in Second Language Acquisition, 14,* 177-195.

Tarone, E., & Swain, M. (1995). A sociolinguistic perspective on second language use in immersion classrooms. *The Modern Language Journal, 79,* 166-178.

Taylor, K. K. (1984). The different summary skills of inexperienced and professional writers. *Journal of Reading, 27*(8), 691-698.

Tchudi, S. N. (Ed.). (1993). *The astonishing curriculum: Integrating science and humanities through language.* Urbana, IL: National Council of Teachers of English.

Tchudi, S. N., & Huerta, M. C. (1983). *Teaching writing in the content areas: Middle school/junior high.* Washington, DC: National Education Association.

Teachers of English to Speakers of Other Languages. (1985). *Statement of core standards for language and professional preparation programs.* Washington, DC: Author.

Tharp, R. G., & Gallimore, R. (1988). *Rousing minds to life: Teaching, learning, and schooling in social context.* Cambridge: Cambridge University Press.

Thornton, S. J. (1994). The social studies near century's end: Reconsidering patterns of curriculum and instruction. *Review of Research in Education, 20,* 223-254.

Tobias, S. (1994). Interest, prior knowledge, and learning. *Review of Educational Research, 64*(1), 37-54.

Tobin, K., Tippins, D., & Gallard, A. J. (1994). Research on instructional strategies for teaching science. In D. L. Gabel (Ed.), *A handbook of research on science teaching and learning* (pp. 45-93). New York: Macmillan.

Tricamo, J., & Snow, M. A. (1994). *Project LEAP: Learning English for Academic Purposes.* (Final report to FIPSE, grant #P116B1-0798.) Los Angeles: California State University, Los Angeles.

Tucker, G. R., & Crandall, J. A. (1989). The integration of language and content instruction for language minority and language majority students. In J. E. Alatis (Ed.), *Language teaching, testing, and technology: Lessons from the past with a view toward the future* (pp. 39-50). Washington, DC: Georgetown University Press.

Turner, J. C. (1993). A motivational perspective on literacy instruction. In D. J. Leu & C. K. Kinzer (Eds.), *Examining central issues in literacy research, theory, and practice* (pp. 153-161). Chicago, IL: National Reading Conference.

Turner, J. L. (1991). *An adaptive model for the development of measures of language achievement in content-based language programs.* Unpublished doctoral dissertation, University of California, Los Angeles.

Tyson-Bernstein, H. (1988). *A conspiracy of good intentions: America's textbook fiasco.* Washington, DC: Council for Basic Education.

U.S. Department of Education. (1992). *The condition of bilingual education in the nation.* Washington, DC: U.S. Department of Education.

U.S. Department of Education, Office of Educational Research and Improvement. (1993). *Language characteristics and schooling in the United States, a changing picture: 1979 and 1989.* Washington, DC: U.S. Department of Education.

Vacca, R. T., & Vacca, J. A. L. (1993). *Content area reading* (4th ed.). New York: HarperCollins.

Van Ek, J. A. (1975). *The threshold level.* Strasbourg: Council of Europe.

Vanniarajan, S. (1987). *Discourse analysis and foreigner talk in the university class.* Unpublished master's thesis, University of Ottawa.

Volker, C. (1995). An English-medium content course: South Pacific studies in a Japanese university. *The Language Teacher, 19*(11), 19-22.

Vygotsky, L. S. (1962). *Thought and language.* Cambridge, MA: MIT Press.

Vygotsky, L. S. (1978). *Mind in society.* Cambridge, MA: Harvard University Press.

Waggoner, D. (1992, October/November). The increasing multiethnic and multicultural diversity of the U.S.: Findings from the 1990 census. *TESOL Matters,* 12-13.

Waggoner, D. (1993). The growth of multilingualism and the need for bilingual education: What do we know so far? *Bilingual Research Journal, 17*(1&2), 1-12.

Walmsley, S. A. (1994). *Children exploring their world: Theme teaching in elementary school.* Portsmouth, NH: Heinemann.

Walqui-van Lier, A. (1995). What makes SDAIE be more than "just good teaching"? *California Association for Bilingual Education Newsletter, 18*(3/4), 9, 23.

Watson-Gegeo, K. (1988). Ethnography in ESL: Defining the essentials. *TESOL Quarterly, 22*(4), 575-592.

Weaver, C. (1994). *Reading process and practice: From sociolinguistics to whole language* (2nd ed.). Portsmouth, NH: Heinemann.

Wegrzecka-Monkiewicz, E. (1992). *High school English as a second language: A comparative study of content based and regular programs.* Unpublished master's thesis, California State University, Los Angeles.

Weimer, M. G. (Ed.). (1987). *Teaching large classes well.* San Francisco: Jossey-Bass.

Weinstein, C. E., & Mayer, R. E. (1986). The teaching of learning strategies. In M. C. Wittrock (Ed.), *Handbook of research on teaching* (3rd ed., pp. 315-327). New York: Macmillan.

Wells, G. (1994). The complementary contributions of Halliday and Vygotsky to a "language-based theory of learning." *Linguistics and Education, 6,* 41-90.

Wesche, M. B. (1993). Discipline-based approaches to language study: Research issues and outcomes. In M. Krueger & F. Ryan (Eds.), *Language and content: Discipline- and content-based approaches to language study* (pp. 57-82). Lexington, MA: D. C. Heath.

Wesche, M. B., & Ready, D. (1985). Foreigner talk in the university classroom. In S. Gass & C. Madden (Eds.), *Input in second language acquisition* (pp. 89-114). New York: Newbury House.

West, R., Stanovich, K., & Mitchell, H. (1993). Reading in the real world and its correlates. *Reading Research Quarterly, 28,* 34-50.

Widdowson, H. G. (1978). *Teaching language as communication.* Oxford: Oxford University Press.

Widdowson, H. G. (1979). Rules and procedures in discourse analysis. In H. G. Widdowson (Ed.), *Explorations in applied linguistics* (pp. 141-149). New York: Oxford University Press.

Widdowson, H. G. (1981, November). *The relationship between language teaching and subject matter.* Paper presented at the meeting of the American International Education and Training Association, San Francisco, CA.

Widdowson, H. G. (1983). *Learning purpose and language use.* New York: Oxford University Press.

Widdowson, H. G. (1993). The relevant conditions of language use and learning. In M. Krueger & F. Ryan (Eds.), *Language and content: Discipline- and content-based approaches to language study* (pp. 27-36). Lexington, MA: D. C. Heath.

Wilkins, D. (1976). *Notional syllabuses.* New York: Oxford University Press.

Williams, J., & Reynolds, T. D. (1993). Courting controversy: How to build interdisciplinary units. *Educational Leadership, 50*(7), 13-15.

Winograd, P. (1984). Strategic difficulties in summarizing tasks. *Reading Research Quarterly, 19*(4), 404-425.

Woloshyn, V. E., Pressley, M., & Schneider, W. (1992). Elaborative-interrogation and prior-knowledge effects on learning of facts. *Journal of Educational Psychology, 84*(1), 115-124.

Wong-Fillmore, L. (1985). When does teacher talk work as input? In S. Gass & C. Madden (Eds.), *Input in second language acquisition* (pp. 17–50). New York: Newbury House.

Wong-Fillmore, L. (1994). *Learning a second language at school: Conditions and constraints.* Plenary address presented at the Rocky Mountain Regional Conference of Teachers of English to Speakers of Other Languages, Phoenix, AZ.

Wood, D. J., Bruner, J. S., & Ross, G. (1976). The role of tutoring in problem solving. *Journal of Child Psychology and Psychiatry, 17*(2), 89–100.

Wrigley, H. (1987). *May I help you?* Reading, MA: Addison-Wesley.

Yalden, J. (1983). *The communicative syllabus.* New York: Pergamon.

Yalden J. (1987). *Principles of course design for language teaching.* New York: Cambridge University Press.

Young, A., & Fulwiler, T. (Eds.). (1986). *Writing across the disciplines: Research into practice.* Portsmouth, NH: Boynton/Cook Heinemann.

Young, R. (1995, March). Introduction. In R. Young (Chair), *Form and function in language learning: Sociolinguistic perspectives.* Academic Session of the TESOL Research Interest Section held at the Annual Conference of Teachers of English to Speakers of Other Languages, Long Beach, CA.

Zentella, A. C. (1978). *Code-switching and interactions among Puerto Rican children.* Sociolinguistic Working Paper No. 50. Austin, TX: Southwest Educational Development Laboratory.

Zikopoulos, M. (Ed.). (1990). *Open doors: 1989/90. Report on international educational exchange.* New York: Institute of International Education.

Index